THE COMMANDING SEA

A wind-rose from a fifteenth-century chart.
Overleaf: A twentieth-century image of the oceans.
The Tuamotu Archipelago area of
the Pacific taken from Apollo 7

THE COMMANDING SEA

by Clare Francis and Warren Tute

British Broadcasting Corporation and Pelham Books

Published by the
British Broadcasting Corporation
35 Marylebone High Street
London W1M 4AA
and
Pelham Books Ltd
44 Bedford Square
London WC1B 3DU

First published 1981
© Nexus Communications Ltd 1981

Designed by Peter Campbell
Picture research by Diana Souhami

ISBN 0 7207 1307 2
ISBN 0 563 17800 0 (Australia)

Filmset by Jolly & Barber Ltd, Rugby
Printed and bound in Italy by
Arnoldo Mondadori Editore

CONTENTS

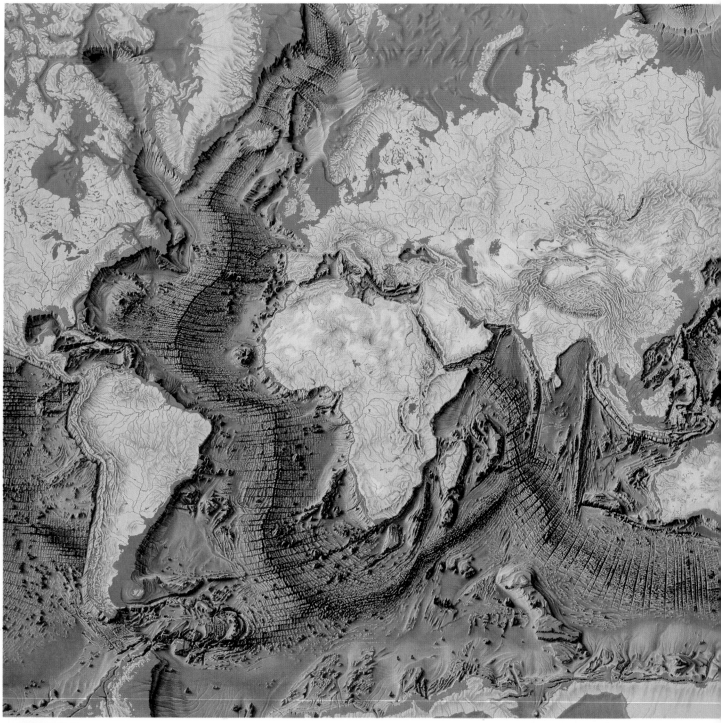

Acknowledgements

Page i Giancarlo Costa; ii NASA/Space Frontiers; iv Susan Griggs/Horst Munzig; vi Paris Match; viii Radio Times; 3 Susannah Fisher; 5 Space Frontiers (chart) Crown copyright; 7 Mary Rose Trust; 10 Aerofilms; 13 Diagram; 14 Giancarlo Costa; 16 SCALA; 19, 20, 23 Susanna Fisher; 25 F. E. Gibson; 30 John Hillelson/Georg Gerster; 31 (rock) Seaphot/J. David George, National Maritime Museum London; 32 University of Dundee Electronics Dept, (chart) National Maritime Museum London; 33 Sonia Halliday, British Museum, Axel Poignant; 34 British Museum/ Michael Holford, Michael Holford, John Moss; 35 (Thebes tomb) Egypt Exploration Society; (Medinet relief) Chicago University Press; (Thera); 36 Giancarlo Costa; 37 Richard Draper; 38 Giancarlo Costa; 39 (reed rafts) ZEFA, (skin boat) Museum of the American Indian, (making a dug-out) National Maritime Museum, London; 40 (Brigg boat) National Maritime Museum, London; (Rhine barge) University of Amsterdam;

(Engersund barge) Viking Ship Museum, Denmark; drawing, Diagram; 41 Giancarlo Costa, National Maritime Museum, London, National Maritime Museum, London; 42, 45 Bob Bentley; 47 Bob Bentley, (view from mast and inside hull) Wexford Films; 49 Richard Draper; 50 British Library; 52 National Maritime Museum, London; 55 National Portrait Gallery, London; 57 British Library; 59 Aerofilms; 61 Science Museum, London, (chronicle) National Maritime Museum, London, (drawing) Bibliothèque Nationale, Paris; 63 National Maritime Museum, London; 65 British Museum; 66 Space Frontiers, (inset) Bob Bentley; 67 British Library; 73 Royal Botanical Gardens, Kew; 75 John Hillelson/Burt Glinn; 76 National Maritime Museum, London, (left) Victoria & Albert Museum, London, National Maritime Museum, London; 77 BBC, National Maritime Museum, London; 78 Barnabys Picture Library, Popperfoto; 79 Milano Cabinetto Numismatica/ Giancarlo Costa, Museo Genoa/Giancarlo Costa;

80 MAS, Barcelona; 81 Museo Navale, Pegli/ SCALA; 82 Map, Museo Navale, Madrid; 84 Folk Museum, Munich; 85 (map) Richard Draper; (canoes) Bruce Coleman/Nicholas deVore; (making canoe) Bob Bentley; 86, 87 Bob Bentley; 88 National Maritime Museum, London; 89 Sonia Halliday/Jane Taylor, BBC Hulton Picture Library, Archivo e Studio Quilici; 91 (parrot and plant) British Museum, Natural History, British Library; 92 John Hillelson/Brian Brake; 93 British Library, Vision International/P. Tatofoulos; 94 National Maritime Museum, London; 96 (inset) Arun Ganguly, (tankers) Shell photograph; 99 Bourne & Shepherd; 101 Arun Ganguly; 102 India Office Library; 103 Mansell Collection; 105 Arun Ganguly; 107 Vision International/Paola Koch; 111 Shell photographs; 112 India Office Library; 113 BBC Hulton Picture Library; 115 Mansell Collection; 119 National Maritime Museum, San Francisco; 121 National Maritime Museum, London; 123 Decca Radar; 125 Bruce Coleman/

INTRODUCTION

Land-living, we tend to take the sea for granted. Making the films on which this book is based was a continual lesson in its immense and unpredictable power. We saw the most costly plans of North Sea oil engineers, the most advanced technology of ocean scientists suffer as much delay and risk as the humble outrigger of Pacific islanders. No man commands the sea.

Yet from earliest days we have struggled with it, learned to cross its surfaces for our profit in trade, and to harvest its resources for food. During the last two decades we have made a huge leap forward in our knowledge of the sea. For the first time this almost unknown element covering seven-tenths of the surface of the globe is being scientifically examined. The excitements of this last frontier of discovery are equal to those of a voyage in space, and far more relevant to our survival.

Our very success is putting the oceans in jeopardy: the dangers of exploitation are already with us. Ultimately we need the waters of the world in order to exist, and we need their fish and minerals and energy for our well-being. Our voyages were timely: this decade – with the conclusion of the world's negotiations on the Law of the Sea, the most comprehensive international legislation ever attempted – is likely to be crucial in man's long relationship with the commanding sea.

Michael Gill

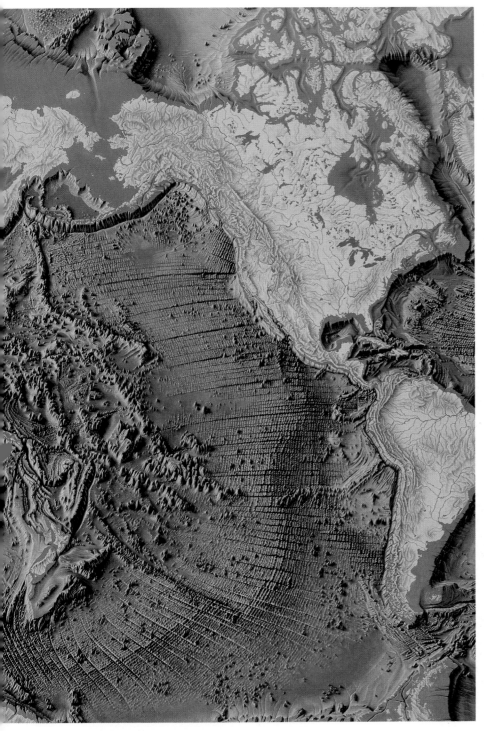

The topography of the ocean floor. If the oceans were drained the ridges would stand as mountain chains, high above the ocean floor. The shallower shelf which surrounds the world's land masses is already being exploited for oil, and has long provided the world with major fishing grounds. Exploration of the deeper parts of the ocean is now advancing fast

Clare Francis sailing *Gulliver G* off the Isles of Scilly

Chapter One

THE EDGE OF THE UNKNOWN

When I was a very small girl on holiday by the sea, my father took me sailing in a dinghy for the first time. To my five-year-old mind it was a terrifying experience: the boat was clearly on the point of tipping over and the waves, which hit the fast-moving hull like bullets, threw curtains of wet, cold spray over my shivering body. I screamed until I was delivered safely back to the shore. As the years passed, my fear of the water was replaced by a fascination with all things nautical. I learnt the rudiments of sailing and then, at the age of twelve, I became the proud owner of a small wooden dinghy, mine to sail fast and free to whatever destination I chose – as long as it wasn't further than the next bay. Once I sailed beyond the limits of safety, to the edge of the shipping channel a mile out from the shore. A strong tide was sweeping me towards the open sea and the waves were dangerously large for my undecked boat. An icy fear suddenly gripped me and, with my heart racing, I turned back for the shore, very frightened yet childishly exhilarated at my own daring. Since then my feelings for the sea have changed little; whether sailing the English Channel or the Atlantic, I still experience that intoxicating mixture of fear and fascination which, despite many temptations to remain landbound, always lures me back for just one more voyage.

Today many people go to sea for pleasure and the small-boat industry has grown to the point where the river below my home at Lymington in the south of England is crowded with yachts and powerboats. Fifty years ago Lymington was a minor commercial port, harbouring a few fishing boats, barges and coasters. Now there are almost two thousand craft kept in the narrow river, and each mooring and marina berth could be filled many times over. Everyone, it appears, wants to get away to sea, to enjoy a brief spell of harsh living in the cramped, wet confines of a small boat. Yet, of all these craft, only a few are taken far out to sea. Despite centuries of accumulated knowledge we still think twice before sailing a long way from land. Even the giant ships which steam past the Lymington river and up the Solent to the port of Southampton are not immune from disaster; experience and technology have improved our seafaring skills, but they have not given us total mastery. We can go to sea with confidence, but not without risk.

Nonetheless, we have come a long way from the days when men first set tentative foot in sea-going craft. The story of man's relationship with the sea, of how he grew to understand it and to use it for his own ends, is a tale of courage, daring and immense hardship. It was this story that Michael Gill was keen to film for a series of six television programmes about the sea. In the programmes we would try to follow the thread of man's relationship with the sea; to tell the story of why he was lured to the ocean and why he faced its awful dangers; of how each step forward was achieved at great cost in human resources, yet brought such enormous rewards that men were encouraged to risk still more in their attempts to master the sea. We wanted to take the story from man's earliest-known sea-going activities in search of food to the great voyages of exploration in search of wealth; from the development of world trade to the necessity to defend the trade routes; from the sea as an open, unexploited expanse to the sea as a vast resource at the mercy of increasing environmental and political pressures. For each use man has found for the sea, he has developed new skills, endured further hardships, enjoyed greater wealth and stirred up fresh problems.

There was no better way to tell the tale than by going out on the ships and among the men at the centre of the story – except where time and history ruled that out, of course. Even so there are replicas of old ships to be sailed in and exciting accounts of past voyages to be re-lived. We therefore planned a series of voyages to take us through the six principal phases of the story, voyages that would take us to the North Sea, the Mediterranean, the Adriatic, the Indian Ocean, the South China Sea, the Sea of Japan, the Coral Sea, the Pacific, the Caribbean and the North Atlantic. Only the first of our programmes presented a difficulty. In a story that began many thousands of years ago, where do you start? I could not go voyaging on an ancient vessel; very few remain, and those which do are carefully preserved in museums. Nor could I refer to written or pictorial records of very early voyages because, except for the occasional scrap left by the ancient Mediterranean civilisations or carved on the wall of a cave, little archae-ological evidence exists. Much of what we know about man's early sea ventures has been gleaned from deduction and anthropological studies. Yet in many ways small-boat sailing can have changed very little over the thousands of years since man first put to sea; the wind and the weather are just as obdurate and almost as unpredictable, the tides continue to ebb and flood, rocky coastlines are still hazardous, and the sea itself is just as variable in mood and behaviour. Why not, therefore, take a small boat along an old sea route and look at the hazards and difficulties of the passage through the eyes of the early mariners? Although I would be sailing in the relative safety of a modern boat, it would be fascinating to imagine passage-making without modern equipment and technology; to re-examine decisions as if they were based on nothing more than observation and empirical knowledge.

For early sailors the chances of making a sea passage in safety were probably not very high, so why did they make them? Even a five-mile voyage, which we regard as fairly short nowadays, would have been hazardous, yet we know that men crossed the channel between Europe and Britain four thousand years ago. Earlier, probably about twenty thousand years ago, migrants crossed a body of water more than twenty miles wide to colonise Australia from Asia. But just as intriguing to me was the discovery that, for thousands of years, men had been sailing to several small islands off the British mainland. I know the Isles of Scilly well – from a distance. I have carefully sailed round them for many years. Lying over twenty miles west-south-west of Land's End, reaching out towards the Atlantic Ocean, they are extremely hazardous to small boats and ships alike. From the sea, they look rocky, inhospitable and infertile; so why did generations of seafarers make the twenty-mile passage to these remote islands?

Part of the channel coast from Lucas Waghenaer's sea atlas of 1584, the first printed book to give both charts and sailing directions

From Lymington it is 200 nautical miles down the English Channel to the Scillies. I would be taking the boat I knew best, my own *Gulliver G*, a 32-foot cruising boat in which I first sailed the Atlantic singlehanded in 1973. *Gulliver G* and I had made the westward passage down the south coast of England on many occasions and each trip had been completely different from the others. That is the one certain thing about the English Channel; you never know what to expect. For most of the voyage I would be singlehanded but, on leaving Lymington and arriving at Plymouth where I planned to stop overnight, the camera crew would be on board. They would then join *Gulliver G* for the last part of the passage from Plymouth to the Scillies.

However well you know your boat and however often you have made a passage, there is still a lot of preparatory work to be done before putting to sea. Equipment has to be checked and maintained, charts must be sorted out, stores and provisions have to be bought and stowed. Sailing in these waters it is essential to have a good look at the tide tables before deciding what time of the day to set out. I wanted an ebb tide for a fast passage out of the Solent, the sheltered stretch of water between the Isle of Wight and the mainland. On the day I hoped to leave, the tables predicted high water at nine in the morning. The ebb would begin to run about an hour before that so I should be out of the Lymington River by eight.

After a last day of preparations *Gulliver G* was ready: fuel and water tanks full, navigation equipment checked, engine running smoothly, sails bent on, provisions stowed, clothing wrapped in plastic bags – an important consideration, this one, because I've never yet met a boat which doesn't get damp below. I had probably forgotten something, but it shouldn't be anything vital since Jacques, my husband, always checks the liferaft, the flares and the rest of the safety equipment.

At six in the morning I peered out of my bedroom window and cast a sailor's eye at the weather. There was a clear sky with scattered clouds, but from the look of the trees quite a bit of wind. Although it was May and almost summer, the air was cold. A northerly wind then – perfect for a west-south-west passage! I did not dare count on it though; that would be tempting fate to make the favourable wind disappear and a headwind take its place. When it comes to the weather I am almost as superstitious as a medieval sailor. But the 0625 weather forecast gave reason for optimism; it predicted north-westerlies of force 5 to 6, with wind speeds of between seventeen and thirty-three knots – a good strong beam wind to give me a fast passage.

Each moment of a fair wind is precious and I hurried down to the marina where *Gulliver G* was berthed. Despite having sailed this coast many times, I still get a knot in my stomach at the prospect of another voyage. The childhood mixture of excitement and apprehension was making the adrenalin flow and as I met the first scent of the sea, sharp, tangy and heavy with a fish-like smell, I was reminded of oceans green with plankton and of long Atlantic voyages. There is a subtle moment when the land and all its complexities are forgotten and the sea, in all its simplicity, stretches challengingly ahead. In the independence and isolation of a small boat the problems of the world can be left behind, at least for a while. That is why, perhaps, small boating is so popular today.

Walking down the marina pontoon, my eye searched out the familiar sturdy mast covered with worn gold anodising and topped by a radar reflector. *Gulliver G* is not the smartest boat, and certainly not the fastest, but she is my own and has served me well. To me at least she is beyond reproach. Built in 1966 out of fibreglass, she can be described as a long-keeled Bermudan sloop. Her lines appear old-fashioned now but they are very graceful; and her displacement, though heavy by today's standards, is a great asset when trying to claw through a large sea. When *Gulliver G* took me across the Atlantic in 1973 I had no intention of trying to break any records and the two of us made a sedate but safe 37-day crossing. Since then I have sailed other yachts over greater distances, but none has challenged the special place that *Gulliver G* holds in my affections.

Down in the mahogany- and pine-lined cabin I took out Admiralty chart number 2675 covering the English Channel, and had another look at my route. The sailing time for the whole voyage could be as little as thirty-five hours or as much as eighty. Everything depended on the weather. With a 24-hour stop-over at Plymouth I should reach the Scillies within three to five days. I put the chart on the chart-table and, since it was positioned right beside the main hatch, covered it with polythene to keep the water off. I turned on the master switch which fed the electric power to the engine's starter motor, the radios, and the lights. I put on sweater, down-quilted waistcoat and oilskins. Although the sky was bright with sunshine the strong wind had a high chill factor. In these latitudes they say there are only two known conditions on a boat: cold and very cold.

At last I was ready to start the engine and reverse *Gulliver G* out of her berth. The romantic sailor dislikes the use of an engine, but only the foolhardy – or those with light, highly-manoeuvrable boats – try to leave a densely packed marina under sail. Parking boats in neat rows beside pontoons is not a pretty way to fill a river, but it provides easy, quick access to your boat. Those who mourn the sight of boats swinging

E

Hardy Mo
°240

Weymou
Chesil
Beach
27
19
S.Sh.R.
Bill of Portla
14
'1 Gp Fl(4) 20s 29M
& F.R 13M Dia(1) 3
44

S.G.Sh
52

M   A

61

A satellite view shows the coast of Britain, but a mariner needs more than a picture. The detail of Admiralty chart 2675 gives information about soundings, tides, lights and hazards

to their moorings forget the miseries of rowing a small dinghy from yacht to shore on a wild, wet night. In early times, long before the invention of heavy-link chain to moor a boat to a heavy weight on the river bed, North European boats had to be light enough to be dragged or carried ashore, or robust enough to take the mud with the rise and fall of the tide. Quite heavy vessels can be pulled ashore by rolling them over logs and, with strong enough rope, a large boat can be tied to trees overhanging a river bank, but in both cases the hull must have a flattish bottom to take the ground – and this is not the best shape for a craft propelled by sail.

It was eight o'clock and I was late; it would take half an hour to motor down the river and I wanted to make the most of the six-hour ebb tide. The Lymington River meanders in wide sweeps through flat marshland down to the Solent. By today's standards river transport, with all its twists and turns, does not seem very efficient. Yet rivers have provided men with their primary means of transport for thousands of years and, in many parts of the world, still do. Almost without exception, men could travel quicker over water than land and, in densely wooded countries, boats were often the *only* way to travel. Even the simplest of craft – a few logs strapped together – could take a man downstream or, with the use of a paddle, enable him to cross a lake.

Men would only have taken to the water if the benefits had been worth the considerable trouble of building a craft. Food would undoubtedly have been the prime motive, not only because boats provided access to fish, but because hunters could use rivers and lakes to extend their hunting territory. Barter, escape from enemies, famine or flood, and the waging of war would also have provided strong incentives.

We can only guess at the design and structure of early craft. Because they were made of highly perishable materials virtually none, except a few of those fashioned from heavy timber, have survived. Cave paintings and rock carvings provide clues as to what they may have looked like, but the best indications come from craft still being built in various parts of the world today. Just as early men used whatever natural materials were to hand, so boats of all shapes and types are still being built out of reeds, bark, skin, or wood – although many are fast disappearing under the onslaught of the outboard motor and the plastic hull. Rafts can still be found in India, South-East Asia and South America, and consist of either logs or reeds or even inflated animal skins strapped together. The skin boat, of which the Welsh coracle and the Irish curragh are examples, is more sophisticated, the stitched hide being stretched over a light wooden frame. Where suitable timber is to be found, bark boats are made, while those fortunate enough to live among forests of large trees can fashion dug-outs out of the trunks. Everything depends on the materials available.

Light, frail craft were safe on rivers, small lakes and estuaries if the weather was good. But even a sheltered stretch of water like the Solent can be extremely choppy in a gale. The secret of survival in a small boat was, one would guess, not to venture too far from the shore. Yet the proximity of the shore is no guarantee of safety; today many a small boat gets into trouble within yards of the beach. Large vessels, too, have sunk in harbours and estuaries; even large natural harbours like Plymouth and Falmouth are littered with wrecks of ships which dragged their anchors and ran on the rocks. Fifteen miles to the east of Lymington, at the other end of the Solent, lies the wreck of a beautiful sixteenth-century ship, the *Mary Rose*, the flagship and pride of King Henry VIII's navy. A mighty ship of 600 tuns cargo capacity (tuns being casks of wine), she carried 400 crew to man her twenty heavy and sixty light guns. One day she sailed out to fight the French and, in full view of the King, was caught by a squall of wind, heeled over and, with her lower gun ports open, quickly filled up and sank. The importance of

The Edge of the Unknown

The *Mary Rose*, from a list made in 1536 of Henry VIII's ships. A diver surveys the wreck, from which finds – like the arrows on the right, boots, clothes, medicines and weapons – are providing unique material evidence of Tudor life

this particular wreck is that one side has been almost completely preserved in mud and, using sophisticated new methods, marine archaeologists hope to bring it to the surface.

Once clear of the river mouth and into the Solent, I prepared to raise sail. First, I needed to engage the self-steering gear. This wind-guided, water-powered gadget is vital to singlehanders, for it enables us to study charts, to cook, to raise and lower sails, and generally to get on with the boat's business while the yacht holds a steady course. It has been developed in the last thirty years and has revolutionised short-handed sailing. With the boat steering herself under engine power I hauled up the mainsail and put in a reef. Reefing, or reducing the size of the sail, is necessary to present a smaller amount of sail to a stronger wind so that the yacht is not overpowered. I could not be certain of the wind strength out in the English Channel, but it was better to be undercanvassed. (Anticipation is said to be the secret of good seamanship; if you can foresee the worst and prepare for it, you will rarely be caught out.) Next, I raised the jib (or foresail) and went back to the cockpit to sheet (or pull) it in. Now we were away! As the jib filled *Gulliver G* leapt forward through the water, heeling gently. Down below there were sounds of bottles settling in the confines of the galley lockers, of water slurping in the kettle, and the clatter of a spoon falling across the cabin.

Here in the shelter of the land there were no large waves, just small wavelets which *Gulliver G* cut through with ease. From the feel of the boat, the urgency with which she pushed along, I reckoned we were doing about six knots or nautical miles per hour, a good speed for us. (A nautical mile, incidentally, is 1.1515 times a statute mile. It makes a better measure of distance at sea because it relates to latitude; sixty nautical miles equal one degree of latitude.) Once clear of the land I would trail a taffrail log – a kind of spinner – which measures distance through the water, and therefore speed, more accurately than I myself could. But for the moment it was sufficient to use what the Americans call 'eyeball navigation', that is, looking, observing, gauging distance from the shore by the apparent size of land objects, and estimating speed by watching buoys or other fixed objects against far-off shore features. All you need for 'eyeballing' are good powers of observation. It also helps to know the area like the back of your hand. The men who fished these waters in frail boats would have come here day after day, month after month; they would have learnt the currents and eddies of the tides, the meanders of the channels through the marshes, and the meaning of the cloud patterns overhead. Long experience and constant vigilance were the allies of the fishermen.

Nowadays all seafarers have the benefit of weather forecasts. Meteorology is a difficult and inexact science, but it has been greatly improved by satellite photographs, which reveal complete weather systems and provide an essential overall picture to supplement the more traditional data sent by ships and shore stations. However, it is impossible to predict winds with complete accuracy: the gradations of atmospheric pressure and temperature are too complex and volatile. You can get a useful idea of what the weather is likely to do from a weather forecast, but you are still wise to take the wind as you find it. When out of reach of weather forecasts, the barometer provides the best guide to bad weather. A sharp fall in pressure usually brings a gale but the highest winds come with the first rise, as an old rhyme relates:

> First rise after low
> Foretells a stronger blow.

Even after receiving a forecast and checking the barometer, I find I still search the sky for weather portents, just as sailors have done since the beginning of time. The formation, colour and height of the clouds can give warning of strong winds:

> If clouds look as if scratched by a hen
> Get ready to reef your topsails then.

Another of my favourites is

> Mackerel sky and mares' tails
> Make tall ships carry small sails.

Today the clouds were moving steadily across the sky and, though a few promised rain and gusts, there were no mares' tails in sight. *Gulliver G* was approaching the entrance to the narrow Needles Channel, through which we would pass from the Solent into the open sea. This channel is a real bottleneck and, as the tides rise and fall, so the water is desperate either to rush into the Solent or to escape from it. As a result the tidal streams are strong, running at up to five knots. Approaching the channel on the ebb, I already had a knot or so of tide helping me along. Once we got into the narrowest part, it would increase to about three knots, pushing *Gulliver G* out of the Solent like a cork out of a bottle.

The phenomenon of the tides must have been a great unfathomable mystery in early times. The sea, a vast alien element with an unpredictable nature, was terrifying enough, but its strange rhythmic movements, the great rising and falling of the water level and the onrush of currents of such force that craft were swept along helplessly, these must have been more awesome still. Early man would have realised that the tides were linked to the moon in some way – simple observation would tell him that the rise and fall of the water was greater when the moon was full or new than during its other phases. But that must have made the phenomenon more mystifying still! No wonder the sun and moon were worshipped for centuries and ancient Britons built strange stone monuments to the sun, like Stonehenge.

Any seafarer who wants to make a fast, easy passage – and that is every one of us – makes the maximum use of the tides. Occasionally there can be disadvantages, and I was about to meet one now, as *Gulliver G* tore through the narrow channel in the grip of the fast-flowing ebb. At the mouth of the narrows lie the Needles, a series of tall white rocks that stand out from the Isle of Wight like a row of jagged teeth. Extending from these rocks almost all the way across the mouth of the channel is a shallow bank. It is not so shallow that it cannot be sailed across, nor so extensive that ships cannot pass through, but it is sufficiently obstructive to cause a tide-race; water builds up behind the shallow bank and, if there is a strong wind blowing against the current, they combine to create short, steep seas with breaking crests. Such waves can be awkward; they come at you from a variety of directions in small vertical walls and can break over a yacht or small boat.

As we approached the tide-race I realised it was looking angrier than usual. The wind was also gusting strongly and *Gulliver G* would do better with a smaller jib up, but not now – at the moment all my attention was focused on the sight ahead of me and the necessity to brace myself against something solid.

There is something absolutely terrifying about the vision of white water. To the mariner it means only one thing – trouble. It means rocks, or shallows, or strong currents. Although I knew there was plenty of water under the keel, emotional reaction overcomes reason at the sight of breaking water. As *Gulliver G* sped into the confused jumble of waves my heart was in my mouth and I felt the familiar taste of fear. It brought back memories of other moments when I thought I'd run out of luck. There was the time I inadvertently sailed into the Nantucket Shoals and was faced by a wall of white surf; the night off Ireland when I thought I had struck a rock; the moment when *Gulliver G* touched a dangerous bank after we had wandered out of a deep-water channel – terrible moments and vivid memories which clutch at the heart.

Gulliver G trembled and shook as the small but awkward waves came at her from all directions, throwing spray on her decks and rolling her sharply from side to side. The confused water hissed and roared as the unseen current pushed against the flow of the waves. A large sea reared up and threw *Gulliver G* a powerful punch. Another clout and then, quite suddenly, we were through and the boat settled into the rhythmic rise and fall of the regular Channel waves.

The Needles. The lighter colour of the sea over the shallows shows in this view from the air

It is the unpredictable nature of the sea that makes it frightening. I had sailed over that bank many times, but it had never given me such a buffeting before. One should always think ahead and be prepared – but I had broken the rule and given myself an unpleasant surprise! When sailing in familiar waters there is a danger of becoming complacent, as I should have remembered. Once, returning from a foggy and frightening crossing of the Channel, I relaxed in the safety of the Solent and promptly went aground in the Lymington River. Although it's important to prepare yourself for anything that the sea may throw at you, I have sometimes found it difficult to strike a balance between healthy anticipation and excessive imagination. When I set out on my first solo transatlantic crossing in 1973 it was here, at the Needles, that the enormity of what I was about to do struck me. In my mind's eye all I could see were enormous waves, hurricane-force winds and a terrible end to my venture. So great was my fright that I was physically sick. In the event, the largest waves I ever saw were half the size of those in my imagination, but the anxiety continued to dog me until I arrived within sight of America.

How much greater must have been the fear of the early sailors. They had no scientific understanding of the sea; the cause of tides was a mystery, charts were unheard of, and the horizon marked the limit of the known world. For the peoples of Northern Europe sea-voyaging was a particularly hazardous undertaking. The westerly winds that sweep in from the Atlantic bring gales, storms, rain and poor visibility. The northerlies bring clear skies, but strong, cool winds, while the easterlies carry the icy cold of the Arctic in their grasp. There is none of the predictability of the trade winds found in the equatorial zones. In northern waters fog can descend in a moment and encompass the land and the sea for days. Calms can last for hours or minutes. The water, too, is very different: it is not clear and translucent, so that rocks and shoals can be seen with the naked eye, but opaque with silt and plankton, hiding most dangers that lurk beneath the surface. The tidal streams are strong, particularly in the English Channel, and difficult to plot. All in all, it is an inhospitable place for the mariner. Even in summer the weather can be ferocious; in winter only a madman puts to sea for pleasure.

As *Gulliver G* and I headed out into the open Channel, the weather was kind. Although it was a rumbustious force 6 with occasional squalls, the wind was still fair – that is, it was coming from a direction other than ahead. You cannot ask for more when heading west down-Channel. The most common winds around Britain blow from the west or south-west, necessitating tacking (or zigzagging) to achieve a westerly objective. When tacking upwind against the tide it is difficult to make any progress at all and the cruising man is tempted to find a snug harbour until the tide turns. During the age of sail it was common to anchor during a foul tide and sail only when the stream was favourable. This was known as 'tiding over'. But in a fierce westerly wind most sailing ships did not even attempt the passage and waited in port until the wind changed. Sometimes they waited for weeks, even months. When Drake set out on his circumnavigation of the world in 1577, he waited two weeks for a favourable wind before leaving Plymouth, was driven back by gales, and finally left six weeks after first setting out. This kind of delay was not unusual and sailors had to be patient men.

Faced by such difficult weather the first mariners who sailed these coasts would have been very careful about venturing out of sheltered waters. Given a calm day, there was no reason why the flimsiest of craft could not be paddled along an exposed shore. However, to do so day in day out, in a variety of weather conditions, required the development of sturdy boats. Skin, bark or raft boats would not have withstood even moderate waves for very long and fishermen would have needed wooden craft if they were to go to sea regularly. Surprisingly sophisticated ancient boats have been discovered in Northern Europe. Dating from about 1500 BC, the boats found at Ferriby in Yorkshire were made of planks sewn together with yew or willow. The Scandinavian Als Boat (300 to 200 BC) and Björke Boat (AD 100) were developments of the dug-out, having a dug-out base with frames and planking added to the sides to increase their height. It was this mastery in wood which enabled men to put out to sea. But even with a wood-built boat the early mariner would have taken care to stay near the shore so that he might beach his craft if a squall threatened. Small open boats are easily overwhelmed and the shore offers the only haven from large waves.

From coast-hugging it is a short step to what I call coast-hopping. Hopping from river mouth to estuary, from haven to harbour, has always been a popular way to travel – and still is today. Once boats were strong enough to withstand the odd squall there was no reason why they shouldn't go straight for the next safe haven, rather than following the line of the shore. Leaving the Needles I had put *Gulliver G* on a compass heading of 260°. This would take me straight down-Channel towards Plymouth, and keep me well clear of the headlands, some of which had dangerous tide-races to seaward. But if I hadn't been so anxious to get to the Scillies, I would have broken my journey at Poole, a pleasant three-hour sail away, then waited for slack tide to round Anvil Point and St Alban's Head before heading for Weymouth and a night in harbour. I was restricted to deep-water harbours because *Gulliver G*'s long keel draws over five foot of water. Early sailors were not so limited: the Vikings, who sailed the length and breadth of the North European coastline a thousand years ago, built large ships, yet they kept them shallow-draughted so that, by swinging up specially adapted rudders, they could drag their longships on to the shore. This had drawbacks – vessels without deep keels cannot sail well to windward – but when you were plundering and raiding, the ability to land on any beach and creep up on your victims from behind had obvious advantages.

Sailing close to the shore is comforting, yet in many ways it is much more dangerous than going out to sea. Rocks and shoals are usually found inshore, as are tide-races and strange currents. Waves are often steeper and more prone to break in shallow or disturbed water. Once away from the coast, on the other hand, the waves become more regular and predictable, and there are fewer dangers to worry about. Many a sailor breathes a sigh of relief when land drops out of sight astern. At the same time the offshore sailor must be prepared to take the weather as it comes and ride out gales at sea. For this he needs a robust weatherly craft. Thor Heyerdahl has demonstrated that it is possible to cross oceans on simple wooden rafts or light papyrus boats. But these experimental voyages were made in the trade wind regions where wind and current are constant, enabling a craft to drift many miles a day in one direction. In northern waters the weather is not so kind and the true sea-going boat has to have a strong watertight hull, with a high prow or some form of decking to keep out the waves. *Gulliver G*'s hull is made of fibreglass reinforced with wooden bulkheads (or internal cross-sections) which maintain the boat's shape and strength. The keel keeps fore and aft rigidity as well as providing ballast and minimising leeway. The hull is completely decked, except for the open cockpit which drains into the sea, ensuring all stays dry below. In these waters primitive boats were not suitable to be taken offshore until they too acquired rigid backbones, in the form of carved or hollowed-out timber, and strong hulls made of planks joined by reliable fastenings. Plant or leather lashings were short-lived as fastenings because they rotted. Wooden pegs were an improvement, but copper and iron provided the real breakthrough. Once planks could be nailed, bolted or clipped together hulls could be made watertight and built to a much larger size with a high prow. The ultimate triumph of early northern boat-building technology was the Viking ship, developed over thousands of years among the fjords, islands and lakes of Scandinavia. As long ago as the Stone Age, ancestors of the Vikings were voyaging far

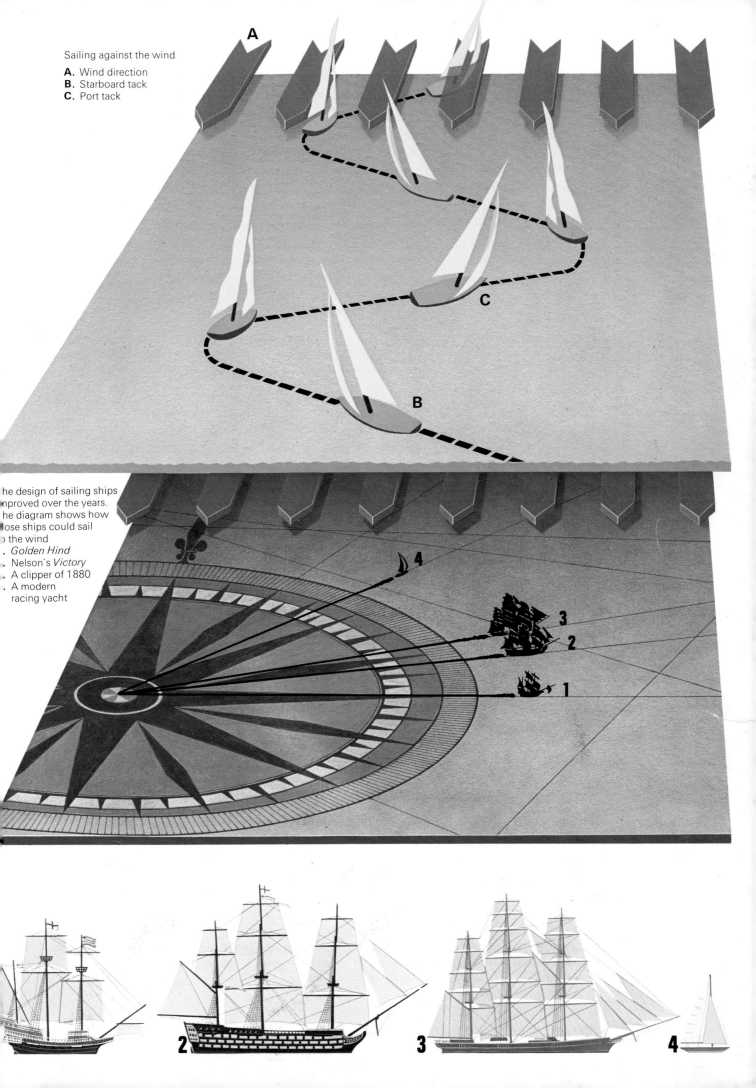

Sailing against the wind

A. Wind direction
B. Starboard tack
C. Port tack

A

C

B

he design of sailing ships
nproved over the years.
he diagram shows how
lose ships could sail
o the wind
. *Golden Hind*
. Nelson's *Victory*
. A clipper of 1880
. A modern
  racing yacht

4

3

2

1

1

2

3

4

offshore; the bones of deep-sea fish species have been found in a Stone Age settlement at Stavanger in Norway. By the eighth century AD when the Vikings began to break out of Scandinavia and voyage hundreds of miles, they had become highly skilled in both boat-building and sailing. Their ships were clinker-built, the overlapping planks being riveted together and fastened to the ribs with lashings of spruce roots. It is not known exactly how they were rigged, but the single square sail could certainly be flattened to allow them to make use of beam as well as tail winds. Just as *Gulliver G* was flying along before this strong north-westerly wind, so the Viking ships would have made excellent speed in such conditions. In 1893 a replica of the famous Viking burial ship found at Gokstad was sailed across the Atlantic and achieved a speed of ten knots on a beam reach.

The replica of the Gokstad burial ship which sailed the Atlantic in 1893

Once such ships had been developed, seas and even oceans could be crossed. Not only did the Vikings sail the length and breadth of the Baltic and the coast of Western Europe, but they were the first Europeans who are known to have crossed the Atlantic. They colonised the Faroe Isles, then Iceland and Greenland, and finally but briefly the mysterious Vinland, thought to be Newfoundland. The distances between these colonies was not enormous – perhaps three or four days' sailing under good conditions – but considering the ocean was unknown and the routes lay in the path of the worst North Atlantic weather, the achievement was magnificent.

We don't know when men first started sailing around the coasts of Northern Europe, but it has been deduced that significant sea voyages were made elsewhere in the world tens of thousands of years ago. Australia had been separated from Asia by water for a long time before it was colonised some 20,000 years ago. It is also thought that western Europe was settled by Mediterranean people who crossed the Straits of Gibraltar from North Africa. Until late in the Middle Stone Age Britain was part of the continental land mass, but then, at some time between 6000 and 5000 BC, the land bridge to Europe was cut by the sea and Britain became an island. For more than a thousand years it remained isolated until in about 2000 BC Neolithic immigrants from Western Europe settled, introducing a new lifestyle based on organised agriculture and flint tools. Later, in the Bronze Age, another movement of peoples into Britain brought settlers from the low countries and the middle Rhine with their new burial customs.

The occasional cave painting or rock carving gives us a vague idea of what the boats of these early seafarers might have looked like but how did they navigate across open sea? The probable answer is that, in the modern sense of the word, they did not navigate at all; they just set off in the right general direction. On leaving the Needles I carefully noted the reading on my patent log and paid out the logline with its spinner astern. This would give me my distance sailed through the water. The magnetic compass beside the main hatch gave me my course. Allowing for the effects of the tide, which I could estimate from the tide tables, I could now plot my dead reckoning position on the chart. To check this I took some compass bearings on two prominent headlands – St Alban's Head and Portland Bill. I was glad to see the two positions differed by only half a mile – an awful lot less than they do on a dark stormy night. Coastal navigation in a small boat is an approximate science at the best of times. Yachts pitch and roll a good deal, making the compass swing back and forth, so that readings of the boat's heading and of the bearings of landmarks are never more than good estimates. There is an old joke among small-boat sailors: a navigator is asked by his skipper if he knows where they are. 'Of course!' he replies. 'I know *exactly* where we are.' Placing a hand palm down over a large area of the chart he cries triumphantly, 'We're here!' However, despite the inaccuracies of small-boat navigation one can usually fix one's position to within a mile or so.

The idea of dead reckoning and position-fixing developed with the increasing use of the compass and the first charts towards the end of the Middle Ages. Before that sailors had little to go on but their eyes and simple observation of the sun and stars. The Pole Star was well known to classical astronomers and seafarers. The Phoenicians, who may have sailed as far as Britain in search of tin, were accomplished navigators. In the Mediterranean the winds are fairly predictable and wind navigation, or gauging course from wind direction, was sufficient. But further north the winds become more variable and, after hugging the coast as far as northern France, the Phoenicians would probably have got their bearings from the Pole Star on a clear night before sailing in the general direction of western Britain and the tin-producing areas. Navigation of this kind was very much a hit and miss affair. Yet the Vikings managed not only to discover Iceland, Greenland and Vinland in latitudes where visibility can be poor for days but to sail back and forth between them. One can only assume that, if lost in mist and fog, they hove to until the weather cleared and they could see the Pole Star again.

The New Stone Age farmers who spread over Britain as far as the Shetland Islands, a hundred miles north-east of the Scottish mainland, voyaged impressive distances, but only, it would seem, as far as they could see. The Shetlands are linked to the mainland by a chain of islands with no more than twenty miles between them, so that in clear weather one is visible from another. Similarly it was not difficult to find the way across the English Channel when the cliffs of Dover can be seen from the French coast. It seems unlikely that these people made ocean passages – but we will never know for sure because, if they did, they either perished in the attempt or left no trace of their voyages.

By mid-afternoon I was abeam of Portland Bill, the most notorious headland on the south coast of England. It is safe for a small boat to sail very close to the headland, as any early mariner would choose to do, or to pass a good two miles clear of it, but anything in between can be disastrous: the tide race off Portland is vicious and many a boat has been lost there. By my estimate we were a safe four miles off with the clear expanse of Lyme Bay ahead. It is fifty miles across the bay, too great a

A Portolan chart of Europe and North Africa, 1557. Coastal navigation by a combination of shore sights and dead reckoning is still familiar to small-boat sailors. In charts like this one the shapes of land masses are inexact, but the information on coastal features abundant

distance for an early boat to sail in safety, and the first navigators would have taken the much longer route around the edge of the bight. With a good wind *Gulliver G* could reach the other side in seven hours but it was obvious that on this voyage it was going to take us a lot longer. The wind was dropping fast and, despite putting up my largest foresail and unreefing the mainsail, *Gulliver G*'s speed was already down to three knots. When faced by a calm it is best to summon all your patience and settle down for a long wait. Many a sailor – myself included – finds calms harder to bear than storms, particularly when caught in an area like the doldrums. As the Ancient Mariner observed:

> Down dropt the breeze, the sails dropt down,
> 'Twas sad as sad could be;
> And we did speak only to break
> The silence of the sea!

There is nothing to be done to bring back the wind, except whistle for it. This ancient superstition is still widely practised. I have whistled myself hoarse on many occasions – not always to great effect – but it did at least vent some of my feelings of frustration at sitting helplessly on a mirror-like sea. Of course, one mustn't whistle when the wind is already blowing – that produces a gale! When becalmed in the doldrums I have also tried giving Neptune a tot of best Scotch. This pouring of malt whisky on to the water had absolutely no effect and it was only later that I discovered he much preferred Burgundy; a whole bottle dropped over the side brought the wind within minutes. I do not regard myself as particularly superstitious, yet I'm always careful to make sure I have my St Christopher medallion safely around my neck. If that were to be lost I would be very cautious – and probably wouldn't put to sea at all.

Myth and superstition have always surrounded the sea and, despite the scepticism of the scientific age, they still survive. Most sailors know it's unlucky to sail on a Friday and to have flowers on board. In the past women have had a somewhat chequered reputation for luck. For a while they were thought to make the sea grow angry, then they enjoyed great popularity as figureheads. This was because, by a convenient stroke of fortune, they had the opposite effect when half-naked and caused an angry sea to calm down. These superstitions have, I am glad to say, largely been forgotten! Countless superstitions have existed, some contradictory, many unusual, but all of them dreamed up by sailors to protect themselves from the hazards of the sea. After bad weather and rocky shores, mariners probably feared darkness most. My early seafarer would almost certainly want to avoid night sailing and, wherever he was along the coast, would have found a place to drag his boat ashore by now. In later times vessels could make for port, anchor in sheltered waters, or, if approaching a dangerous coast, heave to well offshore until dawn. Few would choose to keep moving at night, particularly in unfamiliar waters.

At 50° north the nights are becoming short in May and twilight does not fall until after nine o'clock. As the darkness envelops you, it is easy to believe your boat is a cocoon of safety. The contrast between the velvet blackness of the sea and the warm lamplight of your small cabin creates a sense of security that is entirely misplaced. Night is the time when your guard is down and your reactions slow. It is the time when you long to sleep but cannot. Being singlehanded I had to keep watch through the hours of darkness and into the next day until I arrived at Plymouth. As the night descended I put *Gulliver G*'s navigation lights on: a white light on the stern and, up on the bow, a red light to port and a green to starboard. These lights would tell other vessels that I was a small sailing craft and, depending on which lights were visible to them, the direction I was travelling in. Similarly I could identify another vessel as a fishing boat, a tug or a ship, and see which direction she was moving in. Between us, we should then be able to avoid each other.

The land, too, is well lit nowadays. After the threatened calm some wind returned and shortly after midnight I saw the loom of Start Point Lighthouse on the far side of the bay. It was flashing three times every ten seconds, so there was no mistaking it. Along any one stretch of coast each light has its own individual signal, its own combination of flashes which makes it different from every other light, so that, once you have it in view, you can establish a rough position. In many ways, night sailing is easier than day sailing: headlands and land features have an unpleasant habit of looking very similar in daylight and it's all too easy to confuse one with another, but at night pilotage is made very easy for the navigator – quite the reverse of the old days.

The summer night had started mild but now, at two in the morning, the air was cold and damp. I wore a woollen hat, towelling scarf, mittens and, on my feet, extra thick socks. I was still shivering slightly, so I went below to make myself a cup of tea. While waiting for the water to boil I sat in the companionway looking out through the dark night for the lights of ships. I could see two away to port which would pass well clear, while to starboard, just inside Start Point, the lights of a small trawler hovered over the Skerries Bank.

With the hot cup of tea in my hand, I reflected on the rarity of moments like this: a clear night, a fair wind, a reasonably fast passage, no ships breathing down my neck and the light of a familiar headland ahead, which, with the help of a fair tide, I should round by dawn. It is not often the English Channel allows a boat such fine sailing conditions. Indeed, I was enjoying the moment for the very reason that I knew it wouldn't last. According to the weather forecast the light north-westerly wind was due to shift around to the west.

Weather forecasts are a mixed blessing. It is a great advantage to have warning of strong winds so that if you are near port you may dash for harbour, but when well offshore I would rather not know I'm in for a rough time, because the anxiety of waiting for the gale can be more wearing than the event. On a night like this it would have been fun to guess which way the wind might go; now I knew for sure – for sure because contrary winds always seem to turn up when predicted, while favourable winds do not!

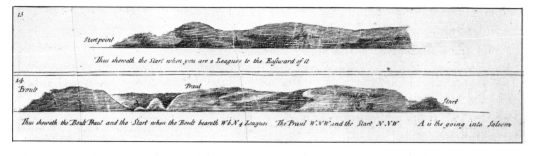

Start Point from the sea – from *Great Britain's Coasting Pilot*, Greenvile Collins, 1693

As the dawn grew yellow and Start Point became a soft grey outline ahead, *Gulliver G*'s sails started to flutter and lift as a faint but increasingly firm breeze came out of the west. I sheeted in the sails until she was sailing as close to the wind as she could go. No sailing vessel can sail directly into the wind, but the modern yacht can sail at an angle of 45° to it, or closer if sea conditions permit. By tacking (or zigzagging) the yacht can thus progress towards an upwind objective.

The Edge of the Unknown

Plymouth now lay upwind and the remaining twenty miles would now take about six hours to cover, instead of four.

The phenomenon of upwind sailing – albeit in a zigzag fashion – is one that the yachtsman takes for granted. Yet it took a long time for men to adopt even the simplest form of sail power, let alone one that could take a boat upwind. The Vikings had to rely on oars to take them to windward and, even during the heyday of sail, the galleon, the ship-of-the-line and the tea clipper were far from efficient on this point of sailing. In 1905 a sailing ship, the *Susanna*, took an incredible ninety-nine days to fight her way round the Horn from east to west, tacking back and forth for days just to hold her ground.

It was not that the principles of building close-winded vessels were unknown five hundred years ago – the ancient lateen rig found on Arab dhows is very efficient to windward. But when adapted for use on medieval European vessels the rig, with its exceptionally long yard or spar, was found heavy and difficult to handle. The problem was one of scale. As sea trade and sea power developed, vessels became larger and larger – trading ships to carry more cargo over greater distances and fighting ships to carry more men and weapons. By medieval times vessels were already so cumbersome, with their unwieldy fore and aft castles, that most of their windward ability was outweighed by the tremendous resistance they presented to the wind. Later sailing ships had better sails for upwind sailing as well as slimmer, faster hull shapes, but speed downwind was so highly valued and masts got so tall and crowded with rigging, that the windage problem was still considerable.

Only with the development of light, immensely strong modern materials has it become possible to sail boats really close to the wind. One thin stainless steel wire now does the work of many hemp shrouds and doesn't rot or stretch. A thin aluminium mast is as strong as a thick wooden one. A sail of man-made fibre is vastly superior to anything made of cotton, flax or hemp; it is light, flexible, immensely strong and doesn't stretch or blow out at the first puff of wind. *Gulliver G* is not exactly a racing machine but, with her steel rigging and terylene sails, she performs better to windward than a crack tea clipper of 150 years ago.

My early mariner would now, with the wind against him, be at a great disadvantage. Even if his craft possessed a simple sail, it would be of little use, so he would be forced to paddle or row. Another solution would be to sit on the shore and wait until the wind changed. It had taken *Gulliver G* twenty-four hours to do 100 miles, but I doubted if my mariner could have done more than twenty-five. Since he was making slow progress anyway, he might as well stop and await more favourable conditions.

When ports developed they grew around the needs of ships, commerce and trade. In the fifteenth century the major English ports were the Cinque Ports of Dover, Hastings, Romney, Hythe and Sandwich, towns well placed for trade with the European continent. But with the opening up of the New World in the late sixteenth century these ports diminished in importance because they lay downwind of the Atlantic. Harbours which lay at the western end of the English Channel, convenient for an easy departure and a minimum of windward sailing, grew in prominence. The most significant and famous of these is Plymouth, where I was now heading. It was from here that Drake set out on his circumnavigation in 1577, and from here, eleven years later, that he helped lead the English fleet to victory against the Spanish Armada. It was also from Plymouth that the *Mayflower* sailed with the Pilgrim Fathers to America in 1620.

To me – as it must have been to many sailors before me – Plymouth Sound was a welcome sight when it finally came into view at midday. It had taken me not six but eight hours to cover the last twenty miles, the wind having dropped to a faint breeze again. But now the great expanse of water, two miles long and two miles wide, opened up before me. Ahead lay Plymouth Hoe, the small hill behind which shelters the old town and inner harbour. To the north-west was Drake's Island, marking the mouth of the Tamar, one of the three rivers which flow into the Sound. Beyond the island and a short way up the Tamar lies Devonport, a major British Naval base and dockyard.

It's always a relief to make harbour; yet, like most people who go to sea, my feelings for the land are ambivalent. For the yachtsman, who sails in cramped and uncomfortable conditions, the contrast between life on sea and land is strong. After a long hard passage he is apt to embrace terra firma with open arms, crying 'never again!' It takes several weeks or months of comfortable living before he gets the itch to go to sea again. In the old days sailors might be away for years at a time, dreaming of a wonderful homecoming. But as often as not the reality of life ashore fell short of expectations, their refuge was taken in drunkenness, money ran out, and the girls were not so friendly. Poor Jack Tar found himself longing for the sea again.

In early times fishermen, seamen and those who lived off the sea were regarded as people apart. By the very nature of their work, seamen did not mix with the mainstream of land-based society. Their customs and way of life were therefore poorly understood and even held in contempt. Sometimes they deserved their poor reputation, for sea-based communities could be lawless and thieving, but generally it was the isolation of the sea-going life that alienated them from the landsman. Later, as trading ports developed, landsmen learnt to cater for the special needs of seafarers and to understand them better, but in more primitive communities the barriers remain.

My requirements in Plymouth were simple – a berth for my boat, a hot shower and a long sleep, then the purchase of some fresh provisions for the rest of my voyage. I found a quiet berth at a small marina and, twenty-four hours later, was ready for sea again. Once ready I am always keen to be away. The lure of the sea does not seem so strong when the wind's blowing from the south-west, the sky is overcast, and rain threatens, but conditions are rarely as bad as they seem. Once clear of the Sound, I found the wind was blowing no harder than force 3 and the sailing was not nearly as bumpy as I or my stomach had feared. Seasickness is not something you grow out of: you simply learn to live with it. I try to avoid it by staying on deck and keeping busy until the feeling wears off – normally after a few days.

Once again the wind was coming from ahead, not the best direction for a fast passage. *Gulliver G* is a well-built lady and needs a good, strong headwind to get her going. Only in force 8 – a full gale – does she really excel, making progress when other boats have long since turned tail. In this light wind she was inclined to stop dead on each wave. The ninety miles to the Scillies might take a long time.

Plymouth to the Lizard, from Waghenaer's sea atlas, 1584

The Edge of the Unknown

My first landfall after leaving Plymouth was the Lizard, which I weathered at dawn the next morning. This famous headland is the most southerly point of the English mainland and known as the 'gatepost' of the English Channel. Its rocky promontory and attendant reef standing a quarter of a mile out to sea held many memories for me, some of them less than pleasant. Twice I had raced around it at night in thick fog, once in a gale, and when becalmed I had sat staring at it for the best part of a day. Yet at other exhilarating moments it had been my first sight of England after many long weeks at sea, and therefore had the happiest of associations. For the sailors of old, too, the Lizard was usually their first sight of home. For many years Lloyd's of London had a signal station on the headland and ships would sail close enough to read the code flags which relayed orders for their final destination; some went too close and foundered on the hidden rocks. After a long seventeen-hour beat up to the Lizard I took care to stay well away from the headland; the tireder one is the greater the margin of error one should allow in one's navigation. As I always say, when in doubt take the corners wide. There was also a dark cloud coming up. It could mean a squall, or just rain, and in case of a squall I prepared to reef the mainsail. I did not concern myself with the jib; if the wind really blew up I could drop it on to the deck within seconds. Although I was singlehanded, the simplicity of the modern yacht's rig permits me rapid and large changes in sail area. It was a very different matter for the old sailing ships; shortening sail and manoeuvring were so difficult and time-consuming that they needed to maintain sea room at all times.

When the squall came it was not severe, but the wind was strong enough to warrant a reef in the mainsail. The sky grew black and driving rain obliterated the Lizard, a couple of miles to starboard. Bad visibility and a sudden squall are a dangerous combination, particularly when a vessel is uncertain of her position. Curving back from the Lizard is Mount's Bay, edged by rocks and craggy cliffs. It sweeps around in a great arc to Land's End, where the Longships reef and Runnelstone rock lie in wait. The entire south Cornish coast is littered with wrecks, but here there are such vast numbers they are impossible to count. On the Runnelstone alone there has been an average of one wreck a year for at least fifty years. This coast is everything the mariner fears: it is often his first landfall after a long passage, it is rocky and treacherous, it is frequently shrouded in fog and, worst of all, it is often a lee shore. Many great sailing ships found themselves driven towards the rocks by strong south-westerly winds and were unable to fight their way off. Sometimes ships were embayed between two headlands and tacked back and forth for days, only to founder when the crew tired or some piece of gear failed; on other occasions the danger was spotted in good time but, during the attempt to drive the ship to windward, a mast was lost and the ship drifted helplessly on to the rocks.

The loss of ships and life over the centuries was appalling, yet continued almost unabated until well into this century. The waters around Cornwall have always been among the busiest in the world as shipping bound for English, North Sea and Baltic ports makes landfall on the Lizard and then proceeds up Channel, mingling with the cross-Channel traders and fishermen. Yet, more than the sheer volume of traffic, it was the lack of navigational aids that contributed most to the terrible slaughter. Often ships would drive straight up on to the rocks, completely unaware of the proximity of land. After long periods of bad weather, navigators could easily be many tens of miles out in their reckoning, let alone the mere one or two that is needed to make the difference between safety and disaster.

Today many brilliant devices are available to the navigator: sonar to read the contours of the ocean floor, radar to guide him through darkness and fog, satellite navigation systems to pinpoint his position to the nearest yard, automatic pilots to maintain an accurate course, and gyro compasses unaffected by the earth's or ship's magnetism. Even on *Gulliver G*, which is simply equipped, there is a depth sounder, a radio direction-finder and, most important of all, a sextant, to fix the boat's position by the sun and the stars. All the technological wizardry available today makes navigation inestimably safer than it was a hundred years ago. Yet there is one factor that does not change and cannot be remedied by invention – the human element. Ships bristling with every conceivable gadget still run into danger because equipment fails, because someone is asleep, or because captains misjudge a situation and take an unjustifiable risk. In recent years we have seen shipwrecks on a massive scale, not in numbers of vessels, but in the size of them. Just fifteen miles west of Land's End, between the Scillies and the mainland, lies the Seven Stones shoal. The channel between Land's End and the Seven Stones is well marked by major lighthouses and, near the shoal itself, a lightship. Yet, on the night of 18 March 1967, in fine weather, a large oil tanker of 61,263 tons steamed straight on to the Seven Stones shoal. Over the next ten days, the *Torrey Canyon* slowly bled to death, spilling out her lethal cargo of black oil to kill or choke the sea life around her. Since then there have been other major shipwrecks in the Channel. Doubtless there will be more.

The early mariner needed all his skill to sail this coast. Thus far the voyage had probably taken him fourteen days. Now he had to choose his weather carefully because good beaches are further apart and there are many rocks and high cliffs to be dashed against. Here off the Lizard he was probably doing better than I. Paddling his light craft close inshore he could be round the point within a couple of hours, while *Gulliver G* flopped about like a stranded whale further offshore, making very little progress. There was a large lumpy sea running, quite out of proportion to the gentle westerly wind that returned after the squall. It looked as though I might have to spend a second consecutive night at sea because, if I did not make the Scillies before darkness, I would have to stand off until dawn. The entrance channel into the inner sound and anchorage is unlit and, without local knowledge, I didn't dare enter at night. Occasionally strong gusts sent *Gulliver G* surging up to windward but most of the time I had to sail her well off the wind and build up enough speed to push her through the waves. I tacked in order to take advantage of a small shift in wind direction, and took a leg into Mount's Bay. Ahead was Land's End, the south-west tip of the English mainland. From here it was twenty-one miles to the Scillies, not a long passage but quite a tricky one. The tides in this area are difficult to plot accurately because they change direction frequently, flowing towards almost every point of the compass during each twelve-hour period. Also, the visibility was down to about two miles and the Scillies are hard to see at the best of times. On a clear day the islands can be seen from the high cliffs above Land's End, which explains how early seafarers knew they were there, but at sea-level these low-lying windswept islands are hard to spot until you are almost upon them. The next tack took me out towards the isolated Wolf Rock which claimed many a ship until it was well marked by a tall lighthouse. The Wolf also stayed in sight for a depressingly long time as a foul tide pushed us south-eastward. The wind remained gusty and variable and, as *Gulliver G*'s faithful self-steering followed each wind shift, our course meandered through twenty degrees on the compass. My dead reckoning was not going to be very accurate. If he had any sense at all, my early mariner would have sat on Land's End until the wind turned to the north or east, and then sailed or paddled the distance in a fraction of the time it was taking me.

At long last, when I was beginning to think I wouldn't make the islands by nightfall, the wind freshened and shifted to the south, so that *Gulliver G* was able to lay her course. The visibility improved a little and I finally glimpsed land ahead. That first sight of the Scillies through a curtain of misty rain was characteristic; jagged rocks showed black against a low smudge of grey which was just discernible as an island. Fortunately I was coming in from the north-east, a fairly safe approach because here, unlike other parts of the Scillies, the rocks and dangers are mostly visible above water. *Gulliver G* was now flying along with the help of a favourable tide – making this one of those rare moments when everything is going right. Never having sailed in among the islands before, I wanted to establish my position before we got much closer. An hour later I was able to pick out the characteristics of St Martin's, one of the five inhabited islands in the group. Then, away to port, I saw St Mary's, the largest of the islands. But I kept checking the landmarks against the chart just in case I'd made a mistake; it's very easy to believe you are seeing what you expect or want to see. So-called distinctive features like craggy headlands or unusual rock formations can look confusingly alike.

The Isles of Scilly from the sea. Greenvile Collins, 1693

The Scillies cover about forty-four square miles of sea. There are five inhabited islands and about one hundred rocky islets. The main islands form a distinct group; indeed, most of them were one island thousands of years ago. Further to the south-west the islands become more fragmented until they break up into vicious rocks and ledges, some showing above the water, others hidden just beneath, waiting, one would almost think, for their prey. For centuries the Scillies have been a graveyard of ships. It is not just their position in the western approaches to the Channel that make them so dangerous, it is their lack of height, their spread and their terrible reefs. The highest island, St Mary's, reaches only 160 feet above sea-level, and it was easy for ships to find themselves on the Western Rocks before ever seeing land. The tides, too, are dangerous because they sweep across the ledges and between the islands. On several occasions I have raced around the Scillies bound for Ireland or America, and each time I have breathed a sigh of relief when they were safely past. Once, when singlehanded and short of sleep, I sat in thick fog somewhere off the Western Rocks knowing that the tide was pulling me towards them. Although one's ears always play tricks in fog, I swear I heard the thunderous sound of breaking waves. Despite the cold, dank air, I sweated in my oilskins until a breeze blew me free. In the hours I sat waiting for the wind to come I could not stop myself imagining what would happen if I was swept on to the nearby reef. In my mind's eye I saw the rocks appearing through the curtain of dripping white fog and tearing into the hull as the yacht pounded and thudded on each long rolling Atlantic swell. It was a very gruesome picture!

And so, indeed, must have been the reality for the thousands of people who have drowned on these dreadful western rocks of Scilly. After a long ocean voyage, ships would often be a matter of hours from harbour when they struck. Some sank immediately, others pounded to death over several days, spilling cargo and debris into the water and on to the island shores. For the people on board the choices were impossible: either they stayed with the ship and died with her, or, if they found the courage, they could leap into the icy waves and try to swim for safety with little chance of success. Very occasionally they were able to launch boats and make for the shore, but for the vast majority the end was drowning.

Lord, Lord! Methought what pain it was to drown!
What dreadful noise of waters in mine ears!
What ugly sights of death within mine eyes!
Methought I saw a thousand fearful wrecks;
Ten thousand men that fishes gnaw'd upon;
Wedges of gold, great anchors, heaps of pearl,
Inestimable stones, unvalued jewels,
All scattered in the bottom of the sea.

The bodies that were washed ashore were buried by the Scillonians who waited with barrows and carts to claim whatever cargo might come their way. Nowadays we would find the idea of wreck-stripping fairly unsavoury, but in those days it was an industry in Scilly and Cornwall. The inhabitants had a very simple view of life: you did what you could to help and thereafter you helped yourself. If the weather was not too bad the Scillonians would row their small gigs out to look for survivors. Otherwise they sat and waited on the shore. Over the years they gleaned a rich harvest of timber, figure-heads, cannon, silver, gold and general cargo, for hardly a winter or severe gale went by than some ship found her way on to the jagged teeth of the Scilly rocks.

Of the many shipwrecks on the islands the most disastrous in terms of life, ships and British morale was the loss in 1707 of the pride of the British Navy's fleet. Under the command of Sir Cloudesly Shovel fifteen ships-of-the-line were returning from the Siege of Toulon. After several days of bad weather the sailing masters were uncertain of their position, but the majority believed the fleet was somewhere off Ushant and Western France. In fact they were off the Scillies. Setting a course north-eastward up the English Channel – as they believed – nearly all the fleet sailed straight on to the rocks. Nearly 2000 men were lost, four times as many as the British lost at the Battle of Trafalgar. Sir Cloudesly's flagship, *Association*, was sunk and his body washed ashore. There is a story that he got ashore alive, only to be killed for his jewellery.

Another serious loss, but of a different kind, occurred in 1798 when one of Nelson's men-of-war, the *Colossus*, dragged her anchors and was wrecked on one of the smaller islands. She was carrying sick and wounded from the Battle of the Nile, all of whom were saved. But she was also carrying Sir William Hamilton's irreplaceable collection of archaeological treasures and Etruscan vases, all of which were smashed and went to the bottom in small pieces.

It is said that the Scillonians used to send up a prayer: 'We pray thee, O Lord, not that wrecks should happen, but that if any wreck should happen, Thou wilt guide them into the Scilly Isles for the benefit of the inhabitants.' The *Friar Tuck*, wrecked in 1863, must have been an answer to that prayer, for she was loaded with tea from China, a valuable cargo in those days. Nearly all the tea mysteriously disappeared from the wreck, to the islanders' material benefit, and even today descendants of the Chinese geese carried by the *Friar Tuck* can be seen on the island of Tresco.

But of the countless wrecks around the islands the one that most shocked the world was the loss of the 3400-ton *Schiller*. Bound for European ports from New York, she was a crack passenger steamer carrying nearly 350 passengers and crew. In thick fog on the night of 7 May 1875, she sailed in among the Western Rocks and hit the Retarrier

The wreck of the *Tripolitania*, Porthleven, 1912. One of the many photographs of wrecks taken by the Gibson family of the Scilly Isles

Ledge. She fired ten guns to attract attention but only one was heard. It was assumed by those on shore to be a signal that the *Schiller* had passed the islands safely. Over 300 lives were lost and only forty-five saved. Nowadays there are far fewer wrecks on the islands, but they still occur. Trawlers and yachts, those without sophisticated navigation aids, still come to grief with loss of life.

When sailing it always seems that events happen with frustrating slowness or baffling rapidity. Having made slow progress between Plymouth and the outer Scillies, *Gulliver G* was now flying along so fast that I almost passed St Mary's Channel. After a quick look at the chart I realised I must turn immediately or miss the entrance. A heavy cloud brought early darkness and a deluge of rain. Craggy Peninnis Head became a vague blur to starboard and I scanned the murk ahead for the black shape of the Spanish Ledges buoy which should be visible to port. Peninnis had a light on it which I could see flashing dim yellow through the rain, but the buoy was unlit. I thought I had missed it until, with startling abruptness, it appeared ahead. Within seconds we had roared past and were flying on to the next buoy. The wind was vibrating in *Gulliver*'s sails and her bow wave showed in a curve of white foam to leeward.

In the open roadstead the wind dropped as suddenly as it had increased and, amid heavy curtains of rain, we floated slowly into St Mary's Harbour and dropped anchor. The accumulated tiredness of almost two days' hard sailing had taken their toll and I needed a long sleep, but first I would enjoy a hot meal and a small tot of whisky. This was the moment when I enjoyed being a twentieth-century sailor; I could open a can, heat it quickly on my little gas cooker, and then fall into a warm sleeping bag which, thanks to being wrapped in two thick polythene bags, was guaranteed dry.

The early mariner would not be doing so well. After his long voyage down the coast he would be waiting patiently for good weather before attempting the open crossing to the islands. After some days he might be lucky; the wind might drop and the sky look settled. He would then start his seven- to eight-hour row or, if he was really fortunate and an easterly wind came up, he could raise a simple sail and enjoy an easy passage. The tides would be difficult to judge unless he knew this area well and, as he approached the islands, he would keep clear of swirling or disturbed water, a sign of rocks just beneath the surface. Eventually he would make land and the long and hazardous voyage would be over. I reckoned that it would have taken a small wooden or skin boat at least ten days to make the voyage and probably well over two weeks. Ten hours' rowing a day would have been a lot when food had to be caught, prepared and heated, and a safe place found for the night. Even when boats became stronger and seafarers more confident, the voyage to the Scillies was no mean undertaking. So why did they come?

The next morning I awoke to the gentle sound of lapping water and the sight of sunshine streaming in through the open companionway. From the deck I could see St Mary's Roads, the open anchorage in the centre of the main group of islands. The sparkling water, a dazzling clear aquamarine, hid secrets about the early settlers to these islands. Until about 500 BC the sea level was lower and most of the islands formed one large piece of land, but then the water gradually advanced until, about AD 400, the pattern of the present islands was formed. Lines of stones run down the beaches and into the sea, remnants of old walls that marked out ancient fields. There are probably dozens of ancient villages under the sea between the islands but, to the chagrin of the archaeologists, they have long been buried by shifting sands.

Clues to the earliest visitors do exist, however. I walked through Hugh Town, the capital of St Mary's, to the Isles of Scilly Museum. Here there are a number of Stone Age axe-heads which have been discovered on the islands and possibly date from as early as 3000 BC. They are made of a type of flint which is still found on the island of St Martin's. Flint, an opaque variety of quartz, was extremely valuable to Stone Age man: it could be fashioned to make axe-heads, arrowheads, and other implements, but at the same time it was very hard and strong, enabling men to kill animals more efficiently. The possession of flint could make all the difference between survival and death in the harsh competitive life of early times, yet it was rare in the west of England. It is no wonder then that men should come here to find it. There is no evidence that anyone settled on the islands before 2000 BC but, once the flint had been discovered, men probably sailed to the Scillies regularly and took back quantities of the stone for barter. Here, then, was a powerful motive for taking to sea: to reach hitherto unobtainable materials of great value.

The first people known to have settled on the Scillies were early farmers who, it is believed, spread from the Mediterranean into Western Europe and then to Western and Northern Britain. We can only guess at why they felt it necessary to migrate across water, but they must have had powerful reasons. Possibly they were fleeing from plague, from famine, or from war. These people brought strange new burial customs with them: near their settlements they built great stone chambers in which to bury their dead. One such megalith can be found at Bant's Carn on St Mary's. I walked along the coast path from Hugh Town to the site and had no trouble in finding the burial chamber. Although it is not large – I had to stoop to walk in – it is angular and quite definitely man-made. Rows of stone slabs form the walls and heavy stone rafters the remains of the roof. It must have been a difficult job to build such a long-lasting monument and one can only wonder at the importance these people attached to being properly housed in the after-life.

Similar tombs have also been found in Cornwall and Ireland, but they are few and far between. Here on the Scillies, however, there are an amazingly large number – fifty have been discovered so far – which has led to much intriguing speculation. The legend has it that the Scillies were the sacred isles of the dead, where people were brought from the mainland to be buried. Lying as they do to the west, towards the setting sun and eternal rest, the isles may well have held special significance. It was often believed that the dead could not cross water so any of the living who had just inherited power and wealth would have been glad of a watery barrier to prevent the return of their dear departed. More practically, the remoteness of the islands would have given the mortal remains and the treasures buried with them a better chance of escaping the attention of grave robbers.

Fascinating though the idea of spiritual motivation might be, there is another theory behind the popularity of Scilly as a burial place. Scilly may well have been a first base for the Megalithic people before they moved east and north into Britain. The settlers who remained on Scilly, isolated from the others, retained the old burial customs for hundreds of years after the people on mainland Britain had forgotten them. Certainly the Scillies would have made an excellent first base for migrants; there was plenty of land for farming, there was fresh water, and the islands were remote. Nowadays we think of remoteness as a disadvantage because we value travel and communications so highly, but many hundreds of years ago it was much sought after. Isolation provided some protection against invasion, raiding and pillaging. A treacherous sea crossing was a small price to pay for safety and peace. As a sanctuary and resting place there can have been few places to equal the Scillies.

However, the islands were not totally isolated during this burial chamber era. In one very important respect the islanders had contact with the outside world: they were involved in trade. Evidence of a trade route stretching as far as the Mediterranean has been found in the form of faience beads dating from about 1300 BC. On the English mainland extensive trade is known to have occurred even earlier in the Bronze Age; artefacts found in the rich graves of Wessex chieftains show commercial links with Ireland and Cornwall in the west, and Central Europe and the Baltic to the east. That trade should have forged such widespread links between different lands is a reflection of man's strong desire for a better life; only by exchanging raw materials and artefacts could he hope for an improvement in his living standards. For island people those exchanges had to be made by sea.

One of the most sought-after commodities which was pursued over long distances was tin. Mixed with copper it made the hard metal, bronze. There has been much discussion over whether or not the Scillies were the famous Cassiterides or Tin Islands, the identity of which the Phoenicians hid for over five hundred years. In about AD 18 the Tin Islands were described as 'opposite to the west parts of Britain, situate as it were in the same climate with Britain, are ten in number and lie near each other. . . .' Modern geologists believe there was never much tin in the islands, nor is there evidence that the Phoenicians ever came here, but the Scillies may well have been a trading centre for tin from Cornwall and elsewhere. Again, remoteness would have been an advantage for trade, which relied on peace and security for success.

Further down the hillside at Bant's Carn are the remains of a village dating from the Roman era. The neat circular bases of what were huts and storage chambers and the existence of drainage ducts suggest a tidy, well-organised community. However, an earlier and more interesting village from Roman times has been found on the tiny island of Nornour, towards the east of the group. Since it was a beautiful sailing day with a fresh breeze and clear skies, I walked back to Hugh Town and set sail for the island in *Gulliver G*. From St Mary' Road we sped into shallow Crow Sound, where I could see the sandy bottom through the clear water beneath the boat. The sunlight showed the islands to be much greener and more fertile than they appear from the open sea. White beaches rise to hedged fields where the famous Scilly flowers are grown. Even the more barren islands were yellow with flowering gorse.

I anchored well off the shallow approaches and rowed ashore in the rubber dinghy. Nornour is a small hill, just over 100 yards across, covered in heathers, grasses, brambles and gorse. I walked through the excavations, which consist of a series of rooms and a workshop dating from the earliest years of the Roman occupation. It is here that some 300 pieces of jewellery dating from the first and second centuries AD have been found. The Romans did not settle the westernmost part of the English mainland, but they did find a new use for the Scillies which has since been adopted for other islands. They made it a place of banishment, a sort of penal settlement. It is tempting to think that the jewellery, which was mass-produced to a similar design and traded far afield, was manufactured by prisoners, just as mailbags were sewn by prisoners in more recent times.

When it was in use as a factory Nornour was linked to other islands, but St Helen's, another larger hill that rises out of the sea, was already isolated when a later settler chose to live there. The day after my visit to Nornour I sailed as close to St Helen's as *Gulliver G*'s draught would permit me and then hitched a lift from local boatman Mike Hicks, who pointed out the site of some ruins, hidden deep in the bracken. When the Romans had gone from Britain and the Dark Ages of disorder descended, many

Britons forgot their conversion to Christianity and slipped back into pagan beliefs. To stem this movement, devout and zealous Celtic missionaries sailed from Ireland to teach the gospel. Others sought wild and lonely places to live a solitary, contemplative life and convert the non-believers when they could. Nowhere could be more suitable for a hermit than St Helen's, and it was here that a holy man named St Ilid came. He built himself a stone hut to which was added a church and oratory; the lower levels of the walls remain and the altar at the east end of the oratory still stands. Legend has it that St Ilid played a key part in the spread of Christianity. Ólaf Tryggvason was a Viking leader, later to be king of Norway, and in about AD 993 he came to Scilly, a perfect base from which to sail on raiding parties or trading expeditions. According to a well-known Norse saga, Ólaf Tryggvason heard it said that the hermit of St Helen's could foretell the future with accuracy. After putting the holy man to a test which he passed with flying colours, Ólaf asked St Ilid to make prophecies about his future. When they came true the future king was so impressed that he agreed to be baptised a Christian. He took the new religion back to Norway where he insisted – at the point of a sword – that everyone else be converted. Thus Scandinavia became Christian and Scilly played a major part in the spread of the religion. However, the new beliefs seemed to have little effect on the Vikings; they continued to raid and pillage unabated!

I sailed *Gulliver G* slowly westward through the islands and thought back to the early mariner, and the long and difficult voyage he had made to get here. He could have had any one of a number of strong motives for making the journey. Like the earliest visitors he could have come in search of mineral wealth such as flint or, if fleeing from war or famine, in search of peace and safety. He might have been a trader bringing goods or, in later times, a holy man trying to spread a belief. As a Viking he would have sailed here with acquisitive and warlike intentions.

In time men made short sea passages with regularity and confidence. Coastal trade became an accepted part of life and invaders were not as frequently discouraged by small stretches of water as people like the Britons would have liked. This increasing use of the sea resulted not only in the movement of migrants and goods, but also in contact between peoples and lands that would otherwise have remained isolated, making possible the spread and interchange of skills and ideas. The Ancient Britons possessed both tin and copper yet they did not discover how to make bronze until the knowledge was brought in by migrants. Without communication with Europe it might have taken them another thousand years to find the secret. For lands cut off by sea, the new contacts brought a much faster rate of advance.

But despite the considerable development of coastal trade and offshore fishing during the Middle Ages, European man remained essentially land-based. He was not interested in voyaging beyond the world he knew. Before leaving the Scillies I sailed *Gulliver G* out towards the Western Rocks, the jagged outer teeth of the islands. Dominating the broken jumble of reefs and islets is the tall, lonely Bishop's Rock lighthouse, which was to become famous as a first landmark for generations of ocean sailors. But to early inhabitants, the rocks marked the limit of the known world. The wide Atlantic and vast New World lay unsuspected far to the west. They must have wondered what lay beyond the reefs, beyond the hard line of the horizon and the glow of the setting sun, but it was not until the fifteenth century that men had both the means and the motives to find out.

TIDES AND CURRENTS
ANNIE HOOD

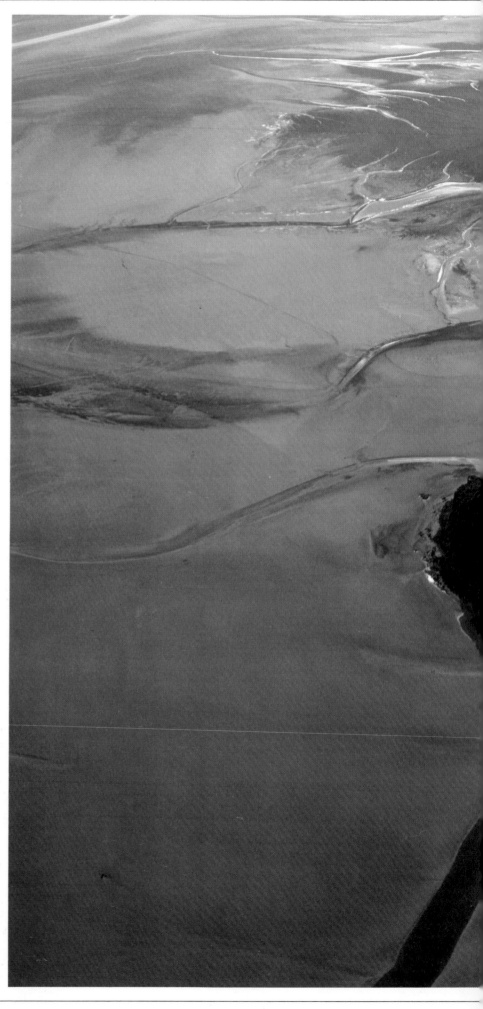

The seas and oceans of the world are subject to a variety of forces which combine to create a complex system of tides and currents. Close to the shore it is the effect of the tides that is most pronounced, whilst currents become dominant in the vast expanses of the oceans.

The gravitational attraction of the sun and moon, acting on the waters of the rotating earth, give rise to a periodic rise and fall in the level of the sea (the tides). Although the sun is very much larger than the moon, some twenty-six million times its mass, its greater distance from the earth reduces its tide-producing effect to only four-ninths of the moon's. When the sun, moon and earth are all aligned the tide-producing forces are complementary and this gives rise to a large tidal range, with high 'high tides' and low 'low tides'. These (known as Spring tides) occur twice a month coinciding with the new and full moon. When the three bodies are at right angles, with the earth at the apex, the tide-producing forces are in opposition and the tidal range is consequently reduced, resulting in low high tides and high low tides (Neap tides). Further variations are produced by the position of the moon relative to the earth, for when it is at its closest point its tide-producing effect is most pronounced. The greatest tidal range, however, occurs during the Spring tides closest to the Equinoxes, in March and September, when the sun is passing over the equator.

In the open ocean the difference in height between high and low tides may be only one or two feet, but in the shallow marginal seas it can increase to thirty feet, and in a constricted estuary even more. The highest tidal range known is that of the Bay of Fundy in north-eastern Canada where, at the head of the bay, up to a seventy-foot range has been recorded. On the other hand in some partially enclosed seas, such as the Mediterranean and Baltic, the tidal range will be reduced to as little as two or three feet. Tidal streams, horizontal water movements resulting from tidal action, will vary in strength according to the tidal range experienced. Thus, whereas in the Mediterranean they are negligible, along the shores of north-west Europe they can reach speeds of three to four knots. When offshore these tidal streams are generally rotary in nature, but in rivers and straits the

movement is restricted and translates into a rectilinear or reversing flow, in such cases an even greater speed of up to seven or eight knots often being reached.

The moon takes twenty-four hours and forty-eight minutes to pass over the same point on the earth, during which time most parts of the world experience two high and two low tides: any tide is, therefore, about fifty minutes later than the corresponding tide of the previous day. Over much of the Atlantic each pair of tides within the same day will attain about the same level (semi-diurnal tides). In contrast, for most of the Pacific and Indian Oceans the same day's tides are of different amplitudes, either the two high or the two low tides being unequal (mixed tides). In a few special areas, including parts of the Pacific and the Gulf of Mexico, there are only single, diurnal tides, with one high and one low tide every twenty-four hours.

There is considerable movement of water within the oceans which is non-tidal in nature. Differences in density at various depths give rise to vertical exchange which also promotes horizontal movements. The density of seawater depends both on salinity and temperature – low salinity and increased temperature reducing it, whilst high salinity and decreased temperature raises it. The overall trend is, therefore, for the polar seas to be of high density and the tropical seas of low density. This would theoretically give

Tidal range may be negligible, as in the Mediterranean, or very substantial
Left: Mont St Michel, on the Brittany coast, stands on a sandy plain at low tide
Above: The 'flower-pot rock' in the Bay of Fundy, Nova Scotia: a 70-foot tidal range has been recorded here

Below: An early device for calculating the times of high and low water. This one was produced in 1766

rise to a poleward movement of warmer surface water from the tropics with the cooler polar water moving equatorwards at depth. In fact these movements are greatly modified both by winds and by intervening land-masses preventing exchange, especially in the northern hemisphere.

Although such vertical movements are important, most surface currents are drifts caused by friction between the winds and the water at the surface. These move more or less in the direction of the winds and will vary in position and strength with the seasons. Land-masses often modify these currents: for example, when an ocean flow is forced through a narrow gap it will increase in velocity to form a stream current, relatively narrow, deep and fast-moving compared to the broader, shallower and slow-moving flows of the open ocean. One such instance is the Florida current flowing between the Florida peninsula and Cuba which, on issuing from the strait, forms the Gulf Stream. It is one of the strongest major currents known, being about two miles in depth and flowing at almost three knots.

As a result of the action of winds on the oceans a series of circulatory systems or cells called gyres are set up, each based in one of the major ocean basins. The trade winds, the steady persistent winds of the low latitudes found between the doldrums and the oceanic anti-cyclone belt, are the main motivating force. They are generated by the rising hot air at the equator being replaced by heavier air from the south and north, the earth's rotation causing them to be deflected to give south-east trades in the southern hemisphere and north-east trades in the northern. Rotation of the earth causes further deflection of the currents themselves and the overall result is a series of anti-clockwise systems of currents in the southern hemisphere (in the South Atlantic, South Pacific and South Indian Oceans), and two clockwise systems in the northern hemisphere (in the North Atlantic and North Pacific Oceans). The North Indian Ocean, with its triangular land-mass and monsoonal weather pattern, forms an exception and a double gyre is created here, moving seasonally in opposite directions. Seasonal weather changes also affect the pattern in the other ocean basins although not to such a high degree. Beyond the main systems to the north are several smaller cells, formed principally of Arctic currents moving south, although the encroaching land-masses restrict and complicate these. In contrast in the Southern Ocean there is a relatively simple flow based on the west-east circumpolar movement of water under the influence of the prevailing westerlies.

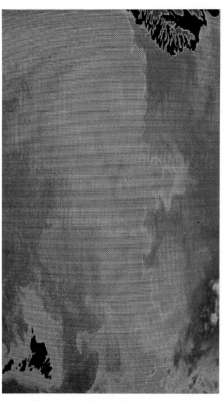

Above: The colour-coded satellite picture shows warmer ('green') water surrounded by the colder ('blue') water of the North Atlantic. The Faroes and Iceland show black.
Below: The first chart showing ocean currents was made by E. W. Happel in 1675

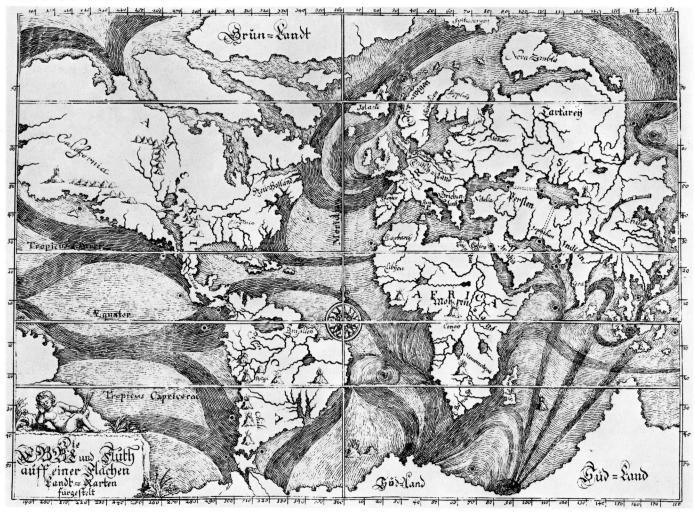

MYTH AND LEGEND
FRANCIS HUXLEY

A friend of mine, when still a child, would get ready for sleep by taking a walk down to the shore and diving into the blue and lucid sea. Beyond the breakers, a dragon awaited him with open jaws; and having let himself be swallowed, he found he was in a green land of pristine beauty, were he did amusing things until it was time to wake up again.

Mankind has known of this land beneath the sea since the beginning. It is peopled by dragons, who sometimes turn into mermen and mermaids (whose beauty makes one forget that they are dragons at heart and have no souls), and by numerous monsters such as the sea-serpent, the water-horse and water-bull, the leviathan and the kraken. Most of these have the ability to change shape when they are hard-pressed, as when they are forced to grant a wish or give a truthful answer. This must be why the leviathan has now been shown to be nothing but a whale, the kraken a giant squid, and the mermaid a seal. Not that this explains why a sober fisherman, who knew his seals, swore that he had seen a mermaid in the Hebrides in 1947.

A mermaid with her measure of seduction

There are various ways of reaching this land beneath the sea. Bran the Blessed got there in a boat, seeing many extraordinary things on the way, as many a Viking hero must have done when his corpse was set sailing aboard a burning longship. You can get there by drowning, the usual fate of a man who has been seduced by a mermaid, or by being sucked down by a whirlpool here called Charybdis, there the Maelstrom. Once in it, amongst what Herman Melville called 'the unspeakable foundations, ribs, and very pelvis of the world', you will see the house the Cherokee Indians say is filled with a great assembly, all beckoning you, or which the Norse called the palace of Aegir the sea-god, whose wife fills the cups of the dead with divine liquor.

Jonah and the Whale – a seventeenth-century wall painting from a church at Sumela, near Trabzon (Trebizond), in north Turkey

Since what is swallowed by the gorge of the sea must at last come out again, it is not surprising that the Polynesian hero Maui-tikitiki-o-Taranga once went fishing with the jawbone of his grandmother as a hook. Also called Maui's fish, it caught in the doorway of that old fellow Tongarui's house, and when he had pulled it up it turned into New Zealand.

The Hindus say that the gods took a bit more trouble over a similar affair, when they plunged a great mountain into the Vase of Ocean and churned it around amidst storms of fire and water. At last the Vase produced the goddess of life, the horse of the sun, the magic wishing jewel that controls the tides of fate, the physician of the gods, and the cup of Soma or immortalising Moon-juice.

The Babylonians also held that this birth from the navel of the sea was a stormy one. They told how Tiamat, the salt-sea mother, declared war on her children because of the commotion they kept making inside her. For her army, she begot a cohort of monsters, whose children appear to be still with us; to combat them, the gods chose one or their number, Marduk, who drove his storm-chariot into her entrails and split her open like the two halves of a mussel. That was how heaven and earth were made. Then he took the Stone of Destiny from Tiamat's captain, beheaded him and made mankind out of his blood. In this way he became king of gods and men, as he had wished.

Marduk's father was Ea the fish-god, also called Oannes, and Noah, and maybe even Jonah. He is the Old Man of the Sea, who is as wise as they come and who appeared in the Red Sea at least seven times before the Flood. He emerged waist-high from the water in the mornings, giving the people assembled on the shores detailed advice on how to live the best life, and disappeared at night. That they paid heed to what he said speaks volumes for his wisdom, since his appearance was such that they called him 'The Repulsive' and 'The Abomination'.

The Babylonians also worshipped sharks, and presumably offered them human sacrifice as many another people has done, to propitiate the anger of the sea. But one must

A Viking stone relief showing Thor and the giant Hymir fishing for the world serpent with an ox head

The immortal, Ma-Ku, creating a mulberry orchard from the sea. Painting by Hsiang Kun, second century AD

not forget that Plutarch wrote that sharks were the ancestors of the human race, presumably because the female does not lay eggs but gives birth to her young complete with placenta and umbilical cord.

The Greeks might better, one thinks, have taken the whale to be our common mother, since it is warm-blooded like us and, it is said, has often been mistaken for dry land. Mariners who not only disembark but light a fire on its back soon find that this particular land sinks quickly back into the sea. The Eskimo certainly think that the sea-mother is warm-blooded, since they tell how she was once a woman, was seduced by a stormy petrel, and rescued by her father in a boat. When the petrel brewed up a tempest in revenge, however, the father threw the girl into the sea and chopped off her fingers when she tried to climb back in again. These turned into seals and whales and fish of every kind – a picturesque way of saying that life originates in the sea, as is still the common scientific view.

It is picturesque because there is also a sea in the human imagination, from which our consciousness takes life. Its waters are apt to become as vexed as any on Earth, and breed an unconscionable number of monsters that mankind has found good reasons to fear and science to explain away. Not that either fear or explanation has much sway over a child who enjoys being rocked in the cradle of the deep, being too young to have been much buffeted by the sea of experience.

Above: A Raratongan fishermen's god known as 'big ears'

Figure head, *Cutty Sark*
A modern incarnation of Amphitrite 'who calms the waves upon the misty sea and blasts of raging winds' (Hesiod's *Theogony*)

SEAFARING IN THE ANCIENT MEDITERRANEAN

JOHN MORRISON

I Early Ships and Voyages

The Aegean and the Levant are the scenes of the first sea-going voyages. Obsidian from the island of Melos, radio-carbon dated to the seventh and sixth millennia, is found in the Argolid, in Cyprus, in Crete and in Thrace. The boats that fetched it were possibly reed-bundles, more probably dug-outs. In the third millennium King Sahure's quite sophisticated ships, pictured in his temple near Cairo, sailed regularly to Syria and the Levant, probably for the timber and metals Egypt lacked. The twin-pole mast and massive rope truss suggest a keelless hull developed from the reed-boats of the Nile. In contrast to Sahure's ships are the contemporary long and slim Aegean war-galleys developed from the dug-out which exhibit the two features henceforward characteristic of Greek oared ships, the high stern and the projecting forefoot, the former enabling the helmsman to sit high above the oarsmen (or paddlers), the latter the forward projection of the kèel. Ships of both these types, the longitudinally symmetrical and the asymmetrical, are to be seen on Cretan seals of the third millennium. Prehistory establishes the main types of Mediterranean sea-going ship: (i) the round symmetrical sickle-shaped ship of Egypt, Crete and Syria, possibly deriving from riverine craft, and (ii) the long asymmetrical galley, possibly deriving from the dug-out.

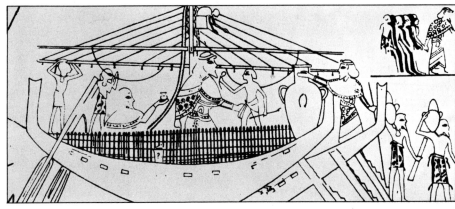

Frieze on the tomb of Kenamun, about 1400 BC. Small Syrian trading vessels of the symmetrical type

The oared ships of the Egyptian queen Hatshepsut, shown on a relief of the second millennium at Deir el Bahari, are, apart from the oars, little different from Sahure's. By the third millennium Cretan traders were sailing throughout the east Mediterranean and as far west as Apulia in Italy, Sicily and the Lipari islands. Contemporary with Hatshepsut's fleet are the (symmetrical, paddled) ships shown in brilliant detail on a miniature fresco at Thera. Small Syrian trading vessels of the symmetrical type are shown on the tomb of Kenamun in Egypt of about 1400.

If the eastern Mediterranean was for the greater part of the second millennium a Mycenaean lake, this was the result of maritime communication for trade, colonisation and war. The Trojan war, described, and certainly exaggerated, by Homer three centuries later, may have been the actual or the imagined epitome of these voyages. It is significant that Troy VI (the predecessor of Priam's city) had more trading connections with the Mycenaean cities than with the Hittites of the Asiatic hinterland.

The migrations of the twelfth century swept away the Mycenaean and Hittite powers, and a seaborne ripple of this surge reached Egypt where its repulse by Rameses III is recorded on a relief of 1176 BC. Another ripple is recorded on the Pylos tablets of the late thirteenth century which speak of the dispositions of men and ships made by the king of Pylos to meet a seaborne invasion. A clay box from Pylos (1200–1100 BC) shows the kind of ship invaders and defenders might have used, one with a high stern and helmsman's seat, a fo'c'sle and projecting forefoot, and twenty-three oarsmen's benches.

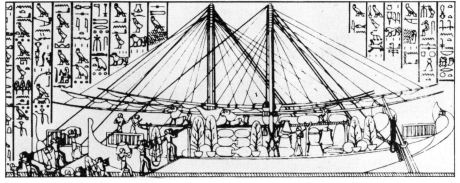

Above left: A ship from Queen Hatshepsut's fleet, about 1500 BC. They have just returned from a voyage to Punt (Somalia) with a deck-cargo
Left: Detail of a fresco at Thera, 1500–1400 BC. A number of passenger-carrying ships are approaching a harbour with sails lowered and powered by twenty-one paddlers a side
Above: Relief at Medinet Habu, Egypt, 1176 BC. The invading ships with mast up and sails furled are undecked and symmetrical, and carry fighting men equipped with sword and shield. They are surrounded and driven ashore by oared Egyptian ships carrying archers

II The Longships of Greece and Rome

Homer, writing in the eighth century, describes voyages of ships manned with twenty, thirty, fifty and on one occasion 120 men. Oars are used for getting out of a harbour or off a beach; then mast and sail are raised. The increase in the number of oarsmen and the development of two levels must be seen together with another innovation, the arming of the forefoot with a metal sheath, which converted the war-galley from a transport of armed men, as it had been hitherto, into an offensive weapon in itself. Ramming as a battle tactic required power and manoeuvrability. The modification of the war-galley rapidly went further, probably at Corinth, where the trireme (the 'three') was evolved at the end of the eighth or the beginning of the seventh century by adding a third fore-and-aft file of oarsmen to the two fore-and-aft files of the two-level ship. The device which made this possible without an increase in the length of some of the oars was the outrigger.

The trireme fleets were expensive luxuries which, in the straitened economic conditions of the seventh and eighth centuries, few states could afford. Corinth and her western colony Corcyra (Corfu) had some, so did Necho of Egypt under Corinthian influence, so did the Phoenician cities of the Levant and the Greek cities of Ionia. Thucydides says that the tyrants of Sicily and the Corcyraeans had large numbers of them at the beginning of the fifth century, the former probably because of the threat to her of the growing power of the Phoenician colony of Carthage. When Persia extended her power over Asia Minor, the Levant and Egypt, she acquired a large naval potential which now threatened Greece in the east as Carthage did in the west. Athens repelled the first Persian invasion on the beaches of Marathon; and by the time the second arrived in 480, she had acquired under Themistocles (by the wise use of a windfall from the silver mines at Laurium) a trireme fleet which formed the backbone of the allied naval force which defeated the combined Ionian Greek, Phoenician and Egyptian trireme fleets at Salamis.

With her triremes, which she had the economic capacity to commission and the skill and seamanship to employ as ramming weapons, Athens dominated the Greek world until the defeat of her crack naval expedition in the cramped conditions of the harbour at

Below: A Roman bireme (top) from a mosaic in the Palazzo Barberini at Palestrina, early first century BC, and (bottom) a trireme, from the Lenormant relief, about 400 BC. The ship in the relief can be projected (see facing diagram) to show the outrigger and the position of the oarsmen *en echelon* to one another

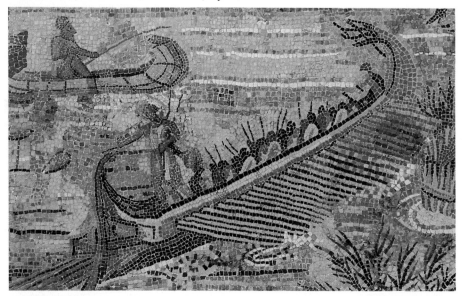

A quadrireme:
four files of rowers, oars at two levels

A quinquereme:
five files of rowers, an outrigger, oars at three levels

Syracuse ultimately brought that domination to an end. The innovative genius of the Greeks in naval matters was not, however, yet worked out.

The Syracusans, who had repelled the Carthaginians in the same year as Salamis, felt themselves again threatened by Carthage at the beginning of the fourth century, and began to build new types of warship. The first of these, the quadrireme (or 'four') , was probably borrowed from the Carthaginians. The second, the quinquereme (or 'five'), was probably the invention of Dionysius I of Syracuse. Both are said to have been built by him in 398. His son, Dionysius II, included a 'six' in his fleet in 356. There is good reason to believe that these ships employed an oar system in which the new factor was the double-manning of oars, which gave them four, five and six fore-and-aft files of oarsmen respectively on each side of the ship.

The new types soon spread to the Aegean, the Levant and Egypt, and the naval rivalries of the Hellenistic kings who succeeded Alexander led to still further evolution, with great increases in the number of men working each oar (and hence of the number of fore-and-aft files of oarsmen on each side of the ship), although the number of levels never seems to have exceeded three for good practical reasons. The concept of the oared ship as an offensive weapon in itself had now given place to the concept of the warship as a platform carrying armed men into a hazardous kind of land battle on the sea. When Antigonus of Macedon assembled a fleet of

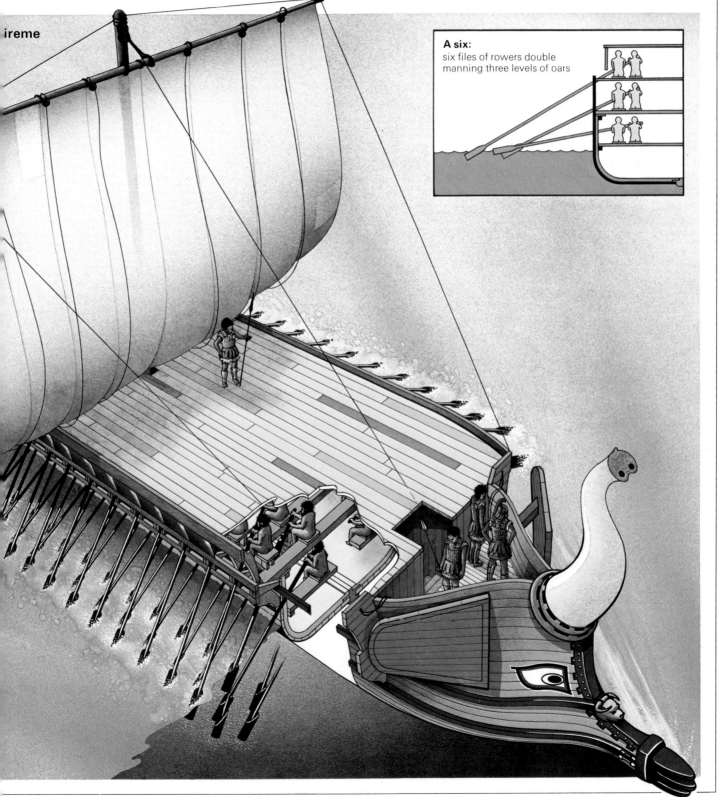

ireme

A six: six files of rowers double manning three levels of oars

240 ships in 315 BC to challenge Egypt's sea power, he had ninety 'fours', ten 'fives', three 'nines' and ten 'tens'. Nothing larger than a 'ten' seems ever to have been committed to battle. Demetrius, Antigonus' son, was an obsessive naval innovator. He used the capture of Cyprus to acquire the long timber needed for an 'eleven', and went on to build 'thirteens', 'fifteens' and 'sixteens'. Not to be outdone, Ptolemy II of Egypt, in the first half of the third century, had two 'thirties' and one 'twenty', in addition to 'thirteens', 'twelves', etc. Finally at the end of the century came the *reductio ad absurdum*, the double-hulled 'forty' of Ptolemy IV (221–204). Some details are preserved of this monster, and it is described, not surprisingly, as moving 'unsteadily and laboriously'. The two hulls would have given the required stability, but with huge oars at three levels the forty fore-and-aft files on each side must have been divided into gangs at each level of 13–14 men half pulling and half pushing each oar (a practice attested in the big Renaissance galleys).

The naval warfare between Rome and Carthage towards the end of the third century was carried out with 'fives' and 'fours' and one or two 'sixes' employed as flagships, and so were the Roman civil wars. The battle of Actium marked the end of the larger polyremes. Antony's fleet contained a few 'threes' and the rest were 'fours' up to 'tens'. Octavian, employing a normal Roman fleet of ships up to 'sixes', defeated his opponent. Antony's ships, nevertheless, were said to have been 'in height ten foot above the water'. Even the 'tens' then were not more than two foot higher than the Athenian 'three', i.e. they were ships of three levels of oars but needing more height to accommodate the uppermost level, not outboard of the other levels and using an outrigger as in the 'three', but directly above them and without an outrigger. When Octavian, now Augustus Caesar, established the network of imperial fleets and squadrons throughout the Mediterranean, these were and continued to be made up of 'fours', 'fives' and 'sixes' (as flagships) supported by smaller galleys, called liburnians, with one fore-and-aft file a side rowed at two levels. Finally, in the naval war between Constantine and Licinius in AD 323, Licinius' fleet of 350 'threes' was ultimately defeated, fifty of Constantine's thirty-oared ships (probably=liburnians) routing 200 of Licinius' 'threes'. Even the 'three' thus became obsolete and the navies of the Byzantine emperors were composed of two-level 'dromons'.

III The Round Ships of Greece and Rome

Throughout historical antiquity the Mediterranean was the scene of intense maritime commercial activity interrupted only by wars or by periods when the naval weakness of the great powers allowed pirates based on the south coast of Asia Minor, on the Illyrian coast and north Africa to proliferate dangerously. The Phoenicians were the earliest traders in historical times and by the eighth century had established trading posts in North Africa and Sicily, and founded Carthage. They are likely to have sailed in the symmetrical 'round' ship. Greeks from the city of Phocaea in Asia Minor are said by Herodotus to have made long voyages to the Adriatic and Tyrrhenia and Iberia and Tartessus (I 163): 'and they sailed not in round ships but in pentecontors'. Another story in Herodotus shows that the Phocaean pentecontors (50-oared ships) had plenty of room for passengers and cargo. They were presumably employed instead of the normal 'round' ships because the Phocaean voyages were colonising adventures, like so many at this time. Both types of ship are illustrated in the cup in the British Museum of the late sixth century. Cargo ships of this kind were called in Greek 'round', also *'holkades'*, i.e. towed ships, because they had no oars and had to be towed in and out of port. They were lead-sheathed and so were not beached like long ships but rode at anchor. In these ships the Milesians and Samians traded with Egypt through Naucratis, and with the Black Sea coasts which they colonised extensively; in these the Euboeans traded with Syria through Al Mina. The increase in prosperity and hence in population in the Greek cities after the repulse of the Persians and Carthaginians led to a demand for imports of grain, and thus for ships of greater tonnage. Massilia and Syracuse in the west and Piraeus in the east became the main trading centres. Grain fleets sailed between the Hellespont and Piraeus.

The conquests of Alexander in the fourth century shifted the economic centre of the eastern Mediterranean from Piraeus to Alexandria and Antioch, and the defeat of Carthage by Rome concentrated the trade of the western Mediterranean on Italy. Throughout the late Republic and Empire Rome derived her corn-supply from Sicily, North Africa and Egypt, and her supply of luxuries from the east through Egypt and Antioch and from the west through Spanish and Gallic ports. Big grain-carrying ships were built for the Alexandria corn-fleet. A number of Roman cargo ships which have been excavated were carrying wine in amphorae.

To conclude, those who built the warships and trading ships in which the Mediterranean sailor played his not unimportant part in ancient history deserve more credit for practical ingenuity and effective design than they are usually given. The sailors again in war and in trade displayed a degree of skill and seamanship and of practical ability to use the sea to their advantage greater than that usually attributed to them.

Right: This oared merchantman, shown in a mosaic of the early fourth century AD, from Tébessa in Algeria, carried its cargo on its deck, the hold being occupied by oarsmen. Such a ship, which had a sail for the main voyage, would have been independent of the towage usually required by round ships

Below: A Roman warship of the first century BC, probably a quadrireme

WATER TRANSPORT BEFORE 1400

SEÁN McGRAIL

Above: Reed raft on Lake Titicaca, Peru, and (right) the same kind of raft under construction

Earliest Times

By the time of the last retreat of the ice sheets some 10,000 years ago, Man had come to occupy much of the inhabitable world. Rafts or boats would have been essential for some of this movement – for example, the settlement of Australia before 30,000 BC – but even in areas accessible by overland routes, water transport would have enhanced Man's ability to explore and to exploit natural resources. There is no surviving evidence for such early craft: however, before *c*.30,000 BC Man had the skills necessary to build rafts of bark and of logs, and by *c*.8000 BC in Europe, and comparable technological stages elsewhere, reed rafts, bark boats, skin boats and logboats (i.e. dug-out canoes) were within his capabilities.

development, with a variety of shipbuilding traditions arising in different parts of the world. Nevertheless, rafts and the other forms of boat were never entirely replaced, and today, for example, reed craft are used in Arabia and South America, bark boats in Africa and Australia, and skin boats in Ireland and the Arctic. Log rafts and logboats were used in Europe until recently.

A North American Indian skin boat

Log rafts on a beach in northern Portugal

North American Indians making a dug-out canoe, from a seventeenth-century engraving by Theodore de Bry

It is likely that the technologically advanced plank boat originated later than these other forms, possibly during the Neolithic phase of technology, although it is not until the European Bronze Age that we have direct evidence for this. Initially planking was fastened by sewing or lashing with withies or grass ropes, or by wooden fittings such as tree-nails: not until the Iron Age were metal fastenings used. The earlier techniques never wholly disappeared and sewing is in use today in such areas as Lapland and the Indian Ocean.

The plank boat was capable of the greatest

Europe from c.2000 BC to c.AD 400

Logboat remains dated to this period have been found in several European countries: they had been used on inland waters probably as ferries and for fishing, fowling and the collection of reeds. Skin boats have not survived, but their use at sea and inland has been documented by Roman Age authors. Log rafts are also known from this time.

Plank-boat remains have been dated to this period, and Classical authors have described aspects of their building and use. On present evidence these boats may be grouped into four traditions:

a. Flat-bottomed, keelless boats with flush planking edge-fastened by sewing. Examples are the prehistoric Ferriby and Brigg boats of the Humber estuary.

b. River and coastal craft, possibly of Celtic origins, from the Rhine/Thames area dated to Roman times, flat-bottomed and keelless, generally with the planking fastened to an internal framework.

c. Sea-going and inland craft of the classical Mediterranean with flush planking edge-fastened by wood (as described on pages 35–8).

d. Round-hulled, keelless Scandinavian boats suitable for sheltered waters, with overlapping (clinker) planking edge-fastened by sewing.

Sail was in use from at least 2000 BC in the Mediterranean, but its use in northern Europe is uncertain until the first century BC.

Some of the evidence for the earliest European craft. Top and above: The Brigg boat of *c.* 650 BC, excavated from near the River Ancholme. The detail shows some of the planking which was edge-fastened by sewing

Left: The remains of a Roman Age Rhine barge excavated at Zwammedam, Netherlands

Below: The drawing is of a reconstruction model of one of the Bronze Age (*c.* 1500 BC) sewn boats from the foreshore of the River Humber at North Ferriby. The photograph is of a reconstruction model of a medieval (*c.* AD 1000) ferry from Egersund, Denmark, which has affinities with the Ferriby boat and the Zwammedam barge

Medieval Europe up to c. AD 1400

Throughout this period river barges, log-boats and log, and even reed, rafts were in use on inland waters: skin boats were used at sea but with decreasing importance. From the plank boats and ships in use in the pre-medieval period four traditions of seagoing ship appear to have emerged: others may remain to be identified.

a. *The Viking tradition*

Finds in Scandinavia and Britain, dated from the fifth to seventh centuries AD, reveal a type of boatbuilding which found its classic expression in the Viking Age. From excavated remains and other evidence we know that in this latter period there were longships (warships), ocean and coastal cargo ships, and small boats. Although these differed in some respects to suit their different functions, they had many characteristics in common: bow and stern similar in form with pronounced sheer at the ends; a hull built in shell sequence with overlapping (clinker) planking fastened together and to keel and stems *before* the distinctive internal supporting structure of floor timbers (ribs), crossbeams and knees was fitted in position; propulsion by oars and by single rectangular sail on a mast stepped amidships; and steering by side rudder.

With the ability to operate off beaches and to go well inland up relatively shallow rivers they were used to maximum effect by both raiders and traders. Longships were narrower and shallower in relation to length than cargo ships, and with a well-matched sail or a powerful crew of oarsmen achieved high speeds in favourable conditions of wind and sea. The sea-going ability of cargo vessels is demonstrated by the regular contact maintained between Scandinavia, Iceland and Greenland. For a period of about 300 years from *c.*AD 800 ships built in this tradition were evidently the most prominent in the north European economy.

b. *The Cog tradition*

The Cog appears to have emerged from a ninth-century Frisian boatbuilding tradition to become the dominant seagoing ship of northern Europe in the late twelfth

Above: The Osberg Viking ship. Below: A Hulc is seen on the relief carving of the Winchester font

A cog, depicted on the Straslund seal of 1329

and the thirteenth centuries. A flat bottom and high clinker-built sides gave great cargo capacity and the ability to take the ground easily and sit upright on an ebb tide. The Cog was also simpler and cheaper to build than vessels in the Viking tradition – an added attraction for Hanseatic merchants. Ships and large boats of this tradition have recently been excavated in Germany, Denmark and the Netherlands, some of them having a distinctive method of fastening the clinker planking with twice-turned nails.

c. *The Hulc*

Although no ship of Hulc type has yet been excavated, documentary and iconographic evidence indicate that in the fourteenth century ships of this tradition began to replace the Cog. Once again this design seems to have originated as a small boat in the Low Countries, but, apart from the distinctive banana shape in outline and the apparent lack of stems, details of construction are not yet known.

d. *The Mediterranean tradition*

In the Mediterranean there appears to have been a continuity in building techniques from the Classical world into medieval times. However, there are early signs of a form of skeleton building in which planking was fastened to a pre-erected framework. The lateen and the square sail were used from Roman times onwards, as were two-masted and even three-masted ships. By the early fourteenth century, techniques used in northern Cogs began to be adopted in the Mediterranean.

e. *Europe in the 15th century*

From this amalgam of traditions emerged the three-masted, non-edge joined, skeleton-built ship which enabled Europeans of the late fifteenth and early sixteenth centuries to 'discover' all the seas of the world. The immediate antecedents of these Caravels and Carracks are not known however, but may become clearer as archaeological research progresses.

Chapter Two

THE WORLD ENCOMPASSED

The warm Pacific trade wind blew gently across the deck and formed the indigo blue sea into neat rows of sharp wavelets. High on the yard above my head a figure balanced precariously on a footrope and grappled with a flogging sail. From the fo'c'sle a voice echoed faintly down the ship, 'Anchor's a-weigh!' The captain leant over the poop rail and shouted into the waist of the ship, 'Loose the clews and buntlines! Stand by the brace!' Three men ran across the main deck and, from the tangle of lines that spread down from the spars to the belaying pins below, selected ropes to pull in and ropes to let out. The deafening sound of the cracking, whipping sails diminished and the first shudder of movement spread through the timbers of the ship. The *Golden Hind* was under way.

I stood on the poop deck, well clear of the principal activity. Though I call myself a sailor, I knew far too little about a sixteenth-century ship to be of any use during this tricky manoeuvre. A three-masted square-rigger is a far cry from a small single-masted yacht, but it didn't take an expert eye to see that this ship was bulky, heavy and squat for her short length. As she slowly gathered way it was several moments before she answered the helmsman's touch and came up on to her course. She was obviously cumbersome and difficult to manoeuvre and, although she would go well enough downwind, it was hard to imagine her sailing to windward. Yet it was in ships like this that men first sailed across the great oceans of the world, to reach all the habitable regions of the globe. After the Viking voyages to Newfoundland it was more than 400 years before Europeans again ventured into unknown waters and began the great outward movement that spanned roughly 250 years, from the early fifteenth to the late seventeenth century; the period known as the Age of Discovery. The first exploratory voyages were made by those hardy, skilful Atlantic sailors, the Portuguese, who sailed down the west coast of Africa and out into the Atlantic as far as the Azores. But it was not until the 1490s that exploration really got going. After Columbus conquered the Atlantic and discovered the New World in 1492 it took only twenty-seven years for every major ocean to be crossed: in 1497 da Gama reached India by the all-sea route; and in 1519 Magellan achieved the greatest triumph of all, the crossing of both the Atlantic and the Pacific. Although Magellan himself was killed in the Philippines, Juan Sebastian de Elcano, with a handful of men, took the *Victoria*, the last surviving ship of the fleet, the rest of the way round the world.

The second ship to circumnavigate the world was the *Golden Hind*. She was captained by Francis Drake, who has been variously described as an adventurer, a rascal, a brilliant seaman, and a common pirate. He was probably all those things, but to the English-speaking peoples – and certainly to me – he is a hero. The ship on which I was sailing was not, alas, the real *Golden Hind*. When Drake returned from his three-year voyage in 1580, the *Golden Hind* was put in a special dry dock at Deptford, where she slowly rotted away until her timbers fell apart; nothing of her remains except a couple of chairs made from her timbers. The ship which was carrying me across the waters of the Pacific was a replica built in 1973, and now circumnavigating the world in celebration of the 400th anniversary of Drake's voyage. After crossing the Atlantic and passing through the Panama Canal, this modern *Golden Hind* had spent four years in San Francisco before sailing across the Pacific to Japan. Now, as she was continuing her circumnavigation, I and the camera crew were joining her for a week's sailing through the South China Sea to Singapore. The next leg of her voyage would take her to Sri Lanka, the Red Sea, the Suez Canal and then, by way of the Mediterranean, to the Atlantic and England.

Drake's route had been very different. Sailing west, there was only one way to reach the Pacific, and that was by passing through the straight that Magellan had discovered at the tip of South America. From there Drake sailed up the west coast of America, plundering every Spanish ship he could lay his hands on and, from San Francisco, crossed the Pacific to the Spice Islands in what is now Indonesia. To reach home he had to round the Cape of Good Hope and sail the length of the Atlantic for the second time.

Drake was never a true discoverer, like Columbus or Magellan. He made no real attempt to explore such unknown places as the south Pacific, nor to investigate the legendary southern continent which was believed to extend from the Magellan Strait southward. He made only two discoveries, and the first – the realisation that the Atlantic and the Pacific were linked by open sea south of Tierra del Fuego and that the southern continent, if it existed, did not start there – was a pure accident. His second discovery, the existence of the stretch of coastline near what is now San Francisco, was

incidental, for Drake sailed this far north only to find a quiet spot away from the angry Spaniards he had robbed to the south. Nor is Drake remembered for his seamanship, brilliant though it was. His real achievement was, quite simply, to be phenomenally successful at almost everything he did, whether it was piracy, robbery, sailing, or outmanoeuvring the Spanish; and this at a time when England was a second-rate power frightened of the might of Spain. Drake's audacity in voyaging into waters which Spain regarded as her private property badly shook the Catholic country's morale, and was both a sign and a cause of England's emerging confidence as the first powerful Protestant nation in Europe. But Drake's success reached beyond politics. His exploits excited and inspired the whole English nation and encouraged the spirit of independent adventure which was to become so dear to the Elizabethans. Stories were written and songs composed about him until he became a legend in his lifetime. The legend inspired generations of Englishmen to follow his example and sail to the furthest corners of the world in search of fame and fortune. When the time came to establish colonies in the New World, England was never short of emigrant adventurers.

The sixteenth-century legend naturally embroidered on the best of Drake's achievements and left out some of the unhappier aspects of the tale; by the time the *Golden Hind* reached the western Pacific waters where I was now sailing, Drake had executed a friend in order to quell a mutiny, endured a fifty-two-day storm near Cape Horn, and lost four of the five ships he had set out with. However, it should be said that this was not a bad record for a long voyage at this time. Legend built Drake up to what we would now call superstar status when, like so many heroes, he was a complex personality, with glaring faults as well as superhuman virtues. Yet it is this very mixture of strength and fallibility, of luck and misfortune, of brilliant seamanship and human miscalculation, that makes him a fascinating character and his circumnavigation a remarkable achievement. The voyages of this period did not result from a great movement involving whole states or organisations – indeed, many rulers doubted that exploration was worth either money or encouragement; they came about through the inspiration, the daring and the ambition of individual adventurers or entrepreneurs. There was no one better suited to the role than Drake.

When I joined the replica of the *Golden Hind* and saw her for the first time, I was immediately struck by her size. Just 102 feet in length, she is tiny when you consider that the original ship carried a crew of between sixty and eighty men on a voyage lasting nearly three years. Anchored amid dozens of modern merchant ships the *Golden Hind* looked like a toy boat and it was only when the tender got within hailing distance that she appeared more substantial; one could see that her hull had the bulk and solidity of a small fortress. Her masts were tall and stout as oak trees and the rigging dense enough to support the largest of sails. As we climbed up the side and over the rail we were welcomed aboard by Captain Peter Haward, who introduced us to his crew of fifteen – considerably fewer than Drake carried. By profession Peter Haward is a yacht delivery skipper and this, he admitted, was the most unusual vessel he had yet delivered. His crew – mainly students, professional yacht crew and ubiquitous 'world travellers' – had flown out with him from England to Japan to sail the replica back to Plymouth. From the way they swabbed the decks and prepared for sea, they appeared to be enjoying their lives as twentieth-century Elizabethan adventurers.

After two hours of hard work the *Golden Hind* was under way, but it was another half-hour before all the sails were set and a hot, tired crew finally climbed down the

On board the *Golden Hind*. Captain Peter Haward (top right), and (bottom right) inside the stern of the *Golden Hind* during construction at Hinks' Yard, Appledore, Devon

ratlines to take a breather on deck. She was a magnificent sight under full sail, pushing through the bright blue water at a steady six knots, and it was hard to believe she was not really a sixteenth-century vessel. In fact, although she had been built in Appledore, England, in 1973, every care had been taken to use authentic materials whenever possible: the sails are made of flax, the plant fibre used in early sailmaking, and the rigging of hemp, the fibre of the cannabis plant. Hemp is strong, but it stretches a good deal when new and shrinks when wet, so that constant adjustment is necessary. In Drake's day they regularly altered the tension of the rigging by means of ropes and tackles. In the twentieth century the problem was solved by running steel wire through the core of the shrouds. But few other steel gadgets are to be found; certainly there are no highly-geared winches to make the crew's job easier. The sails are hoisted and trimmed by manpower augmented only by the purchase of block and tackle. The hull is wooden, the massive forty-foot half-frame timbers made of oak, and the keel timbers of elm. Only the wood for the planking – the African hardwood iroko – would not have been used in Drake's time: sixteenth-century shipwrights would have used well-seasoned oak, impossible to find in long lengths today. The planking is fastened to the half-frames, or ribs, by bolts and the completed hull made watertight by caulking (filling the gaps between the planks) with oakum and pitch. The fine quality of the woodwork extends to the ornate rails and galleries of the upper decks, and to the carved figurehead of a golden hind high on the bow.

Although most of the materials are authentic it has been impossible to copy Drake's ship exactly because no plans or dimensions of the vessel survive. The design of the replica is based on available references and educated guesswork. For this reason only tentative conclusions about the performance and sailing qualities of the original can be drawn from sailing her, particularly when, as Peter Haward pointed out, Drake's men would have had a lifetime's experience handling such ships. But the size at least of the two ships must have been similar: plans of the housing at Deptford which was going to be built round the *Golden Hind*, and her weight, which was between 100 and 120 sixteenth-century 'tuns', fix the length at 90–100 feet. The beam and draught have been deduced from contemporary references. For our purposes – to find out what it was like to sail on a sixteenth-century galleon – the replica was ideal.

Some of the trappings on the new *Golden Hind* are modern; nowadays a crew expects a certain minimum standard in their living conditions, such as bunks, pump-flushed lavatories, a well-equipped galley, and above all some space to call their own. Nor can the modern navigator be denied radar and position fixing systems to keep his ship off the rocks. Deep in the hold there is an engine, a generator and water and fuel tanks. The crew, too, could only be twentieth-century; they were wearing jeans and smoking cigarettes. One of them was even a woman – something Drake would never have allowed!

The plan of the ship is simple. Above the hold is a gun deck, then a main deck; at the forward end of the main deck is a forecastle and aft an aftercastle which rises two decks higher. The gun deck on the replica contains no guns, just twelve wooden bunks ranged along the sides. However, on Drake's ship this deck was the home not only of eighteen demi-culverin, or 9-pound guns, but of sixty men. They had neither bunks nor, it is thought, hammocks, although these had been introduced from the West Indies by Columbus who saw them used by the Carib indians. To sleep, the men had to curl up on the hard deck in the space between the guns and, even when half of the crew was on watch, it must have been very cramped. When moving about the gun deck they had to stoop, for the headroom was probably less than five foot. The only other living

San Francisco
June/July 1579

Plymouth Dec 1577
Sept 1580

Mogador

Cape Verde
Islands
Feb 1578

Panama

Sierra
Leone
July 1580

Lima

Arica
Feb 1579
Coquimbo
Santiago Dec 1578

Rio de la Plata
April 1578

Port St Julian
June 1578

Philippines

Java
March 1580

Celebes
Jan 1580

space for the men was the main deck or the forecastle, both open to wind and weather. Columbus's crew fared even worse: they had to sleep either on the main deck or on the ballast in the hold, for there was no intermediate gun deck on the *Santa Maria*. The aftercastle on Drake's ship contained the main cabin where the twenty or so officers and gentlemen lived, ate and slept, their conditions only a little less cramped than those of the men. On the new *Golden Hind* this main cabin contains only three large bunks, a well-equipped galley, and an eating area, luxurious by sixteenth-century standards. The galley has a cooker, a refrigerator, and plenty of stowage room, but on fifteenth- and sixteenth-century ships there was neither a galley nor an eating area. When a hot meal was required a cook box, little more than a box of sand on which to make a fire, was brought out on deck, a meal prepared, and the food eaten in the open. When the weather was bad it is doubtful if there was any hot food at all.

Aboard the new *Golden Hind*, the crew had settled into their working routine of three watches and regular meals. I asked them what they thought of their living conditions. 'Pretty basic,' someone replied, 'and I really miss fresh vegetables when we've been at sea for a while.'

'And ice-cold beer.'

'And we could do with more ventilation below decks; it gets really hot down there.'

But, they added, they would not have missed the opportunity to sail a sixteenth-century ship for the world. It was an adventure of a lifetime, and an unusual way to see the world.

The motives of Drake and his men went beyond pure adventure, otherwise the hardships and the grave risks would not have been worth it. Sailing into the unknown, without adequate charts or an idea of how long they might be at sea, they faced a strong chance of dying from starvation and thirst, if tropical disease, a native's arrow or that scourge of the great voyages, scurvy, did not get them first. The mortality rate on these early voyages could be very high. On Magellan's voyage ninety per cent of the crew perished; da Gama, too, lost the majority of his men during his voyage to India. Faced by such risks, why did European men leave their familiar and insular medieval world? What prompted them to risk everything for unknown waters?

The answer may be put in one word: opportunity – the opportunity to find fame and fortune on a vast scale. In the fourteenth and fifteenth centuries conditions in Europe were ripe for an enterprising mariner to make a mint of money: all he had to do was find a short route to the East. Europeans had an insatiable demand for the silks of India and the spices of the East, yet the Arab middlemen who controlled trade from the Indian Ocean across the land route to the Mediterranean squeezed ever-higher prices out of their customers. Moreover, the Christian countries resented having to buy from Muslim infidels, their traditional enemies. If an all-sea route could be found, then supply could be increased and the Arabs excluded. By Drake's time the Portuguese had discovered and monopolised the route round the Cape of Good Hope and the

Spanish had seized both the Americas and the western route to the Indies, which led over the isthmus of Panama by mule and then across the Pacific by ship. The Iberian nations had thus grabbed a monopoly of Eastern trade and, as if that wasn't enough, the Spanish had also stumbled upon vast quantities of silver and gold in the Americas. The newly-emerging Protestant nations were excluded from these riches and over-shadowed by the power of their Catholic neighbours. However, one man was deter-mined to change all that, and he was Francis Drake.

Drake had no reason to like Catholics – his father, a Protestant preacher, had been persecuted for his faith when England was still a Catholic nation – and his dislike had changed to a burning hatred and lust for revenge after an incident in the Caribbean when the Spanish had tricked him and his shipmates into a bloody ambush. In 1572 he made a daring raid on Panama and captured some bullion the Spanish were transport-ing across the isthmus. This expedition made Drake rich and famous, but it was not enough. He wanted to hit Spain much harder, in the place where their bullion ships were unprotected, where no one since Magellan had dared to sail – into the Pacific through the strait at the tip of South America. Such an audacious venture would be a powerful challenge to Spain's immense power.

Religious zeal and the desire to avenge dead friends were laudable motives, but Drake had other reasons for embarking on such a voyage. He was an ambitious man and he wanted wealth, position and status. Born of respectable but modest yeoman stock, he wanted to raise himself to the highest ranks of society and become a gentleman. Such motives are not unusual. Columbus burned with a desire for wealth and self-aggrandisement. Before setting off across the Atlantic to discover what he believed would be the western route to India, he struck a hard bargain with Isabella of Spain whereby success would earn him and his descendants high rank, titles and wealth. Rulers wanted results and they were only too happy to reward the adventurers for producing them. No one was very concerned about the means that were used. Drake was an opportunist who traded, robbed or raided to achieve his aims. In the 1570s he had been a slave-trader, but Elizabeth I and her court condoned almost any activity as long as it furthered England's ambitions. If Drake was a bit of a rogue he still felt superior to the Spaniards, who had institutionalised torture under the guise of the Inquisition. In Drake's eyes, these practices reduced them to the level of inhuman criminals.

Drake was consumed by the idea of sailing into the Pacific, but having the idea was one thing and getting it off the ground quite another. He needed his queen's permission and financial support; both were a long time coming. Ninety years before, Columbus' determination had been put to the test; it took him ten years to persuade anyone to back his first voyage to the west. He hawked his idea around England, France and Portugal, before Spain finally put up the money. Magellan renounced his Portuguese citizenship in order to settle in Spain and win support for his voyage. Drake was not known for his patience but he had to exercise every ounce of it while he waited for the right moment to gain Elizabeth's approval. The Queen's dislike of decision-making was second only to the rapidity with which she changed her mind. After waiting several long years for the go-ahead Drake drew close to despair in case someone should pre-empt his plan. But at last, in 1577, Spain again threatened to overrun the Protestant Netherlands and angered Elizabeth so much that she gave Drake *carte blanche* – money, ships, men and secret instructions, which undoubtedly gave him permission to strike at Spanish treasure ships and colonies in Peru and Chile.

The task ahead of Drake, even sixty years after Magellan's voyage, was still an immensely difficult one. To reach the Pacific he had to take his fleet down into the South Atlantic, which was largely uncharted, and then find the narrow Magellan Strait. The passage of the strait could take as long as a month, depending on the ferocity of the winds. Once through, he would face the full fury of the Southern Ocean until, with a bit of luck, he could fight his way north into the more temperate regions near northern Chile and Peru. Here he would be in enemy territory. He could not rely on help from the natives because, if not actually under Spanish rule, they were often too unpredictable to trust; Drake well remembered that Magellan had been killed during an inter-island squabble in the Philippines. Replenishment of food and water would be difficult, particularly for a long voyage across the Pacific. On Magellan's expedition only thirty-five out of 280 men had survived, many of them dying on the Pacific crossing.

The problems involved in launching such a large undertaking were many. The preparations for these expeditions were fraught with delay, double-dealing and money troubles, as well as intrigues which could bedevil crew relations throughout the voyage. Drake had to do business with the port suppliers who, given the opportunity, would have filled his ships with rotten meat, old biscuits and leaky water barrels. With a fleet of five ships to provision for a voyage that would take at least two years, it was a mammoth task. The total complement of over 160 men had to be chosen from the many volunteers who undoubtedly flocked to Plymouth on hearing about the voyage. It was rumoured that Drake was making for the Mediterranean and Alexandria for trade, which, if it had been true, would have been a pleasant trip. Because the admiral was Drake, the crew assumed that piracy would bring them plenty of prize money and this was an enormous incentive at a time of widespread poverty.

In addition to the working crew a number of gentlemen explorers were to sail with the ships. One of them was a parson, Francis Fletcher, who wrote a vivid account of the voyage. The rest were courtiers, noblemen or relatives of the ship's officers who were going along for the adventure, the glory, or to represent one of the expedition's sponsors. They were led by Thomas Doughty, an educated and polished courtier who had used his influence at Elizabeth's court to gain favour for Drake's idea. Drake, who was neither well-educated nor polished, had great admiration for Doughty, as well as gratitude for the help he had given him. These emotions were to prove misplaced.

A detail from an engraving by Theodore de Bry of Drake at the River Plate

Drake finally sailed from Plymouth on 13 December 1577. *The Golden Hind*, or the *Pelican* as she was called during the early part of the voyage, was the largest vessel in the fleet, but by sixteenth-century standards, she was not big. Even in those days the capacity of a large merchant vessel might be 1000 tuns, ten times more than the *Golden Hind*'s. Standing high on the quarter-deck watching the new *Golden Hind* surge forward before the push of the powerful north-east trade winds, one is aware that she is immensely tall for her small size. At the stern the poop rises high out of the water like a drunken apartment block while the forecastle, the protuberance on the forward end, is only a little less extreme. The hull is voluminous, wide and obstinate, sitting in the water like a fat barrel. Over 4000 square feet of sail on three masts propel it along. Sailing downwind the ship makes good speed, but upwind her height and bulk create great resistance to forward motion. 'She's reasonably fast downhill,' Captain Haward confirmed, 'but windward sailing is not her strongest point! She sails at about 70° to the wind if you're lucky but with leeway – well, we don't make much progress!' He gave a new course to the helmsman. 'Look, I'll show you.' The ship slowly came up into the wind and there was a flogging of canvas aloft. The crew moved to the braces to haul the yards and trim the sails. With the yards as close to a fore-and-aft line as they would go and the sails trimmed as flat as possible the ship was now hard on the wind. Peter Haward indicated the angle of the ship's wake, which gives a crude indication of the amount of leeway or sideways motion the ship is making. It looked considerable. 'We're lucky to make any ground at all,' he said wistfully. He was not happy to be sailing a ship that could not claw itself off a lee shore, the dread of all seamen. 'We'll just have to give the land a wide berth and hope for the best. They talk about lee shores being graveyards of ships – well, we're right back in that era and I've had to adjust my thinking accordingly.'

Why then did Drake choose a relatively bulky, inefficient ship? Sixteenth-century shipbuilders knew how to construct lighter, faster vessels that could sail to windward; the caravels used by Columbus were light, shallow-draughted and manoeuvrable, and, with the benefit of the lateen rig adapted from the Arab dhow, they were better windward sailers. However, these small vessels had two disadvantages; they had limited accommodation for men and supplies, and they had absolutely no room for cargo. Drake intended to bring back many tons of gold and spices; he wanted a ship that could be loaded to the gunwales with booty. The *Golden Hind* was just what he needed – a voluminous cargo-carrier. He was happy to sacrifice some speed, windward ability and manoeuvrability to achieve his ambitions.

The *Golden Hind* was rigged in the style that came to be known as a barque; she had square sails on her two forward masts and a lateen sail on her mizzen, or aft, mast. Her hull design was a compromise between the heavy, rounded tradition of Northern ships and the slimmer, faster lines of the Mediterranean. This blending of traditions during the fifteenth century resulted in vastly improved sailing ability. Although the *Golden Hind* was not a good windward sailer, her all-round performance was very much better than that of medieval ships. The ships used for the voyages of discovery were not built specially for the job; they were ordinary trading vessels that were designed for short or medium passages. It is a great credit to the shipbuilders of the time that even a few of these ships succeeded in completing long voyages.

Why Drake should have chosen such small ships is not clear from contemporary accounts. Most likely he wanted vessels large enough to carry everything that might be needed on a long voyage, but small enough to be beached and repaired en route. In the days before antifouling paints, a ship accumulated thick growths of weeds and barnacles on her bottom and in warm waters the hull was attacked by a woodborer called the teredo worm. To clean the bottom and cover it with grease to discourage the worms, the ship had to be careened. This involved grounding her at high tide, emptying her of her ballast, cargo and supplies, and pulling her over on her side by tackles to the mastheads. It was a long, difficult process which would have taken very much longer with a bigger ship, increasing the danger of surprise attack by the Spanish while the ship was defenceless.

The first part of Drake's voyage took him along the well-established route to the south which used the Atlantic trade winds to best advantage. From Plymouth he headed south until he picked up the north-east trade winds that took him down the Moroccan coast and out to the Cape Verde Islands. Sailing before the wind, progress was fast and smooth, enabling the crew to settle into the routine of shipboard life.

Here on the replica of the *Golden Hind* the crew was divided into three watches of five men each and they kept what is now considered the standard watch system: four hours on and eight hours off, with one four-hour period broken into two two-hour 'dog' watches, to rotate the hours a particular watch is on duty each day. In Drake's time they changed watch every four hours too, but the idea of dog watches had not yet been introduced. The duties of the crew on the replica were not very different from those of Drake's men. They had to pump out the bilges, wash the decks, repair the sails and work on the gear, perhaps tarring the shrouds or splicing some ropes. The sails had to be trimmed as the direction of the wind varied, the amount of sail had to be increased or reduced according to the wind strength, and a good course steered. The new *Golden Hind* is equipped with a wheel for steering and, under normal conditions, one man can manage the job. In the sixteenth century the wheel had not yet been developed and even the largest ships were steered by tillers attached to the head of the rudder and operated through a port cut into the stern on the main deck level. Standing in the steerage, deep in the dark interior of the main cabin, the helmsman could not of course see ahead. He steered by means of a compass and verbal instructions from the officer on the quarter-deck overhead. In bad weather many more men had to be put on the tiller to keep the ship on course and prevent her from being caught by a beam sea. In the early seventeenth century the system was improved by the development of the whipstaff, which extended the steering to the quarter-deck level where the helmsman could see ahead. But nothing was really satisfactory until the wheel was introduced in the eighteenth century.

Working ship was a labour-intensive business. Yet here on the replica the total complement numbered only sixteen, and one of them was a full-time cook. How did they manage? 'At the beginning – with difficulty!' said Peter Haward. He freely admitted that when he took over the ship for the return trip to England he knew little about sailing a square-rigger. 'Didn't know a buntline from a bullrope,' he laughed. Eventually his crew had worked out how the complex web of lines controlled the various sails and how to operate them most efficiently. However, setting sail still took a long time because, compared with the number of men Drake carried, they were very short-handed. Perhaps sixty men was going to the other extreme, but Drake knew he would probably lose many on the way and, if he was going to get involved in skirmishes with the Spanish, he needed to manoeuvre his ship fast.

In high winds and seas the dangers of working aloft could be considerable. Watching Captain Haward's crew moving out along the yards, it looked precarious up there, but the crew assured me it was surprisingly secure most of the time. It was only when the ship rolled and the masts started to whip from side to side that it became difficult. So far only one of the crew had fallen from aloft – while carrying out maintenance in port. Fortunately he hit the water and not the deck where, the crew were quick to tell me, he would have made a lovely mess.

Drake's fleet made good time on their passage down the North Atlantic, stopping only to steal food or ships from the Spanish or Portuguese. Progress slowed only when the wind faltered and the weather grew stormy and unpredictable, signalling the

FRANCISCVS DRAECK NOBILISSIMVS EQVES ANGLIAE AN° ÆT SVE 43

Habes Lector candide fortiss. ac invictiss Ducis Draeck ad vivum Imaginem qui toto terrarum orbe, duorum annorum, et mensum decem spatio, Zephiris fauen: tibus circumductus. Anglium sedes proprias, 4. Cal Octobr, anno à partu Virgi: nis 1580 reuisit cum antea portu soluisset 1d. Decem: anni. 1577.

The engraving of Drake is attributed to Jodocus Hondius, the great
map-maker. The miniature is by Nicholas Hilliard and was painted in 1581

beginning of the doldrums. Throughout the Middle Ages sailors believed that the sea boiled near the equator, that dreadful demons, serpents and ghosts lay in wait, or even that they would fall off the edge of the world. The sixteenth-century sailor was better informed, but he still regarded southern latitudes with deep suspicion. Drake's crew, who had only learnt their true destination when they were past the entrance to the Mediterranean, had every reason to feel discontent. Yet the grumbling and quibbling among the ordinary men was no worse than usual on a long voyage out of sight of land. The presence of a Portuguese pilot, whom Drake had captured in the Cape Verde Islands and forcibly pressed into service to guide them down the South American coast, may have given the men extra confidence. Finding Nuño da Silva had been a great *coup* for Drake because pilotage – that is, the art of taking a ship from place to place within sight of land or navigation marks – was still the most popular and trusted form of navigation. Detailed knowledge of a particular coastline, acquired by experience and observation, was highly valued in the absence of reliable charts or written information. In northern Europe rutters, or pilot books, were in general use by this time but these sailing directions, which listed courses, dangers, soundings and landmarks for a variety of passages, were not available to Drake for Portuguese waters. Faced by the choice of groping his way down the coast using compass and sounding lead, or pressing the pilot into service, Drake grabbed the pilot.

With the fleet making fast progress and the crew content, all should have gone well, but at this early stage the expedition almost ended in discord and disaster. The problem did not lie with the ordinary seamen, but among the gentlemen adventurers. Extraordinary though it now seems, a ship's captain did not enjoy outright authority in those days. Fighting ships were commanded by soldiers and tactics decided by generals. Only the working of a ship was left under the control of the ship's master. In these early voyages of exploration the highest-ranking gentlemen expected to be given command of a ship while the master ran it. To make matters worse, the gentlemen did no real work; as befitted their social status they sat around amusing themselves while the ship's crew sweated away aloft. In this kind of atmosphere it only needed one troublemaker to create a dangerous situation and one now appeared: no less a man than Thomas Doughty, whom Drake had believed to be his friend. Doughty was an accomplished intriguer. Working behind Drake's back, he tried to undermine the crew's loyalty and confidence. He suggested the plan for the voyage was his idea and that he had the greater right to lead the expedition. Considering the degree of provocation Drake was patient, transferring Doughty first to one ship then another. But as the fleet sailed down the coast of South America it became increasingly clear that he would have to take action to prevent discontent developing into mutiny.

For Drake the situation was a nightmare. He undoubtedly felt the humiliation more keenly because of his aspirations to be a gentleman himself, although, to the well-born, he probably appeared nouveau-riche and ridiculous. Now the very man he had looked up to as the epitome of good breeding was challenging the position he had struggled so hard to win. Not that crew troubles were unexpected – they seem to have been the rule on early voyages. Drake carried the account of Magellan's voyage in his cabin, but he needed no reminding that, in order to crush a mutiny, Magellan had executed two men at Port St Julian, the very harbour Drake was now approaching. Should he also take such drastic action?

Many people have criticised Drake for his decision to try Doughty and, having found him guilty of mutiny, execute him. But Drake had to establish his authority or, as he told his men, they would fight among themselves and none of them get home alive. The importance of unity and authority is paramount on a long voyage. Even today, in events like the Round the World Yacht Race, crew members are sometimes replaced at stopovers to establish a harmonious working atmosphere on a yacht.

A commander demands loyalty and obedience, for there can only be one leader. After this near-mutiny Drake decided to lay down some principles regarding discipline and behaviour, so that everyone in the expedition would have a clear idea of what was expected of him. In so doing he unwittingly laid down the precepts which would govern shipboard discipline and organisation for centuries. He overturned the old idea that the gentlemen would have no part in the running of the ship. In future, he said, 'I must have the gentlemen to haul and draw with the mariner and the mariner with the gentlemen.' He also established that the officer-gentlemen would be subordinate to the captain and that they would enjoy no special privilege or rank. From this time on, the captain and not the military commander was the supreme authority on board an English fighting ship, an innovation that was to have important consequences ten years later when the English fleet, brilliantly led by Drake and other sailor-commanders, trounced the Spanish Armada which was under the inefficient command of the military.

After this important declaration at Port St Julian, Drake encountered no further serious challenges to his authority. Nor, it was clear, would his twentieth-century counterpart, Captain Haward. If there is a human equivalent to a dynamo then Peter Haward was it. No sooner did he give an order than he launched himself at the rigging and swarmed up to the topmost yard to haul with his crew. Back on deck, he pored over charts in the chart room or took a trick at the wheel. Only the arrival of a steaming mug of tea made him pause. Natural authority inspired by example, professionalism and hard work is always more effective than authority imposed by mere rank. Columbus was hampered by being an Italian trying to run a Spanish ship yet, due to his qualities as a leader and a sailor, his crews never mutinied. It was only when he tried to set up the administration of a colony that he met failure and returned to Spain in chains. Magellan, a Portuguese, met great resistance to his authority from his Spanish crew and only after the show of strength at Port St Julian did he establish his position as a leader. None of these great voyages of exploration could have taken place without a strong character in command. Drake had his weaknesses – his impatience, his love of pomp and ceremony, his ambition – but he had qualities which set him apart from other men: clarity of purpose, boundless energy and stubborn tenacity. Though his restless ambition found him few real friends, he was adored by the ordinary crewmen and, after the events at Port St Julian, grudgingly respected by the gentlemen who considered themselves his social superiors.

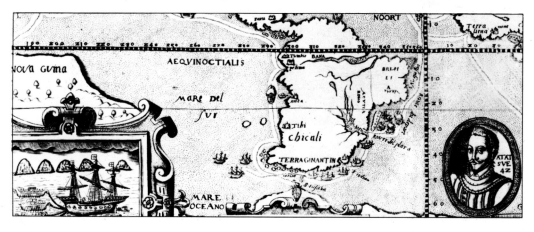

This map, by Nicola van Sype, shows Drake's route – and how little help contemporary charts were to a navigator approaching the Pacific

Having abandoned one ship because it was unseaworthy, Drake now pressed on to the Magellan Strait, which promised to be the most testing part of the voyage. Nuño da Silva led the fleet to the entrance of the strait but from then on Drake had only Magellan's journal to guide him through the tortuous passage. The Magellan Strait is 334 miles long – roughly the same length as the English Channel. It twists and turns between snow-clad mountains, massive glaciers and rocky islets. The wind pounces down from the mountains in sudden squalls which bring gale-force winds and blinding rain. A ship can be moored in the lee of an island one moment and in danger of being swept against it the next. Westerly winds predominate, so that westbound vessels may have to wait days for a favourable wind. Strong currents swirl through the strait, sometimes making progress impossible even when the wind is fair. Magellan took thirty-eight days to make the passage, averaging under nine miles per day. Now Drake was going to attempt it at the worst time of year, in the depths of the southern winter. Faced by the choice of pressing on in bad weather or waiting at Port St Julian and risking further discontent, he decided on positive action which would keep his men occupied and happy. At first it seemed it would be a difficult passage – for two days strong headwinds prevented the fleet from entering the strait – but then it blew from the north-east and, after surprisingly few problems, the ships completed the passage in just seventeen days. They even managed to eat fresh meat on the way, having come across hoards of what the Welsh crew members called 'pen gwyn', or 'white head'.

Luck is an essential part of success, and Drake had been very lucky. But as every sailor knows, good weather only lasts so long. Hardly had Drake's ships sailed into the Pacific, which had been named for its benign winds, than they met the full fury of a terrible storm. Nowadays most sailors think of this region as part of the Southern Ocean rather than the Pacific, for the very reason that the weather is very much fiercer than the conditions found among the blue waters to the north. If Drake had any illusions about this unexplored part of the world, they were soon dispelled. The storm was severe even by Cape Horn standards. With only brief lulls it raged for over fifty days. As Parson Fletcher wrote:

> '. . . we continued without hope at the pleasure of God in the violent force of the winds intolerable working of the wrathful seas and the grisely beholding (some-times) of the cragged rocks & fearful height, & monstrous mountains being to us a lee shore where we were continually drawn by the winds & carried by the mountain-like billows of the sea. . . .'

The storm was a supreme test of men and ships. To escape the clutches of the lee shore they had to claw their way off for day after day, keeping a small amount of sail set, constantly trimming the sails. Fighting the sea in this way, the ships took a terrible punishment. Yet it is great credit to the design and construction of these trading vessels that only one, the *Marygold*, actually foundered. The men on the *Golden Hind* heard the *Marygold*'s crew cry for help over the din of the storm, but nothing could be done and she went down with all hands. Those who remained were in a terrible state, worn down by scurvy, lack of sleep, and exposure to the bitter rain and wind. Faced with the strong possibility of drowning they had every incentive to keep going; nevertheless the resilience and the tenacity of these men was remarkable, and their seamanship outstanding. They managed to drive their ships against the kinds of winds and seas that even the great nineteenth-century sailing ships had difficulty in overcoming.

When the wind finally dropped Drake anchored at some islands far south of the

The Straits of Magellan

Magellan Strait and, seeing ocean where the mythical *Terra Australis Incognita* was meant to be, rightly guessed that the Atlantic and the Pacific were joined by open sea. However, he explored this unknown region no further; his interests lay in the wealthy Spanish possessions to the north. During the storm he had lost contact with the other remaining ship of his fleet and, after waiting in vain at a rendezvous, the *Golden Hind* set sail alone.

For his voyage up the coast of Chile and Peru, Drake appears to have used a Spanish chart that he had acquired at some time during his travels – probably by theft. The chart proved to be little better than useless, and one can see why. In the captain's cabin high on the poop of the new *Golden Hind* we sat and looked at a reproduction of an Ortelius chart, the type which the Spanish were using in the 1570s. 'Beats me how he found anything using this,' said a crew member who regularly navigated. Compared to the modern Admiralty chart lying next to it, the continents certainly sported some strange shapes. Chile bulged out into the ocean while the west coast of North America stretched halfway across the Pacific. It is possible that the Spanish deliberately encouraged the publication of misleading charts to discourage their enemies from entering the Pacific, but this is unlikely. Although Ortelius became Philip of Spain's personal geographer in 1575, he was based in Belgium and published his atlas in Antwerp in 1570 when independent of Spanish patronage. The atlas was a compilation of many cartographers' works and was based on the ideas of the great Ptolemy, whose second-century maps were rediscovered in 1400. Thanks to Ptolemy's observations of the stars, these charts managed to show the Mediterranean with some accuracy, but the mapping of the new discoveries relied more on conjecture and imagination than scientific observation. Chart-makers relied on information brought back by explorers, but the early navigators were severely hampered by one major problem – they could not determine longitude and so were unable to fix the position of their discoveries. Knowing this, one can see why the Americas appeared so awry. Longitude could not be calculated until the time at a fixed point – Greenwich – was exactly known. In the second half of the eighteenth century, the 'lunar distance' method of establishing Greenwich time was developed and, a few years later, John Harrison constructed the first reliable sea-going chronometers. Captain Cook used both methods to chart the Pacific and other regions accurately for the first time. On board the new *Golden Hind* the chart room, which lay at one end of the tiny captain's cabin, possessed a quartz chronometer whose accuracy Peter Haward regularly checked against radio time-signals. At the moment it was one second slow but, not having gained or lost time for many weeks, it was extremely accurate. By using a modern sextant to measure the heights of the sun and stars and noting the exact time of the observation, the navigator can calculate his position from precomputed tables to an accuracy of a mile or two, or even better in calm conditions.

A second major problem for cartographers was how to show a roughly spherical object like the earth on a flat piece of paper, so that a straight line drawn between two points represented a constant compass bearing. As early as 1569 this problem was solved by a Fleming called Mercator but, like so many revolutionary ideas, the new method did not come into general use until much later, in the eighteenth century. The Mercator chart was the father of the modern chart, which still bears the description 'Mercator projection'.

Despite the lack of a good chart, Drake sailed safely up the coast and began to look for silver and other riches that he could steal from the Spanish. He didn't have to look

The astrolabe (the example on the left is German, made in the sixteenth century) enabled the mariner to find his latitude – his position north and south. The crucial problem of finding longitude was not solved until the eighteenth century. Then the development of the marine chronometer – a timepiece which remained accurate whatever the conditions in which it was carried – meant that the mariner knew the time at the Greenwich Observatory. He knew the local time from solar observation and the difference gave him his position east and west. The chronometer below is Harrison's fourth, which was the model for the one used by Cook on his later voyages. Taking bearings is still the most foolproof test of a ship's position when it is within sight of land: the illustration below – showing the process taking place on land – is from a treatise of 1583 by Jacques de Vaulx

far. In the previous thirty years the Spanish had built up an extensive network of trading posts and merchant ships in the Pacific to extract and transport the vast wealth of Peru and Chile. The merchant ships, which were built on the west coast of central America, were not equipped with guns because there was no one to fight – or so it was thought. Drake had an easy job: all he had to do was find a ship and demand surrender. The Spanish were taken completely by surprise and, raiding and pillaging, Drake stormed up the coast filling his hold with treasure. Having stirred up this hornet's nest, he then looked for somewhere safe to hide and chose to go north, beyond Spain's reach. Using the Spanish chart that showed the land stretching away to the north-west he sailed miles into the Pacific before doubling back and finding the coast again, near to what is now San Francisco.

From San Francisco there was only one way to go and that was across the Pacific. Although it was a massive undertaking to cross this largest of all oceans with its scattering of low-lying islands and hidden reefs, it was a far better proposition than trying to return home through the Magellan Strait. Better to run the risk of meeting a few Spaniards than sail through those storm-tossed, icy southern waters again. But there was another, more important, reason to go west. Drake was greedy for more wealth. Having got this far he wanted to round off his triumph by bringing back a commodity that was worth, weight for weight, more than gold. This most valuable of substances was the humble clove. In those days it grew in only one place, the Moluccas, better known as the Spice Islands.

To cross the Pacific Drake would have to rely on navigation by the sun and stars. Astro-navigation was still regarded by most seamen as a fancy new skill that was quite unnecessary for most sea passages. But explorers and ocean sailors had of necessity to be numerate, literate men who could master the art. For centuries astronomers had known how to calculate latitude from the Pole Star, and fifteenth-century navigators adapted and simplified astronomers' instruments to measure the height of the star at sea. However, use of the Pole Star was limited; south of about $9°N$ it cannot be seen. Sailing over the equator required the use of another star and the most convenient was the sun. But obtaining latitude from the sun was not a simple matter for, unlike the Pole Star, it is not 'fixed' in the sky but 'moves' around the earth daily, and north or south of the equator with the different seasons. The daily movement was solved by measuring the sun's height only at local noon, when it is at its highest point; the seasonal variation, on the other hand, had to be precomputed by mathematicians and published in tables which gave the position of the sun in relation to the equator for each day of the year. By means of some simple calculations, latitude could then be found.

However, sun sights taken at sea could err by as much as sixty miles – quite enough to put an overconfident mariner on the rocks. The instruments used for measuring its height were simply not very accurate. Curious to see if I could obtain any results with a sixteenth-century instrument, I had brought a replica of a cross-staff on board the *Golden Hind*. Never having used one before, I had taken the precaution of going along to the National Maritime Museum at Greenwich for a short course of instruction before leaving for the Pacific. The museum staff warned me against trying a sight with an astrolabe, although this instrument was also used in Drake's time, and after inspecting one I could appreciate why. The astrolabe has to be kept perfectly perpendicular – on a heaving deck! – and a bar rotated until the sun shines through a tiny hole on to a back plate. It sounded wellnigh impossible to me and instead I gladly absorbed what they had to tell me about the cross-staff. This instrument uses the horizon as a reference point and is one of the forerunners of the modern sextant. It consists of a single piece of wood, shaped rather like a long ruler, with a cross-beam that slides up and down its length. All you have to do is hold it to your eye and slide the cross-beam back and forth until you sight the horizon under one end and the sun over the other. You then read the height of the sun in degrees off the main rod. It sounded simple, but I soon discovered that it was a lot more difficult in practice. As the *Golden Hind* rolled gently along on a beam wind, I braced myself against a rail and, roughly at noon, tried a few sights. After ten minutes my eyes were half-blind and my arms were aching. What was more, my sights were inaccurate, to put it mildly. Not too bad for a beginner, but the subject of polite mirth from the crew: we calculated that they would put us somewhere on the Asian mainland. Doubtless Drake was more skilled. Nevertheless, it was only on land that explorers could obtain really accurate calculations of latitude.

Using the cross-staff – a plate from an early eighteenth-century manual of seamanship

We discussed how Drake would have made the long Pacific crossing and decided he would have sailed down to a given latitude, as recommended on the chart he had acquired, and then sailed along it until he reached land. The given latitude would be the one the Spanish galleons, bound for the Philippines to load silk and spices, had found to be reasonably clear of islands and reefs. Tracking longitude would have been the most difficult part of the operation, and Drake would have used the ancient art of dead reckoning, that is, plotting a position from estimates of direction and distance travelled in relation to time. Columbus traversed the Atlantic using nothing *but* dead reckoning, even for latitude, but since no one knew what was on the other side of the ocean anyway, it didn't really matter. In Drake's day, the width of the Pacific was very roughly known, so dead reckoning was important to give him an idea of his westerly progress.

In the days when sailors could not read or write they could not record course and speed in a written log. Instead, at each half-hour of a four-hour watch they would go to a wooden block known as a traverse board and insert two pegs into holes, one to record the course steered and one to show speed. At the end of the watch the navigator could calculate the average course and speed sailed during the four hours from the sixteen pegs on the traverse board. I have an old traverse board which sits on a bulkhead in *Gulliver G* but, though it looks very decorative, I have never had occasion to use it; pencilled positions on a modern chart are more efficient.

Keeping local time was not too difficult in these early ships. Half-hour-glasses were turned eight times during a four-hour watch (coinciding with the pegging of the traverse board) and this local time could be corrected daily by calibrating the moment when the sun was at its highest with local noon. Magnetic compasses, too, were quite efficient, and by Elizabethan times men had begun to gain an understanding of magnetic variation, the phenomenon whereby magnetic north differs from true north by an amount that varies according to position and time.

Speed was perhaps the most difficult factor to calculate. Columbus, like many a sailor, estimated his speed by the look and feel of the ship as she sped through the water. Most masters who know their ships well can guess their speed to within half a knot. The new *Golden Hind* carries a mechanical spinning log (similar to though larger than the one on *Gulliver G*), but I asked Peter Haward to estimate our speed without looking at the log. 'Ah,' he murmured, looking over the rail at the bow wave and glancing aloft to feel the push of the sails. A final look at the water and he ventured 'five and a half knots, I should say.' He was quite right.

The problem with estimating speed was that, until a century or so after Drake, no one knew exactly how long a nautical mile should be. Until the size of the earth was established, the length of one degree of latitude subtended from the earth's centre on to its surface could not be properly calculated. In the fifteenth century the nautical mile was thought to be 5000 feet long, and in the sixteenth century 6120 feet (it is in fact 6080 feet long). But so long as everyone agreed on a single measurement at any one time, a standard unit of measurement did at least exist. By Drake's time the common log was in use. A wooden board attached to a log-line was thrown from the stern of the ship and, over a fixed length of time (usually thirty seconds measured by a special sandglass), the number of knots tied on the log-line were counted as they ran through the fingers, the space between each knot representing a nautical mile per hour. This is how the word 'knot' came into use.

The combination of latitude and dead reckoning would have given Drake a rough idea of his position as he crossed the Pacific – but only a rough one. He would have done well to take on a pilot from the Caroline Islands which he sighted towards the end of the crossing. Here were some of the most remarkable navigators the world has ever seen. The people of the Pacific had mastered the art of finding their way across the vast ocean after colonising hundreds of its many islands thousands of years before. By the time Europeans reached these waters most of the island people had forgotten how to navigate long distances, but the few that did remember passed their knowledge on through father and son for generations. Today there are still men in the Caroline Island group who can find their way between many scores of islands without the use of even the simplest navigation aids like compass or log. Mau Piailug is one such man. In 1976 he navigated the replica of a Polynesian double canoe 2500 miles from Hawaii to Tahiti, from the north-east trade winds through the doldrums to the south-east trades. The canoe was accompanied by a powered vessel that kept an accurate position check; astonishingly, Mau Piailug's estimated position hardly varied from his true position, even after 2000 miles.

Historians suggest that the islands of the Pacific were discovered by accident and that many voyages must inevitably have failed to find land and died in the attempt. They imply that, on venturing into the unknown, the navigators could not have found their way back home and should not, therefore, be called true explorers. Having heard of Mau Piailug's achievement and knowing how fast and seaworthy these canoes were, I felt this could not be true. No navigator in his right mind would sail off without noting the way he was going to be sure of finding his way home again. There is no

The western hemisphere, from Gerardus Mercator's world map of 1587, shows how uncertain Pacific geography was many years after the first circumnavigations

Polus 9|0 Arcticus

Oceanus

Mare dulce

Estotilant

El ftreto de Anian

Anian regnum

Circulus Arcticus

AMERICA SIVE INDIA NOVA
Anno 1492 a Christophoro Columbo nomine Regis
Castellæ primum detecta.

Tolm reg.

Quiuira reg.

Tolm reg.

sierra neuada

Nova Francia

Chilaga

Lat des hermanas

Anacal

Tontonteac

Canada

Florida

La Bermuda

Tropicus Cancer

Archipelago di S. Lazaro

Circulus Aequinoctialis

MAR DEL NORT

Golfo Mexi

Mexico

Caribana

Trinidad

MAR DEL ZUR

Nova Guinea
nuper inuenta quæ an
sit insula an pars conti
nentis australis adhuc incer
tum est

Peru

Amazones

Brasil

Tropicus Capricorn

Insulæ incantad.

PACIFICO MARE

Chili

C. de S. Maria

Rio de la plata

Archipelago minor

Hanc continentem
Australem nonnulli
Magellanicam regi-
onem ab inuento-
re nuncupant

Estrecho de Magellanes

Terra del fuego

TERRA AVSTRALIS

Circulus Antarcticus

Polus Antarcticus

DE MVNDI CREATIONE ac constitutione breuis instructio.

Studiofus Geographiæ ante omnia confideret mundi creationem, hoc modo. Deus conftituto puncto, quod nunc mundi centrum eft, ero fede et quiete grauem maffam informem creans, quã chaos uocant, illi eam iniecit, excitatoq̧ uehementi fpiritu eam agitauit, agitando crafsiora grauioraq̧, difcreuit, quæ centro fe ad æquilibrium applicantia, terram ac mare in unũ corpus figuræ fphericæ dederunt, cuius centrũ punctus ille qui fedes eft grauium exiftit, fupra hoc corpus ut leuiora et nobiliora quæq̧ ita fuperiorem lucum obtinuerunt, lucidaq̧ materia globos paulatim collecta, lunam, folem, ftellasq̧ reddidit, quæ ratione primi mobilis fupra inquam cœli fuper polis æqui-noctialis fiue mundi ab ortum occafum rapiuntur, noctem diemq̧ diuidentes, at fuper aliis polis, eclyptiçæ uidelicet, proprio motu ab occafum in ortum, aliæ citius, aliæ tardius circumuoluuntur. Vt autem terra habitationi animalium accommoda fieret, fpiritus ille quo placuit Deo undiqȝ circumfufus...

huiusiam fphærici corporis conuexam fuperficiem contemplaturus Geographiæ ftudiofus aftris illud fubiici et pro illorum fitu uaria ipfi accidentia contingere obferuet, quæ ratione circulorum, quibus aftrorum motus diftantiæ et tempora determinantur, illi obueniunt. Sunt autè circuli ad Geographiam cognitu necefsarij, Æquinoctialis ſiue Parallelus ſiue æquidiftantes, et Meridiani. Porro quia hi circuli in plano non eodem modo quo in fphæra expri-mi poſsunt, quod fphæræ fuperficies in planum feruata eadè partium ad inuicem habitudine depingi nequeat...

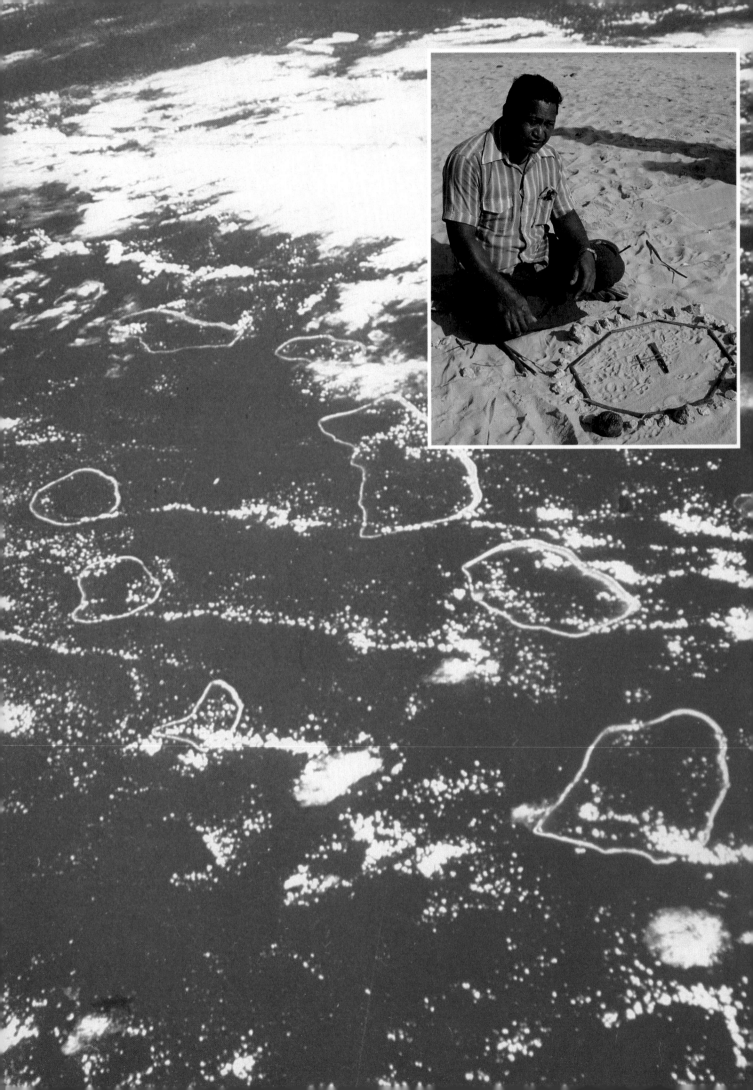

written history to tell us how many boats or people set out on the voyages of exploration, but great navigators like Mau Piailug still exist and can fill many gaps in the story the anthropologists have managed to piece together.

Before setting out for the Pacific we had contacted Mau Piailug in Hawaii, where he was preparing to navigate on another expedition. I was very pleased when he agreed to meet us at Singapore. After a long flight in a large jet – the first he had ever taken – Mau was a little dazed on arrival, but he soon recovered when we picked him up from the bustling, bewildering city and took him for a day's sail on the *Golden Hind*. He stared at the great masts and the square sails of the ship and shook his head in wonder; the *Hind* was quite the most extraordinary vessel he had ever seen, the antithesis of the fast, light Pacific canoe which flies over the water; she was cumbersome and far from fast. Nonetheless, Mau indicated, she was a fine and beautiful vessel. His broad, brown face broke into a wide smile and he settled in a corner of the main deck to watch the crew working the ship. Later, on a quiet beach, he sat on the sand and told me, in halting English and vivid signs, how he could find at least fifty islands – maybe more when he thought about it. He had started his training as a small boy on the island of Satawal, and had graduated as a fully-fledged navigator at the age of eighteen, after memorising the star compass bearings of every island. He illustrated the star compass by making a circle of stones in the sand. Each stone represented the position of the set or rise of a named star. Mau then added palm fronds to show the different swell patterns and winds that could occur. Different winds create a series of different wave types. The underlying swell shows the direction of the prevailing trade winds, while smaller cross waves indicates a temporary wind from a different direction. The presence of islands over the horizon can be deduced from small counter-swells, as well as from the flight paths of birds at sunset. Using all the data available Mau explained how the canoe, which he depicted with a criss-cross of small fronds, could follow exactly the right direction.

Some Carolinians remember the guiding stars for an island by dance or chants. But Mau shook his head. No, he just remembered them in his head, he said. To remember the swells, waves, currents and guide stars for each and every island, one from another, was a prodigious feat of memory. Yet Mau had done it, and proved that it worked. Only historians ignorant of the deep knowledge and understanding the Pacific peoples have of the stars, the winds and the waves, could doubt the possibility of charting and exploring an ocean in this way. I would happily sail in a boat navigated by Mau Piailug, even if it were voyaging into the unknown with little possibility of finding an island ahead. I would feel confident that he was charting our course in his head and could find his way back along the track to the island we had started from.

We said farewell to Mau Piailug after two days; he had to return to Hawaii and the preparations for his next voyage. He was not sad at leaving the bustle of Singapore; to a quiet island man the big city was a symbol that men had gone mad. As he left he smiled and, doubtless thinking of the *Golden Hind*, shook his head once more.

Polynesian double canoes: a drawing made by an artist on one of Cook's voyages

Satellite view of the Hawaiian chain. Mau Piailug shows, with stones on the beach, how he is able to use star bearings and wave patterns to find his way from one island to another

No amount of skill in seamanship or navigation could defend the islanders against the slow but steady European encroachment on their Pacific territory. As men like Drake were able to find their way across the vast ocean using scientific navigation methods, so it was only a matter of time before colonists followed explorers. That is not to say there was an immediate rush of Europeans anxious to set sail for the Pacific; until the problem of health and nourishment could be solved the mortality rate on long voyages remained high. As Drake prepared his ship for the Pacific the provision of health-giving food must have been his greatest headache. On setting out from Plymouth nineteen months before, the *Golden Hind* had been well stocked with salted pork and beef, dried beans, peas and lentils, flour, onions, vinegar, cheeses, honey and ship's biscuits, as well as some live hens and pigs in pens. During the raids up the American coast, the crew had managed to capture food from the Spanish and in California seals and deer were caught and preserved in brine ready for the long crossing ahead. But even salted meat did not last long in a hot climate and it could be expected to go rotten in a week or so. Any honey, cheese and onions loaded in England would have been finished months before. From the original stores probably only the ship's biscuit, known as hardtack, remained. This was the staple carbohydrate carried by sailing ships until this century. It was a hard, dry biscuit which would have kept well in sealed, dry conditions. Since no container was properly sealed and no hold dry, the biscuits soon became infested with weevils. If men were to live, they had to eat the biscuits, weevils and all. Some, it is said, waited for nightfall so that they would not have to look at what they were eating. Others put their biscuits in hot broth to cook the worms a little. Brave men just ate them uncooked in broad daylight.

Drake probably stocked his ship with some form of root vegetable provided by the Indians who inhabited the North American coast, thus protecting his crew against scurvy, the disease caused by lack of vitamin C. But it was not always possible to find fruit and vegetables, and in the Magellan Strait virtually all Drake's crew suffered from this unpleasant disease. At the slightest exertion victims complained of exhaustion and faintness. Their teeth began to feel loose and their gums became swollen and tender, making eating difficult. In its advanced stages the disease was terrible; the gums became so swollen and putrid that teeth dropped out and, though a man might feel reasonably well lying down, he could drop dead on getting to his feet. During Magellan's 99-day crossing of the Pacific, his men were reduced to eating rats and biscuit powder full of worms, to chewing leather and drinking putrid water. Nineteen men died. It seems strange that it was rarely the captains or officers who suffered from scurvy until one discovers that they usually had a personal store of sweetmeats like crystallised fruit or quince which provided the essential vitamin.

Scurvy was not the only disease the men faced; yellow fever and malaria took a heavy toll in mosquito-infested ports, while dysentery struck on the longer voyages as the bilges became more and more putrid with an accumulation of rubbish and sewage that settled in the loose stone or sand ballast deep in the hold. Short of emptying all the ballast and washing it down, which the more efficient captains carried out when careening, there was little that could be done to keep the bilges clean. Most men did not associate an insanitary ship with illness and the word hygiene had not yet been invented. To complete the picture, rats had a free run of the ship and lice, bed bugs and fleas were everywhere. The men had probably only one complete set of clothing, with an extra jacket for cold climates. In warm waters they enjoyed the occasional swim, but washing as such was not a regular pastime.

Faced by such conditions one wonders what possessed the ordinary sixteenth-century seamen to go on these voyages; they had neither comfort, nor adequate food, they were riddled with disease, and they faced a good chance of dying before the voyage was over. However, this harsh shipboard life was not much worse than their lives in England where they faced a good many uncertainties and hardships. Harvests could fail and, even in a good year, the winter diet was very meagre. Death from disease was almost as common on land as at sea. Rats, lice and insanitary conditions were a part of everyday life. To these men, enduring adversity was a small price to pay for the enormous riches they hoped to find; Elizabethan men were, simply, very tough individuals who would have found conditions on the new *Golden Hind* luxurious in the extreme. Not that they enjoyed long and dangerous voyages: they needed constant reassurance both as to the purpose and the likely rewards of the expedition. Drake, a master of psychology and timing, would choose the right moment to make a short speech, ask the parson for a prayer or, his *pièce de résistance*, quote from Fox's *Book of Martyrs*, a work of Protestant propaganda which described in horrifying and lurid detail the burning and torturing of Protestants by Catholics. Discontent about shipboard conditions would turn to hatred for the vile Spanish, and Drake would have a united and purposeful crew once more.

Drake had planned his Pacific crossing well and, though his ship was out of sight of land for sixty-six days, the passage was made without serious outbreaks of scurvy. Nonetheless the crew were relieved when they finally came across some islands whose inhabitants brought out fruit, fish and coconuts. Drake was wary, however, because it was here, somewhere in the west Pacific, that poor Magellan's crew, almost dead from hunger and disease, had been attacked by natives intent on theft. The islanders soon lived up to Drake's fears. They demanded more and more payment for food and he had to warn them off with cannon fire. Sailing on to other islands (probably in the Caroline group) there was more trouble: Drake was certain he had found Magellan's 'Islands of Thieves'. In fact, Magellan's islands were further north, in the Marianas, but many of the Pacific islands would have given Drake the same reception. Sometimes encounters between natives and Europeans started on a happier note with friendly gestures, the exchange of gifts, feasting and liaisons between sailors and the local beauties; but before long relations usually went sour. The natives would grow impatient for their visitors to leave and would start to help themselves to the sailors' belongings. Nowadays we appreciate that the islanders were not the only ones intent on theft; the appropriation of these new lands by Europeans for their empires developed into a sophisticated form of robbery. In so-called trade the local people ended up with useless baubles and beads, as well as the terrible afflictions of measles, smallpox and venereal disease. This exploitation has left a rightful residue of guilt in Western minds. But at the same time it would be wrong to think of the native as 'the noble savage' who was innocent, virtuous and gentle: often he was far from noble and very savage indeed. Inter-island wars were frequent and bloody, while cannibalism was common in many parts of the East Indies.

Even today a small ship must be careful. It had been planned that the new *Golden Hind* would visit the Philippines, just as Drake had done. But Peter Haward decided it was too risky; Black Beard may be long gone but piracy is still commonplace in the South China Sea and around the Philippines. The pirates use motorised junks nowadays and have developed a variety of tactics: sometimes they shadow their victims for days before suddenly striking at night; or they may pretend to be in need of help; or they may sail straight up with guns blazing. Many yachts have mysteriously disappeared in these waters and huge numbers of Vietnamese boat-refugees have perished at the hands of ruthless pirates. Captain Haward was not taking any chances. In Hong Kong he had bought two shotguns, ammunition and 150 sandbags, which were piled high on the quarter-deck, the main deck and the fore deck to protect crouching crewmen from gunfire. The crew had also prepared a number of petrol bombs which they planned to throw unlit at a pirate vessel. If the vessel refused to stand clear, they would follow up with a match or two. The crew showed me the battle plan which was pinned to the notice board in the main cabin. Each of them had a position, a weapon, and strict orders on the chain of command. The little *Golden Hind* could be turned into a battleship within minutes. 'We don't exactly want to meet any of these guys,' said one of the crew, 'but I tell you, if we do we'll give them a hell of a good fight!' Seeing the thoroughness of their preparations, I had no doubt the pirates would come away empty-handed. In the event we saw no suspicious vessels and the first which dared to approach was a curious Indonesian gunboat, full of laughing sailors who cheered the sight of a sixteenth-century ship.

Warning of other vessels was given by the lookout, high on the foreyard. Those of us who were ignorant of square-riggers assumed he would sit in what we called the crow's nest, properly called the foretop, but a lookout coming off watch put us right. 'Can't see a blind thing from the foretop,' he pointed out. 'There's a sail bang in front of you. The best place is right out on the yard. It's quite comfortable up there,' he added, 'but I usually take a radio up with me to pass the time.'

A good lookout was essential to Drake, not only to give warning of Spanish or Portuguese vessels, but to prevent the *Golden Hind* from running on to a reef. After taking on water in the Philippines, Drake sailed tentatively southward, searching for the Mecca of the early explorers, the fabled Spice Islands. This small group of islands, now known as the Moluccas or Maluku, lies between Borneo and New Guinea in the vast Indonesian archipelago. Drake had no charts of this region and only a vague idea of where his goal lay, yet, so determined was he to reach the spices, that he was prepared to risk a voyage through treacherous reefs and scattered islands. To avoid running aground and losing the ship, the lookout had to give plenty of warning of danger signs ahead – brown water, breaking surf or disturbed waves. Then the *Golden Hind* had to manoeuvre quickly and sail clear of the reef, hauling her yards and sailing as close to the wind as she could. Fortunately Captain Haward had never had to take drastic action of this kind because he never let his ship sail anywhere near reefs or small unlit islands. His echo-sounder, which gave warning of a shallowing bottom, was useless over much of the Pacific because coral atolls and reefs often rise steeply from great depths, offering no warning of the danger. Similarly Drake's lead line, simply a piece of lead on a line, would usually have touched bottom too late. However, Drake did manage to find the Moluccas safely, although it took him thirteen days to sail a distance that could have been done in two.

Leaving the new *Golden Hind* for a few days, the film unit and I caught a plane to Jakarta and then on to the South Moluccas. We wanted to visit the famous Spice Islands and see for ourselves some of the tiny aromatic berries and nuts that had drawn Drake and so many others to sail halfway round the world. We went first to the island of Ambon, which produces cloves, cinnamon, nutmeg and mace, but the harvest had already been picked there, so we took a boat on to the smaller island of Saparua where we were assured that the spices were still hanging on the trees.

Approached from the sea, Saparua looks like a single mass of dense jungle: vivid, green and lush. We went ashore at a beautiful village in a bay ringed by golden sands and palm trees. Huts built of sago stems and roofed with palm leaves stood haphazardly along the shore. Beside the landing place the village women were washing themselves, their children and their clothes in a stream of fresh water that surged up through an outcrop of dead coral. It was a timeless scene. Just as Drake and Magellan had been a source of amazement to the local people, so were we. Within minutes of our arrival all activity ceased and we were surrounded by a crowd of giggling children and smiling women. The children, whose skin was a lovely golden brown, thought our white skin was very funny. The older women, more used to white people after many years of Dutch colonial rule, just nodded and muttered greetings.

Yet the Dutch were not the first to colonise these remote and valuable islands. Nor indeed were the Portuguese. For hundreds of years before Europeans arrived the Chinese and the Indians traded for spices with the Javanese kingdoms which ruled the Moluccas. Then Muslim traders settled in India and sailed on to colonise the Spice Islands. By the time Vasco da Gama and the other great Portuguese explorers opened up the Cape of Good Hope route the islands had been under the rule of Muslim sultans for some 200 years. The Portuguese used the rivalry between two sultanates to establish a fort and trading post at Tidore in the North Moluccas, but their position was shaky and Drake hoped to usurp them and trade with the sultans himself.

Having arrived on Saparua, we asked through our interpreter where we could find the spices. There was some discussion, a great deal of nodding, and we set off up a very bumpy road in a decrepit truck towards the main village. There we were shown a packing shed where a large pile of black cloves lay waiting to be put in sacks ready for transportation to Java. (Ironically, most of the cloves would come back to the Moluccas after being mixed with tobacco to make the spicy cigarettes which the Moluccan men chain-smoke all day long.) By now it was midday and we stayed in the village to have a meal: rice, smoked fish, unidentified meat and gado gado, a light Indonesian salad. The fish and meat were delicious, having been transformed by a subtle, tangy, spicy sauce. After a short siesta to avoid the worst of the midday sun, we went in search of the spice trees again. When the truck finally ground to a halt we found ourselves in the most unlikely of places: cool, spacious woodland that looked like an English birch forest on a fine summer day. Tall, delicate trees rose high into the sky, their dainty leaves dappling the ground with shade. There was no pattern to the forest; paths meandered among the trees in haphazard fashion. Only the presence of small storage huts suggested industry. Clove and nutmeg trees were growing side by side and by reaching up we could pick the fruit from the lowest branches. Nutmegs grow inside firm green fruits protected by thick rough skins which dangle from the branches like pom-poms, while on the clove trees small clusters of hard green berries hide the unexpanded flower buds which are dried to produce the pungent spice. Why clove trees should have grown here on the Moluccas and nowhere else is a mystery but, until the English smuggled some trees out and broke the Dutch monopoly many years later, these islands provided their owners with enormous wealth and power. Today it is hard for us to understand how such a mundane commodity as spice could be so immensely valuable to those northern Europeans who could afford them. The diet of the colder countries was limited and monotonous; animals were slaughtered in the autumn and their flesh, in various stages of decay, had to be forced down during the winter months. Pepper and cloves hid the taste of putrid flesh and could be varied with other spices to relieve the monotony. Spices were also sought as a primary ingredient of medicines; plague doctors in the seventeenth century wore hoods with beaks containing spices to ward off disease. Nowadays the supply of spices far exceeds the demand and, on the more remote islands like Saparua, most of the harvest is left on the trees. The Moluccas have become unimportant in European politics. The transition has not been easy for the Moluccan people; after many years of foreign domination the Dutch pulled out in the 1940s leaving them to fight for their much-wanted independence against the Javanese who were intent on creating the vast new country called Indonesia. After a bitter struggle the Moluccans lost the war and are now, once again, dominated by another power.

When Drake arrived in the Moluccas in 1579 he was eager to load as many spices as possible. In his enthusiasm, he dealt direct with the local suppliers and thereby upset the sultan who normally received a commission. However, this problem was soon smoothed over, the two made a bargain of friendship and a trade treaty, and Drake sailed away with a hold bulging with gold and cloves, worth the equivalent of many millions of pounds today.

Drake now had to prepare his ship for yet another long passage – this time across the Indian Ocean to the Cape of Good Hope from where, after replenishing his water supply, he would make for home. His main task was to careen the ship and clean her bottom. A sheltered uninhabited island was found where the unprotected ship could be hidden from Portuguese and pirates, and the job done in safety. With the crew weakened by heat, humidity and disease it was twenty-six days before the *Golden Hind* was afloat again. A lesser captain might have scrimped on the job, but never Drake. There were no half-measures for him; his thoroughness, his planning and his seamanship were impeccable. He was more than a captain, he was a superb manager and strategist.

But no amount of good planning could protect Drake from the lack of a pilot and a good chart. He finally ran out of luck as the *Golden Hind* sailed south through the East Indian islands. After successfully avoiding numerous shoals and dangers and within a short distance of clear water, she ran on to a reef off the Celebes. Fortunately it was not exposed to a large sea or the ship would have pounded on the sharp coral and broken up. Drake tried to pull her off with anchors, he pushed guns over the side to lighten her, and eventually – and how it must have broken his heart – he jettisoned three tons of the valuable cloves. It was all to no avail. Drake ordered prayer after prayer to be offered up by Parson Fletcher to quiet the angry, critical men. Then the parson did something the captain didn't order; he prayed for forgiveness for those who had condemned and executed Doughty so many months before. Drake was of course furious, but he said nothing. That afternoon the wind that had held the ship against the reef dropped and miraculously she floated free. But Drake did not accept that Fletcher's prayer had anything to do with it; he believed the parson had been blatantly disloyal. His reaction was typical: in full view of the crew he chained Fletcher to the forehatch, excommunicated him and put a notice round his neck which read: 'Frances Fletcher ye falsest knave that liveth.' However Drake was not a man to hold grudges and after a while the parson resumed his place among the crew. Here again, Drake had reasserted the strong leadership so essential on a long and hazardous voyage.

Drake now hurried homeward. When the *Golden Hind* reached Plymouth on 26 September 1580 she had been away two years and nine months. Drake's first question was whether the Queen still lived. She did. He breathed a sigh of relief. In such politically volatile times a new monarch might have looked on his enterprise with very

The World Encompassed

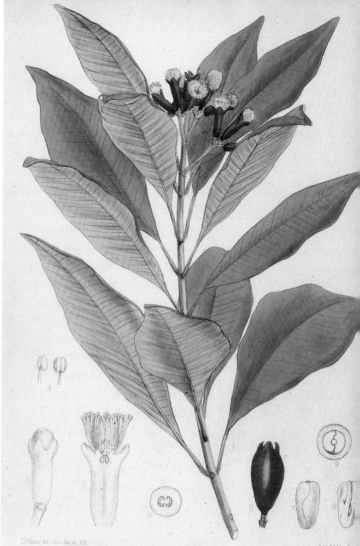

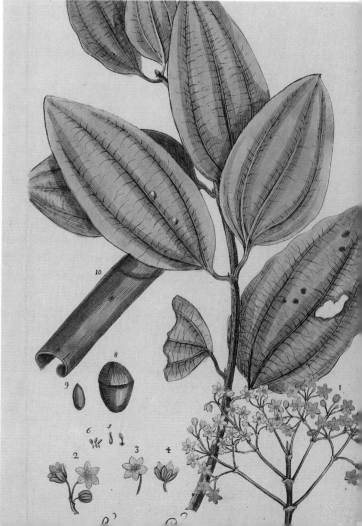

unfavourable eyes. But Elizabeth was delighted with Drake's achievement and so she should have been; he had brought back enough valuables to give his backers a 4000% profit and pay off the entire national debt! He had also made himself a very rich man. He bought himself a large house, Buckland Abbey in Devon, and surrounded himself with the beautiful things he craved. Not that success kept him away from the sea; there were still Spaniards to fight and new oceans to sail. His career did not end until he died of fever in the West Indies at the age of fifty-three.

Drake was a cocky, self-made man who had the ambition, the zeal and the self-assurance to lead his crew into the unknown. The success of his and the other voyages of discovery inspired an increasing amount of exploration which culminated in the great voyages of Captain Cook two hundred years later. Cook marked the beginning of a new era. Whereas Drake was a pirate adventurer, motivated by riches and revenge, Cook was a pure explorer whose motives were scientific. A magnificent navigator, who used newly developed techniques to fix longitude, Cook charted vast areas of the Pacific. Accurate charting made the oceans safe for ever more traffic and trade and changed for ever the isolated, untouched worlds of the Indian and island peoples Drake had encountered.

Before returning to England I joined the replica of the *Golden Hind* at her anchorage off Singapore for a last day's sail to a nearby island. The north-east wind was blowing strongly and the crew climbed up the ratlines to the yards with more caution than usual. Their feet braced against the footropes and their bodies bent over the yards, they began unfurling the sails. From the quarter-deck Peter Haward's customary yells rang across the ship. 'Brace the yards to windward! Stand by the anchor!' After ten minutes of intense activity, the sheets were hauled and the *Golden Hind* slowly gathered way.

'She's not the easiest boat to handle,' was Peter Haward's final comment. 'But I'm enjoying the challenge of sailing in her.' We looked ahead, to where the sails were full and taut as ripe fruit, and to where the bow threw the waves aside as it pushed firmly through the water at six knots. The ship must have made a fine sight. Later, as the *Golden Hind* approached Singapore Harbour and threaded her way through the dozens of anchored merchant ships, watching sailors must have thought so too, for they cheered and waved as we passed. Certainly it was an achievement, now as in Drake's day, to be sailing a small galleon round the world.

Ahead, Singapore's skyscrapers formed an incongruous background to the *Golden Hind*'s tangle of rigging and spars. In the days of exploration Singapore hardly existed. The great port – now the fourth largest in the world – was the brainchild of Sir Stamford Raffles. When he arrived to administer it in 1819 there was little but swamp and jungle, but its position midway between India and China made it ideal for his purpose. Raffles' aim was to build 'a great commercial emporium and a fulcrum where we may extend our influence'. He succeeded. A thousand workmen a day laboured to clear the jungle and build the new city; within a year its revenue was sufficient to pay for its administration, and it is now run most efficiently by the descendants of those who built it for the British.

The growth of ports like Singapore was a symbol that the age of exploration, of daring voyages by a few reckless adventurers, was over. The way was now open for the next stage of man's conquest of the seas – to make possible the carrying of goods on a vast scale. A new era of mighty trading companies, large fleets of ships and great empires had arrived.

Singapore

MARINE TECHNOLOGY IN THE FIFTEENTH CENTURY BASIL GREENHILL

The development of the three-masted, skeleton-built sailing ship in the fifteenth century made possible the expansion of West European man's activities all over the world. It was this vessel, the 'space capsule of the Renaissance', as I have called it elsewhere, which was the vehicle by which geographical knowledge was within forty years increased out of all recognition. In 1480 Europeans' experience of sea travel was virtually confined to European and North African waters. By 1520 the world had been encompassed, the Indian Ocean visited by way of the Cape of Good Hope, and the Spanish and Portuguese were established in the new world.

The causes of this great change were very complex and included, among others, the nature of the Castilian society which conquered Granada and freed Spain from Muslim rule in the late 1400s, the desire for quick wealth – best achieved by the seizure of land – reinforced by religious zeal, a combination which has been summarised as 'Serve God and grow rich', and developments in the

structure of trade and in financial organisation. The expansion took place by sea, and it could not have taken place had the sea-going vessel and the means of navigating it across the oceans not been available. The invention of the sailing ship was one of man's most significant and far-reaching achievements.

We still do not really know how, when or where the three-masted ship was developed. There appear to have been three dominant shipbuilding traditions in Northern Europe in the 1200s and the 1300s. The best known today was the round-hulled clinker tradition – the vessels built with planks overlapping at the edges – one branch of which comprised the Viking ships in all their variety. The second was represented by the family of the cog, vessels developed from Dutch and German traditions of building flat-bottomed ships with high, clinker sides and straight stems and stern posts; these developed into the famous cogs of the Hansa Community, almost the standard merchant vessels of

The tools of Renaissance exploration.
Left and above: The three masted sailing ship, under sail and under construction. The plate is fifteenth-century Iberian, and the builder's yard a detail from the Barberi map of Venice.

The navigational tools: the compass (top right is a sixteenth-century Italian one); the cross-staff (the one shown opposite, with matching scales, was made by Thomas Tuttell around 1700); the lead line gave soundings (the seaman shown below is from a decoration on a seventeenth-century chart)

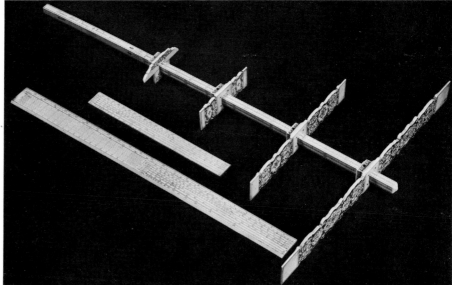

northern Europe for a century or more, until they were replaced by vessels of the third tradition, which was perhaps a British one. This was the hulc, which appears on British town seals and on British coins, a carrier of cargoes from England which was adopted as a preferred European ship type in the 1300s.

Although very different from each other in shape and details of construction, these three types of ship had in common that they were shell-built (the planks which made up the outer skin of the ship were joined together first and the strengthening skeleton of ribs then shaped to match the shell and fitted into it). They were also all equipped with one mast from which a single square sail was set. Vessels built in this way were limited in size and strength and the single square sails were unsuited for prolonged regular ocean sailing.

The development of the ship involved a double revolution. Bigger and stronger ships were built by reversing the building process and first erecting a skeleton of frames and then wrapping it around with a skin of planks, not joined together at the edges. Then these new ships were rigged with three masts. They could beat against the wind (very inefficiently at first) and were capable of making long ocean voyages.

Such indications as we have at present suggest that the three-masted, skeleton-built sailing vessel may have come to northern Europe from the Iberian Peninsula and western France – certainly it seems to have spread through northern Europe from west to east, or rather from south-west to north-east – and that perhaps the techniques of

skeleton building had originated in the northern Mediterranean some time after the year 1000. The Portuguese may have been the agents by which the knowledge of skeleton construction spread to northern Europe. It was perhaps they who first combined the new building technique with the three masts, at first rigged with three-cornered Mediterranean lateen sails, and then these sails combined with the square sails which were so much more efficient for ocean sailing. What is possibly the earliest identified depiction of a three-masted, square-rigged sailing ship is probably Spanish from the early 1400s, but the three-master seems to have been well established in Britain by the middle of the 1400s and to have moved into north Germany in the second half of the century.

But it would have been little use to have the ships if there had been no means of navigating them. Though the Vikings had made relatively long sea voyages, for centuries the art of conducting a ship had depended on extended pilotage – on sailing by the guides provided by the environment on the surface of the earth itself – coastal landmarks, local

winds, tides and the nature of the seabed and its depths, called soundings and a compass course. In the late fifteenth and early sixteenth centuries, at the time when the skeleton-built, three-masted ship was being fully developed, a simultaneous development took place in the science of conducting a ship across the ocean, out of soundings and sight of land, for long periods.

The spread of printing and of literacy and the circulation of pilotage books rapidly extended the areas in which men could sail by pilotage alone. But the really great leap forward was the use of observation of the stars and the sun to fix a ship's position north and south (centuries were to pass before Captain James Cook proved the success for the first time of two separate ways of fixing position east and west). Very simple instruments – the quadrant and the mariner's astrolabe – were used at first. With these tools the three-masted sailing ship of the early 1500s could be taken anywhere in the world – at a cost for those on board, in terms of hardship from cold, wet, starvation, filth, shipwreck and the actions of enemies, almost unimaginable today.

COLUMBUS
WARREN TUTE

The most spectacular geographical discovery in recorded history, ironically enough, turned out to be an accident. The enterprise undertaken by Christopher Columbus in 1492 was predicated on finding a sea route to 'The Indies' – Eastern Asia – by sailing west. Today we honour Columbus for something he never intended to do and never knew he had done. Indeed, he died in 1506 still under the impression that the lands he had partially explored during his four great voyages between 1492 and 1504 were the offshore islands of China and South East Asia. Even the name America was later credited to another Italian, Amerigo Vespucci, although the islands of the Caribbean – the West Indies – are now so named because of Columbus' belief. How did this come about?

The eldest son of a moderately prosperous Genoese family of wool weavers, Cristoforo Colombo was born in 1451, nine years before Henry the Navigator died. This was a period when a remarkable expansion of the mind – the Renaissance – began to be matched by an equally astonishing territorial expansion of Western Europe across the oceans of the world, an outburst of discovery and empire-building which was to last for some four centuries. In the fifteenth and sixteenth centuries Europe awoke after a dark night of nearly a thousand years.

Those first great voyages of exploration received their impetus from the astronomical, mathematical and hydrographic work of Henry the Navigator's 'marine intelligence office' at Sagres in the Algarve. This extraordinary Prince, himself an ardent geographer, assembled the best Arab, Jewish and Christian talent, constructed the first observatory in Portugal, and by force of personality made exploration profitable and thus popular. He set the climate for the Portuguese, Spanish and Italian navigators of the latter part of the fifteenth century. They blazed the trail and the Iberian monarchies reaped the rewards. Later on, English, French and Dutch adventurers broke this initial monopoly, but the process by which all these major voyages came about remained essentially the same: the active support of the monarch concerned had first to be obtained and later paid for because without royal patronage nothing on such a scale could be attempted. Columbus epitomises this method by which Europeans opened up the entire globe.

The story begins in Genoa where family feeling was strong – Cristoforo's brothers and nephew were to join him in his later voyages – and where it soon became obvious that the Discoverer was not cut out for the wool trade, since he took every opportunity

Above: Henry the Navigator leads his captains – from the Monument of the Discoverers, Lisbon
Below: The private chapel of Henry the Navigator at Sagres

inside the Mediterranean to the Greek islands. He also married Dona Felipa Perestrello e Moniz, the daughter of the hereditary captain of Porto Santo in the Madeira group and the grand-daughter of Gil Moniz who had been a knight companion of Prince Henry the Navigator. This marriage gave him an entrée to the Court, a somewhat unpredictable asset as it turned out, but one he put to the test in 1484 by seeking to interest the King of Portugal in his revolutionary project. The King, intensely interested in new discoveries, nevertheless thought this Genoese a big fancy talker and gave him small credit. The King passed the project on to a committee who turned it down flat. Then in 1485 Doña Felipa died, leaving Columbus with a

Ferdinand and Isabella, royal patrons of Columbus, on coins of their reign and (below) a portrait of Columbus, attributed to Ghirlandaio

of going to sea. His formal education was negligible and he could neither read nor write until well into his twenties. Little is known about this part of his life, but in May 1476 he reached a turning point when shipwrecked off Portugal, later going to Lisbon where his brother was employed in one of the new chart making establishments. Portugal was then the most lively and progressive country in Europe. Apart from being a centre of learning, Lisbon received, digested, and passed on, a wealth of new information brought back by sea captains from Madeira, the Azores and the West African coast, as well as from north-west Europe.

At that time the existence of the American continent had not been suspected. The known world was thought to consist of Europe and Asia surrounded by one continuous ocean. Certainly educated people guessed the earth was not flat, and that you would not fall off the edge, but scientific knowledge was discouraged by the Papacy for reasons of its own. However, if the earth really was a globe, it would in theory be possible to sail round it in either direction. The idea then occurred to Columbus that it would be easier and shorter to reach China and Japan (and the precious Spice Islands) by sailing west on their latitude in the northern hemisphere rather than east round Africa which entailed a long leg to the south.

The Columbus theory might well be sound but it was to take him ten frustrating years to get the backing he needed to prove it. Habit, custom and superstition all worked against him. 'Man should not tempt the Almighty', it was said in 1476, 'by seeking unknown depths of the ocean', just as when the Wright brothers were trying to fly in the first decade of the twentieth century, it was said that 'Man was made for the earth, not the sky'.

During those ten years Columbus became a master mariner in the Portuguese merchant service, voyaging to Iceland, the Azores and

five-year-old son. His status at the Portuguese Court all but disappeared. Accordingly he decided to chance it in Spain.

Based on the Franciscan friary of La Rabida at Palos near Huelva, it took Columbus nearly a year to obtain an audience of Queen Isabella and six more to get his Great Project accepted. Moreover by 1488 there were rival contenders for patronage in both the Spanish and Portuguese Courts. The Portuguese Dias had rounded the Cape of Good Hope and was all set to reach India on his next voyage. The King of Portugal could see little point, therefore, in sponsoring a voyage to the same place by a western route. The Kings of France and England were similarly disinclined to involve themselves. It was an agonising time. Columbus was sure he could do it: the experts said no. Only Queen Isabella remained on his side and she had had to accept advice from the Talavera commission which firmly said no.

Throughout his life Columbus was highly religious, and received more support from priests than he did from Court or commoners. At the end of 1491 when he was about to give up and join his brother in France, the Prior of La Rabida persuaded him to approach the Queen yet again. This time Isabella summoned him to Court and sent him money to buy himself clothes and a mule.

At last the idea had found support. The Royal Council still recommended against on grounds of cost; the Queen was in favour but was in no way helped by the Discoverer himself, for Columbus jeopardised the whole project by stepping up his demands. Now in the event of success he was not only to be ennobled and given the title of Admiral, he was also to be made Governor and Viceroy of any lands he might discover. These titles were to be hereditary and he was to receive ten per cent of all gold, gems, spices or other merchandise tax-free.

The Court was outraged. The Queen said she would pledge her jewels, but this, in the event, proved unnecessary. The Keeper of the Privy Purse, bending to the royal will, undertook to raise the money himself. In any case, it was pointed out, the expedition would not cost more than a week's entertainment of a foreign sovereign. That was the way they thought in those days. Until they succeeded, the four men who put America on the map – Columbus, Cabot, Verrazano and Magellan – were only grudgingly and meanly supported by their sovereigns. Cabot, for instance, who gave half the New World to England cost Henry VII a mere £50.

This first Columbian crossing of the Atlantic was made by three caravels, the largest of which, the *Santa Maria*, was probably only about 100 tuns. The *Niña* and the *Pinta* were smaller, not over seventy feet in length. This tiny fleet left Palos on 3 August 1492 on

Alejo Fernandez, *The Madonna of the Navigators*, in the Alcazar, Seville. Columbus is on her left

the same tide as, and in the luckless company of, the last vessel carrying the Jews whom Ferdinand and Isabella had expelled from Spain and for whom Columbus in all his writings had no word of pity. The world, and in particular the new world about to be discovered, would pay a heavy price for religious arrogance.

The first leg of the voyage to the Canaries was made in less than a week and there final stores and water were embarked, and some repairs made to the *Pinta*. On 6 September 1492 the fleet weighed anchor for the last time in the Old World, every trace of which had disappeared below the eastern horizon by nightfall on the 9th.

Columbus' plan for the voyage was simple and in one sense its simplicity ensured success. He had no intention of braving the headwinds and turbulent seas of the North Atlantic which had already thwarted so many Portuguese. In his African voyages south he had observed that the winter winds in the latitude of the Canaries (28°N) blew from the east. This latitude, he believed, was also that of Japan so that all he had to do was to sail due west on that same latitude, using the easterly trade winds, and he would be bound to hit his target. In fact he did just that, except that his landfall turned out to be the Bahamian island of Guanahani. Columbus, however, remained convinced that it was one of the outer islands of Japan.

In contrast with expeditions which were to follow, this first Atlantic voyage of Columbus proved to be relatively uneventful. For the first ten days the easterly trade winds blew, as anticipated, and he made 1163 nautical miles. But because his basis of calculation was wrong (Columbus assumed that Japan lay 2400 miles from the Canaries whereas the correct distance is about 10,600), he thought he had travelled much further than in fact he had and, when the wind dropped over the next five days and he covered a mere 234 miles, his crew began to mutter and grumble in a mutinous way.

This was understandable. None had sailed out of sight of land before for longer than three weeks and Columbus was a 'foreigner' – a Genoese – whom it might be expedient to throw overboard if he refused to turn back. But Columbus had an iron will and believed staunchly that he was under divine guidance, and he gambled with an astonishing nerve. On 10 October, when mutiny flared up again despite the sighting of flocks of birds, which suggested that land lay ahead, Columbus promised to turn back if, in fact, they did not make a landfall within three days.

At 10 pm the next day Columbus and a seaman on watch thought they saw a light 'like a little wax candle rising and falling'.

Top: The frontispiece of the Book of Privileges given to Columbus by Ferdinand and Isabella, referring to him as Admiral of the Ocean Sea, and (bottom) his coat of arms from the same book

This was an illusion, often experienced by sailors subjected to an overtense watchfulness. However four hours later the lookout on the *Pinta* saw a white cliff in the moonlight and this time the shout of 'Tierra! tierra!' was justified. By noon the next day the fleet had anchored in five fathoms in a shallow coral bay. Columbus and the two other Captains went ashore and 'all having rendered thanks to our Lord, kneeling on the ground, embracing it with tears of joy for the immeasurable mercy of having reached it, the Admiral rose and gave this island the name of San Salvador – Holy Saviour'.

On 15 March 1493, 224 days after setting out, Columbus completed the greatest round voyage in history by anchoring off Palos. Despite a somewhat meagre collection of gold artefacts, caged parrots, and 'Indian' slaves, he had proved his point and was duly acclaimed Admiral of the Ocean Sea by Ferdinand and Isabella and given his contract rewards. More importantly, arrangements were at once made for a second expedition with seventeen vessels to be mounted, and no expense spared.

Illustration for a version in Latin, of 1493, of Columbus' letter to Isabella reporting his discoveries

This time Columbus was away for over two and a half years, discovering twenty large and over forty small islands previously unknown to any European. But the grandiose expectation of meeting the Emperor of China and of returning with vast hoards of gold were not fulfilled. Columbus was as determined and arrogant as ever but the results were disappointing, to say the least. A growing outcry against the Columbus brothers all but caused the Spanish King to abandon them and the Indies as well. However, whilst this was in the balance news came that the King of Portugal was fitting out a further expedition to India and that even Henry VII of England, whose son was soon to marry the Infanta of Aragon, had become interested in finding an ocean route to Cathay. The Spaniards decided to stay in the game.

A third voyage began in 1498. This time Columbus sighted what was later to be called

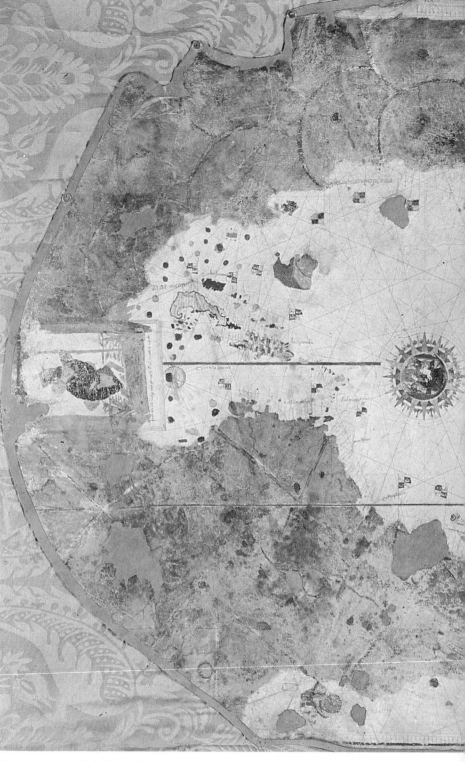

Venezuela and sailed along what would soon be called the Spanish Main, still assuming this area to be offshore China. His deep faith never faltered: God was showing him the way but somehow or other the tally was not correct. Illusion set in and at one stage of this voyage he even thought he had discovered the Garden of Eden. The King of Spain, however, was after gold not Eden, and Columbus' stock continued to fall. There had been a rebellion in Hispaniola, Spain's first colony in the new world, and another Governor had been sent out to quell it. Glibber-tongued rivals were securing licences to explore in

territories Columbus considered exclusive to himself. There was a hot dispute about authority and the voyage ended ignominiously with the Columbus brothers being returned to Europe in chains.

Columbus was a great navigator, a born leader and an instinctive seaman. Administration, however, was not in his grasp. This seems to have been understood by Ferdinand and Isabella who promised him justice and did, after eight months, allow him to keep his now empty titles of Viceroy and Admiral. At the same time, though, they appointed a more competent Governor of the Islands and Main-

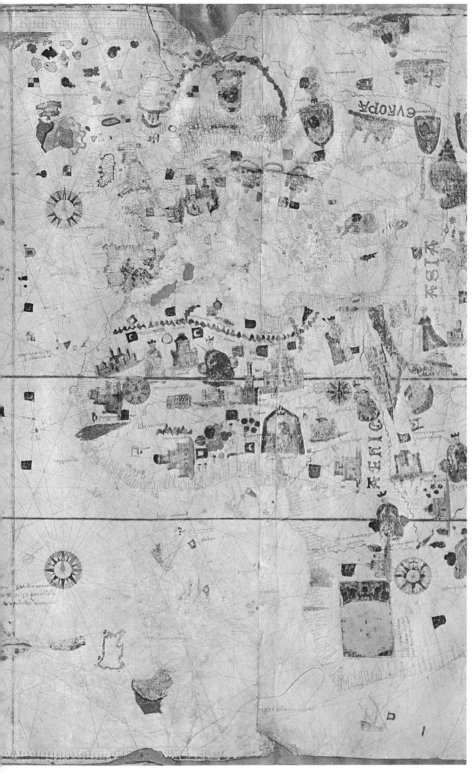

with his brother, his son and twenty-two others. The rest of his expedition chose to stay in Santo Domingo rather than risk another ocean passage.

By the material standards of the time he had failed again. He had not discovered the strait – how could he when none existed? He had unwisely given out that the Isthmus of Panama would be of no interest to the Spanish Crown, and he had found but little gold. Yet he had done his best. Eighteen months later he was dead.

Inadequate as an administrator, Columbus nevertheless launched an era of Spanish domination in the new world which had dramatic results. Initially the huge inflationary influx of gold and silver dictated the course of events, but by the end of the sixteenth century, spices, silks and precious stones became more valuable than bullion in the markets of Europe.

The Spanish and Portuguese established their lead in exploiting the new world a quarter of a century before Luther nailed his famous thesis to the door of Wittenberg Parish Church in 1517. During the fifty years after Columbus Iberians reaped an immense reward. Beginning with the settlement of Hispaniola, Spain moved quickly to conquer, colonise and exploit. Once across the Isthmus of Panama and with the opening up of the Spanish Main, the conquests of Mexico to the north and of Inca Peru to the south were undertaken with a brutality and religious hypocrisy which has appalled the civilised world ever since.

Spain instituted her first Pacific settlement at Panama in 1519 and there galleons were built to trade across the Pacific to the Moluccas and the Philippines for spices and gold. These and other products such as hides, tallow, cochineal and sugar, together with potatoes and tobacco (and the less welcome syphilis) were then transported to Spain in rigidly organised, escorted convoys.

The main cargo, however, continued to be silver and gold, and the great Spanish treasure ships soon became the prey of pirates of all nations, the 'brethren of the coast' as they came to be known, who began infesting the lesser islands of the Caribbean.

After that first great voyage by Columbus the Spanish and Portuguese monopolised the Americas during the sixteenth century. In fact Iberians created two trading empires in the Americas – the silver empire of Spanish America and the Portuguese sugar empire of Brazil. Both depended absolutely on a continuing supply of slave labour, this grisly trade being responsible for the shipping west from Africa during the following three centuries of over ten million slaves.

lands of the Indies who departed in February 1502 with 2500 soldiers, sailors and colonists in thirty sail. Columbus was left behind bombarding the Crown with petitions of one kind or another and perhaps to get him out of the way, a fourth voyage was agreed. He was fifty-one, an old man by the reckoning of the day, arthritic and subject to recurring attacks of malaria.

Nevertheless, the 'High Voyage' as Columbus himself called it was perhaps the most interesting of them all. This time he expected to discover the strait through which Marco Polo had sailed from China to the Indian

Ocean, but once again nothing seemed to tally. In fact he ranged from Honduras to Darien, keeping New Year's day 1503 in the harbour of what is now Cristobal in Panama. He established a trading post and fort at Santa Maria de Belen but the Indian gold he was hoping to acquire did not materialise and the place had to be abandoned. He then ran his worm-eaten vessels ashore on a sandy beach in Jamaica and stayed there a year. After surviving hurricanes, mutinies and the perfidy of Governor Ovando in Hispaniola, Columbus eventually chartered a leaky caravel in Santo Domingo and returned to Spain

INHABITANTS OF THE PACIFIC
DEBBORA JONES

Over 4000 years before Europeans began 'discovering' the Pacific islands, navigators from South-east Asia were embarking on their own voyages of discovery, eastwards across the vast Pacific Ocean. It is the view of most modern archaeologists and linguists that these were the first explorers and colonisers of the thousands of islands we call Oceania – an area covering one-third of the earth's surface. Their swift and stable outrigger canoes were an important invention of the Austronesian navigators – the means of not only reaching, but settling, the outer limits of Oceania. The migration was complete by AD 1000, yet even today their epic feats are honoured in local oral histories.

Nonetheless there are unanswered questions regarding the motivation for such long-distance voyages, the kind of planning they involved and the problem of how people came to cross great stretches of open sea. There are, for example, nearly 2000 nautical miles between the Marquesas Islands and northern New Zealand. Yet artefacts exist which date the journey to the first millennium AD. We know that Pacific navigators could read wind and wave patterns and calculate the positions of sun and stars. They were also capable of steering into the prevailing wind and of navigating by 'dead reckoning'. Although accidental 'drift' voyages must have been common, it is apparent that return trips were planned and carried out.

By studying the 'cultural baggage' which survives from these journeys, we are able to trace the paths of human progress through the three culture areas of Oceania – through Melanesia and Micronesia to Polynesia. In particular, the distinctive 'Lapita-style' pottery and implements are evidence of an exceptionally expansionist group of Austronesians. They were probably the founders of Polynesian culture.

However, contending theories abound of discovery routes from south-east China, Japan and the Americas. Thor Heyerdahl's highly-publicised crossing to eastern Polynesia from South America proves the possibility of culture contact. And the mysterious presence throughout the Pacific of the New World sweet potato has yet to be explained convincingly.

Whatever the path of discovery, both the domestication of plants and animals, and the more sedentary residence patterns which remain a feature of Pacific island subsistence patterns, coincided in South-east Asia with

A fishermen's god from the Pacific island of Raratonga, and (below) fishing from sailing canoes in the Caroline Islands

the era of expansion into Oceania. Tubers were cultivated in Melanesia; tubers and tree crops in Micronesia and Polynesia; in all places supplemented by fishing, hunting, and gathering. Pigs, followed by dogs and fowl, became the most important domestic animals. Implements of shell, bone and stone (some in the New Guinea highlands predating the coastal Austronesian explorers by over 20,000 years) were produced along with other objects of fine artistic quality and functional elegance, both before and after steel tools were introduced by Europeans. Social organisation ranged from the egalitarian, non-hierarchical power structures of Melanesia, to Micronesian and Polynesian social stratification with power based less on persuasiveness than the hereditary right to command.

However, the continuing legacy of the ancient Pacific colonisers was the value they placed on communication with other islands through the transport of people and, as populations spread, what those people made and grew. The Lapita expansion, and economies everywhere oriented to exchange between lands, epitomise the drive for off-island contact (and the world view which supported it). This drive remains a vital component of ethnic identity in the Pacific – even where lifestyles are pervasively coloured by the intrusion of European values and technology.

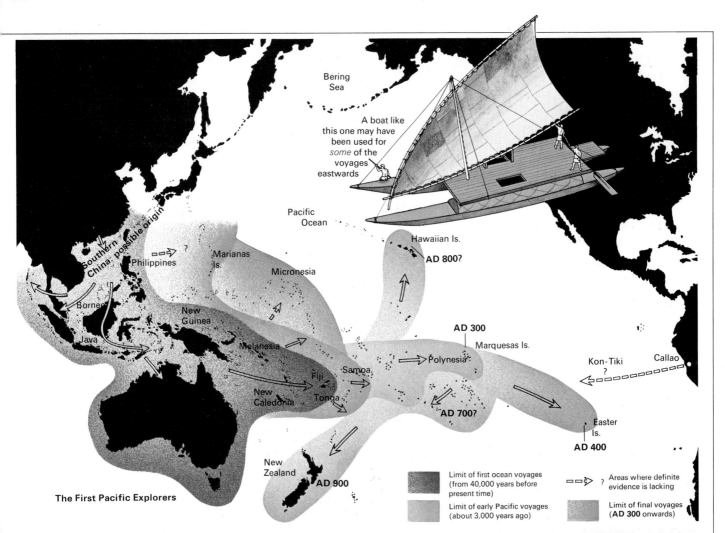

Bering
Sea

A boat like
this one may have
been used for
some of the
voyages
eastwards

Pacific
Ocean

Southern China, possible origin

Philippines

?

Marianas
Is.

Micronesia

Hawaiian Is.
AD 800?

Borneo

New
Guinea

Java

Melanesia

Polynesia

Fiji

Samoa

AD 300

Marquesas Is.

Kon-Tiki
?

Callao

New
Caledonia

Tonga

AD 700?

Easter
Is.

AD 400

New
Zealand
AD 900

The First Pacific Explorers

■ Limit of first ocean voyages (from 40,000 years before present time)	⇢ ? Areas where definite evidence is lacking
■ Limit of early Pacific voyages (about 3,000 years ago)	■ Limit of final voyages (**AD 300** onwards)

The Pacific islands were colonised by means of sea
voyages. The outrigger canoe – the one below is from
an engraving made in 1815 – used by the pre-
European navigators is still made (right) and used for
travel between islands. A single hollowed-out log
forms the hull. The smaller log lying alongside, with
its connecting trellis of sticks already in place, will form
the outrigger

Bateau des îles Carolines

XVIII

Yams are the staple crop. The highest compliment to a woman is to say that she is as beautiful as a yam

After making a record catch the fishermen prepare to celebrate by painting traditional patterns on their faces and donning garlands of palm leaves

An island off mainland Papua New Guinea was chosen as the film location. Here the traditional way of life has persisted unchanged for centuries
Above right: The women wade on the reef, nearly a mile from land, throwing out their hooked lines
Left: Much of the fishing is done from outriggers within the lagoon (surf is breaking on the boundary reef on the horizon)
Right: Every day families sail two miles across the open sea to their gardens on a neighbouring island
Middle right: Boys learn the principles of sailing from model boats made for them by their fathers or uncles. Cats are valued pets
Far right: Water (too salt to drink but useful in cooking) has to be brought every day from underground caves deep in the centre of the island. It is carried in glass and plastic floats, washed up on the sea shore from other fishermen's nets

And, despite that intrusion, there are still, sprinkled through the archipelagoes of Papua New Guinea some strikingly traditional societies, where we can glimpse, from life on a sliver of coral atoll, the premises of stone-age living and the ancestral blueprints for bridging the inherent isolation of islanders. With inter-island warfare no longer an obstruction, this bridging is done through elaborate trading networks, and ceremonial exchanges of garden food, pigs and valuable objects. These exchanges constitute the realm of political power, and enmesh people from different islands and clans in a web of economic and ritual obligations. The items of currency in one such area are greenstone axe blades – no longer utilitarian objects – and red shell necklaces. Especially during harvest men and women sail the archipelago in search of these valuables to finance feasts in honour of the ancestors. Luxury and subsistence goods are often sought at the same time, but the latter become the main reason for voyaging in the lean months.

However, even the everyday tasks of life – fetching fresh water, or yams from the gardens, coconuts or sago for cakes – can involve frequent voyaging to islands where people own property – often miles away across stretches of deep water.

So that as well as providing an abundance of fish, shells for currency or to sell for money, coral for limepowder or seaweed for canoe paint, the sea provides paths. These wind through the coral reefs – like paths over land – connecting people with nourishment as well as with other people.

Today, then, as always, the sea presents communities with the challenge of survival – and the promise of achieving it through relationships with other lands.

CHINA AND THE SEA
BASIL GREENHILL

The European expansion of the late fifteenth and sixteenth centuries, which marks the frontier between medieval and modern history, was really the discovery, through the three-masted, skeleton-built sailing ship, that the seas and oceans of the world are all interconnected. The early voyagers were not interested in exploring the unknown, but were concerned with new sea routes from known areas to known areas for commercial purposes. In fact they came across a great deal that was unknown on the way.

Nevertheless it was a long time before technology and social attitudes were such that sailing ships could go anywhere in the world and come back again as a matter of course. A second frontier was provided by the voyages of Captain James Cook, who demonstrated that the late eighteenth-century wooden merchant sailing ship, properly managed, was capable of prolonged operation at extreme range and of returning with almost all her crew alive. With this experience, when the expansion of world trade which resulted from the Industrial Revolution followed, the patterns of the European-based commerce of the pre-steamship age rapidly became established.

The discovery of the continuity of the high road of the sea was a western European achievement. But when they reached eastern seas, the Europeans found sophisticated indigenous local water transport already in operation and they depended on local people's highly developed knowledge of local pilotage. From the East Indies the early Portuguese traders used Chinese ships and merchants for their new trade with China.

The Chinese had a highly developed shipping economy long before the European expansion and in the 1300s their ships were more efficient than European vessels. In the early 1400s Chinese ships were showing the flag on a series of special voyages, sailing even in the northern Indian Ocean. An immense country, with rivers thousands of miles long and a coastline of over 2000 miles, China is bisected by the great river Yangtze-Kiang. To the north of its mouth the coastline is low, the seas shallow; to the south the seas are deep, with a rugged coastline with many deep indentations. These differences had their effect on the development of the vessels of the north and of the south, but they had in common a basic structure which can be compared with a modern plywood pram dinghy, with its flat bottom, sides curved only in one direction at time, broad transom

The evolution of the junk
Above: Model of a Formosan sailing raft: these were up to thirty-five feet long, and already have the curved sides and broad stern of later junks
Right: A model of a Pechili (South China) trading junk, made in 1938 as a copy of a vessel lying in the harbour
Bottom: A model of a Foochow pole junk, made at the same time by the same man

stern and smaller transom bow. In place of the frames of European ships, either inserted or set up as a skeleton at an early stage of construction, Chinese vessels had solid transverse bulkheads of which the bow and the stern transoms might be regarded as the terminating units. Classical Chinese craft appear to have been built by laying bottom planks on baulks lying athwartships on the ground. These bottom planks were joined edge to edge and the bulkheads, prefabricated nearby, were then secured to the bottom

planks and the side planking added, also joined edge to edge, using the bulkheads to give the shape of the final boat. Big Chinese wooden sailing vessels of as late as the 1930s could carry 400 tons of cargo in the numerous watertight compartments made by the separate bulkheads, each containing the property of a different merchant. These vessels ran up to 180 feet long, and were very much larger than the ships of the European expansion.

These vessels and their predecessors were steered with balanced rudders, which appear to have been in use in China by the second century AD. They were rigged with three, four or five masts, from each of which were set very large, efficient and controllable lugsails of a type quite different from anything which had developed in the Western world. One of the big latter-day vessels, the *Keying*, sailed in the nineteenth century from Shanghai to New York and then on to London, and she behaved well under the normal con-

Above: Modern junks on the Li River
Right: A nineteenth-century drawing of the first junk
to sail to Europe, seen on the Thames
Bottom: Modern junks with beautifully cut sails

ditions to be expected in the North Atlantic.

With such ships the Chinese established extensive trade in the east and continued it for many centuries. The vessels were sailed with the help of charts of local areas and with the aid of the compass, which had been known in China before it was developed for sea use in Europe. A seventeenth-century copy of a Chinese chart of the coasts of the Indian Ocean dating from the early fifteenth century, believed to have been compiled from the data brought back by the great flag-showing voyages of twenty years before, follows different conventions from European charts, but gives many compass bearings. It also gives the altitude of the Pole Star at various places as well as the distances between them. In its different way, the chart conveys its information as fully and as accurately as contemporary European charts: it gives more information and, of course, the Chinese voyages of the early 1400s covered vastly greater distances than anything that was being attempted in Europe at the time.

Since the Chinese had the ships and the navigational techniques and the basis of a trading structure needed for them to make as great voyages as those made by the Europeans in the late 1400s and the early 1500s, why then did they not 'discover the sea'? Perhaps the question should be put the other way round. Since the Chinese – and perhaps the Arabs as well – were equally well or better equipped than Europeans, what was it that made the Europeans of the period think in terms of world travel, rather than being content with what they had? What is certain is that the long-term results, the inauguration of an age in which control of the world's trade, and with it political and cultural domination, passed for centuries into the hands of Western Europe, was not foreseen by the pioneers and played no part in their motivation.

CAPTAIN COOK
WARREN TUTE

'The study of Cook is the illumination of all discovery' wrote Professor J. C. Beaglehole in his *Exploration of the Pacific*. 'No man ever understood better the conditions of success.' But that is only a part of the truth. Indeed it would be fair to say that Captain James Cook (1728–79) remains to this day the most famous and successful sailor there has ever been – a prodigious man and the first of navigators.

Consider the range of his life, his achievements and the mark he left on the world. If talent repeats and genius creates, Cook possessed an astonishing measure of both qualities. Had there been an eighteenth-century Book of Records, Cook would have qualified as King of the 'Firsts', not the least of these being that he was the first working class boy – he was the son of a day labourer in an inland Yorkshire village – to rise without the benefit of privilege or class to a unique position at the top of the mariner's profession.

Today the rags to riches syndrome – or the possibility of it – is taken for granted. Anyone can do it provided the talent, the will and the readiness to work are there. In 1755, if you came from Cook's background, you had to be very sure of your fate to turn down the offer of your first command of a merchant ship and instead volunteer for the Royal Navy as an Able Seaman. Cook did just that.

Captain James Cook by John Webber, artist on the third voyage
Below left: Detail of a chart, probably drawn by Cook himself

The Navy is an exacting profession but one which offers the individual a number of opportunities not available to those ashore. In the mid-eighteenth century, however, not so many of those opportunities were open to the lower deck. In that sense, therefore, Cook was the first of the meritocrats. His quality quickly brought him advancement to Boatswain and shortly afterwards to Master first of HMS *Solebay* and then of HMS *Pembroke*, in which ship he sailed, in 1758, on the expedition to capture Quebec.

In those days Masters of HM Ships were responsible for their ship's navigation and pilotage, the latter to include any survey required of uncharted waters. So it began. Cook astonished his superiors by meticulously surveying the St Lawrence river under the most tricky conditions. This survey enabled the big ships of the Royal Navy to sail up the St Lawrence – the first ever to do so (another first) – and thus to play a decisive part in the capture of Quebec and the later conquest of all Canada.

This success led to him being appointed Master of the Flagship of the North Ameri-can Squadron and, during the next three seasons, he completed surveys of the St Lawrence River and of the Nova Scotia and Newfoundland coasts which are still in use today. From then on he never looked back.

The two centuries separating Drake from Cook saw ships and the guns they carried become larger and more efficient, the techniques of seamanship and sea-keeping improve, and the oceans of the world – with the exception of the Pacific – charted and known. But three major problems remained to be solved – longitude, health and the Pacific itself. Cook tackled and solved all three problems in eleven short and brilliant years from 1768 to his death in 1779. It was an amazing achievement.

For 300 years after Henry the Navigator, an ocean pilot's equipment changed in essence very little. He had a compass, a lead and line, a log, a formula he could carry in his head for correcting the elevation of the Pole Star, and a cross staff or astrolabe. This latter instrument had been refined by John Hadley into a Quadrant in 1731 and then by Captain John Campbell RN into a sextant in

1757. With this equipment and in clear weather, a navigator could calculate his approximate latitude.

Longitude, however, required the accurate measurement of time. The standard half-minute, half-hour, hour and four-hour sandglasses were by no means accurate enough and no clock or watchmaker had been able to provide an instrument which would function to chronometer standards at sea in all parts of the world, in equatorial heat or arctic gale. The knotty problem of longitude had indeed so exercised the Admiralty that fourteen years before Cook was born Their Lordships had appointed Commissioners for the Discovery of the Longitude at Sea and had offered a hefty prize – £20,000 – to anyone who could come through with a workable solution.

This prize was won by another humbly-born Yorkshireman, who was twenty-one when the Board of Longitude was established in 1714, the year that the first Hanoverian came to the throne of Great Britain. John Harrison, a carpenter and self-taught mathematician from Foulby in Yorkshire, won the Admiralty prize outright (although it was only paid over to him three years before he died in 1776 and then only after the personal intervention of King George III).

The feat was considerable. Harrison had

An important aim of Cook's voyages was the increase of scientific knowledge. Sydney Parkinson's drawings of a New Zealand plant *(Olea apetala)* and a red-rumped parrot from Tahiti. Parkinson also made the spirited drawing (left) of the *Endeavour* at sea and the drawing from which the illustration of vessels of the Society Islands (below) was engraved

already invented the bimetallic pendulum for long-case clocks before setting his mind to work on the longitude prize. Between 1735 and 1760 he completed four time-keepers. The first was a massive mechanism of brass and wood weighing 72 lbs. The last was a watch about three times the size of a pocket watch of the day. All of them easily fulfilled the Admiralty requirement and all four chronometers are still working today in the National Maritime Museum at Greenwich.

Cook used a copy of Harrison's watch by Larcum on his second voyage of Pacific exploration. It gave him an error of less than eight miles in calculated longitude when making his final landfall at Plymouth on 29 July 1775 after circumnavigating the world. It was, perhaps, the first instance of 'Give me the tool and I'll finish the job'.

The second great problem solved by Cook was the human one of the health of his ship's company at sea. Cook realised very early on

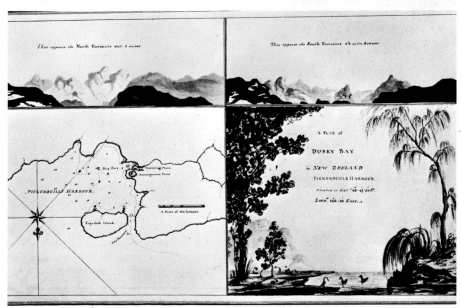

Charting in the Pacific was the great task of Cook's voyages. Detail of a chart of Dusky Bay, New Zealand, 1773

that exploration across a great ocean meant keeping to the sea for very long periods. Accurate navigation would be useless without the backing of stable administration. Scurvy was the ancient enemy and Cook defeated it by instigating new standards of cleanliness on board – such as occasionally washing – and by forcing his officers and men to eat fresh vegetables whenever they were available and drink lemon juice, 'Sour krout' and his Special Portable Soup when they were not. The results were dramatic.

When Anson, who later became First Sea Lord, had taken a squadron of six ships round the world in 1743–4 four men had died from enemy action but over 1300 from disease, mainly scurvy. On Cook's last voyage only five men were lost through disease, and three of them left England 'in a precarious state'.

The third problem – the exploration and charting of the Pacific ocean – stands without doubt as Cook's greatest achievement and perhaps as the single most remarkable feat in the long story of man and the sea. There were three Pacific voyages in the eleven years between 1768 and 1779, when Cook was stabbed to death in Hawaii. The first came about because Cook's observations of the eclipse of the sun in Newfoundland in 1766 had been brought to the attention of the Royal Society. This influential body – then just over one hundred years old and very much under Royal Patronage – made him one of their official observers to be sent to Tahiti to record the transit of Venus, due on 3 June 1769. Then came a stroke of luck.

The Royal Society's own choice for a commander of the expedition – Alexander Dalrymple – was vetoed by the Admiralty because he was a civilian. There was more to

The Pacific as Cook found it – the panorama of Tahiti was engraved from drawings made on the spot. Many of the places Cook explored – like Milford Sound, in the South Island of New Zealand (below), and Cook Bay, Moorea, Tahiti (right) still look much as they did when he first saw them. The effect on the inhabitants and their way of life was, however, incalculable

this simple prejudice. When Cook, the obvious service alternative, was appointed and had opened his secret orders he discovered that in addition to the scientific objects of the expedition, he was directed to sail south from Tahiti to search for Terra Australis Incognita. This was the vast southern continent which was then believed by geographers to exist. Cook was also ordered to explore the coast of New Zealand, discovered by Tasman in 1642 but still thought to be part of the great southern land mass. The point of all this was that the British Government, with the world-changing victories of the Seven Years War only just behind them, wished to be the first to claim suzerainty over a new piece of the burgeoning Empire.

Cook left Plymouth on the first voyage on 25 August 1768. He anchored again in English waters three years later on 12 July 1771. He could own to a partial success: he had not disproved the existence of Terra Australis Incognita, but he had discovered New Zealand to be two islands instead of being a part of that nebulous southern continent he had been told to find. He had also surveyed the east coast of Australia encountering his first 'primitive, hostile and implacable' aborigines in Botany Bay. In other departments the voyage proved less of a success: although they had rounded Cape Horn in the outward direction without a single case of scurvy, malaria and dysentery wreaked havoc in Batavia on the way home.

Cook also learnt the hard way on this voyage never to leave the smallest detail unattended – and never to trust a naval dockyard – when preparing his ships for sea. He had digested these lessons when setting out on the second voyage a year later in July 1772. He also had with him the chronometer mentioned above. However his standards of accuracy were such that he felt he could never trust the requirements of exactness to a single instrument. When he surveyed Nootka Sound on the west coast of North America, for instance, he checked the chronometer readings with no fewer than 137 lunar observations. By the time he reached home three years later, in July 1775, he had ranged from Alaska to the Antarctic, discovered the New Hebrides and New Caledonia, and finally disproved the existence of Terra Australis Incognita.

Cook was now promoted post Captain and elected a Fellow of the Royal Society, which awarded him the Copley Gold Medal. Within a year he was off again. This time he had instructions to make for what is now California by way of Tahiti, and search for that 'will-o-the-wisp of the age of discovery', the North-West Passage.

The two ships touched at Tasmania and Queen Charlotte's Sound and the Cook and Palmerston Islands were discovered before making Tahiti where the native Omai who had been brought to England as a curiosity

on the previous voyage was returned to his habitat together with a gift from King George III of live cattle and poultry. The expedition then went on to the south-western extremity of the Alaskan peninsula and through the Bering Straits before being turned back by an impenetrable wall of ice. Finally on 17 January 1779 the two ships anchored in Kealakekua Bay, Hawaii, to carry out a very necessary refit.

Now the final tragedy began. Cook was mistaken by the islanders for a Polynesian God whose return in 'a large island with trees, bringing gifts including swine and dogs' had been prophesied in Polynesian legend. This was all very well but there is a time for everything: the strain of welcoming such a god proved too much for local resources and there was heartfelt relief when the two ships sailed away again on 4 February. Then came another stroke of luck but this time very bad luck indeed. Two days later *Resolution* sprung her foremast, thus forcing the two ships to return.

This time they were greeted with no welcome but only a smouldering, sullen dislike. Cook had always found the natives to have a light-fingered attitude to property but this time thieving increased to alarming proportions and culminated in the removal of a large ship's boat. An affray followed. Cook's normal and rigid control of his passions suffered a momentary lapse and he was unwise enough to fire his shotgun. This provocation was fatal. He was immediately overwhelmed and brutally stabbed to death.

Cook's death was all the more tragic because he had proved himself unique in always trying to deal with native peoples gently and with strict honesty. 'It has ever been a maxim with me,' he wrote, 'to punish the least crimes any of my people have committed against these uncivilised nations. Their robbing us with impunity is by no means a sufficient reason why we should treat them in the same manner.' In other words – and anachronistically – the buck stops here. As Professor Beaglehole remarks, Cook was a passionate man who held himself well in check. Whenever he did lapse he immediately deplored his action. His last lapse he did not live to deplore.

Thanks to Cook the entire Pacific was opened up, and in essentials the modern map assumed its present form. Surveys of the Arctic and Antarctic wastes had necessarily to wait until the nineteenth century, but in Cook's life, by general accord, lies the consummation of the spirit of scientific navigation. 'In those few elected spirits, such as Cook, is the complete equipment of Genius. Fortune coincides with their appearance and the face of the world is changed.'

Top: Cook (the tall figure in the group of four) in Queen Charlotte Sound, New Zealand, by John Webber
Bottom: Double-hulled Tahitian war canoes, painted by William Hodges on Cook's second voyage

Chapter Three

CARGOES

Thousands of small, round shrubs clung in orderly pattern to the hillside which sloped sharply away to a river far below. Across the deep valley the land rose in steep waves; foothills green with vegetation climbed to rocky grey mountains. In the far distance, so tall and brilliantly white that they dominated the sky, were the peaks of the Himalayas. I was standing on the highest point of the Soom tea plantation in the Darjeeling region of Northern India. Around me were the ancient mountain kingdoms once known as The Forbidden Lands; Nepal lay ten miles to the west, Tibet fifty-five miles to the north and, just in front of me on the other side of the valley, Sikkim. From a point just above the 7500-foot-high town of Darjeeling it is even possible to see Everest itself. It is on plantations like Soom, clinging to the steep slopes beneath the town, that Darjeeling tea is grown. One hundred and fifty years ago this area was covered in dense jungle. Even now the thick, green vegetation of the ravines and escarpments which cut the plantation create a strong contrast with the smooth velvet carpet of tea bushes.

Clare Francis on board the paddle-steamer *Chaibassa*, which still transports goods on the Hooghly. At the other end of the scale the Shell tanker *Batilus* is too big to enter most ports and unloads its cargo into a smaller ship

The clearing and planting of these hillsides were no easy tasks. Today the remoteness of the region still makes tea production relatively expensive, but as any tea connoisseur will tell you, Darjeeling tea is worth the trouble. Its delicate flavour has earned it the description 'the champagne of teas'. In the blended teas that most of us drink, it is Darjeeling that provides the scent and bouquet.

Camellia sinensis, the tea plant, was probably first brought overland to Europe from China by the Russians. It appeared in England over 300 years ago but it cost so much – £10 per pound, the equivalent of two years' wages for most people – that it was drunk by just a few of the very rich. Like many imported products, however, the price only had to come down for the mass of the people to start consuming it. Between 1706 and 1750 tea imports into England rose from 54,000 to 2,300,000 pounds – and that did not take account of the considerable quantity smuggled in from Europe. By the end of the eighteenth century enough tea was arriving in England for two-thirds of the population to drink over two cups a day.

At that time all the tea drunk in Europe was grown in China and transported by the great fleets of the East India Companies, of which the Dutch and the English were the most important. Then, in 1835, the English Company lost the one thing on which its fabulously profitable Far East operation relied: the British Government withdrew the Company's official trade monopoly with China. Faced by efficient competition for the first time, the Company turned its attention to India where, after ousting the rival French and subduing local rulers, it had become very powerful. But how was the East India Company to make the most out of this vast country? Having lost much of the China tea trade, one of the answers was to create a market for tea grown in India. Until this time, no tea was exported from the sub-continent; in fact, the plant was not thought to grow in India at all. But the country possessed the two things needed for tea production – a large, able workforce, and highland regions where the climate was warm yet moist. So the Company imported tea bushes from China and planted them in the foothills of the Himalayas where they flourished. At the same time India was found to possess its own tea plant, which was growing unnoticed in Assam in the north-east corner of the country. This tea was strong, dark and pungent.

Both Chinese and Assam bushes were tried here in Darjeeling and, as the manager of the Soom, Mr Lall, explained, the plantation now has both hybrid and pure Chinese strains growing side by side. It takes 800 men and women to pick the Soom's 550 acres of tea bushes. During the main season, from June to September, each bush must be visited every seven days to catch the new growth of leaves. From the high ridge at the top of the plantation I could see long lines of pickers straggling up the hillsides, filling the baskets on their backs. The laden baskets are then taken to the plantation factory by foot, pony or jeep for weighing and processing. Even today, most tea is packed in the traditional plywood tea chests with silver-foil lining. 'Tea absorbs the smell of plastic, wood, or anything else,' Mr Lall told me, 'so we stick to the old containers.' Quantities of tea still travel down to the plains and cities by river. The Himalayan range is the source of several great river systems. Here on the eastern side of the Indian continent flow the Brahmaputra and the sacred Ganges which, with numerous tributaries and distributaries, intermingle to form the vast Ganges Delta, covering thousands of square miles of Bangladesh and West Bengal. This web of waterways has been used to transport goods and people for thousands of years, but it was not until Europeans sailed to India by the all-sea route that the volume of trade began to expand to reach today's vast scale.

Cheap labour and local boats: the primary produce of India – tea, jute, indigo, opium and so on – has been transported by similar means for centuries

International trade is so much part of our lives that it is difficult to imagine how we would survive without it. Indeed, Britain is more dependent on the importation of basic foodstuffs – and therefore more vulnerable to a shortfall in supplies – than many other nations. In the Second World War Germany brought her to her knees by attacking the North Atlantic convoys in an attempt to starve the country into submission. Trade has enabled certain countries, particularly those of Western Europe, to specialise their skills to a high degree, and to create enormous wealth in the process.

Trade began as the exchange of a few luxuries and, thanks to sea travel, grew to form the basis of life for a great number of people. The carriage of light, high-value commodities like silks and spices was possible over land, though it was a lengthy and costly process, but the movement of large quantities of food and raw materials could never have taken place without ocean transport. One only has to imagine trying to take a ton of tea from Darjeeling to Western Europe by land, river and occasional coastal transport to appreciate how often it would have to change hands from one mode of transport to another, how many people would be involved in the process, and the immense time it would take. The cost of carrying it in a fast modern lorry would still be prohibitively high – even assuming the roads were passable and no countries en route were at war.

The discovery that all the seas were one and that every part of the world was linked by water led not only to a large volume of trade, but to the exchange of an amazing variety of products. Before going to India I carried out a survey of my garden and kitchen with the help of a horticulturist and a historian. My typically English garden turned out to have only four plants which are indigenous to Britain – heather, holly, honeysuckle and mint. All the rest come from abroad. Even the rose, that most English of flowers, was brought from Persia by the Romans. The rockery has flowers and shrubs from New Zealand, South Africa and the Mediterranean. Inside my kitchen there were several foods that could be said to be native to England – meat, fish, cheese and honey, for instance, although much is now imported – but there were a large number of products that originated from abroad: potatoes from the Andes, tomatoes from New Mexico, coffee from Brazil, and chocolate brought back from the New World by the Spanish and kept a secret for many years. Almost all fruits come from overseas, and most spices from the East. Tea, that mainstay of the British, became popular both as a beverage and for its medicinal qualities. As Samuel Pepys wrote:

'Home and found my wife making tea, a drink which
Mr Pelling, the apothecary tells her is good for
her cold and defluxions.'

The beneficial qualities of tea were hotly argued about for years but, whether or not it does you good, tea has long been established as a staple. Certainly I am one of the tea industry's best customers, drinking as many as six cups a day.

Since the seventeenth century, when tea was a curious luxury for the rich, until today, when it is one of the world's basic commodities, trade has changed out of all recognition, in its nature, its size and the way it is carried out. On this, my third, voyage I was going to follow a consignment of tea from the remote Soom plantation all the way to Europe to find out how goods are carried today, over 130 years after tea was first developed in India and 400 years since the first East Indiamen established regular sea routes between West and East. I would be travelling 11,000 miles from this corner of the undeveloped world to Rotterdam, the largest, most modern port in the world and Europe's principal gateway to world trade.

On the final day of my visit to Darjeeling I watched a batch of the highest-grade tea – described by Mr Lall as 'first flush, young leaf, high scent and no stalk' – packed into chests and loaded on to a lorry for the journey to Calcutta. Since the road and railway links were built between the plains and the hill country the best tea, most of which will be exported, travels this way. The poorer grades, however, may still be carried by the traditional river boats which have changed little over the centuries. Built of wood and propelled by simple sails or long oars, they float majestically along, loaded high and wide with anything from hay to timber to tea.

The paddle-steamer
Chaibassa

Another type of craft that has long graced the Ganges Delta is the paddle-steamer. Just north of Calcutta I joined the *Chaibassa*, which has been trading between the hill regions and Calcutta for an incredible sixty years. Built in Glasgow, Scotland, in 1919 she and boats like her revolutionised river transport in West Bengal. Instead of the four to five weeks taken by the sail- and oar-driven craft, the steamers make the 900-mile trip to Assam in ten days and the return journey in eight. The magnificent *Chaibassa* is a sight to gladden the hearts of nostalgic steam enthusiasts everywhere. Her low hull is wide and flat, 230 feet long with a draught of only five feet to take her through the shallows. Halfway down her sides are the immense paddle-wheels which dip and churn through the yellow waters, pushing the steamer at an elderly six knots, her top speed now that her best years and her commissioning performance of ten knots have passed. Above the deck, which is loaded high with cargo, is a giant corrugated-iron canopy surmounted by a bridge deck and a tall thin funnel which belches a thick black plume of coal-laden smoke. The smoke has sealed every inch of the vessel in a coat of crisp black, so that canopy, funnel and deck are uniform in colour, almost as if the boat has been newly painted. Only the bright colours of the cargo provide contrast. The *Chaibassa* will carry anything but on her trips down to Calcutta she normally brings raw materials like timber, jute, bamboo, plywood, spices and tea from the inland regions. On her return journey she carries industrial and imported goods like hardware, pots and pans, fertiliser, cement and all kinds of manufactured goods.

This movement of produce – the raw materials outward and the manufactured goods inward – follows a pattern established long ago. It was the lure of unobtainable goods such as silk and spices that attracted Europeans here in the first place but, as demand for eastern products grew and grew, the British found themselves with a serious problem. They had what we would nowadays call a balance of payments deficit; money was pouring out to pay for the eastern goods but Britain was producing few exports to bring the money in. The solution was to develop products in the colonies which could either be exported straight to other countries or imported into England, turned into manufactured goods, and then re-exported. Cotton was sent to the mills of northern England, woven into fine fabrics and sold abroad; jute was used in carpet-making; and opium was grown in large quantities for export to China where it more than paid for England's operations there. Thus trade engendered more trade, in a spiral of investment, profit and wealth that grew dizzily upwards. The amount of money to be made by those directly involved – the merchants, shipowners, and captains – was enormous. Yet it was because of these very profits that trade and, most importantly, the mechanics of trade – the ships, the ports and the facilities – developed so steadily.

An 1890s photograph of ships on the Hooghly

The largest and most successful organisation in the history of English trade was the East India Company which had a monopoly of commerce with India from 1600 until 1833 when the government threw Indian trade open to all British companies. In its time the Company had enormous power, operating more like a government than a trader, with the right to keep an army, to acquire territory, to administer justice and to print money.

The centre of the Company's operations in East India was Calcutta, which lies on the banks of the Hooghly river, 125 miles upstream from the Bay of Bengal. The Hooghly is the most westerly of the great rivers of the Ganges Delta and gives access to the richest areas of Bengal and East India. After establishing a small factory beside the river in 1690, the Company bought three entire villages which eventually became the large sprawling city that is Calcutta today. (Acquiring villages, lands and peoples was not unusual for the East India Company; in 1835 it obtained the whole of Darjeeling from the Rajah of Sikkim.) Steaming down the Hooghly today, small remnants of the old city can still be seen among the acres of docks, warehouses, coal dumps and petrol wharves. Overlooking the wide yellow river is the occasional ruined palace or colonial residence, reminders of the style in which the administrators and officials liked to live. One of the most famous landmarks – now gone – was the Chandpal Ghat, the ceremonial gateway where the officers of the East India Company would arrive by

The promenade deck of the P & O ship *Rome*, 1895

boat. The gateway afforded them some dignity that their arrival did not; as a British Chief Commissioner of Assam recalled, 'We were ignominiously carried on shore on the backs of coolies who waded through soft and most disgusting mud.'

In the early days Calcutta had few facilities; there were no wharves, pontoons or landing-stages. Most serious of all, there were no pilots to guide the East Indiamen up the long and difficult river. Pilotage is an important service for any port, but it was essential for Calcutta, 125 miles and fifteen sand bars from the sea. Even financial inducements would not tempt the captains of the East Indiamen to bring their ships upriver until pilots were brought out from England, the river properly surveyed, and a reliable service established. In 1672 the 170-ton *Rebeccah* became the first ship to sail to Calcutta under the guidance of one Samuel Hacon, who was rewarded with the sum of 100 rupees. The Bengal Pilots became highly respected and well-paid officials in the East India Company, living in grand houses with numerous servants. Since 1948 the organisation has been known as the Calcutta Pilot Service, but there is one man who remembers it under its old name. After the *Chaibassa* had arrived at her pontoon on the east bank of the Hooghly, Captain Dutta, the last of the Bengal Pilots, joined me for a short trip downriver. 'There are many difficulties in the journey from the sea,' he explained. 'Very strong tides, for example. If the ebb of the spring tide coincides with the monsoon, the current can run at seven to eight knots. Then there is the tidal bore . . . the weather . . . the shifting sandbanks.' The tidal bore is a wall of water created by the tide surging up river. It can be as much as ten feet high and cause ships to break their mooring-lines unless they are safely inside a closed dock. During cyclones the wind can reach speeds of over 100 knots and the monsoons regularly bring torrential rain which cuts visibility to a few hundred yards. It is so shallow in the wide mouth of the river that the pilot must choose the moment when the tide is rising to race for deeper water before the tide falls again. All in all, the pilots' job did not sound an easy one. Captain Dutta had gone through a long and arduous training, first gaining his Mate's Ticket in the British Merchant Navy, then serving his pilot's apprenticeship as a leadsman, standing in the ship's chain taking soundings every three minutes. Once qualified he was faced with a heavy responsibility. As Kipling wrote:

> 'Almost any pilot will tell you that his work is more difficult than you can imagine, but the Pilots of the Hooghli know that they have one hundred miles of the most difficult river on earth running through their hands, and they say nothing. Their service is picked and sifted as carefully as the bench of the Supreme Court, for a judge can only hang the wrong man – but a careless pilot can lose a 10,000 ton ship with crew and cargo in less time than it takes to reverse the engines.'

It could take an East Indiaman up to two weeks to reach Calcutta from the sea, yet there were great advantages in having a port so far inland. The wide estuary with its numerous small islands was a hotbed of pirates and marauders, and it was only when ships took on their cargoes upriver that they could load in safety. A small town so far from the sea could also be more easily defended from enemy forces; there was less likelihood of being taken by surprise when opponents had to sail the length of the river or send a land force. For the ports which had no wide-ranging river system to link them with inland regions it was quicker and more profitable to bring ships as near as possible to the factories, raw materials and marketplaces. Ports like London, Hamburg and Rotterdam developed many miles from the sea; others like Buenos Aires and Oslo grew at the top of estuaries and fjords.

In Calcutta, Darjeeling tea is auctioned every Monday morning at 9.30. Up to sixty per cent is bought by the Russians, who enjoy light fragrant teas drunk with lemon. The next largest buyer is Britain. The consignment that I was following, however, was destined for a buyer in Rotterdam. The buyer used an agent to purchase the tea and now he employed a shipping agent to find a carrier for his cargo. The agent chose the container ship *Monet*, owned by the French Compagnie Générale Maritime (CGM), which was due to call in the next ten days. However, the ship would not be leaving from Calcutta itself; although the port has grown to be the largest in India and handles over forty per cent of the country's exports, it is not suitable for many of today's vessels. In recent years ships, particularly those carrying bulk cargoes like oil, coal, and ore, have got much larger. At the same time the Hooghly has been silting up and, despite constant dredging, Calcutta cannot take anything with a draught greater than twenty-six feet or, because of the limited manoeuvring space, a length of more than 570 feet. To handle large vessels a new port, with bulk-cargo berths and the first container terminal in India, has been created at Haldia, fifty miles downriver from Calcutta.

The *Monet*

Haldia lies on the low west bank of the Hooghly just where the river widens out and starts its final run into the sea. The new terminal consists of little except a transit shed, a large portainer crane, and hundreds of containers. On the day I arrived the flat landscape was overshadowed by a ship with a long black hull and a tall white superstructure: the *Monet*. It is difficult to find much beauty in a container ship. The lines are not sleek or elegant, but strictly functional. The accommodation block seems disproportionately high, rising over 100 feet above sea-level to give the crew a clear view across the three layers of containers and four cranes that cover the deck. This top-heavy look is rather ugly; nonetheless, the *Monet* does have personality. The clipper ship of the last century could be described as a beautiful lady, whereas the container ship is more like a plain but exceedingly efficient secretary. Strictly speaking, the *Monet* is a multi-purpose ship. Principally designed to carry containers, she can take some conventional and some roll-on roll-off cargo, a facility known as 'ro-ro' for short. The essence of ro-ro is that goods can be driven straight on to the ship on forklift trucks. The *Monet* always docks starboard side to the dock so that she can lower the large ramp, on the starboard side of her stern, which gives direct access to the aft section of her hold. However, the bulk of her 20,000-ton carrying capacity is used for containers.

Containerisation was introduced by Sealand, an American company which produced the first standardised metal box for the carriage of general cargo. The advantages of the system were soon appreciated by Western shipping lines. Cargo could be handled much more quickly than before, reducing costs at the dockside: special portainer cranes can lock on to a container and lift it aboard a ship in under two minutes. The long metal boxes – the standard size is $8 \times 8 \times 20$ feet – are designed to fit straight on to lorries or railcars, for direct onward transportation. Delicate cargoes are well protected from rough handling, rain and weather. Frozen goods – principally meat – are carried in specially refrigerated containers which are plugged into compressors on the ship, dockside, or lorry. In addition, as each container is sealed from the beginning of its journey to the end, pilferage, long a major source of loss to shippers and insurers, is reduced to manageable proportions. (In 1806 the London Police reported that cargo in the Port of London was in danger from 'river pirates, night plunderers, light and heavy horsemen, game watermen and lightermen, mudlarks and scuffle hunters, copemen or receivers of stolen commercial property . . .' a terrifying army, by the sound of it. To protect goods, docks were enclosed by high walls and gates guarded by port police, but the 'evaporation' of cargo remained a serious problem until the introduction of containerisation.)

The carriage of general cargo in containers is bringing about a revolution in trade by sea, a change as dramatic as the development of steam in the last century. For countries with high labour costs the advantages are obvious, although some dockers' unions have resisted reductions in manning levels, thus preventing the kind of cost savings that were anticipated. But for undeveloped countries like India the picture is different. She has neither the roads nor the rail stock to take containers onward by land and there is little cost saving at the dockside when labour is anyway relatively cheap. Haldia container berth has been built not because the country needed it, but because the shipping lines and traders insisted upon it, to reduce their costs in a highly competitive industry.

With containers came specially designed ships like the *Monet*. The great advantage for the ship's master is that his cargo cannot shift to one side of the hold and produce a list in bad weather; each container slides down into a shaft and stacks one above the other. Tea is a natural choice for containerisation. The light plywood tea chests are fragile and, above all, must not get wet, so they need the protection of a metal box. As I prepared to go aboard the *Monet*, the Rotterdam consignment was being stuffed into a container on pallets shuttled by forklift trucks. When the container was full, it was sealed with a small lead disc imprinted with a six-digit number. This seal would be checked at various points along the journey so that, should it be broken, it would be known where and roughly when it happened. Many miles away in France, every scrap of information about this container was being stored, checked and rechecked on a computer in the offices of CGM. The container number, seal number, origin, destination, contents and weight were known and had already been relayed to the ship, the local agent, the consignee and the Customs authorities. Oh that airline baggage and foreign mail were always so well looked after!

As the tea container disappeared into the depths of the *Monet*'s hold, I climbed the long gangway slanting up the ship's side. After the steam heat of the dockside it was a contrast to enter the clean, air-conditioned accommodation block, walk into a lift, and step out five decks higher on the bridge. There, in the spacious control centre of his ship, I found Captain Fenouil, master and final arbiter of all around him. Immaculate in white tropical uniform, he appeared almost insignificant amid the banks of consoles,

Containerisation. The goods, stored in sealed metal boxes which facilitate loading, unloading, carriage and security, are piled high on the ship's deck. Highly sophisticated, often computerised port facilities make loading and unloading quick; but this equipment is only found at a limited number of ports

instruments and navigation aids. Yet here was a man of more than thirty years' experience who could control and manoeuvre this 538-foot vessel with a few crisp orders. As dusk fell the cranes were stacking the containers five high below decks, each box locking on to the one beneath, like pieces of Lego. The captain explained how vital it was to get the loading done as quickly as possible, so that the *Monet* could get to sea again. She was due to leave at seven the next morning – as long as there were no hold-ups. 'In port there are factors beyond our control. It is impossible to say everything will go to schedule until we've left!' To handle, organise and maintain this large mobile warehouse, which is capable of carrying 600 containers, Captain Fenouil had a crew of thirty-one, many of whom were highly trained specialists. Each had plenty of work to do during the 24-hour stop; gone are the days when port meant relaxation and long trips ashore. The First Officer, in charge of the cargo-loading, worked most of the night, as did his deputy, the officer in charge of security, Mademoiselle Aline Vassard. Aline is twenty-three, pretty, elegant and very French. She was the first woman to be employed by CGM on one of their ships. Now, she pointed out, there are fifteen, some officers like herself and others stewards serving meals and cleaning cabins. Although women have long served in the Russian merchant marine, it is still something of a surprise to find a girl like Aline in the masculine environment of a cargo ship. But any suggestion that it is a strange job to have chosen and Aline shrugs her shoulders, saying that it is not at all extraordinary to *her*.

The idea of an efficiently run ship with a small well-trained crew came relatively late in the story of sea trade. The East Indiamen were possibly the most inefficient and costly merchant ships that ever existed. Without competition from other companies, the Indiamen had only to deliver their cargoes in order to make money. Speed and cost-saving were unimportant as long as profits were sky-high. When the captain and stockholders of an East Indiaman could make a 400 per cent profit out of one successful voyage, they did not worry if the ship took well over a year to make the round trip to India. Safety was of paramount importance; it was better to wait for a storm to pass, to make a detour around pirate-infested waters, than to try to clip a few weeks off the time. The ships were so massively constructed anyway – they cost almost twice as much to build per ton as non-Company ships – that they were not the fastest vessels even in the best of conditions. Neither did they carry as much cargo as they might; valuable space was taken up by heavy guns to defend them against pirates and enemies. Only in the free-trade areas like the West Indies did trading ships develop into faster, more efficient vessels. Nowadays most ships have to specialise in order to survive in the highly competitive market of world shipping. The *Monet* was specifically designed to carry general cargo between Europe, Asia and the Far East, using ports that range from the very modern, where portainer cranes can shift containers at the rate of one every minute, to the relatively unsophisticated, where the ship must use her own deck cranes to move cargo at a more sedate pace.

At 7.30 in the morning the *Monet* left Haldia dock on schedule. The lock pilot manoeuvred her out of the basin and into the lock, which closed behind us. We waited expectantly for the gates into the Hooghly to open but, after half an hour, they were still firmly shut. The captain eventually discovered the hold-up was due to an industrial dispute. It was the first hitch in what, for him, was going to be a very long day. He shrugged and ordered a cup of coffee; this was something beyond his control. After two hours the gates finally opened and the lock pilot handed over to the Hooghly pilot for the fifty-mile voyage down to Sandheads and the open sea.

The flat expanse of the wide estuary gave no clue to the presence of sandbanks. The water was a uniform yellow and only when the navigating officer called 'five metres' from his console on the bridge did I realise that we were passing over shallow water. The old Bengal pilot, Captain Dutta, had told me that he navigated ships over some of the bars with no more than nine inches of water under their keels. The pilots calculate the depth of water over banks ahead from tide-tables and from semaphore stations on points and islands along the route, which signal the height of the water at a given point. Problems occur with heavily laden ships which start rolling in the swell because this increases the draught of the ship by as much as five feet on each gyration. However, the *Monet* was not fully laden and her draught was chalked up on the blackboard at the rear of the bridge as a mere twenty-three feet at the bow and twenty-five feet at the stern, more than I would care to manoeuvre but nothing to the Hooghly pilots. At Sugat Island, with the open sea tantalisingly near, the pilot looked at the semaphore station through the binoculars, sighed, and apologised to the captain. Due to the delay at the lock we were just too late for the tide and could not cross the last sand-bar. We would have to anchor until nine in the evening. This represented an idle half day in the *Monet*'s busy schedule, time which was worth perhaps £8000 to CGM. But the Captain was philosophical: if he had lost time here, he would pick it up elsewhere. Anyway, there was no possibility of moving the ship; one brush with a sandbank and she had little chance of escape. The swirl of the currents round a stranded ship is inclined to clear the sand away from under the bow and stern until the weight on the midship section breaks her back. Captain Dutta had seen this happen in 1952, when an impatient pilot took a ship over a bank on a falling tide.

At seven o'clock in the evening we sat down to a five-course dinner washed down with good table wine – standard fare on a modern French ship. With attentive stewards at one's elbow, a menu card on the table, and a sea view from the colourful dining-room, one might think this was a three-star hotel. But the modern seaman expects no less than good food and comfortable surroundings to compensate for the lack of family, friends and home life. During dinner the captain was informed that all doors to the main deck were being locked. When the *Monet* anchored a group of river boats had appeared and fastened themselves to the stern. They were hoping to trade, the captain told me, and were after anything, preferably whisky and cigarettes. In exchange they would offer fruit, fish or spices. These people were probably innocent of any intention to steal, but as darkness fell it was impossible to determine who wanted to trade and who to steal. While waiting in the roads off the Bangladesh coast the year before, the crew had discovered a whole party of uninvited guests aboard, and a nearby ship had reported all her mooring lines gone the next morning. Fifteen years before, a CGM ship had been stopped by armed men in a sophisticated navy-style launch off the Philippines and robbed. Here in the Hooghly, pirates used to be a constant problem for the East India Company. The raiders would catch the trading ships at the start of their homeward journey, when sickness and desertions had depleted the crew's ranks and sacks of cargo impeded the use of the guns. On the banks of the Hooghly there is a place which used to be called Melancholy Point, because the bodies of captured pirates were hung there as an example to their comrades. Conventional piracy – the robbing of innocent trading vessels – still flourishes in the South China Sea, the Red Sea, and around Central America.

Nowadays new and more sophisticated forms of robbery have grown up, mostly in the nature of fraudulent insurance claims. A heavily-insured ship may sink in record time, for example, although quite miraculously the crew manage to escape without injury. If the ship had been losing money the insurers may suspect she was scuttled, but without proof there is little they can do. Another ship may sink while carrying a valuable and well-insured cargo which never actually existed. A case which is fast gaining notoriety is the story of the *Salem*, a supertanker which secretly discharged her cargo of oil in South Africa, sailed empty up the Atlantic and sank suddenly off the coast of Senegal without loss of life. At first it was believed that she had gone down with her cargo, insured at Lloyd's for £30 million, but then the truth slowly emerged. The possibility of large-scale fraud such as this exists because the destination of a cargo can be camouflaged by a mass of paperwork, the owners of a ship cannot be identified, and in some countries a vessel can assume a new name without too many questions being asked.

After the evening meal the captain encountered his third problem of the day. The pilot was upset because he had not been invited to sit on the captain's right at dinner and he now refused to come up to the bridge. Eventually, after numerous diplomatic entreaties by the captain, he agreed to guide the ship over the last of the sand-bars and the risk of missing yet another tide was averted. The relationship between pilot and captain has always been a delicate one. It is the captain who has the ultimate responsibility for the ship, yet within harbour limits he must hand over all control to the pilot. If the pilot makes an error, it is the captain who is liable. But should the captain decide to overrule the pilot he risks everything: charges of negligence, enormous fines and disgrace. Normally captain and pilot have what Captain Dutta described as 'a most cordial relationship', and this type of upset was, everyone assured me, most unusual.

Once through the shoals the *Monet* anchored again, this time to await the boat which would collect the pilot at dawn. It never approaches ships at night, I was told, for fear of being mistaken for a pirate vessel and getting blasted out of the water. At seven in the morning we finally got under way for Madras, the next port of call. To make up for lost time the engines were run at full cruising revs, which gave a speed of eighteen knots. Down in the engine control room the chief engineer was watching the temperature gauges closely. The heat of the two 12,000-hp, oil-fired engines was the limiting factor on speed, because here in the Indian Ocean the sea water is warm and not very effective as a cooling agent. At eighteen knots the *Monet* was using a lot more fuel than at speeds of just fifteen or sixteen knots but, if she slowed down, there was a danger of losing her berth at Madras to another ship and having to wait. Speed versus fuel costs, economy versus delay: the captain had to weigh up these factors and decide his tactics. To show a profit, the *Monet* had to be fast yet efficient, carrying a large volume of goods at minimum cost.

It was not until the mid-nineteenth century that cost-efficiency became important in Eastern trade, and it was brought about by competition. First the East India Company was forced to compete with other British companies when it lost its monopoly of trade with India and China. Then in 1849 British ports were thrown open to foreign shipping. It was not long before the East India Company, its ships and organisation so large and unwieldy, lost business to the more economically run free-trading ships. On the India route the medium-sized, moderately fast vessels proved most efficient. Although the beautiful, sleek clipper ships developed by the Americans are the best-remembered sailing ships of the last century, they were not suitable for general trade, having high running costs and a large number of crew. They were used only when speed was important – in the China tea trade, for instance, when a much

Firefighting training on board the *SS Meta*, and the bridge of the Shell training ship *SS Opalia*. New ships need new skills

higher price was obtained for the freshest tea. However, these ocean greyhounds did inspire ship designers to streamline the traditionally beamy free-trader, thus improving performance and helping the common sailing ship to compete effectively against steam for many decades after the 'iron sail', as the engine was nicknamed, was introduced.

The *Monet* was steaming effortlessly through the calm blue waters of the Indian Ocean. Out on the stern of 'F' deck some of the crew were enjoying a swim in the ship's small pool; others were relaxing in deck-chairs. The scene was reminiscent of a cruise ship rather than a cargo-carrier. CGM is in fact an amalgamation of two old companies which ran passenger services, The French Line and Messageries Maritimes. So why don't they carry any passengers today? 'It was considered,' the First Officer told me, 'but what passenger would be happy with just twelve hours in port? And a port that is probably a long way from a city? We, the crew, never get time to go ashore – but we can't complain. A passenger would, I think!'

Early traders soon realised that, as far as making profits were concerned, people were just another form of cargo. Sixteenth-century adventurers like Drake and Hawkins were quick to join in the lucrative triangular Atlantic trade, carrying sugar and other products from the West Indies to Europe, then sailing to West Africa with cheap manufactured goods to exchange for slaves for the return journey to the Indies. The East India Company carried people too, though of their own free will. Since imports from India always exceeded the quantity of goods exported to the country, East Indiamen had plenty of room on the outward journey for passengers and all their luggage. According to a passenger's rank – and the cost of his fare – he or she could have between one and a half and two and a half tons of baggage space. Accommodation was in either the great cabin or the round house above it, the bunks being separated by canvas screens. Live animals were carried to provide fresh meat. Entertainment consisted of card-playing, conversation and, if there were musicians on board, music and dancing. Compared to the common sailors the passengers lived well, yet most regarded the five- or six-month voyage to India as tedious and slow and few enjoyed it. The passengers to the East were servants of the Company, their families, freelance traders and entrepreneurs, and those curious to see the strange and exotic lands where it appeared that fortunes could so easily be made.

A storm on the Hooghly, 1824, by James Baillie Fraser

In the nineteenth century a new kind of passenger trade developed, catering for a large number of poor, desperate and hopeful people who wanted to travel to new and better lands. Whether Irish fleeing from famine, Jews escaping from persecution, or adventurers hoping to get rich in the Australian and Californian gold rushes, they were prepared to endure the harshest of conditions to reach their objectives. Some unscrupulous shipowners took advantage of the demand and crammed too many people into old and unseaworthy ships, sometimes with terrible consequences. On the North Atlantic run the vessels packed with Irish emigrants were infamous for overcrowding, disease and frequency of shipwrecks. During this era the common sailor, whose life had never been an easy one, enjoyed better conditions than the passengers.

Aboard the modern merchant ship the crew's conditions have never been better. The *Monet*'s crew are given individual cabins, a desk and easy chairs, piped music and private shower-room. Their pay is a little higher than they could expect for a job of similar skill ashore and, for every month spent at sea, they get seventeen days at home although, as many of the crew were quick to point out, they get no more holiday than the average shore worker once weekends and public holidays are taken into account. To keep everyone happy there is even a purser on board whose principal job, after normal watch-keeping duties, is to organise games, sports and film shows. The food, even by the standards of a French ship, is excellent: large, walk-in deep-freezes store French bread, cheeses, meat, fish (including frogs' legs, of course); cool rooms hold mouth-watering fruits and vegetables; and a wine locker contains enough bottles for a six-month voyage.

'It is a golden jail,' said the captain; 'golden because we are so well looked after, and a jail because we are separated from our families and the outside world.' Even the longest-serving crew member found that, after thirty years at sea, he had not become entirely reconciled to being away from home. The radio-telephone has made it easier for men to keep in touch with their families but, the captain explained, it can make the separation seem harder: 'A voice close by, yet far away.' The lack of time in port cuts down on the crew's social contacts and adds to their feelings of isolation. Even on board ship the work, which is increasingly specialised, tends to keep the crew apart and they have to make an effort to meet in off-duty hours.

Why then choose a life at sea? This is the one question a seaman finds difficult to answer. Perhaps because he is drawn to the sea more by instinct and gut-feeling than by analytical thought, he cannot put his motives into words. The captain shook his head in reply, while others murmured about freedom, responsibility and love of the sea. They agreed that most of the adventure had gone, now that they saw so little of the countries they visited; as the captain put it, 'We have the mystery of the sea, but we no longer have the time to enjoy the mystery of the land!' The challenge of the sea is still rewarding enough in itself, although not, it appears, for the next generation. Like most shipping companies, CGM was having trouble in recruiting graduates and school-leavers. Most of the *Monet*'s crew were thirty-five or over; only the navigating officer, a seaman electrician and Mlle Aline Vassard were under twenty-five. Aline knew why she had chosen this career: 'I wanted to travel, I wanted to see the sea, and I wanted to do an original job . . . not in an office where I would write at a desk!' She too missed having time ashore, but found that the responsibility and interest of her job compensated for it. Being at sea for three months at a time meant Aline had no boyfriends; she found that men preferred girls who never went away. This, she said, didn't bother her. She was confident that one day she would find an understanding husband who would be happy to let her continue her career in the merchant service.

In the seventeenth and eighteenth centuries a life at sea had its attractions too. A seaman could earn very much more than he could on land and, at a time when the mysterious, beautiful East was a focus for men's dreams and aspirations, many men joined the merchant service to see the world. However, in practice conditions were often so poor that they took the first opportunity to desert. The food was no better than it had been in the sixteenth century: dry biscuit and salted meat was the standard fare. Disease was rife, particularly dysentery, known as 'the bloody flux', which could kill a strong man in ten days. A major grievance was that wages were paid only for successful voyages; if a seaman fell ill or was captured he received nothing, and, if a cargo was lost or damaged, the crew actually had to pay for it out of their own wages, although losses were usually caused by bad weather rather than negligence. If a seaman was lucky he might become an apprentice navigator and better himself; otherwise his future was not bright. Large numbers of merchant seamen were pressed into the Royal Navy; in fact, the government looked upon the flourishing merchant marine as their unpaid storehouse of labour to be called into service at the Navy's convenience. Press-gangs frequently boarded East Indiamen in the English Channel and, despite the crew's attempts to appear disabled or mad, would grab the fittest men. It was not until 1810 that some limitations were put on the numbers that could be taken from any one ship. But even if a seaman escaped the press-gang and death from disease, he had little to look forward to in his old age: there were no pensions for ordinary seamen unless they were disabled in service.

For the captains of the East Indiamen, manpower was a major problem on the return journey from the East. In 1785 the 755-ton *Manship* left the Thames with 132 men, but on arrival at Calcutta only eighty remained; four had died and forty-eight deserted. Scurvy could still take a heavy toll, and one ship reported losing a quarter of her men to the disease. In an attempt to curb desertion, discipline was harsh. A man might be given the cat-o'-nine-tails or 'flogged around the fleet', receiving a beating on each of the Company's ships in harbour, a punishment that could easily kill a weakened man. In 1788 the ringleaders of a mutiny were given five dozen lashes each.

Just as fights used to break out between the bored, overcrowded crew of the East Indiamen, so incidents occur in the close confines of a modern ship. The night before the *Monet* arrived in Madras the ship held a crew party on the after-deck. Meat was roasted on a barbecue; tables were loaded with savouries, salads and pastries; and the wine flowed freely. The evening passed happily until, most people having left, a fight broke out between two of the crew. Nothing would have been made of it, the captain told me, except that one man pulled a knife, an offence that he could not possibly overlook. A captain's disciplinary powers are limited by law today; he is permitted to lock up a dangerous man until the ship reaches port and, if mutineers threaten the safety of his ship, he is allowed to hold them at bay with a gun. But he cannot impose punishment. In this case, Captain Fenouil informed the miscreant that he would be reported to the authorities in France, who would decide on the action to be taken. In all probability the man's pay would be docked for three months. The captain was not worried about the sailor repeating the offence. 'It was a burst of passion,' he said with a Gallic shrug. 'Such things happen from time to time.'

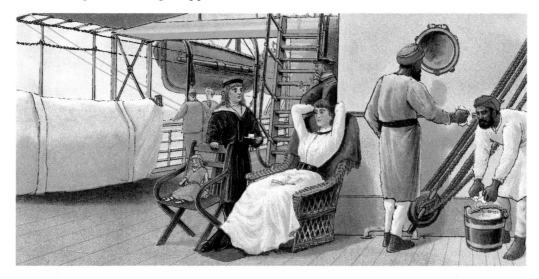

'An afternoon bask in the sun' from *P & O Pencillings*

Sixty hours after leaving Haldia the *Monet* arrived off Madras, picked up a pilot and sailed into the harbour. It was here that the captain managed, as he put it, to earn his year's salary in half-an-hour. The pilot's walkie-talkie had broken down and he tried to communicate with the tugs and the dockers by whistle and hand signals. As a result, everyone's actions lacked cohesion: tugs were pushing in the wrong places, and none of the right lines were run from the ship to the bollards on the dockside. A strong wind started to blow the *Monet* away from the dock and push her across the basin towards another ship. Having waited patiently while the pilot tried to sort out the situation, Captain Fenouil took the unusual step of asking him to stand down and, only seconds before a certain and serious collision, issued the crisp order: 'Full ahead. Hard a-port.' Her engines churning, the *Monet* drifted within yards of the other ship, paused and, as we breathed again, slowly drew away. After issuing further orders the captain brought the ship into the centre of the basin, stopped her dead, and handed her back to the pilot who regrouped the tugs and brought the ship safely into her berth.

In Madras there were sixty containers to be loaded. The cargo included forty-two tons of curry, fifteen tons of seashells, 100 tons of tamarind seeds, 125 tons of drugs, fifty tons of dried animal skins, and, of all things, fifteen tons of human hair. In the ro-ro section twenty buses were to be driven on for discharge in Ceylon. Even the first officer, who was in charge of loading and off-loading, agreed that it was an exotic mixture of cargoes, particularly when the ship already had 120 tons of frozen frogs' legs aboard.

As the cranes started to swing the first containers into the hold, the first officer compared the cargo list which had been telexed from head office against the large loading chart in front of him. He had to check two critical factors. First, each container has to be stacked according to its destination; it would be extremely wasteful and time-consuming to have to dig out a single container from under a whole stack of cargo which was due to stay on board. 'If that happened,' said the first officer, 'first I would be fired and second I would be very unpopular!' Second, and even more vital, the weight of the cargo has to be properly distributed about the ship or her stability will be threatened. Heavier cargo is placed low and spaced well out between bow and stern, but if the ship is fully laden stability can easily become critical. When meeting container ships at sea I have always thought they looked top-heavy, but it was a bit of a surprise to discover that top weight really is a serious problem. It is the three layers of containers above deck-level that make the ship roll excessively in a large sea. Outward bound from Marseilles the *Monet* had carried 3000 tons of cargo on deck and, as the first officer said, 'she rolled like a pig.' But lack of stability may produce more than a bad roll; if certain limits are exceeded, it may capsize the ship. In December 1978 the *Munchen*, a modern barge-carrier loaded high like a container ship, suddenly disappeared in the North Atlantic. It is believed that she capsized in very bad weather and sank rapidly. 'If we got the stability seriously wrong this ship could capsize,' confirmed the first officer. 'At night I think we would have no chance of survival. In the day . . . maybe. She would go down very fast, I think. Anyway, I am going to make sure it won't happen!'

Aboard the *Monet* the stability calculations are not left to chance. In a room off the first officer's spacious office there is a computer programmed to the ship's weight and design characteristics. The weight and proposed distribution of the cargo is fed in and the computer spits out the vital stability ratios. To help trim the ship, the first officer also has a large ballast console at his disposal. By pumping water in and out of tanks that are ranged around the hull, sideways trim can be altered to eliminate list, and fore and aft trim to avoid a large difference between draught at the bow and at the stern. When the ship is to be fully laden, fuel is taken on to increase stability. The *Monet* can carry up to 3300 metric tons of diesel and fuel oil, but, at today's prices, she tries to fill up only at ports where the cost is relatively low. Again, cost has to be balanced against efficiency and, in this case, stability as well.

Occasionally containers carry high-value cargo. In General de Gaulle's day, when France was buying huge quantities of American gold, up to fifteen tons of the metal was placed in a single container and welded to the deck of a ship. More frequently, travellers' cheques and banknotes are transported by container ships. On land such cargoes are generally guarded, but it is unnecessary at sea; no one except the first officer and the captain knows which box contains the valuable cargo. Anyway, even the most daring pirates would find it difficult to attack a large container ship.

After making a stop at Colombo in Sri Lanka, the *Monet* steamed up the west coast of India and into the seas that quite rightly earned themselves the description pirate-infested. For centuries the lucrative Eastern trade had been in the hands of the Arabs, who carried goods from the Far East to India and the Mediterranean. Then the Portuguese, followed by the Dutch, English and French, arrived and cut out the middlemen. Not surprisingly, the Arabs were somewhat annoyed and made a practice of attacking European ships whenever they could. Using fleets of fast dhows, some as large as 300 tons, they robbed East Indiamen over a large area from the Persian Gulf to Bombay and Madagascar. Such was the Arabs' success that the Europeans organised groups of armed ships to search them out. It was no easy task; the corsairs hid in a myriad of inlets and secret harbours along the long Arabian coastline.

One of the ports hardest hit by piracy was Bombay, which England acquired from Portugal as part of Catherine of Braganza's dowry on her marriage to Charles II. The island became the chief seat in India of the East Indian Company. The need to defend this important trade route led to the setting up of the Bombay Marine, a force that was to exist for 250 years. In the beginning it consisted of a few sloops, brigs and dispatch vessels, whose numbers were increased when piracy was rife and reduced when things got better. In 1798 the force became closer to a small navy, with the issuing of regulations and defining of objectives. Finally, in 1830, it was renamed the Indian Navy. The Bombay Marine was too small to stamp out piracy altogether, and it was only when the British and French Navies appeared in force – mainly to fight each other – that the pirates were kept at bay. Nevertheless, the Bombay Marine reduced the East India Company's losses and confirmed the need for a permanent fighting force to protect trade.

Bombay was to be the *Monet*'s last port of call in Asia before she sailed on to the Middle East and Europe. The port's long links with the Arabian and East African trade routes have made it the business and commerical centre of India. However, relative wealth and the high demand for imported goods have also made it the smuggling capital of the sub-continent – nowadays the Bombay authorities are more concerned about contraband than pirates. Ever since countries recognised the need to control trade and imposed restrictions and duties on certain types of goods, smuggling has prospered. India needs all the foreign exchange she can earn from tea and other exports to buy badly-needed fertilisers, machinery and equipment; she does not want foreign exchange squandered on luxuries like jewellery, gold and motor cars. It is easy to stop the import of foreign cars – you just ban them and, since they are too large to smuggle and too obvious to possess, no one breaks the rules. But small items like wristwatches and textiles are easy game for smugglers. The prevention of this trade is a difficult task for the local authorities. As the chief customs officer for Bombay explained, it is impossible to guard every inch of India's long coastline. The smugglers are difficult to identify, too, because they use trading dhows and fishing boats which are indistinguishable from the hundreds of innocent craft which sail the seas between Arabia and India. The authorities are forced to rely on random searches and inside information. One of their favourite ploys is to take a boat they have seized, man it with customs officers and, while pretending to trade or fish, pick out suspicious craft for surprise searches. They also use the speed of fast patrol boats to outrun their opponents. But, like customs authorities the world over, their main weapon is information obtained on the organisations which are running smuggling operations within their own country. Catching boats on their outward journey is important too, because they are fighting a two-way traffic. India's currency cannot be exchanged abroad so, to pay for the contraband watches and textiles, the smugglers take out old silver, jewellery, antiques and wild animal skins. 'Our country is being deprived of all her treasures by the smuggling of these things,' the customs officer sighed. And they are impossible to replace. Tigers and leopards, already much reduced in number and threatened by the deforestation of India's jungles, are being killed merely to finance smugglers' operations.

Smuggling in the West follows a different pattern. In one way it is not so serious: traditionally it has mainly involved luxuries like alcohol and cigarettes, on which governments impose high duties not so much to protect their countries' foreign exchange or home industries as to raise revenue. For centuries the smuggling of brandy, wine and tobacco from the European continent to England was considered a fair and almost honourable occupation. The industry was often the principal means of support for isolated English south-coast communities, and only the severest of measures succeeded in restraining it. In the Isles of Scilly the islanders used long rowing boats, known as gigs, to put pilots aboard inbound ships; they also used them to ferry silks and muslins from the occasional East Indiamen or to collect brandy from France. In 1828 an ordinance was passed restricting the number of men in a gig to four instead of six or eight, so that the boats could no longer outrun the customs cutters. At the same time a large preventive force was stationed on the islands and the trade in drink and luxuries was effectively suppressed.

Today, however, there is a darker side to smuggling; drug trafficking is an international problem which is biting deep into every society. Drugs are easily hidden in general cargo and the Bombay customs take no chances. Every container that comes off a ship has to be opened, emptied and examined within the port limits. There are strict controls over outgoing containers too; some time before, dry-cell batteries exported from India to Canada were found to contain hashish.

Her cargo loaded and cleared by Bombay customs, the *Monet* was free to leave for Djibouti, the Red Sea and the Suez Canal. From Port Said she would sail to Marseilles, Barcelona, Le Havre and Rotterdam. The ship had no final destination; from Rotterdam she would visit three more North European ports and then head south again, through the Mediterranean to the East. She is rather like the *Flying Dutchman* of ancient legend, destined to sail the seas for ever. She stays in individual ports for up to thirty-six hours, but she has no home port, no stopping-place where she rests for months at a time to be overhauled, painted and reprovisioned for her next trip. It is more important to keep her at sea than beautifully painted. After her next three-month tour she was in fact scheduled to go into dry-dock to have her antifouling paint renewed, but this annual chore takes just seven days. All other work is carried out at sea or during the brief stopovers in port. The *Monet*'s schedule is all-important not only to keep her costs down but to attract business. Merchants want their goods delivered quickly and on time. As Captain Fenouil said, 'Everything is so scheduled and well planned that the only surprises come from administration.'

The idea of schedules came in with steam. In the days of sail it was impossible to predict how long a voyage would last. On average the East Indiamen took about five to six months to make the outward journey from England to India, but if, as frequently happened, there were delays, the trip might last months longer. On his first voyage to Madras Robert Clive, who was to bring much of India under the control of the East India Company, had enough time to learn the Portuguese language during a journey that lasted a year.

Until the Suez Canal was opened in 1869 there was, of course, no short sea-route to the East. In the early days of steam, mail ships would go as far as Alexandria to offload their cargo and their passengers for an uncomfortable overland journey to the Red Sea, where other vessels waited to make the onward journey. But the vast bulk of trade

Four barks and two big American schooners loading lumber on the West Coast of the United States. Sailing vessels continued in use longest in the transport of non-perishable bulk cargo

was still carried by sailing ships on the long route down the length of the Atlantic, round the Cape of Good Hope, and across the Indian Ocean. A straight line is rarely the fastest way to travel under sail and ships voyaged in wide arcs to keep a strong, fair wind behind them. From England, they would head south to Portugal to pick up the north-east trade winds which took them as far as the doldrums, just north of the equator. Once through the calms it was best to head for the eastern bulge of South America to keep the easterly winds on the beam. Going south the wind would gradually become more favourable until, at about 35° South, a ship could expect to pick up westerlies and head straight for the Cape. Once in the Indian Ocean sailing ships made another loop. First they would run their easting down, as it was called – heading east along roughly the same latitude to take advantage of the following winds. Then they would head north and catch the south-east trade winds to India or the Far East. The last stage of the journey had to be carefully timed to coincide with the south-west monsoon between May and September, otherwise a ship could take months to sail the last few hundred miles against contrary or light winds. Once in port a vessel might rest there for months, so that the round trip to India and back was not usually achieved in less than a year and a half. The *Monet*, on the other hand, takes just three months to make the voyage to Indonesia and back, and she stops at fifteen or more ports.

Although it was more reliable than wind-power, steam did not challenge the sailing ship for a long time because it was so very inefficient and expensive. The *Victoria* and *Adelaide*, two steamships which raced with mail to Australia, had to be heavily subsidised because they each used thirty-seven tons of coal a day and there was almost no room left in their holds to carry money-earning cargo. Even the massive *Great Eastern*, 688 feet long, launched in 1860 with enough capacity to take coal, cargo and passengers, was uneconomic because she burned twelve and a half tons of fuel each *hour*. Only when the more efficient compound engine was invented did the running costs of steamships come down. The first compound engines reduced coal consumption by a half; then, in 1881, the triple-expansion engine cut fuel usage to one-sixth of the original level. On its own the opening of the Suez Canal was not enough to make steam pay; it was the low cost of running the triple-expansion steam engine that brought about the ascendancy of power over sail. Nonetheless, sail managed to compete effectively for many decades on the more remote and dangerous routes where coaling stations were few and far between. Square-riggers carried grain and nitrates round Cape Horn until well into the twentieth century, sailing through seas and weather conditions that earned both ships and crews the reputation as the toughest and finest in sailing history. The Horn trade was effectively brought to a close by the opening of the Panama Canal in 1914, and in the years that followed most of the magnificent sailing ships were laid up. It was the end of an era.

With Suez behind her, the *Monet* headed across the Mediterranean bound for Marseilles, Gibraltar, and the Atlantic. It was the first time that I sailed in a craft so far removed from the sea, both in body and in spirit. Seen from the accommodation decks the waves appear like a flat corrugated pattern of ripples on a surface far beneath. During a gale the ship would undoubtedly roll a lot and the waves would appear large even to someone high on the bridge, yet the crew are well screened from the spray, the wind and the cold by thick glass, thermostatically-controlled ventilation and the massive structure of the ship herself. Even in the worst of weather meals appear on time, the crew changes watch methodically, and films are shown on schedule on the video-television screen in the sumptuous lounge. In today's merchant ship the sea is not allowed to impinge on the smooth routine of day-to-day business.

At seven in the morning the Chief Engineer and his number two go down in the lift to the lowest level and unlock the engine-room door. The engine room has been unmanned all night: an automatic fault-finding system has been in charge, constantly searching and monitoring temperatures, pressures and flow-rates in a manner more thorough and methodical than men could ever achieve. Linked to the system is an alarm that sounds in the lounge and engineers' cabins. Since even the smallest deviation from the norm is regarded as a fault, there may be an alarm almost every night. The engineers have only to look at a print-out in the control room to see what fault has occurred and when. During their 7.00 am to 6.00 pm working day they carry out maintenance and repairs. If they lack spare parts or expertise, equipment and specialist help will be sent out to the next port. Everything possible is done to keep the ship at sea, earning money.

At 8.00 am the watch changes on the bridge. The navigating officer checks the latest position marked on the chart and adjusts the course as necessary. In these waters I was surprised to find that a sextant was used to fix the ship's position rather than a satellite-navigation system. 'Too expensive and not necessary,' the navigator told me. 'On most of our route we have sun and clear skies, so a sextant is still best. Nearing the coast at night or in bad weather, we have radar to guide us in. Only in the English Channel and North Sea do we use anything else: then we have Decca navigation which automatically gives us three co-ordinates and a position we can read off a special Decca chart.' It is also surprising to discover that ships do not have their radar switched on all the time. In the open sea it is never used except in bad visibility. What about other ships then? 'We keep a good look-out, just like in the old days,' the navigator said. 'There is always one officer and one man on the bridge. The officer may be busy doing many jobs, but the man – his only function is to look out for other ships.' It is possible to keep just two men on the bridge because so many of the tasks that used to be carried out by crewmen are automated. The hydraulic steering mechanism is controlled by the autopilot, which is, in turn, guided by the gyro compass, which always reads true and, unlike the small-

The *Garthsnaid*: the photograph was taken by the second mate after four hands had been sent aloft
to secure a section of the foresail which had come free from the gaskets in very heavy weather

boat compass, is unaffected by the vagaries of the earth's magnetism. The engines are controlled directly from the bridge and, in the centre of the main console, there is a red button, masked by a protective cover, which reads Crash Stop. If pressed, this button will throw the engines into full reverse. On the *Monet* the system has only been tried once, during the ship's commissioning trials. 'I hope very much we never use it again,' sighed Captain Fenouil.

Collision is the main fear of the modern ship's captain. The rules of the road are simple: when meeting head on, both ships turn to starboard; when meeting roughly at right angles, the ship which is approaching from the other's left or port side must turn to starboard; when overtaking, the overtaking ship must keep clear. However, collisions still occur. One of the main reasons is the lack of skilled men on ships and, in all too many cases, lack of any men on the bridge *at all*. Only a few traditional maritime nations insist that two men should be on watch at all times; on ships under so-called 'flags of convenience' there is often just one man in charge – who may be less than conscientious. Flags of convenience are a post-World War II phenomenon, whereby ships are registered in certain countries such as Liberia, Panama, Cyprus, Somalia and Singapore to escape the expensive restrictions on manning and pay that are imposed elsewhere. It is very easy for a ship to be registered in one of these countries; owners do not have to be nationals, nor must they visit the country to effect the registration. Neither do the crew have to be citizens. Best of all for the owner, these countries do not try to create regulations, let alone implement them. This means that crew from low-wage countries can be employed in smaller numbers to reduce a ship's running costs. Flags of convenience have become very popular: in the early 1950s there were about 1000 ships under these flags, with a total capacity of 5–6 million tons. In the mid 1970s there were 6000 providing 75 million tons, almost a quarter of the world's tonnage.

Although many of these ships are well run, it is indisputable that they have a higher than average accident record. Some ships are very old, but a small though terrifying proportion are just inadequately manned. If there is no one on the bridge to spot another ship the rules of the road become irrelevant. There have been occasions when the *Monet* has been forced to alter course although, according to the regulations, she was not the vessel bound to do so. Much is talked about the time it takes a ship to stop, but it is only in narrow waterways that this is important. In the open sea collision can be averted faster by turning. If a ship does want to stop for some reason, it is best achieved by circling. The navigator told me that the *Monet* can crash stop in just over six-tenths of a mile, but she can circle to a halt in under half that distance.

Lack of international agreement over manning levels is only half the problem, however. Even basic safety precautions are not always taken. In 1876 a tenacious and dedicated man called Samuel Plimsoll finally succeeded in getting a bill through the British parliament which was designed to protect seamen from what used to be known as coffin ships. These were old and unsafe vessels which were grossly overloaded by their owners in the hope that either they would manage to make money or they would go to the bottom and bring in a handsome insurance payment on their cargo. Many did go down with their crews. Plimsoll's law made it compulsory for British ships to have marks painted on their sides to show how deeply they were allowed to be loaded, depending on the area and the season in which they were sailing. Ships voyaging in tropical fresh water are allowed to carry the maximum weight and those crossing the North Atlantic in winter the least heavy loads. Since Plimsoll's long and hard fight to bring the law on to the statute book (at one time he called Members of Parliament 'villains' and shook his fist at the Speaker), the Convention on Load Lines has laid down international standards. In the field of safety equipment, the Convention for Safety of Life at Sea has also established certain minimum requirements for the carrying of life-jackets, lifeboats, liferafts and other basic equipment. The problem is that the flags of convenience countries don't have the means to enforce these rules on their ships. They have no direct links with shipowners; much of the time they don't even know who the true owners are because they are hidden behind 'paper companies'. Neither do these countries have organisations to inspect load-lines or safety equipment. 'Yes, it is more worrying to meet a Liberian tanker than a French ship,' commented Captain Fenouil, 'but fortunately I don't usually know the nationality of the ship I am meeting. So I am careful with *everybody*.'

The marine insurance market, which is centred around Lloyd's of London, encourages safety at sea. If a ship is to be highly insured the underwriters want some guarantee that they are backing a good risk. Lloyd's Register of Shipping, an offshoot of Lloyd's itself, classifies vessels according to the quality of the materials and construction methods used. Nowadays the best-built ships win the accolade Lloyd's 100A1. Insurance premiums also reflect factors like the type of cargo carried, the oceans to be crossed, and the safety equipment that is provided. Before marine insurance grew up in the early seventeenth century, shipowners and merchants could be ruined by the loss of a ship and its cargo and people were relatively cautious about investing in such a chancy business. Spreading the risk provided a tremendous boost to both shipbuilding and trade. The *Monet* is insured in France and then reinsured at Lloyd's for £20 million.

From the north-west corner of Spain the *Monet* steamed straight for Ouessant (Ushant), the island off the western tip of France. 'From here on we must be certain of our position,' said the navigator. 'Around Ouessant there are many ships and we must keep in our proper lane.' The English Channel is the busiest waterway in the world; it is used by every kind of vessel from small fishing boats to VLCCs (Very Large Crude Carriers) of over 250,000 tons. Some steam up the Channel, others across it. At the places where shipping converges – in the narrow Straits of Dover or at corners like Ouessant – it has become necessary to organise the traffic into lanes like a motorway system. Between the up and down lanes there is a no-go area to keep ships on opposite

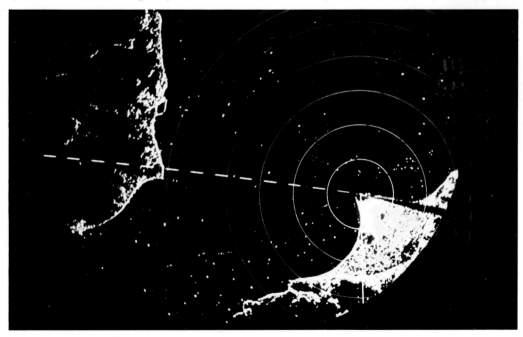

North Sea traffic shows up as blips on a radar scan from the Dungeness transmitter. The concentric rings are at four-mile intervals; the dotted line lies in the direction of Cap Gris Nez on the French side

headings well apart and, should any vessel have to cross the lanes, they have to do so at right angles. On the *Monet*'s bridge the Decca navigation system flashed three sets of numbers, giving a position that was carefully pencilled in on the chart. As night fell the loom of Créac'h Lighthouse on Ouessant appeared in the far distance off the starboard bow. Its two flashes every ten seconds are the most powerful in the world and have a range of thirty-three nautical miles in 74% visibility.

Ouessant has no less than six lighthouses, a reflection of the island's importance at the southern entrance to the Channel. On the northern side are the Isles of Scilly and the rugged Cornish coast, also well marked by lights. Until organisations were set up to build and maintain lighthouses on a regular basis, a ship coming into the English Channel often faced the most dangerous part of what may have been a long voyage. The earliest lighthouse in Britain was built by the Romans at Dover and was lit by an open fire. Until the nineteenth century lighthouses were built and operated on a haphazard basis. In 1517 Henry VIII set up the guild of Trinity House, which was empowered by Elizabeth I to provide sea marks for shipping. Local entrepreneurs would apply to Trinity House for a licence to build and maintain a light, in return for which they would receive light dues from passing ships. However, shipmasters were somewhat reluctant to stop and pay their dues after safely passing a light, so, as operators made or lost money, lights shone or were extinguished. As I had seen in *Gulliver G*, the rocky Scillies were extremely dangerous to inbound ships. For 200 years from 1680 a light burned on the island of St Agnes, but for most of its life it was no more than a coal fire in an iron brazier and frequently went out. At the best of times – when it was least needed – it would have been visible for just a few miles. As ships continued to pile themselves up on the Western Rocks, it was decided that something more effective was needed and, in 1859, a lightweight structure was built on the small Bishop Rock at the westernmost edge of the reefs. It didn't take long for the sea to show what it could do; the light was swept away before ever being lit! The second effort, a stone tower, fared a little better, but it shook so much in bad weather that articles fell off the shelves in the keepers' quarters. The men who lived in it must have been very brave – or exceptionally fatalistic. The third structure, a massive tower of interlocking granite slabs, was built around the second tower in 1887 and still stands 167 feet above the sea, the tallest and one of the most lonely in Britain. Another famous lighthouse is the Eddystone which guards an isolated reef ten miles south of Plymouth Sound. No less than five attempts were made to build on these rocks. The first two towers were designed by Henry Winstanley who had the misfortune to witness the destruction of the second at first hand. When he was visiting the lighthouse a terrible storm blew up and everything – Winstanley, the keepers and the tower itself – completely disappeared. It was not until 1882 that a lasting structure was finally erected.

Lights have been powered by many kinds of fuel, from wood and vegetable oil to coal and limelight. Nowadays nearly all are powered by gas or electricity. When I first visited a lighthouse I was surprised to find that the light itself was no more than a small gas-lit mantle. The intensity of illumination is created by the large lenses which rotate around the light, producing many more thousands of candelas (candlepower). Using the latest carbon arc light, the beam of Créac'h can be boosted to an incredible 500 million candelas so that, when fog reduces visibility to half a mile, it can still be seen at a distance of over three miles. Along busy waterways like the English Channel the coasts are now so well marked that it is possible to sail from one end to the other without losing sight of a light. From the 100-foot-high bridge of the *Monet*, the principal lights are visible at more than twenty miles in good visibility.

The light on the Isle of Islay shows bright through murky weather

Our next port of call was Le Havre at the mouth of the Seine. At one time it was a terminus for the transatlantic passenger trade and the home port of the last great French liner, the *France*, owned by one of the companies now incorporated in CGM. Today Le Havre is a modern, sprawling industrial port and its passenger trade is confined to the cross-Channel car ferries. When the *Monet* docked in the large container terminal next to CGM's offices, it was the end of the voyage for many of the crew. After three months at sea they packed their bags and waited for wives or relatives to collect them. They might never sail on the *Monet* again. Even as they walked down the gangway, a new crew were arriving to take their place. In a large company like CGM crew are allocated to the next ship coming in, although they might never have sailed in that type of vessel before. Specialisation has resulted in greater flexibility, a CGM official told me. An expert engineer can understand any kind of modern engine within half a day and, although the design of ships may differ considerably, a captain has the same tools and controls at his disposal on a modern bridge. Captain Fenouil was staying on the *Monet* until she returned to Le Havre after calling at Rotterdam. He, like all the crew I spoke to, felt that the constant changing of personnel was a good thing. 'Otherwise we would get tired of each other – and less polite, I think!' The chief engineer added, 'In one way it is a pity to build up camaraderie only to break it up, but it is good to have to start again, fresh every time.' The most difficult thing, several men thought, was to get back into the routine of family life. Each homecoming demanded adjustment and, where children were concerned, a lot of effort to re-establish communications. But that was the price they paid for their jobs; part, as always, of the seaman's lot.

Amid an ocean of containers, the CGM office stands square and modern close by the quayside. Inside is a computer terminal linked to CGM's other offices around Europe. Invoices, contracts, freight manifests, customs papers are all printed out at the push of a button, a sophistication necessary to control the 50,000 containers owned by the company and the total of 300,000 it handles during a single year. Like most shipping lines, CGM has faced grave financial problems in recent years. The reason is simply that there are far too many ships chasing too little cargo. Optimism in the 1960s and early 1970s led to an unprecedented boom in shipbuilding, accentuated by the closure of the Suez Canal and the need for large oil tankers for the Cape of Good Hope route. Between 1965 and 1975 world trade tonnage rose 87 per cent, but shipping capacity rose by 130 per cent, or half as much again. This enormous overcapacity has led to aggressive, cut-throat competition. Ships have become more and more sophisticated; in Le Havre we saw the latest addition to CGM's fleet, a banana carrier which brings the fruit from the West Indies in specially-designed containers that are temperature-controlled and air-ventilated to eliminate fermentation. You can't get much more specialised than that. The other effect of competition, CGM told me, was to make them cut back ruthlessly on uneconomic ships and routes. In 1977 the company owned ninety-seven ships; within three years this had been reduced to sixty-five, and by the mid 1980s they expect to own a mere forty. However, the amount of cargo carried has gone up dramatically, despite the reduction in ships. From three million tons of general cargo in 1977, CGM carried four and a half million tons last year. It is ships like the *Monet*, highly efficient and specialised, that have made this possible. 'And less time in port,' the CGM official added. 'We hope to get the ratio of sea time to port time up to 90:10. There has been a trend to cut crews to the minimum, but we will not cut much further because we will be sending more technicians to sea – men who can repair the ship while under way.' Captain Fenouil told me about one effect of this policy. In

France a man who hopes to rise to the level of captain is now expected to be a fully qualified engineer as well as a seaman and navigator. 'I think they hope that one man will be both chief engineer and captain – but I myself do not think this is possible.'

But however efficient shipping lines like CGM become, they find it difficult to compete with ships under flags of convenience. Lack of regulations means that Panamanian or Liberian ships can not only operate with a smaller crew, but they can pay them less. A French crew may cost fifty per cent more than a Liberian one. Many developed countries have tried to protect their fleets by subsidising shipbuilding and repair facilities. Nonetheless, many ships have been laid up – there are still numerous supertankers mothballed in Norwegian fjords; some have been sold or, on the if-you-can't-beat-them-join-them principle, re-registered under a flag of convenience. Thus many Liberian ships are in fact American- or European-owned.

The older vessels which are sold off by companies like CGM work their way down the shipping ladder until they become dilapidated and in some cases unseaworthy. Sooner or later they will almost certainly come under a convenience flag. Most worrying for countries like France and Britain which border busy waterways, more and more large ships and supertankers are coming under these flags. The French will not easily forget the disaster of the Liberian-registered *Amoco Cadiz*, which devastated miles of the North Brittany coast with a thick layer of oil. The British suffered the *Torrey Canyon* wreck and numerous smaller but exceedingly frequent spillages.

'Many Liberian and Panamanian ships are very well run,' repeated Captain Fenouil, 'but there are just enough madmen around to make me nervous about tonight.' The *Monet* was heading up channel towards the Straits of Dover, and for the first time in the voyage the captain looked tense. Ahead lay a passage eighteen miles wide which is transformed into a bottleneck by long sandbanks and shallow water. The lane for large ships coming down from the North Sea is only three miles wide, while the up-lane is five. Through this strait pass an average of 300 ships every day, while another 300 criss-cross the Channel carrying holidaymakers and cars between Britain and the continent. Among these 600 vessels will be about fifty oil tankers, and two of these will be over 200,000 tons. 'Most ships follow the proper flow of traffic,' said Captain Fenouil, 'but about five per cent do not. This is what makes it so dangerous.'

The *Monet* reported in to the French coastguard by radio as she entered the south lane and joined the stream of ships heading north-east. At Dover the British coastguards were monitoring the south-west flow of traffic on their radar screens. As darkness fell and a thousand lights appeared like stars around us, I contacted the Dover coastguard to ask them what we should expect in the way of traffic and hazards as we came to the narrowest section of the strait. It was a quiet night, I was told. At present there were no rogues about; no one going the wrong way up a one-way street. The only hazard was divers working on a submarine cable, but this area was well marked by buoys. However, marking dangers with buoys is no guarantee that ships will keep away. In 1971 there was a gigantic pile-up which, more than any other event, was responsible for making the traffic separation scheme compulsory. A tanker, the *Texaco Caribbean*, was in collision with a ship called the *Caracas* near the Varne Bank at four one morning. The *Caracas* was towed into port but the tanker exploded and sank. Though warnings about the wreck were broadcast a German ship ran into it and sank. The two wrecks were marked with buoys but the following month yet another ship ran into them and went down with the loss of her entire crew. Altogether almost sixty people lost their lives.

Staring out into the darkness from the *Monet*'s bridge, the array of shore lights, ships' lights, buoys, light vessels and lighthouses was dazzling. The captain pointed out various vessels he was keeping an eye on and returned to his vigil over the two radar screens, one showing relative motion, the other true motion. He was keeping track of every moving dot and relating it to the lights around. Each lane marker, whether buoy or light vessel, was identified by sight and radar, and then checked on the chart. Nothing was left to chance. As we neared Calais a rogue appeared, heading south-west down our lane, but fortunately he passed well clear. The coastguard cannot always identify rogues – this one would probably get away under cover of darkness – but in daylight they send out a spotter plane to discover the ship's name. If it's a foreign vessel, they report it to their national authority and hope they are prosecuted. 'Some nations are much more severe with their penalties than others,' added the coastguard significantly. Just as safety regulations are difficult to enforce, so are anti-collision rules. But France is one country that is getting very tough with ships that endanger her coasts; she is currently involved in litigation to recover some of the millions of pounds of damage caused by the *Amoco Cadiz*. The authorities most fear a collision involving a large oil tanker in the narrowest part of the strait. Not only could the resulting oil spillage ruin enormous areas of coastline, but the tanker might block part of a traffic lane or catch fire, endangering many other ships in the process. Only two years before, a British-run tanker nearly ran on to a bank when her gyrocompass, normally a most reliable instrument, went wrong. It was only because she was in touch with the coastguard that they were able to warn her of the danger. Although the captain did not at first believe his ship could be on the wrong heading, he finally checked his compass and turned his ship just minutes before disaster.

'The odds will eventually run out,' said the coastguard. 'It requires just one person to make a mistake.' Only strict international safety and manning laws, properly policed and enforced, can minimise the risk of human error. A few more disasters and some countries may insist that ships conform to basic standards before using their ports – but major collisions seem a high price to pay for a firm policy of enforcement.

The *Monet* was through the strait by dawn and Captain Fenouil could begin to relax a little. We met one further trouble spot where a lot of traffic was crossing the lanes, but then we were clear. Only as we waited at anchor off the Hook of Holland did he allow himself some sleep. The Hook lies at the mouth of a giant canal, opened in 1890 so that the then largest ships could sail the eighteen miles up the waterway to Rotterdam. Now there is an oil terminal opposite the Hook called Europoort, capable of taking today's giants of the sea, 500,000-ton tankers, which have to be half-discharged before they can sail through the shallow Dover Strait and into the North Sea. But general cargo still travels up the canal to Rotterdam and, once the *Monet* had been allocated a berth and a pilot, we sailed into the waterway bound for the largest port in the world.

Rotterdam has grown to handle one quarter of all the European Economic Community's seaborne trade because of its position at the mouth of the Rhine and Meuse rivers, gateway to the industrial heartland of Europe. In the thirteenth century it was no more than a small fishing village, but by the middle of the fourteenth century it had become a major port in European trade. Only the Second World War stopped its growth; the port was flattened first by the Germans then by the Allies. Reconstruction gave the Dutch the chance to build the finest complex of docks and facilities in the world.

The high bridge of the *Monet* provided a first-class platform from which to view the city as it appeared, a gaggle of cranes and tall buildings rising high over the flat lowlands around. With over twelve miles of wharves, ranging from container berths to coal, grain and iron ore quays, two large shipbuilding yards, two dry-dock complexes, more than 200 ocean-going ships and hundreds more barges and tugs, five oil refineries, and mile upon mile of containers, there is a lot of Rotterdam to see.

Here, finally, the consignment of tea that had come aboard in India was unloaded and slotted into the complex onward transportation system that would take it to its final destination. The 11,000-mile journey from Haldia had taken just five weeks, a fraction of the time it took in the early days of trade. The ship that had carried the tea was among the most efficient, functional vessels ever designed, a product of hundreds of years of development. However, trade has involved more than the exchange of goods, immensely important though that has been. Trade brought different peoples into contact with each other on an ever-widening scale and startling new skills and ideas were suddenly available to people whose lives had remained unchanged for centuries. For better or worse, the world has become dominated by Western techniques and to a great extent by Western ideas. From the time the explorers first discovered that the world was linked by sea, the might of power and commerce has imposed its mark on almost every community on earth.

The desire for wealth was the prime incentive in the growth of trade. Yet if profit was the end it was also the means; the richer that merchants became the more they invested in ships, ports and facilities to increase their wealth still further. But, as always, it was the skills of those who lived and worked on the sea that actually made it possible, men who are, even today, a breed apart. 'I think seamen are still not properly understood,' said Captain Fenouil. 'I think it is good if ordinary people can know what our lives are like. That is why I am glad you are making this film.'

However, trade and the exchange of ideas did not grow freely or without disagreement. In the ways of men, some wanted more land, trade and wealth than they already possessed. Others found it necessary to defend what they had managed to win, acquire or steal. Merchant ships could be armed to defend themselves against enemies, but the seas could more easily be dominated by ships specially designed for the job. Fighting ships had existed for centuries, but now they were organised into fleets of armed vessels whose purpose was to defend and further the interests of the maritime nations.

EAST INDIA COMPANY
WARREN TUTE

Eight separate and sovereign nations established East India Companies during the heyday of European exploitation of Asia from the end of the sixteenth century to the middle of the nineteenth. Only two, however, achieved size and importance: Holland and England, with France some way behind. The remaining five – Scotland, Denmark, Sweden, Austria and Spain – dropped out when the competition grew too hot. Surprisingly, the Portuguese never started one at all.

The English and Dutch East India Companies were incorporated within two years of each other – the English by Queen Elizabeth Elizabeth I in 1600 and the Dutch by the States-General in 1602, although on the ground in India and the Far East the Dutch were already in the lead. Both aimed at a monopoly of trade. In effect, therefore, a private war began and continued between the two companies for most of the seventeenth century. This trading war escalated into actual armed conflict between Holland and England at intervals throughout the same period.

East India Companies were brought into being to amalgamate and control a variety of private trading ventures. They were vigorously opposed by other companies and individuals already in the field, notably the English Levant Company which had been trading overland to Persia for some twenty years. Even when established, the companies could not police whole areas in which they operated. Privateering, therefore, continued. Monopoly was a hated word in Stuart England. To a certain extent there was room for all, but neither side gave the other an easy ride.

Both Dutch and English companies were successful from the start. Both Protestant nations were aggressive for trade and with their individuality and independence proved to be more than a match for the Catholic Portuguese who had been the first Europeans to reach the Spice Islands by sea. In the early days the Dutch went ahead, possibly because the English had wasted much time in the latter half of the sixteenth century in a fruitless search amid Arctic snow and ice for the North-West Passage to Cathay.

The first English voyages, known as 'separates', were privately backed by individual shareholders. By 1612, however, when trading posts or factories had been

European expansion eastward
Top: Jahangir sits surrounded by western attributes – including cupids and James I (copied from an English miniature)
Right: The Dutch capture of Laala, Ceram, in 1654

established in Surat, Masulipatnam and Pettapoli in India, and when even Japan had been reached, all voyages began to be financed by the Company as a whole. When these trading ventures began neither individuals nor governments had the capital resources to set up, protect and administer great empires. Nor did the British and, to a lesser extent, the Dutch want to conquest and empire as did the Spanish and Portuguese. They simply wished to trade. Both, however, later found that protecting their commercial interests more or less forced empire upon them.

In the early days John Company – as the Honourable East India Company was known colloquially – did not even own the ships in its service. The owner, known as the 'ship's husband', would sell the ship on completion to a Captain, whose transferable property it then became. The Company would charter the greater part of the space in a ship at stipulated rates, the remainder being at the disposal of the Captain for trade on his own account. This system lasted until 1796, only a few years before the Company's Indian monopoly was abolished. It made a large number of men rich but at the expense of rigged freight rates. With the intense competition of the industrial age it had to go.

The first Governor of the Company was Sir Thomas Smythe, known as 'Customer Smythe' because he farmed Queen Elizabeth's Customs. After seven years the staff still consisted only of a Secretary, a Book-keeper and a Beadle. However after 1710, both the English and Dutch companies grew at a tremendous rate. The Dutch at one time possessed forty warships and employed 10,000 soldiers to protect 150 merchant ships.

In those tentative years the English Company's factories in India were protected by the Islamic Mogul Emperors. 'A war and traffic are incompatible,' wrote Sir Thomas Roe, James I's Ambassador to the Mogul Court, and therefore trade was restricted to those areas which the Emperor could protect. By 1684, however, only ten years after a treaty of alliance of questionable value had been made with the warlike Hindu Federation of Mahrattas, the days of the 'fenceless factory' were over. 'Though our business is only trade and security,' the Company decided, 'and not conquest which the Dutch have aimed at, we dare not trade boldly nor leave great stocks where we have not the security of a fort.' These were the first steps to military and civilian control of the subcontinent of India.

Both Dutch and English Companies developed as a sort of half-way house between medieval private enterprise and the full state control of the twentieth century. Their Charters gave them certain tax exemptions and allowed them to own land, maintain an army and a navy, build and fortify trading centres, declare local wars and make local peace, exercise civil and criminal juris-

Life on board an East Indiaman – an engraving by George Cruikshank

diction, and perhaps most important of all coin their own money.

Right from the start it had proved impossible to sell more than a limited quantity of English woollen cloth in the hot climates of the Far East, as enemies of the Company were quick to point out. However, Elizabeth I and subsequent monarchs wisely allowed the Company to export a certain quantity of coin of the realm, provided that equivalent gold and silver bullion was returned after each voyage. This proved to be a happy device. In 1621, for instance, the £100,000 which had been authorised for export brought back oriental wares worth five times as much. A quarter of these wares was sold in England, the rest being exported to Europe at a great profit. Thus the treasure of the realm steadily increased.

In 1609 the Company set about acquiring its own dockyard at Deptford, where for over 200 years it built the lofty East Indiamen, universally regarded as lords of the ocean. These magnificent ships brought as much

prestige to the country as they did profit to the Company. Indeed it was observed with some force at the end of the eighteenth century that, if Warren Hastings and his successors could dominate all India, they owed their opportunity to the signal excellence of the Captains and sailors of the East India Company's ships which brought them out. Apart from good seamanship, this success was due to the Company's insistence that their Captains' first duty was to save the cargo and bring the ship safely to port.

To service this fleet of ships, the Company constructed the Howland Great Dock at Rotherhithe in 1696. For more than a century this was London's largest dock. Because the actual unloading of cargo was a legally guarded privilege of other quays, the Howland Great Dock was used for repairs and anchorage, since it could be locked against the tide. The dock extended over ten acres and was built by the owners of the land, the Howland family, following the marriage, at thirteen, of their only daughter Elizabeth to

HMS *Essex* about to be rescued by the Bombay Marine

An Indian miniature showing a functionary of the East India Company

the 14-year-old grandson of the first Duke of Bedford, himself to become the second Duke. It was from this dock that a certain Captain Clive sailed for India in 1755. The Howland dock, greatly enlarged, became part of the Surrey Commercial Docks on the demise of the East India Company in the mid-nineteenth century, and continued in operation as the Greenland Dock until 1970.

But trade was what really mattered, and at first the Dutch were well ahead both in the Far East and in Europe, where Amsterdam did not yield supremacy to London as the greatest port until the beginning of the eighteenth century. At the other end of the world the Dutch had begun by driving out, first, the Portuguese who, a century before, had aspired to monopolise the spice trade, and then the English who took their place.

The Dutch established their main capital in Batavia (Jakarta), adding regional sub-

sidiaries in the Malay archipelago, Ceylon, Java, Malacca, Amboina (Ambon) and Ternate. They also set up a fortified trading and staging post at the Cape of Good Hope to secure the route from Holland to the Far East. However, the military costs of enforcing this attempt at monopoly eventually bankrupted the Dutch Company and it was wound up when Napoleon invaded Holland in 1798.

The English concentrated on India. Charles II had married a Portuguese princess, Catherine of Braganza, who brought him Bombay as part of her dowry. After the Restoration in 1660 Charles leased this city of 60,000 to the East India Company for £10 a year and established Bombay, Madras and Bengal as the three 'presidencies' from which the native rulers of India were to be dominated and later subdued.

By about the beginning of the eighteenth

century the Dutch had been driven from the mainland of Asia and from Ceylon. Both British and Dutch Companies, by war and subsequent treaty, had begun to restrict themselves to territories they could effectively control. The British took over India (except for certain French areas); the Dutch strengthened their hold over the Far East. A state of armed neutrality existed for many years between the British Presidencies and the French in Madras, but Clive's victory at Plassey in 1757 during the Seven Years War put most European factories in India under John Company's domain.

In 1759 Clive suggested that the British Government should take over India but British politicians thought it more expedient (and less costly) to leave civil administration in the Company's hands, and it was not until after the Indian Mutiny, which began at Meerut in 1857, that the British Raj was

of equity and humanity which have their existence in the feelings of mankind that are capable of judging'.

Throughout its history the East India Company had always preferred trade to conquest. It discouraged Governor-Generals from territorial expansion even when there was no other way of resisting an enemy – the Mahrattas, for instance – except by destroying their military potential and taking their land. Indeed the Company was so hostile to the Marquess of Wellesley, elder brother of the future Duke of Wellington, who as Governor-General transformed the map of India in seven years, achieving settlements which were to the undoubted advantage of the populations concerned, that he resigned in 1805. His successor was forbidden to take on any new territorial responsibilities but saw at once that the pacification begun by Wellesley must be completed or abandoned. By 1814, therefore, the Mahrattas had been conquered and the Company, in spite of itself, was overlord of three-quarters of India. It has been well claimed that the British Raj was acquired in a fit of absence of mind.

But 1813 saw the beginning of the end. The Company's monopoly in India was cancelled and twenty years later its Chinese monopoly also ceased to exist. Just as the London Guilds lost their exclusive powers and indeed their *raison d'être* as a result of the industrial revolution and the fierce competitiveness it engendered, so the East India Company became an anachronism when trade with the sub-continent became a free-for-all and when their great sailing ships were replaced by the steamships of the Peninsular and Oriental Steam Navigation Company. The Mutiny in 1857 finished it off and the Company was formally dissolved in 1858.

A scene on the Hooghly by Thomas Daniell, 1788, shows trading and pleasure craft of native and European merchants. Records like these were supplanted by photographs – the firm of Bourne and Shepherd took both landscapes and scenes like the one below of the examination of a cargo of opium

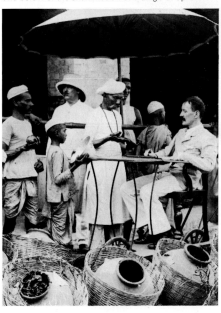

established in the form in which it continued until independence and the splitting of India into two countries in 1947.

By the time George III ascended the throne in 1760, the character and scope of British commerce had begun to assume the form it has today. This was in large measure due to the East India Company's success. A century before, wealthy Londoners had begun frequenting coffee houses such as Lloyd's to enjoy the fashionable new drinks brought over by the East India Company. Early in the reign of George III all classes in town and country were drinking tea in their own homes. Indeed, tea had begun to rival spirits and beer in popular esteem.

From then on the rich rewards of the London and Amsterdam markets tempted Company servants to amass private fortunes at the expense of their employers and the local inhabitants. The 'Nabobs' had arrived.

These rich adventurers were making and marring the reputation of the new Empire in India and they were disliked or envied by all classes in Great Britain. 'India', declared Chatham, 'teems with iniquities so rank as to smell to heaven and earth.'

Indeed, when one successful but arrogant Governor, Warren Hastings, set about making the rich merchants of Bengal pay for the protection under which they lived, an action which coincided with the arrival of a new generation of ambitious, sober and incorrupt young Scotsmen to administrative posts in India, the nabobs and the politicians in their pockets had Hastings impeached. This trial lasted seven years and all but bankrupted Hastings. In the end he was acquitted and India thenceforth began to be governed in accordance with Burke's declaration 'by those laws which are to be found in Europe, Africa and Asia . . . those principles

TRADE AND THE TRADING SHIP
ALAN McGOWAN

The development of the trading ship. Portuguese carracks from a painting of about 1520 (below left). Below: The earliest technical drawings of an English ship, by Matthew Baker, about 1585 – it incorporates the idea that a streamlined (fish-shaped) hull would be most efficient

Although I am mainly concerned with ships developed to carry the cargoes of the rapidly expanding trade of the seventeenth and eighteenth centuries, it is necessary to look also at warships. Except in the case of relatively small, specialised vessels, warships and merchant ships differed very little until towards the middle of the seventeenth century. Innovations in rig were the result of experiments in warships, where the sailing qualities were all-important; for the merchant vessel, whose existence largely depended on its ability to carry the greatest amount of paying cargo at the smallest cost, sailing qualities were far less important. Unless improved sailing enabled another voyage to be made in the season, it was of little consequence to the owner and he was not therefore inclined to experiment. In consequence new ideas were adopted in merchant ships only after their value had been proved in practice.

As a result of the great explorations in the last years of the fifteenth century, the first great oceanic trading nations were Portugal and Spain. The ships they used for most of the century were carracks: large, heavily-built and capacious, with beam, keel and length of deck in a ratio of 1:2:3. They had high fore- and after-castles which made them poor sailers and difficult to manoeuvre. Their rig was fairly simple: square spritsail, fore course, topsail main course and topsail, and a lateen mizzen sail.

Towards the middle of the sixteenth century the Spaniards developed the galleon, in which the forecastle was brought almost entirely behind the stem, a first step in improving the sailing qualities. This type of galleon formed the backbone of the fighting ships in the Spanish Armada. They were met in 1588 by a vastly improved version of the

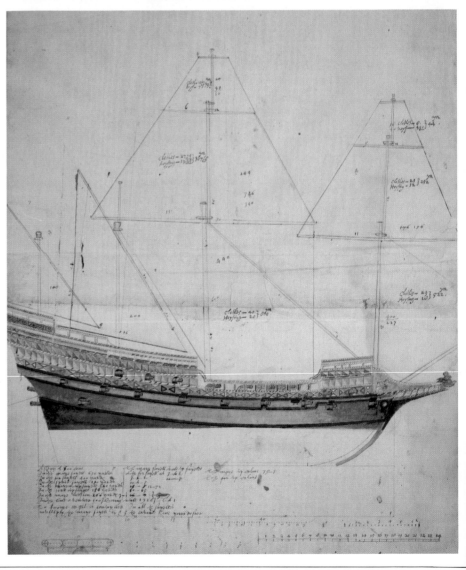

galleon which had been developed in England in the early 1580s. In these ships the height of the upperworks had been so reduced as to minimise windage and the sails given a much flatter cut, both measures which improved the performance to windward to a degree that astounded the Spaniards. As a result the form was copied by all the major seafaring nations of Europe.

In the seventeenth century the trend towards a straighter profile continued. The *Sovereign of the Seas* (1637) was the first 100-gun ship and the first also to have three continuous decks. Although not an unqualified success, she was the real prototype of the great ships of the line of the eighteenth and early nineteenth centuries.

While it is generally true that in the sixteenth and seventeenth centuries the warship was developed first by Portuguese and Spanish and then by English seamen, the cargo-carrying vessel was largely evolved by the Dutch. Early in the fifteenth century the northern provinces of the Netherlands produced the herring buss, specifically designed for fishing with the larger drift-net introduced at the same time. By the middle of the sixteenth century the herring buss could carry

An eighteenth-century Danish timber bark

A collier brig of about 1800 unloading her cargo

well over 100 tons of fish. Its rig was simple: three masts with one square sail on each. The hull form, with flat floors and bluff bows, was designed for maximum carrying capacity consonant with seaworthiness; speed and good sailing qualities to windward were of little consequence. Not least of its virtues was its ability to sit safely upright when grounded at low water, so permitting the loading and unloading of cargo over an open beach. The buss was an ideal cargo-carrier and a succession of similar types followed, the best known being the *fluyt*, introduced about 1600. With these vessels the Dutch dominated the carrying trades of Northern Europe as they had dominated the herring fishery from the late fifteenth century.

This pre-eminence in the carrying trades was broken by the success of England in the three Dutch Wars of 1652–4, 1665–7 and 1672–4. Ships of the *fluyt* type were captured in large numbers and sold cheaply to English owners. When these finally wore out, a new shipbuilding tradition arose in England to replace them, for until the late seventeenth century English shipbuilders had concen-

Charlotte of Chittagong, an Indian coastal trading vessel

trated on the construction of armed, defensible ships. These new vessels developed out of the *fluyt* and used first in the coal and timber trades, led to the north-country 'cat', the most famous example of which was Captain Cook's *Endeavour*.

Because of disputes with rival merchants from other countries, as well as the dangers from piracy, defensible ships had to be used in the trade with both the East and West Indies until the early nineteenth century. European and North American trade, on the other hand, was carried in undefended ships from the end of the seventeenth century.

By about 1710 the main pattern of rig had been established in warships: triangular headsails had replaced the spritsail topsail of the seventeenth century, being introduced soon after the wheel (*c*.1703), which made their use practical. Course, topsail and top-gallant sails were set on the fore and main masts, with a lateen sail on the mizzen mast and square topsail above it. Staysails were set between the masts and were increased during the eighteenth century. Merchant ships adopted innovations only as it became convenient and economical to do so; thus we find vessels in the middle of the eighteenth century still using the whipstaff, the wheel's cumbersome seventeenth-century predecessor.

There was a variety of rigs: coastal traders were one- and two-masted; deep-water vessels were three-masted as ships, or as barks after 1765, or two-masted as snows or brigs. In most trades the rig was kept as simple and easily handled as possible in order to minimise labour costs, while the average size of vessels suited to each type of rig steadily increased. By such economies, in British ships entering London between 1700 and 1766 the average amount of paying cargo carried per crew member increased by more than four tons. An example of simplifying rig may be seen in the development of the bark rig (*c*. 1765) in which the mizzen topsail was omitted. The eighteenth century shows an increasing use of fore-and-aft sails in square-rigged ships, which improved sailing ability and were labour-saving in that they could be handled without anyone going aloft. This trend is epitomised by the development of the schooner, which was no more than a very small coasting vessel in the seventeenth century, had become an established trans-atlantic cargo carrier 100 years later, and which, in the late nineteenth century with five or six masts, was to include the largest wooden ships ever built.

The four-masted schooner *Margaret Thomas*, built at Thomaston, Maine, in 1904

MODERN CARGOES
BASIL GREENHILL

The history of British merchant shipping in the nineteenth century has been much mis-understood. Usually the story is represented as one of slow attrition, with the merchant sailing vessel under continuous threat from the steamship throughout the century. In fact, until 1865 the steamship offered the sailing vessel no serious competition, except on passenger and mail routes which were government subsidised and on short sea routes around the coast and to the Continent. The reason was simple. The engines of early steam-ships used steam generated in primitive boilers at low pressures, and the steam was used once only in one cylinder. As a result they needed so much fuel for long voyages that there was not enough room left to carry any substantial quantity of the cargo which earned the vessel's profits.

So, as late as 1860, although the paddle

Above: The barque *Ellen* under tow, Norway, 1893. Steam could offer reliability, but efficient engines which allowed steamships to carry bulk cargoes economically were not developed until the second half of the nineteenth century.
Below: Clipper ships, unlike the big steel barques and the schooners, ceased to be competitive in the 1870s. This is the famous *Glory of the Seas* ready for launching. Her builder, Donald McKay, wears a top hat in the foreground

and early screw cargo and passenger steamers of the first-grade liner companies could operate profitably with a government subsidy for carrying the mail, and although steamers could make profits, for instance, in the coal trade between the Tyne ports and London, the ordinary merchant ship carrying the bulk of goods moved on deep water and was still a wooden barque of about 500 tons, or a two-masted schooner or brig of less than 100 tons. These ships were very little different from their predecessors of the 1820s or indeed,

in essence, from the ships of the 1760s. They were flat-bottomed, full-lined, narrow, deep vessels, rigged partly with iron wire by now, and often equipped with cotton canvas sails, but with wooden masts and spars. Speed was economically significant in only a few trades, and the tea clippers, fruit schooners and fast packet ships about which so much has been written represented only a tiny and, commercially, relatively unimportant fraction of world merchant-shipping tonnage.

But in 1865 Alfred Holt of Liverpool had three steamships, the *Agamemnon*, the *Ajax* and the *Achilles*, built with compound engines which used steam generated at sixty pounds per square inch, and used it twice over, in two cylinders, with the result that their coal consumption was less than a quarter of that of early steamers. They could travel to China in a regular sixty-four days against the uncertain ninety days of the best sailing vessels, and they could carry three times as much cargo. So the real decline of the merchant sailing vessel after her 400 years of pre-dominance was at last begun.

In 1881 the triple-expansion engine was developed, using the same steam three times over. Soon a steamer could carry one ton one mile by burning no more fuel than the equivalent of a sheet of heavy Victorian writing paper. Under the stimulus of this competition the sailing vessel in Britain developed out of all recognition, from the small wooden ship to the large steel four-masted vessel able to carry 5000 tons of cargo, while in America the great wooden four-masted schooners were built for the coal and timber trades.

The passenger liner, now able to make profits without subsidy, went through a similar revolution. Early passenger steamers had had their best accommodation in a stern cabin with windows looking out on the ship's wake – a relic of sailing ship days.

Above: The four-masted barque, *Lawhill*, one of the most successful later sailing ships, built in 1892, contrasts with the contemporary steamer, *Powhatan* (left), built in 1900. The little schooner *Susan Vittery*, seen in Falmouth Harbour with the *Powhatan*, was built in 1859 for the Azores orange trade

Above: The increasing luxury of travel by ship – the dining saloon of the *Lucania*
Right: The *Aquitania* on the stocks in 1914

Other accommodation was to be found in long deckhouses, standing between the high bulwarks like railway carriages in a cutting. But in 1870 the *Oceanic*, with a compact compound engine low in her hull, began the conversion of the passenger steamship into the travelling palace. Her principal accommodation was amidships and her dining saloon extended the full width of the ship. The old main deck was covered over with two further decks and the staterooms were much larger than anything seen at sea before. The model of the *Oceanic* was copied and developed into the great liners of the late nineteenth and the twentieth centuries, the *Lucania*, the *Himalaya*, the *Saxonia*, the *Aquitania* and *Mauritania*, and in due course the first 'Queens'.

The building of big sailing ships virtually stopped in Britain in 1897, though in North America and parts of Europe it continued until after the First World War. British sail tonnage, still over two million in 1900, was down to just over one million by 1910, with 10½ million tons of steamers. The *William Mitchell*, the last big deep-sea steel sailing ship owned in Britain, was broken up in 1927, and the last of the old wooden square-rigged ships, the *Waterwitch* of Fowey in Cornwall, ceased to sail in 1936. The Ålanders of Finland ended the history of the sailing ship in Europe with great steel vessels like the magnificent barques *Herzogin Cecilie*, and the *Pommern*, which is now preserved in Mariehamn, and the wooden *Sigyn* of Wårdö, now preserved in Åbo. These ships sailed until the late 1930s.

Meanwhile the turbine and the diesel engine had gradually developed to take over from the triple-expansion steam engine. After 1950 a great revolution, born of technical developments forced on during the Second World War, rapidly took place. In the early 1960s economical and efficient jet aircraft rapidly rendered the passenger liner uncompetitive and obsolete. But merchant ships generally have developed out of all recognition in the last twenty-five years. As costs have risen, vessels have grown bigger and bigger to benefit from the economies of scale; they have become more specialised and more efficient, needing small crews and less fuel, and spending less and less time in port where no money is earned. Gas carriers, giant tankers, container ships, barge carriers and car carriers, ore carriers, roll-on roll-off ships, have accompanied a total revolution in the world's cargo-handling methods. Merchant shipping today is the result of this great revolution rather than of the long evolution ending in the middle of this century.

The Atlantic run became the most prestigious of the passenger routes
Below left: The *Mauritania* in 1907
Left: Arriving in New York in 1955; by 1961 the first big jets could carry as many people across the Atlantic in one week as a liner at a fraction of the cost. The *Queen Elizabeth 2* (right) now plies as a cruise ship, and bulk carriers like the one below are, in size at least, the new rulers of the ocean trade routes

THE INSTITUTIONS OF THE SEA

ALAN PEARSALL

The most obvious aids to mariners are light-houses and lightships and the buoys which mark the entrance channels of a port. A ship will also, for the first and last stages of her voyage, take on a pilot with local knowledge of the approaches. In England and Wales, all these aids are supervised by that ancient body, the Corporation of Trinity House.

Founded by Royal Charter in 1513, probably on the framework of an earlier guild of 'shipmen', Trinity House was in 1594 granted powers over lights along the English coasts, many of which were nevertheless provided by private individuals and only gradually taken over by Trinity House. Even so, they remained relatively few in number until, in the early nineteenth century, much more attention was given to safety at sea. Trinity House established many new lights, its efforts being paralleled in Scotland and Ireland by independent Commissioners. Able engineers brought into being many fine works, particularly the great rock lights such as the Bishop Rock Light. While the majority of the present-day lights are creations of the nineteenth century, much technical progress has since been made in improving the efficiency and economy of the lights, and in adapting them for remote control. A few new lights have also been built.

The Longships lighthouse in Cornwall illustrates the great problems involved in building and maintaining rock lighthouses

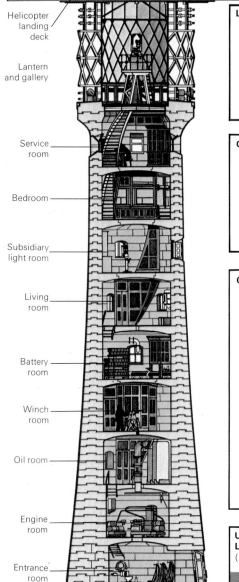

Helicopter landing deck

Lantern and gallery

Service room

Bedroom

Subsidiary light room

Living room

Battery room

Winch room

Oil room

Engine room

Entrance room

The International Association of Lighthouse Authorities. Combined Lateral and Cardinal System A (for Europe, Africa, India, Australia and most of Asia). (System B for N and S America, Caribbean and parts of Asia)
Lateral marks: Used generally to mark the sides of well-defined navigable channels
Isolated danger mark: To mark any small isolated danger with navigable water all round
Safe water mark: Used in mid-channel or landfall
Special marks: Any shape permissible
Cardinal marks: Used to indicate the direction from the mark in which the best navigable water lies, or to draw attention to a bend, junction or fork in a channel, or to mark the end of a shoal

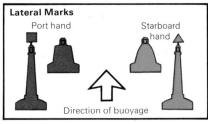

Lateral Marks
Port hand
Starboard hand
Direction of buoyage

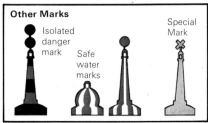

Other Marks
Isolated danger mark
Safe water marks
Special Mark

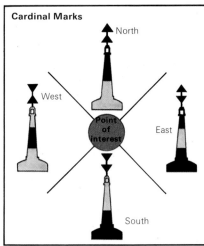

Cardinal Marks
North
West
Point of interest
East
South

Unattended Lightship
(21 metres long)

The optic of a lighthouse, showing lamps and lenses

From the outset Trinity House concerned itself with the qualifications for pilots, and became in the eighteenth century somewhat of a 'nautical adviser' to the Government, examining the Navy's navigators, the masters. In the early nineteenth century, it was given powers to supervise and license pilots, which it still exercises in many ports, although in some places there are local pilotage authorities. Pilots themselves, however, are regarded as self-employed.

The detailed examination of ships to ensure their seaworthiness is nowadays the concern of two organisations, one governmental, the other a non-profit-making corporation. The latter appeared first as an offshoot of those with a direct interest in the subject, namely the underwriters who insured ships and cargoes, a practice going back to medieval times. By the mid-eighteenth century, underwriters and others concerned with marine insurance had established Lloyd's Coffee House as an influential centre

A pilot coming aboard from a modern Trinity House pilot cutter, shore-based rather than working as before from a cruising cutter
Below: Lloyd's coffee house where marine insurance began to take its present form

for the profession, and in the 1760s a Register of Ships was established, providing also an assessment of the quality of each ship. Its advantages were also appreciated by merchants and shipowners, although rivals appeared at times. In 1834, the last of these was absorbed, and the Register became an independent body. Since then, it has greatly widened the scope of its information, and this has involved establishing standards of construction and maintenance of ships and the inspection by its own surveyors of hulls and machinery at all stages of construction and throughout a ship's life to maintain the 'class' which is allotted. From 1852 surveyors were appointed overseas, and, although other countries have established similar societies, Lloyd's Register of Shipping still leads, as does Lloyd's itself in the sphere of insurance.

The British Government department principally concerned with merchant shipping was the Board of Trade, now the Department of Trade and Industry. Its regulatory powers over shipping are largely a product of the mid-nineteenth-century concern over

A customs search – a magazine illustration of 1893

the poor state of the British mercantile marine. The first legislation requiring ships to meet certain standards was sponsored by the Colonial Emigration Commissioners in response to the many abuses practised upon emigrants. The Board of Trade first entered the fray with concern over the qualifications of officers, instituting voluntary examinations in 1845 and compulsory ones in 1850, in which year the Board set up a Marine Department. In 1854 a great Merchant Shipping Act consolidated previous legislation and added much new. The Marine Department continued its activity by instituting examinations for engineers in 1861, and establishing a Rule of the Road and the International Signal Code. From this beginning the Board's concern with shipping has grown wider and more detailed, and now involves much international negotiation in such matters as safety at sea, lifesaving equipment, wireless and radar standards, and the construction of ships, which the Board had left to Lloyd's Register until it became clear that legal powers were needed to cope with overloading and unseaworthiness. The outcome was Plimsoll's famous Load Line Act, for which the Board of Trade had to establish its own surveyor branch.

A cartoon from *Punch*, published in 1880 when Samuel Plimsoll, the great advocate of safety at sea, left Parliament

On its arrival at port or an inland destination cargo is subjected to the inspection of HM Customs and Excise, whose presence is equally familiar to the traveller overseas. The raising of revenue by taxing the commodity of trade is a very ancient 'custom', and to that was very soon added the task of enforcing controls or prohibitions either on particular goods or on those of particular countries, such as those embodied in the seventeenth-century Navigation Acts. These tasks remain the principal duties of the Customs, whilst the Excise concerns itself with internal duties such as those on spirits.

Above: A rescue made by the Ramsgate lifeboat,
powered by oars only, in 1860
Left: The St Ives lifeboat

Since 1671 Boards of Commissioners have controlled these departments.

A logical consequence of these activities is that attempts at evasion of duty are made, and in the eighteenth and early nineteenth centuries the Customs maintained a considerable force both ashore and afloat to prevent smuggling, and there are many stories of daring efforts to bring in wines and spirits across the Channel. Today's preventive forces are much different in character but nevertheless exist.

The Customs have many other tasks connected with the sea. Wrecks have always been their concern, and from 1786, when that registry was introduced, Customs officers acted as Registrars of Shipping. The Customs also became concerned with signing crews on and off, the collection of light dues, and the enforcement of much of the nineteenth-century legislation, as well as the supervision of immigration and emigration. Many of these duties are still performed by them.

A word should finally be said about lifesaving. The Coastguard, once mainly a watch against smugglers, increasingly became a lifesaving and patrol body during the nineteenth century, and since 1918 almost entirely so. It co-ordinates the efforts of its own men ashore, the lifeboats, administered by the Royal National Lifeboat Institution, still voluntarily funded, the helicopters and aircraft of both Navy and Air Force, and other ships, whether naval or merchant.

Chapter Four

SEAPOWER

There is a deafening roar, a sheet of flame, and a deep thud that sends vibrations through the vast length of the USS *Saratoga*; another $18 million plane has been catapulted into the air, reaching 150 knots in $2\frac{1}{2}$ seconds and disappearing quickly into the pale blue Mediterranean sky. Almost immediately, another jet is blasted off the angled deck, dipping slightly before it gains height. Pressed back in their seats by the iron hand of the 6G acceleration, the pilots momentarily suffer blacked-out vision and distorted features, but retain control to guide their planes on to the allotted course. Twelve aircraft can be launched at a rate of three per minute off four catapults. The four-acre flight deck is a scrum of running men, moving planes, walls of white steam, grey smoke – and noise, noise, noise. Men in green (technicians), men in white (in charge of safety), and yellow-jacketed controllers move about quickly but carefully. They get extra money for working on this dangerous airstrip; despite the water-cooled jet-blast deflectors which are raised behind each flame-belching exhaust, a man can be hurled across the deck if he's careless. Caught near a plane's air intake he will be sucked in and, in the words of one of the air controllers, 'never be returned as issued'.

Suddenly the noise stops. The neat array of parked, folded planes is moved, one by one, along the deck, in readiness for another group to land. In the tower the air boss – his official title – controls the incoming wing of aircraft, invisible to the eye but just minutes away. I am taken across the flight deck to stand with four men on a tiny platform sticking out from the side of the ship, my eye on a level with the flight deck and the arrester wires which will catch the planes as they touch deck at 130 knots. The men watch dials, talk into radios, press buttons, as each plane approaches. The buttons give the pilots either a green for safe to land or a red for overshoot. The first plane is coming in too high despite the lighted Fresnel lenses at the end of the runway which show the pilot the correct angle and descent path for a hook-up on the third of the four wires. The controller shouts into his radio and the plane lurches downwards as the pilot quickly adjusts height at a speed hovering on the manoeuvrable side of too slow. Then the craft is down and the engine roars as the pilot puts on full throttle, ready to take off in case of a missed wire. The plane jerks to a halt on the three-wire, the throttle is eased and the aircraft is quickly pulled over to the parking area. They land in quick succession now, some too high and catching the four-wire, one or two looking dangerously low, risking a landing on the curved ramp at the leading edge of the deck – a mistake few aircraft or men survive. But the conditions are good and no one misses, no one overshoots, although later there will be plenty of critical discussion as the pilots view their landing performance on video playback. A night landing in bad weather is the real test for pilots; adrenalin and heartbeat are at top level as they face fear, excitement, split-second decision-making. If they miss a wire and can't get airborne again, they must eject immediately or die. On this tour the *Saratoga* has lost four planes. The crews of three managed to eject; the fourth died when their plane missed the wires at night, caught the wing of a parked aircraft, turned over, and plunged off the flight deck into the sea.

While she is stationed here in the Mediterranean, the USS *Saratoga* is at sea for fifty per cent of the time. And at sea she exercises. Day and night, hour after hour, planes take off and land in giddy rotation, an endless succession of flying, maintenance and refuelling. This 1046-foot-long ship is a moving airfield. Most of her 4500 men are here to keep the airfield, the planes and the weapons they carry in working order, to fulfil the *Saratoga*'s function as central cog in the US Sixth Fleet. The flyers are the principal actors on this stage; they are the men who go off to fight, to exercise and to gather intelligence. The captain himself is a flying man who has had a two-year training in running, handling and navigating a ship before taking this job. Admiral Sanderson, Commander of Task Force 60, the fighting-ship arm of the Sixth Fleet, is also a pilot.

The United States Navy is as far from the traditional Nelsonian navy as you can go. By official proclamation the men call their ship 'it' rather than 'she' – although a few forget from time to time. They often refer to the navy as 'the military'. Most of the crew are technicians, engineers, operations men; few are seamen. Nowadays it is more important to be able to fix an aircraft's radio transmitter than tie a bowline, and to refuel a $30 million reconnaissance plane than to steer a course. In one respect the aircraft carrier operates in the same way as the medieval warship. In those days, war at sea was carried out by soldiers; sailors merely worked and navigated the ship in order to transport them from place to place. On the aircraft

he flight deck of the USS *Dwight D. Eisenhower*

carrier the sailors' job is to move the floating airfield around so that the fighting men, the flyers, can operate.

The *Saratoga* is one of thirteen carriers in the US Navy, but when I visited the Sixth Fleet she was the only one present in the Mediterranean. She wasn't meant to be – the principal warship should have been the *Nimitz*, one of America's three nuclear-powered maxi-carriers. But the thin blue line of US power is stretched; the *Nimitz* had been called to the Indian Ocean supported by two cruisers. Task Force 60 was reduced to one carrier and twelve cruisers, destroyers and frigates. The submarine fleet must have been similarly reduced, but no one was saying by how much. Normally the Sixth Fleet, which includes amphibious craft, service ships and surveillance vessels, as well as fighting ships and submarines, numbers about forty-five vessels, 200 aircraft and 23,000 men. The total strength of the US Navy in 1980 was 1123 ships and auxiliaries, of which 202 were frigate size or above; the largest fleet in the West and, although reduced from its World War II numbers, still an impressive force. It is also a very expensive one to run. Yet now, as for much of history, major powers consider a navy to be an essential tool of national policy, a political weapon with which to further their aims, or thwart the ambitions of their enemies.

National navies organised along modern lines did not appear until the Age of Discovery. Before that time countries generally banded together groups of ships as and when they needed them, or permitted merchant vessels to operate in their name against enemies – piracy, murder and pillage were endorsed and encouraged by many. Some early navies were well organised, however, and pursued distinct aims; those of Greece and Rome, for instance, were used to enlarge and defend empires. But for the most part fighting ships were manned by lawless, uncontrolled marauders. Only with the rush for control of the newly-discovered sea routes around the world did navies become firmly established as instruments of national policy.

Today the political aim of the West is, in simple terms, to deter war by achieving a balance of power with the Soviet Union. Peace is the objective and, according to Admiral Sanderson, 'Our job is to be *ready*, and to *be* here. Readiness and presence; these are the functions of our navy in peacetime.' With a depleted force, the admiral's job is difficult, but he and his men take it very seriously. Seeing the pitch with which the day-to-day exercises are carried out and sensing the atmosphere of tension and purpose, you realise that for them the front line still exists. As far as they are concerned, war might be just days away, an attitude that a peace-loving observer like me finds rather frightening, but one that is necessary to them if they are to remain at a peak of readiness. 'Our essential problem', said the admiral, 'is reaction time. And that's what we're working at.' In the era of missiles and jet aircraft, a defending force has no time to make elaborate plans; it must defend itself immediately or be lost.

When the *Saratoga* is not at sea working on her readiness and her reaction time, she is carrying out her second peacetime function – presence. The ship's symbol is a fighting cock, appropriate for a vessel which spends half its time on display, in the hope of creating good will and influence where it is needed in the ports of allies, neutrals and countries that might favour a Western alliance. During visits, the ship puts on her best plumage in the form of colourful flags and awnings, impresses the opposition by her size and strength, and promotes concord with the local population by friendly gestures and the spending of dollars. But it is not only in port that presence is required; one of the most important jobs of the Sixth Fleet is to establish itself in areas where the free movement of ships might be threatened. The concept of the freedom of the seas is an old one, largely created – and enforced – by the powers who stood to gain most from trade. Today, a worldwide shortage of fish and the realisation that mineral wealth may lie under the sea floor is leading many countries to claim 200-mile limits around their coasts. But some nations are trying to extend their rights beyond fish and oil, and are demanding that peaceable foreign warships ask permission before entering their 200-mile waters. 'We go right in there and show them that we don't buy that idea.' says Admiral Sanderson. 'We just anchor off their coast for a few days every few months.' The US Navy also uses favourite Russian anchorages regularly, 'just so they don't begin to think they own the place'. One area of particular interest is the Black Sea which, the admiral maintains, would quickly become a Soviet pond if the US didn't go there regularly. After asking permission from the Turks to pass through the Bosporus and Dardanelles (the Russians also have to ask permission to go through), American ships enter the largely Soviet-bordered sea to visit Constanta in Rumania.

The Sixth Fleet's area of operations is a particularly sensitive one; not only does it touch Russia itself but also many of the countries Russia would like to influence. Here at the meeting point of East and West the two superpowers are locked in a battle of prestige and influence. Naval leaders and politicians alike have no doubt as to the importance of this bloodless war. As the Greek statesman, Themistocles, wrote around 480 BC: 'He who commands the sea has command of everything.' It was Themistocles who led the Athenians to victory over the Persians at Salamis. Throughout history domination of the sea has been an essential adjunct to domination of the land. Once a nation has lost its sea power, defeated by an enemy navy or suffering a decline in its capabilities, its victories ashore have been short-lived. Historians are emphatic on this point; there has been no exception. Apparently the USSR has learnt the lesson, for she is in the process of building the largest navy in the world, intent, the Americans say, on gaining influence over weak countries, particularly in the Third World, on establishing naval bases wherever she can, on controlling trade routes, and eventually on dominating the world. 'Grab a little here, pinch a bit there . . . they'll have us in no time!' said one sailor who had no doubts as to the opposition's intentions.

The importance of sea power to wealth and prosperity was never more apparent than in the mid-nineteenth century, when Great Britain had the largest navy the world had ever seen. This vast force supported a merchant navy whose tonnage exceeded that of all other countries put together. After Nelson's defeat of the Franco-Spanish fleet at Trafalgar, and before the rise of the rival German, American and Japanese fleets towards the end of the century, the British navy dominated the world trade routes and helped the country to exploit its empire to the full. Queen Victoria's Diamond Jubilee Fleet Review in 1897, when the British Navy paraded off Spithead, was a staggering show of naval strength. Seeing the scratchy old films of the event today, line upon line of mighty battleships steaming in formation, one can only be impressed by the enormous force collected in one small stretch of water. Yet it was the swansong of Britain as the supreme naval power; the Germans built a fleet to rival that of the British, and since then no single nation has ever dominated the seas. The British knew the importance of display in achieving their objectives; they showed the flag around the world, just as Admiral Sanderson was doing in the Mediterranean. Only now the US does not have as many flags to fly as it would like. Ship for ship their navy is outnumbered by the fast-growing Soviet fleet and the threat of Russian domination is a very real one.

'And their navy has changed from a defensive role to an offensive one,' says the admiral. At the end of World War II the USSR had a small navy designed to operate near their coasts. Then came Cuba, humiliation, and a determination to have an effective deep-water navy. Not only have they built a large number of ships quickly, but the sophistication of their technology is beginning to catch up with the Americans'. On slides projected against the wall of his day cabin, Admiral Sanderson pointed out the Soviet Kresta-class cruiser, which brims with no less than nine weapons systems ('they've got so much fire-power there can't be much room for the men on board'); the Kara-class cruiser, which is gas-turbine driven like the most advanced frigates in the Royal Navy; submarines – they have a staggering 313 against the Americans' 122 and they are turning out new ones at the rate of two a month; and countless intelligence-gathering ships, known as AGIs. Until recent years the Russians were behind on two fronts: they could not refuel while under way at sea but had to stop and moor alongside a fueller; and their submarines had to surface to fire missiles accurately at precise targets. The first defect has been remedied: Soviet warships are no longer sitting ducks when refuelling, but steam alongside their supply ships in the manner perfected by Western navies. The Russians are still working on the second problem, to guide missiles accurately from beneath the surface, 'but it's only a matter of time,' the admiral stated bluntly.

The aircraft carrier, unwieldy and some say undefendable against modern weapons, is still the magnificent centrepiece of the US navy. The theorists argue that carriers would be the first to be blown up in an all-out war, but strategists increasingly believe that limited war, involving specific targets and conventional or small nuclear weapons, is more likely. Carriers would be central to this kind of action, just as they were in World War II. Certainly the Russians think so; they are building their largest carrier yet, a ship of over 60,000 tons, which will join their existing fleet of two aircraft and two helicopter carriers, and greatly extend their air power. The defence of the *Saratoga* does not seem to worry Admiral Sanderson. Around the ship is a ring of frigates and destroyers, unseen over the horizon, whose job is to protect the carrier and her aircraft from attack, particularly from the most deadly of modern warships, the submarine. 'If the enemy gets past them we can still defend ourselves,' he maintains; 'whatever they throw at us, we have a counter-weapon. Everything has its antidote.'

Today the counter-weapons are incredibly sophisticated and extremely expensive. One surface-to-air missile can cost $8 million. Sailors talk in a rich jargon of baffling phraseology to describe their jobs and the complex electronics and mechanics they control. The essential functions of navies remain unchanged; it is only the techniques that have altered, and with increasing rapidity. Ships die not only from old age, but from obsolescence. Each new idea is superseded by another as each power seeks to outmanoeuvre its enemy. The *Saratoga* is an old ship now – she was launched over twenty-five years ago in 1955 – but she has been maintained as an effective fighting unit by frequent and expensive refits. Her original designers could never have imagined the amount of equipment and weaponry that would be pushed into her frame, nor indeed the number of men – 1000 more than she was built to carry. Soon the *Saratoga* will go in for yet another service extension programme at the staggering cost of $526 million, twice her original cost. Obsolescent equipment and systems will be removed or improved, and living quarters will be made more tolerable. But, expensive though these changes are, they are nothing compared to the replacement cost of such a ship. Built to the same high standard, the *Saratoga* would cost $4500 million today – twenty times her original cost. The latest addition to the US carrier fleet is the nuclear-powered *Carl Vinson* and, though she does not possess the same armour-plated, double-skinned, hulk-like quality of a 1950s' ship, her cost is over $1700 million. These

Top: USS *John F. Kennedy* steaming at thirty-five knots
Bottom: The steam catapults fire aircraft to a speed of 150 mph within 130 feet; the arrester hook of one of the planes in the foreground on the left

massive amounts of money reflect not only inflation but the sophistication of the myriad of complex systems in the modern ship. While Nelson's ships bristled with guns, the warship of the 1980s bulges with electronics and computers. Cost is the greatest limiting factor on the technological development of the warship, and indeed on the size of navies. Every advance costs millions in terms of research, development, installation and adaptation.

An early nineteenth-century engraving of the interior of a midshipman's berth

The other great limitation is the ordinary seaman. For centuries the sailor's job was to sail ships and fire guns, but now over sixty per cent of the *Saratoga*'s crew are technically-skilled ratings whose work is complex and demanding. Most often their jobs affect the safety of their fellow men and even the whole ship; never before have seamen had to be so highly trained or responsible. However, with the abolition of the Draft it is difficult for the US to attract men of the right calibre into the armed services; skilled men can earn twice as much in jobs ashore and without the disadvantages of life at sea. After the Vietnam War the popularity of the navy in relation to the other services fell and it is now the Air Force which collects the most volunteers; 'because it's largely home-based and least likely to see action,' the *Saratoga*'s captain explained. Aboard the carrier manning levels are about ten per cent down and in some departments as much as twenty per cent. For example, the engineering department has charge of the four main engines, each producing 70,000 hp, as well as a mass of subsidiary generators, pumps and motors. It must ensure that the ship can produce its maximum thirty knots or, for flying operations, a steadier twenty knots or so; 350,000 gallons of water must be desalinated each day once the shore-loaded supply has run out; steam pressure must be maintained for the catapults; hot water and ventilation must be provided for the men. The engineering systems are vital to the ship, yet the chief engineer has only eighty per cent of the men he needs. Also, turnover in skilled men is high; they come in for training, then leave for better jobs ashore. The skilled men who remain end up doing two jobs, their own and the trainees'. 'My men work a twelve- to sixteen-hour day,' said the chief. 'Sometimes longer when there's a job to be done.' The skilled men who stay in the navy work for the love of it; down in the propulsion spaces it is hot, steamy, noisy and, amid the web of pipes, boilers and condensers, cramped. After a long day, a man just wants to eat and sleep before starting work again. Once, it is said, there was a man who never saw daylight for six weeks. 'The work *is* hard,' said a young trainee engineer, 'but I like it that way. It's a challenge and real satisfying. And sure, I *do* make the effort to get up top and see the sky.'

Overcrowding, long hours, moderate pay; not surprisingly the US Navy collects its fair share of roughnecks and no-goods. The chief petty officer in charge of the Human Resources Department observed, 'Enlistment depends on the economic situation, the prestige of the military, and the need for a military.' At the beginning of the 1980s all these factors are contributing to a low level of recruitment. A ship of 4500 men is a small town, a micro-society. 'Like in every society we have a small percentage of hoodlums and thugs,' said Captain Flatley, commanding officer of the *Saratoga*. 'It's always the same men who get into trouble.' But the Navy tries hard to keep its men on the straight and narrow, as well as happy and motivated. The Human Resources Department offers college courses given by civilian university professors on board the ship; training methods are studied to make learning easier for the men (they find that most recruits cannot cope with the written word and absorb information from slides and spoken words more readily); drug and alcohol rehabilitation courses are provided ('a new treatment of old problems; we try to stop them at the top of the hill rather than sending an ambulance when they get to the bottom,' said the chief of department). The food is plentiful and all-American: Coke, hamburgers and ice cream abound. Every night there's a different film showing in seven different parts of the ship; and there are two shops, a library, gym, TV station, chapel, and a fast mail service home.

It is not only the ordinary seamen's abilities which limit the efficiency of a large, complex ship like a carrier, it is the managers', too. The *Saratoga* is run like a corporation rather than a warship. She has an executive officer – akin to a managing director – who sits behind a desk, does much of his business by telephone (there are 2300 on the ship) and has department heads reporting to him. Normally he works office hours and has a large In tray full of papers. He is, in effect, running a community, all of whom have to be fed, accommodated, clothed and entertained ('Call me a hotel manager'). He is in charge of keeping the ship supplied – no easy task when producing 15,000 meals a day. But the greatest problem – and the ship's most vulnerable need – is fuel. She uses an incredible 660,000 gallons a day, half to power the ship and half the aircraft, and is refuelled every third day. (Not including wages, the running costs of the carrier are $1 million per day.) But keeping the *Saratoga* at sea is only one part of the problem. The introduction of new techniques into systems that are already incredibly complex makes enormous demands on management. The ship's operational systems – the gadgets and machines that are used to find, track and destroy the enemy – have to be constantly updated and improved. Procedures must also be kept under review. So sophisticated is the new technology that, in terms of cost, Admiral Sanderson says, 'you're talking megabucks.' But the money is ill spent unless the systems can be well installed, properly implemented, and capable of repair.

'We rely on sophistication to make up for our lack of numbers,' says the admiral. 'But once you add NATO's forces, we have the numbers too. Let there be no doubt, we are committed one hundred per cent to NATO.' In the Mediterranean, America's NATO allies do not have large navies but the admiral insists that the contribution of even the small gunboat navies is invaluable. 'Only the Greeks have vessels suitable for hunting and hiding among their own islands.' However, the fact remains that the US shoulders most of the burden here.

The situation is different in that other great theatre of sea power, the North Atlantic, where eight nations share the responsibility for defence. About once every two years NATO stages a major exercise there; I was now leaving the *Saratoga* to follow Exercise Ocean Safari, involving 17,000 men, seventy ships and 200 aircraft.

During my visit to the *Saratoga* (I had, incidentally, been allowed to stay overnight, despite my sex), I had hardly seen a tenth of the ship – probably less. But then she has more than 1500 compartments and even the longest-serving crew members haven't been in all of them. 'There are many new recruits who are just plain terrified of a ship this size,' I was told. 'They say some men never venture out of their own section all the time they're aboard.' There is a system for finding your way round such a ship – each compartment is numbered according to its deck, its location in relation to the 245 frames of the vessel, and its distance from the centreline to port or starboard. The system works, but it takes quite a time to get used to it. As I prepared to leave I was grateful for an escort up to the flight deck – otherwise I might have missed my flight by an hour or two.

I had arrived on the ship from Sicily by helicopter – or heelo, as the US Navy calls it – but now I was to leave by turboprop aircraft which, though it normally took off under its own power, was on this occasion to be catapulted off the deck due to lack of space. Wondering if my insurance covered this kind of thing, I donned crash helmet and life jacket and, on getting into the plane, was told to strap myself into the backwards-facing seat. When the nose tilted up, that was the signal that we were about to go, and I must lower my head otherwise my neck would snap forward. After what seemed a long wait the plane finally got into position, the nose tilted up, someone shouted 'OK, here we go!' and, quite suddenly, the world disappeared for a second or so. My body was flung against the seat belt and I felt as if I'd been fired from a cannon like a leotarded lady in a circus act – which I had in a way. Being fired off the deck in a jet at twice the speed was unimaginable; it was a sensation I had no ambition to try!

As the plane banked to the north towards Sicily I could see the *Saratoga* beneath me, her long, anvil-shaped body steaming steadily through the blue sparkle of the Mediterranean waters. Minutes later we passed over a frigate, one of the carrier's protectors, even now keeping a watchful eye on possible enemies. Not an easy job when the Sixth Fleet's responsibilities cover more than a million square miles of ocean, bordered by a number of politically sensitive countries and a dozen potential trouble spots.

The task of NATO in the North Atlantic is more clear-cut, yet just as difficult to achieve. Northwood, England, is the headquarters of Admiral Sir James Eberle, who is Commander-in-Chief of the Royal Navy's Fleet as well as one of the three major NATO commanders. He has special responsibility for the Channel and Eastern Atlantic. He explains the importance of the North Atlantic: 'It is the key link between the powerhouse of America, with her enormous economic and military resources, and ourselves here in Europe.' The main purpose of the NATO Atlantic fleets, and of large exercises like Ocean Safari, is 'to show the Soviets that if war should come we could still get the necessary supplies and reinforcements from America to Europe'. If the USSR is not convinced of this, then the West's policy of deterrence fails. What makes the defence of the Atlantic so critical is the West's dependence on trade. 'For the West, the use of the sea is essential for our economic survival. For the Soviets this is not so.' The United Kingdom, in particular, relies very heavily on international trade for her food and raw materials; this makes her particularly vulnerable to warfare that cuts her supply lines. Yet she is a vital rear base in NATO's defence strategy; in a European war Britain would serve as a giant depot, airfield and missile launcher from which to attack the enemy on the European continent. Equally important is Norway, a territory that would give the Soviet Union a long and valuable coastline. Countries like Britain and Norway die if their trade dies.

The need to defend sea trade led to the birth of the first nationally-organised navies. The protection of merchant shipping and the free use of trade routes was – and is now – a primary function of sea power. Spain, Portugal, then the Netherlands and England tried to establish their trade monopolies through the power of their fighting ships. Spain's hold over the Americas began to decline after the defeat of her Armada off England in 1588. Fighting between the other three trading nations continued until the early nineteenth century; the English and Dutch fought no less than three wars for control of the East Indies during the seventeenth century. In the end it was Britain that emerged as the greatest naval power, enabling her to consolidate her position as the world's major trading nation.

Today the merchant vessels of every country can move freely across the seas because no one nation dominates the oceans to the exclusion of others. Peace has come through the balance of power between the Soviet Union and the NATO allies, and nowhere is the balance more critical than in the North Atlantic. Because Europe is so dependent on the movement of raw materials and food and Russia is not, the Soviet build-up threatens to exploit our weakness while they stand to forfeit nothing themselves. Most naval commanders I talked to are convinced that it is Russia's intention to press any advantage she may gain. All quote history; they believe that the present Soviet threat is merely an extension of Russia's long-held imperialistic ambitions which date back to the Tsars. Nowadays these aspirations are bound up in an ideology which serves to make them stronger.

The Soviet Union has an impressive naval force based on its northern coast. It is, says Admiral Eberle, 'one of the most powerful fleets in the world'. However, NATO does hold some of the cards, thanks to geography. The Russian Baltic fleet has to pass through the narrow straits between Denmark and Sweden to get into the Atlantic, an exit that is closely controlled by NATO. Its Northern Fleet which is based around the Arctic port of Murmansk is not so tightly constrained, but it still has to sail into the Norwegian Sea and through one of the gaps in the Greenland-Iceland-Faroe-Shetland chain to reach the open Atlantic. It is the control of this second exit that NATO's North Atlantic forces are working on. The purpose of a major exercise like Ocean Safari, says Admiral Eberle, is to test the effectiveness of NATO procedures and tactics that would come into play in times of tension or war. A key part of the exercise would be the passage of military supply and reinforcement shipping from North American ports across the Atlantic to the Norwegian Sea in the face of determined attacks by 'enemy' forces – NATO forces in disguise, of course. Each of the seventy ships and 200 aircraft had been allotted a role, friendly or unfriendly, and are ignorant of their opponents' strategy. It was to be an enormous game played with expensive toys – but a very realistic one and, if the strategists are right, a vital one too.

HMS *Blake* is with the friendly 'Blue' force. She is the last of the Royal Navy's cruisers and, in an effort to extend her usefulness, has been converted to carry helicopters. Originally, in the days of sail, cruisers were fast ships which were used for reconnaissance. By the early twentieth century, the battle cruiser, combining speed with the carrying of large guns, had been developed. There is no role for the big-gun cruiser in the modern navy – much smaller vessels like frigates can carry light but immensely powerful weapons in the form of missiles, and, by using gas-turbine propulsion, can maintain high speeds for long periods. Even as a helicopter carrier *Blake* is not efficient by today's standards; a new breed of ships purpose-built to carry vertical take-off aircraft and helicopters is coming into commission. *Blake* has outlived her usefulness. This will be her last major exercise before she is decommissioned and sent to the scrapyard, a victim of age and obsolescence.

Originally laid down in 1942, work on *Blake* was suspended at the end of the war and she was not finally commissioned until 1961. Approaching her by helicopter, you get some idea of how elegant she must have looked when she was launched. Her forward section is slim and clean, her decks uncluttered except for two large gun turrets. But her aft section is an aesthetic disaster: a tall, square hangar and landing platform have been added to the afterdeck. 'It's our secret weapon actually,' said the commanding officer, Captain Mackenzie. 'The enemy don't know which way the ship is going.' I was also to hear *Blake* described as 'a frigate towing a garage'. The hangar contains four Sea King anti-submarine helicopters, while the ship's main armament consists of two Seacat missile launchers with four missiles each, two 6-inch and two 3-inch guns. The 6-inchers are the last big-calibre guns in the Royal Navy.

Crammed into *Blake*'s 538-foot length are more than 800 officers and ratings – as on the *Saratoga*, the increasing numbers of men needed to handle the sophisticated technology has led to overcrowding. But there's no doubt that the crew love her. 'She's always been a very happy ship,' says Captain Mackenzie, 'and a ship with real character.' *Blake* was built with two expansion joints in her and as she goes along the hull flexes, leaving a wake that is not straight but wiggly, a characteristic which has earned her the affectionate nickname 'Snakey Blakey'.

Most of the officers are attending a briefing on the role *Blake* is to play in Ocean Safari. This ship is part of Task Group 408.1, whose first job in the two-week exercise is to guard the gap between the Shetlands and the Faroes. A convoy of merchant ships is on its way from America to Norway and the Blue forces must protect it from the enemy, who will try to slip through the gaps and sink the merchantmen before they reach Europe. The opposition's principal weapon is the submarine, and *Blake*'s main job will be to track and kill any she finds. She must also keep an eye open for surface ships of which there will be both pretend-Russians and real Russians. The real Russians want to have a close look at the exercise, to learn all they can about NATO operations; to this end there are twenty Soviet ships in the area, some warships, some support vessels, and the rest AGIs, ostensibly involved in research or fishing, but easily identifiable by the mass of radio antennae with which they hope to pick up NATO signals. The exercise is a game within a game. Later, when I went aboard a Royal Navy frigate for a day, we came across an AGI and circled it. No one waved, no one shouted; the crews of each ship just lined the decks and stared at each other in eerie silence. It was rather a chilling scene.

Aboard *Blake* the ship is in an official state of 'tension' or readiness. The operations room hums with activity as men peer over dim-lit machines in the darkness, watching blips and tracks on radar screens. Each dot is tagged with a code number, identifying every vessel as Blue, Orange, Soviet or innocent merchantman. High in the sky overhead Nimrod aircraft equipped with long-range radar sweep the seas, pinpointing and identifying every object for miles around. Even higher, satellites probe the surface of the oceans with cameras, listening devices and a host of secret equipment. It is because aircraft carriers are such large targets, so easily found, that they are said to have outlived their usefulness. During a Sixth Fleet exercise the *Saratoga* had managed to hide for one and a half days, one of her men had proudly told me, but he admitted that, even with radar and communications closed down, the ship cannot hide indefinitely from such devices as the heat detectors carried by Soviet reconnaissance planes. Even the smaller warships like minesweepers can be sought out in this way. Aircraft sent in support of surface vessels are also tracked on radar over hundreds of miles. Nothing on or above the surface is safe. Only the shadowy, sinister submarine can move around the earth in secrecy. As Admiral Eberle says, 'The main Soviet threat is their submarine fleet. If we had to fight another large-scale war it would be against the submarine.' The Russians would probably say that they have been forced to build a large submarine fleet to counter the threat from NATO's, a threat that has far outweighed anything the West could muster before. There are several ways that nuclear weapons can be launched at an enemy but only the submarine can lob a missile at a city or military target from an unknown location before anyone realises it. Similarly, it can slink up on an enemy warship or merchant vessel and destroy it before a defensive shot can be fired.

A Royal Navy Wessex helicopter investigates a Russian warship during a NATO exercise in 1978

The submarine is the king of modern sea warfare. It is the latest in a long line of what have been, in their day, invincible vessels. From the time of the early fighting ships there has usually been one design and type of vessel that has been master of all others. From about 3000 BC until as late as the eighteenth century the oared galley, armed with a ram and later guns, was the principal fighting vessel of the Mediterranean. In Atlantic waters the galleon, a streamlined version of the sixteenth-century three-masted sailing ship, sailed rings around ships that were encumbered by high forecastles. By the seventeenth century the ship-of-the-line – generally a vessel carrying more than seventy guns – had been developed solely for warfare. Iron-clad battleships had their day but were in turn superseded by the dreadnoughts which, combining speed with big guns, outclassed all other warships in one sweep. But even their days were numbered by the arrival of the aeroplane for they were particularly vulnerable to air attack. The aircraft carrier then became the capital ship of most navies, but now it too is vulnerable and the submarine has taken its place.

After three days patrolling the Shetland-Faroes gap watching for submarines, HMS *Blake* will go to meet some of the merchant ships which are crossing the Atlantic, escort them to Scapa Flow in the Orkneys and then to Norway. Again, her principal task will be to seek, track and kill submarines. Her primary weapons are the four Sea King helicopters which carry radar, sonar, and torpedoes with automatic homing devices. In the main operations room, men are plotting the position of known submarines and surface ships on two tables: one for vessels within a twenty-mile range; the other for those farther away. At the other end of the room they are plotting aircraft movements.

Blake does not carry sonar herself; she relies on her four helicopters to sweep the waters around her for signs of approaching submarines. Even then, she relies on information from other sources for most of her initial contacts. 'The best anti-submarine platform,' says Admiral Eberle, 'is the submarine itself.' It is a case of setting a thief to catch a thief. The admiral rates the nuclear submarine as the most significant development in naval warfare since the last world war. The great weakness of the conventional submarine is that it must surface regularly to use air for recharging its batteries; and then it is detectable. The nuclear submarine, on the other hand, can stay submerged indefinitely. It can also sustain high speeds for a long period of time – although it's rather noisy when going flat out. More usually, the nuclear submarine cruises at moderate speed, making as little noise as possible, and hiding where she can.

How exactly do subs hide, I asked? And how, if at all, can they be detected? These were the two questions that received the least answers. The methods used to track and destroy surface and air units can, it seems, be revealed, but anything to do with submarines is, like the vessels themselves, shrouded in secrecy. But the basic tactics of the game *are* generally known. To search each other out submarines use magnetic anomaly detectors, and passive and active sonar. They can significantly reduce the likelihood of their own detection by placing themselves in a cold-water layer, which deflects the opposition's sonar. These cold layers are created by the meeting of ocean currents of different temperatures, in this case the warm Gulf Stream and the cold Icelandic current. Subs can also hide behind mountains rising from the sea floor. Here in the North Atlantic the subsea terrain is pitted with ravines, ridges and plateaus, and offers plenty of places for even the largest subs to hide. How then does NATO keep tabs on the large Soviet Northern Fleet which, in 1980, boasted 50% more submarines than the NATO Atlantic fleet. Apart from the US which has 116, Britain is the only other NATO power to have nuclear subs – and she has a meagre four – not many to track the numerous Soviet vessels. The answer, it seems, is to put a dense net of listening devices across the Greenland–Iceland–Shetland gaps so that nothing can escape from the Norwegian Sea undetected. Sonar buoys dropped from Nimrods, and other secret devices, constantly monitor the submarine movements of the Russian Northern Fleet.

In the ops room aboard *Blake* a constant stream of information and intelligence flows in from the Task Unit's command ship, the Royal Netherland ship *Tromp*, from

Northwood and numerous other sources. 'Everything's involved in anti-submarine warfare nowadays – ships, aircraft, subs,' said an officer. 'It's just a question of getting the mix right, to make the best use of all your units.' Modern fleets are highly inter-dependent and work closely together, although not in the physical sense of sailing in tight formation as the ships-of-the-line used to do, delivering broadsides at the enemy. The last time two fleets met in formal combat was at the Battle of Jutland in World War I, and then the result was inconclusive. Today, the interdependence is in com-munications and information, in gaining a clear picture of the opposition's positions and tactics. At the same time, radio and satellite communications are the first things the enemy would try to deny the NATO fleet. 'We have to assume that they would jam all our known working frequencies,' I was told. 'That's what all those AGIs are doing – trying to find out what our frequencies are. So we have to plan a way round that. One of the signalling methods we still use is the Aldis lamp – and we might even be reduced to flags. They can't interfere with those – short of blowing us up, of course.'

Until Morse code and radio were invented, communications between ships of war were very poor. Unless they were in tight formation it was impossible to read flag signals in anything but the finest weather. The flagship would have to fire a gun to attract attention to her signals, and the others would converge until they could read them. Or, more frequently, one of the smaller vessels would be sent to each ship of the line with verbal or written instructions. If the admiral wanted a meeting with his captains, it might take all day to arrange. When a ship was working in isolation, her captain was really on his own, and had to display a high degree of initiative, not to mention political acumen. With the introduction of efficient communications the day-to-day actions of ships of war came under the direct control of the Fleet Admiral, regardless of location. Today, strange to say, certain officers in a ship must once again show the type of individual initiative required in Nelson's day. Though signals have never been transmitted faster, neither have destructive weapons. When a missile is winging its way towards a ship, a captain must make a split-second decision or lose his vessel. A gunnery officer must decide which weapons to deploy against the several enemy missiles that might be converging simultaneously – and there's no time to discuss matters with the captain.

After three days patrolling the Shetland-Faroe gap, *Blake* leaves for a position 100 miles south of Iceland. Sadly, I cannot be on board during these manoeuvres because, like Cinderella, I must be gone by midnight each day – which is impossible to arrange. The Royal Navy, ever aware of its great traditions, does not permit women to stay in warships overnight. 'Lack of facilities' is often quoted as the reason, but I feel it goes deeper than that. Warships are for fighting men; women would confuse, even hinder the workings of the ship. As the executive officer on the *Saratoga* had said, 'Women are like alcohol – my men can't handle them.' In response to the powerful feminist lobby, the US government is trying to integrate women into the fighting sectors of all the armed services. In the Navy the experiment has not been a great success – many doubt it ever will be. As one sailor put it, 'When a man works and lives alongside women there's one problem they'll never be able to overcome – and that's basic chemistry!'

During the patrol, *Blake* herself did not find any of the Orange submarines in the area. Nor did she make contact with any real Russians. The key to tracking these sub-surface vessels is sheer weight of numbers. As Admiral Sir Raymond Lygo, former Vice-Chief of Naval Staff, has said, 'On land a ratio of 3:1 *against* the defenders is not a bad balance, whereas at sea the balance needs to be between 6:1 and 8:1 in *favour* of a defending force.' The point is well illustrated by *Blake*'s next task. She is going to meet some of the merchant ships which are sailing from America bound for Scapa Flow, where they will group into convoys for the final phase of the journey to Norway. There are six hundred ships which, for the purposes of the exercise, are assumed to be twenty – many of whom could be sunk within a short space of time by just one nuclear submarine. Yet to have a reasonable chance of protecting the ships from that one vessel, the defenders would have to deploy between six and eight vessels to sweep a 150-mile circle round the convoy. If ten subs were surrounding the group, then a force of sixty to eighty ships would be needed. When the Soviet submarine fleet is larger than all NATO's put together, the statistics become alarming.

Before aircraft and submarines came on the scene, in the days of galleys, men-of-war and dreadnoughts, a ratio of 1:1 provided a reasonable chance of success for either side, and superior strategy could win the day. Nelson's fleet was outnumbered by the Franco-Spanish fleet at Trafalgar, but his brilliant manoeuvre of cutting through the enemy's lines brought him victory. But throughout history merchant ships have always suffered very heavy losses in times of war and, to protect them, the convoy system appeared as early as the twelfth century. It became a well-proven technique, used regularly up until the twentieth century. For some reason, the allies did not use convoys in the First World War until 1917, by which time their merchantmen had suffered terrible losses. In the Second War the system was used from the beginning, but a shortage of warships still led to heavy losses, almost all at the hands of the ubiquitous submarine.

On Ocean Safari a task group is escorting a military convoy up from Southern Norway to Narvik in the north. A force of marines is being landed on the Arctic Circle coast of Norway to what they call 'sanitise' the area, clearing it of enemy forces who might be attempting to move south and occupy key ports. Navies have been used to support or hinder armies from the earliest times – to land them, supply them or, in the days of the big guns, bombard the enemy lines. The largest operation in support of an army was, of course, the D-Day landings, which demanded a very high level of co-ordination, organisation and plain old-fashioned luck.

Navies have also played a vital role in preventing invasion. When Drake and the English fleet sailed from Plymouth to chase the Spanish Armada in 1588, it was to stop the enemy from meeting up with its army in the Netherlands and invading England. Trafalgar, too, was the culmination of an anti-invasion campaign, but this time it was the French headed by Napoleon who waited on the Channel shore for a chance to conquer the English. Today the functions of modern navies are the same – it is only the means they use to achieve their objectives that have changed.

The Blue forces are told 'War has been declared'. *Blake* goes to Defence Stations – just one step short of Action Stations. The crew divides into two watches and works longer hours – instead of five watches of four hours each with two dog watches, there are just four watches: two of five hours and two of seven hours. The men will have less sleep and hurried meals. The aircrew have been told: 'Grab what sleep you can, where you can, and eat properly.' During the next week *Blake* has to defend herself against both air and submarine attack as well as protecting the merchant vessels in the convoys. Later, I had a chance to see an anti-aircraft operation. The enemy planes had been reported by shore radar. For the exercise they were simulating incoming missiles. The ship picks up the 'missiles' on her radar and, as they come within her own missile range, the four Seacats on the port-side launcher track through the air, guided by a radar-controlled computer which reads trajectory and speed, then calculates height, angle and range for firing. The men in the GDR, the gun direction room, have only to check that the computer is following the right target and is functioning correctly. This time everything is okay and the missiles can be fired. But they don't go. Not only because the target is a real plane and not a dummy, but because missiles are far too expensive to fire frequently. Once in a while a ship might be allowed a live shot, but the rest of the time the crew must be satisfied with pretence. If by any chance her missile should fail to destroy its target – an unlikely possibility – *Blake* can fall back on her large guns in the World War II manner. But, the gunnery officer admits ruefully, they're not much of a substitute.

Trained as a gunnery officer himself, Admiral Eberle sees the precision guided weapon as the second most important development in sea warfare after the nuclear submarine. 'In the days of naval gunnery it was actually extremely difficult to hit things. You aimed at them for a long time and you had to fire a hell of a lot of shells before you ever hit anything. But today it's very easy to hit things.' The problem now, he feels, is to know *what* you are hitting when you are rarely within visual range of your target and might indeed be fifty miles away. A far cry from Nelson's time when ships not only relied on visual sightings to locate the enemy but, having spotted each other, slowly converged over perhaps several hours and then tried to blast each other out of the water at almost point-blank range. Fighting was conducted at close quarters until the introduction of the shell and the armoured vessel in the mid-nineteenth century, when opposing ships could no longer get near enough to grapple and board each other. Today ship-to-ship combat is conducted out of visual range by missile.

Blake escorts her convoy towards the Norwegian coast and makes contact with Orange submarines. Her Sea King helicopters have been sweeping the sea for sonar contacts for seven days; now at last they have found an 'enemy'. The submarine they are tracking is unaware of their presence – the great advantage of helicopters is that they make no noise under the water. By the time the sub realises she has been found, it is too late. A homing torpedo dropped by one of the Sea Kings is about to destroy her – at least it would in a real situation, the umpires decide, and a 'kill' is declared. The convoy reaches Stavanger safely. Others get into Sogne Fjord and Bergen. The exercise is over.

Not many submarines have been 'killed' during the exercise, but it doesn't seem to matter. The important thing, says *Blake*'s captain, is that a multinational force has worked together well; different navies have used each other's supply ships to refuel, and have strengthened their procedures and their common bond. But just how effective would the manoeuvres be in a real war? Would convoys really get through the large numbers of enemy submarines, and survive the onslaught of precision-guided missiles? At his Northwood headquarters, Admiral Eberle admitted that initial merchant shipping losses would probably be very high, but in time he was confident that sufficient supplies could be got through. He could not estimate casualties. Nor could he comment on the likelihood of nuclear weapons being used; this was a matter for the politicians. The Navy, like the other services, is a tool of government policy, and its officers are never put in the position of making important political decisions. Once a decision has been taken, however, the execution of that task is then the Navy's responsibility.

Exercise Ocean Safari has also been a test of procedures and routines on each individual ship. A warship lives, fights – and possibly fails – by its routines. Back in HMS *Blake* I was once again bound to the 'Cinderella Rule', and could stay aboard for no longer than a day. It is one of many rules which are made *not* to be broken. As Master-at-Arms Brennan, the most senior chief petty officer in the ship, says,

'Most people like being told what to do – they like to have their lives ordered, to know what their next job is, when their meal times are.' As the senior rating directly responsible for discipline to the ship's executive officer, the master-at-arms is always known as 'crusher', a name that dates back to the days when ships had corporals who carried battens with which to crush miscreants' heads. 'The title stuck,' he says, 'but we don't go round crushing any more.' Something of an expert on the old forms of punishment, the master went on to recount how proven murderers used to be tied to the bodies of their victims and thrown into the sea. Robbery was just as firmly dealt with; the thief lost a hand, was tarred and feathered, and then put ashore at the nearest point; 'not amusing nowadays if one got landed in the Falkland Islands'. Nowadays discipline is treated in a more merciful way and is, the master explained, fairly straightforward. If a man is late back from leave, misses musters, or doesn't get to his work place, he'll most likely get Number 9, which is extra work duty – fourteen days of working from dawn till late at night. 'That's usually enough to make them think twice.' To come into line with the other services, the Royal Navy has now introduced fining, a punishment that also seems to work well. The ship's executive officer is Commander McPhee, who is second only to the captain. He deals with the great majority of disciplinary matters that come before him; only about five per cent of cases – the really serious ones – are referred to the captain. Offences ashore (drunkenness or theft) are dealt with strenuously, while military misdemeanours (wearing the wrong uniform or failing to salute) are treated in a minor fashion. Persistent wrongdoers who normally work hard and cheerfully are treated with tolerance. 'Every ship needs a few of these characters,' said the commander. 'When on board they work long hours without complaint. Trouble is they attack their periods ashore with equal enthusiasm, and forget when and where to find the ship.'

The relationship of officers to men has also changed significantly since the old days. An ordinary seaman was never allowed to speak to an officer and any failure to show proper respect was treated very harshly. Once, it is said, a seaman was severely punished for daring to grab the arm of an admiral to prevent him falling into the sea. As recently as World War II there were rigid class barriers between officers and men, but now, the master-at-arms said, the divisions are more relaxed and certain freedoms are allowed. Certainly a rating can talk to an admiral. Admiral Eberle has described the relationship as being less formal and more professional than in the past. He illustrated the new relationship with a story about an admiral who found a sailor having a haircut in the ship's barbershop during working hours. 'You're having your hair cut in working hours, I see,' said the admiral. 'Yes sir,' replied the sailor, 'it grew in working hours.' 'But not all of it,' countered the admiral. 'No sir,' said the sailor, 'but I'm not having all of it cut off.' The successful officer today relies on force of personality rather than the letter of the regulations to enforce commands. Nonetheless, the master-at-arms insisted, the basic discipline hasn't altered. 'Woe betide the rating who behaves with contempt. He quickly suffers the consequences.'

Though many rules and punishments have altered over the years, some of the traditions have stayed. The captain still does his rounds once every three weeks or so, while the commander goes through the eighteen mess-decks every evening when the ship's at sea. The main reason is to make sure everything is clean and tidy, but it also gives the senior officers a chance to meet the men. Few traditions remain unless they serve a useful function – which is possibly why the grog ration was finally discontinued in 1970. When large numbers of seamen used to be pressed into unwilling service and conditions were little short of appalling, a strong dose of alcohol kept the men happy.

Proper pay and conditions eliminated the need for rum-induced courage.

Procedures are particularly important during highly technical operations, for example when undertaking replenishment at sea, known as RAS. The taking-on of fuel and supplies from another ship while under way is vital to a ship's independence and safety, allowing her to stay at sea for long periods of time. When ships became dependent on fuels instead of wind-power they inherited a great weakness as well as a great strength. Though they were able to maintain consistently higher speeds, they also had to meet up with supply ships regularly or steam for base to re-bunker. Stopping alongside another ship at sea was not very good for the ships – they lost a lot of paint that way – and, as the commander pointed out, any World War II U-boat captain would have thought he'd won the pools if he'd come across two stationary ships in the middle of the ocean. Supply bases were therefore an important adjunct to a powerful navy, and to a great extent still are. The British Navy's command of the seas in the nineteenth century depended as much on the size of its fleet as its possession of ports like Cape Town, Gibraltar, Malta and Bermuda. Today, bases around the world are still highly prized and much sought after – yet the Soviet Union manages to run its large navy with virtually none. To get round the refuelling problem, the Russians do what kings and governments used to do in the past; they call their merchant fleet into service. In the old days merchant ships were called upon to fight, but now the Russians merely order them to refuel or resupply their naval ships. From having one of the smallest merchant fleets in the world, the USSR now has over 8000 merchant vessels sailing the oceans, part of its policy to become a major maritime power. The use of this large fleet has given the Soviets the ability to extend their navy across the world.

Western navies rely on their own fleets of naval auxiliaries for resupply but, even though the ships' crews are well practised in the RAS manoeuvre, it can be a tricky business. The ship-handling is critical because the two vessels must maintain a constant distance between each other, as well as keeping to the same speed. The various drills for passing over the fuelling hoses have to be rigidly adhered to, otherwise there can be serious accidents. Seamen and engineers have to carry out a set of procedures in exactly the right order or fuel can suddenly gush over the deck, making it like an ice rink. Since the guard-rail has to be removed during the manoeuvre, a man can easily slip over the side and be lost. The strain on the holding gear at either end of the hoseline is tremendous; tons of heavy wire and hose can suddenly part and thrash about, breaking a few heads in the process – the men wear hard helmets and keep a wary eye on the danger points. As an example of the unexpected, the *Saratoga* was refuelling one night when she discovered a small vessel between herself and the tanker! It was a fishing boat whose crew, on waking up to their predicament, suddenly put on their previously darkened lights and gave everyone a surprise. They were lucky to float clear astern of the two large ships.

Marine engines have been developed to give ships ever-greater speed and efficiency, but all have relied on frequent refuelling – with the glaring exception of nuclear power. But this apparently ideal form of propulsion has one huge disadvantage; it is immensely expensive to install. While the cost is justified for submarines and aircraft carriers, it is too high to be practical for cruisers, destroyers and frigates. However, with the increasing cost of oil, this situation may rapidly change.

Every captain would like to command a modern ship equipped with the latest weapons and the most efficient technology, but more than anything he values a good crew. The sailor has been described as the most important single factor in an effective navy. But if the abilities of the ordinary seamen are important, then so are those of the

NATO exercise. Refuelling at sea (top), gun drill, and fleet operations for the NATO Standing Naval Force Atlantic

men who lead them. Admiral Eberle has confidence in the modern sailor: 'I have no hesitation in saying that now they are of a very high quality indeed, in their achievements, in their dedication to their tasks, and in their sheer professionalism.' These sentiments were echoed down the line, though with more critical appraisal. 'The mechanic joining today is a brighter boy than when I joined the Navy,' said *Blake*'s master-at-arms, 'though a good many of them still suffer from the non-ability to write or spell.'

The Battle of Trafalgar is still the glorified ideal of everything that is brave, loyal and true in the fighting sailor. The ordinary seaman was known as Jack or Jack Tar, deriving from the tarred canvas which he wore to protect him from the weather. In the days of sail he led a harsh life. Even in a first-rate ship like the *Victory* he lived, slept and ate beside his gun. His possessions were limited to whatever fitted into a small chest and he had to buy his own clothes out of his pay – which he did not receive until the end of a voyage. Disease was rife and thirteen times as many seamen died from illness as from battle injury during the Napoleonic Wars. Things had not really improved since Drake's day. With little to attract men into the Navy, recruitment was not sufficiently high, and half Nelson's men had been forced into service by the notorious press gangs. Once in the Navy, however, the ordinary English sailor was immensely courageous and fought to the death. Doubtless this was largely due to the extraordinary qualities of Nelson himself. He had an almost god-like aura about him – today we would say he had charisma – and such were his powers to inspire loyalty and trust, such was his reputation for invincibility, that men loved him with a doglike devotion. After the battle it was reported that the men 'have done nothing but Blast their Eyes and cry ever since he was killed . . . chaps that fought like the Devil sit down and cry like a wench!'

Nowadays officers can hardly expect such blind loyalty from men who are sometimes as well, or even better, educated than they are. They have to work much harder for the respect due to their authority. 'A sense of humour helps,' says Commander McPhee, 'and an officer should be loyal, honest and enthusiastic. He should want to do his job well. A certain amount of grey matter between the ears is useful – we're beyond the days when a gunnery officer should be able to read or write but not both!' In Nelson's day, a commission in the Royal Navy was considered to be a fine if poorly paid career for a gentleman. Today the Navy is still regarded as 'The Senior Service', a legacy of Trafalgar which serves to attract men towards it and, once in, gives the British naval seaman a special pride in his job.

Conditions have vastly improved since 1805, of course. Like the *Saratoga*'s crew, the men in *Blake* have good food and accommodation, and entertainment in the form of films and TV. There is a doctor, a dentist, a padre, a ship's newspaper known as the 'Oily Rag', in which the men can write anything they please – short of treasonable statements; there is a Chinese laundry, tailor and barber; and pay is for once not lagging too far behind that in Civvy Street. The disadvantage of family separation remains, but there is no complaint about it. Says Master-at-Arms Brennan, 'I think the vast majority still love going to sea, still love travel and still love going to foreign places.' For many, too, life on land is complex and sometimes hard to cope with, while life at sea is ordered and familiar. As one ordinary seaman said, 'It's escapism, I think. If you're hitting around in port for a few months, it all gets a bit heavy, and there's nothing like getting out to sea. You know you can clear your mind. It's a good feeling.' The master observed that 'one is always looking forward to something in the Navy, either looking forward to going away to a new place or looking forward to coming back home again. It helps to keep everyone young and happy!'

After the NATO exercise *Blake* goes on a last tour, visiting Gibraltar, Italy, France and Portugal. It's a popular itinerary: lots of shore leave, sunshine and not too much hard work. After three months she steams back to England, towards decommissioning and the end of an era. In Plymouth she stops to take on some special guests for the last leg of her voyage to Portsmouth – nine ex-captains who have commanded *Blake* during her thirty-five-year service. They are aboard not only to say goodbye to the ship, but to witness a historic event – the last occasion on which big-calibre guns will be fired in the Royal Navy. After leaving Plymouth there is a special dinner held in the ward room and the officers and former captains toast the ship for the last time. The next morning I joined *Blake* by helicopter, in time to watch the 6-inch guns fire their last shells. When first installed these weapons were revolutionary: with shells that were loaded and primed mechanically, they were the first fully automatic guns to be used in the Royal Navy. Most suitable for shore bombardment, they are not just out of date, they are completely outmoded. A 170-ton structure firing 130-pound shells is no match for a lightweight missile. With all eyes upon them, the giant guns suddenly swivel through the air and lock on to a still-distant target being towed by a Canberra jet high in the sky. In the gun-direction room they check that the radar-controlled target-finder is not guiding the guns up the tow-wire on to the plane itself. (If the shells get a bit close, the pilots radio down, 'Could you tell your guys we're pulling this thing, not pushing it!') The command is given to fire and, with a deep thunderous roar, the mighty barrels kick out their steel-encased explosives which blossom into white puffballs across the sky. For over an hour the Canberra makes runs overhead and the guns roar out, cascading shell cases across the deck at the rate of eighteen rounds per minute per gun. Finally the Canberra has to return to base and the guns fall silent. The men who watch are nostalgic, but fully appreciative of the reasons why both the guns and *Blake* must go. 'She's very labour-intensive,' says Captain Mackenzie, 'the machinery's old and it needs a lot of men to keep it going.' 'Really, all she carries now are four Sea King helicopters,' added the commander, 'and there are modern ships which can do that with far fewer men.'

The costs of running *Blake* have been high. If cajoled up to her full speed of thirty-one knots ('not something we care to do very often for fear of shaking the ship to pieces,' said the commander), she uses a ton of fuel per mile. At a cost of £50 per ton, it would cost over £18,000 for half a day. At cruising speed the fuel usage is much more economical. Pay and allowances total £250,000 per month for the 840 men on board. And then there are victuals on top of that: every day the ship consumes 100 dozen eggs, $\frac{1}{2}$-ton of potatoes, 100 loaves of bread, 400 lb of meat, 4 gallons of liquid soap and 40 toilet rolls. Some fascinating statistics have been published in the last edition of the 'Oily Rag'; in two and a half months 1.52 miles of sausages, approximately 2,321,400 individual baked beans and $71\frac{1}{2}$ gallons of tomato sauce have been consumed. The 'Oily Rag' boasts many kinds of contributions, including poetry. One poem is titled 'Farewell to Blake'. The last verse reads:

> My big guns then will speak no more,
> To keep the peace nor fight a war,
> For missiles now appear to be
> The weapon of the ships at sea,
> But should England need Sir Francis Drake,
> Then beat his drum and bring out *Blake*.

As the old cruiser approaches Portsmouth Harbour she flies her long paying-off pennant, just as Nelson's ships used to do. Her crew line the decks, facing outwards, ready to salute the C-in-C Naval Home Command for the last time. Helicopters hover overhead, one of them streaming a banner which reads 'Goodbye Snakey!' The sad call of a lone bugle echoes down the ship. It is an occasion which cannot fail to move the hardest of people and I have trouble keeping a trembling lip in order.

Soon *Blake* will be stripped of her valuable equipment and readied for her new reserve status; she will be sealed off and subjected to MDH (or massive dehumidification) to keep her in perfect condition. After a few years, if no war threatens, she will be scrapped. Ironically, sailing astern of *Blake* as she enters Portsmouth is the newest addition to the Royal Navy's fleet, the minesweeper *Brecon*. Just as *Blake* once encompassed new technology, so does *Brecon* – she is the first Royal Navy ship to be built of fibreglass. The old cruiser, last in a direct line which can be traced back to the armoured cruisers of the early twentieth century, is saluted by the first in a new tradition.

But how relevant is a navy in these days of long-range missiles and nuclear warheads? Defence experts believe it has never been more vital. Not only does it possess the one weapon launcher that is still relatively undetectable – the nuclear submarine – but a navy retains one great advantage over land installations. It can keep moving, and therefore presents a more adaptable and less vulnerable force. If, as many believe, a limited war is most likely, navies would play a vital role. But as Admiral Eberle explained, the cost of keeping an effective defensive force will never be cheap. He did foresee a change in what he called the quality-quantity equation, however. 'In the past we've tended to use technology to improve our performance, building bigger and better ships and missiles. Of course the bigger they get, the more expensive they get. I believe that we should now use technology differently, to maintain present performance in smaller, more reliable and less costly ships and weapons.' However, improvements in performance will inevitably occur, and if one superpower develops a new system then the other is bound to follow. With planes 'invisible' to radar, laser weapons and ever more sophisticated ideas in the pipeline, it is hard to see what kind of navy will develop. Most intriguing of all is to guess what will happen if the nuclear submarine becomes completely detectable. Will an antidote inevitably be found, as Admiral Sanderson suggested? Or will submarines lose their invincibility and be superseded by another type of vessel? Fans of *Star Wars* can probably make the best guess.

HMS *Blake* came alongside the dock at Portsmouth and lowered her gangway to the crew's wives and families for the last time. In the grey drizzle, the crew began to take their leave. Few of them left without a final look at 'dear old Snakey', a real character among ships: faithful, long-serving and true – as well as 'hellish difficult to keep clean', cramped and run-down. But shortcomings or no, everyone agreed that she had possessed that most important of qualities, something quite indefinable – she had been a happy ship.

Sea power grew out of men's desire to use the sea as a means of transport. But a long time before trade developed, the sea was being used as a provider of food. For thousands of years fishermen sailed the seas with freedom, taking care only to keep out of enemy's waters. Now the situation has changed and, as a result of our urgent need for food and energy, the sea's harvest is giving rise to new conflicts.

The Spithead review which took place in 1977 as part of the Queen's Silver Jubilee celebration

DEVELOPMENT OF THE WARSHIP
DAVID LYON

The development of the warship 1830–1945
One hundred and fifty years ago the sailing warship was reaching the end of a long but unspectacular process of development. The different types of fighting ship were distinguished from one another by size, gun power and function rather than by any fundamental differences in design. The largest and heaviest armed ships were the 'line of battle ships' (later simply 'battleships') which were intended to fight in fleets for maritime supremacy. Next down the scale in size and power were the frigates, followed by corvettes and sloops, the vessels which extended and exploited the command of the sea won by the ships of the line.

The introduction of steam in the 1820s and 1830s at first made little difference to this picture. The engines used were unreliable, consumed vast amounts of coal in return for very little power, drove paddle-wheels which were vulnerable to gunfire, and took up large amounts of the broadside which could otherwise be occupied by guns. Smaller types of ships, sloops and frigates, could afford this weakening of their offensive capabilities in return for the advantages of steam power, and could act as tugs to the battleships which remained purely sailing ships until the adoption of the screw propeller in the 1840s solved the problem of combining steam propulsion with a full broadside of guns. Masts and sails, however, remained a feature of nearly

The evolution of the modern fighting ship. Left: HMS *Warrior*, the first British sea-going ironclad. Above (top to bottom): American Civil War: The Battle of Hampton Roads, the first battle between ironclads – USS *Monitor* and CSS *Virginia* (ex-*Merrimac*). HMS *Thunderer*, a turret ship – one of the first battleships to be built without sails. TB No. 2, one of the earliest torpedo boats in the Royal Navy. HMS *Dreadnought*, the first 'all big gun' battleship, and the first big warship to be powered by turbines

all warships until well into the last quarter of the nineteenth century. This was less a matter of unthinking conservatism than a result of the continuing but ever-decreasing lack of fuel economy of steam engines, and the consequent lack of endurance.

During the Crimean War the French built the first ironclads, intended for shore bombardment. The addition of armour soon spread to sea-going ships and introduced the first real change in ship types, since the appearance of the French *Gloire* and then the British *Warrior* meant that all battleships thenceforth had to be ironclads.

Iron had already been tried as a structural material for warship hulls, but the introduction of armour was the signal for the final replacement of wood throughout the world's navies. Protection by armour meant the development of bigger guns in order to defeat that armour, and the confusing variety of types of battleship built up to the beginning of the 1890s can be understood as trials of various systems of mounting a few heavy guns with adequate protection. The old broadside system was no longer relevant; instead three basic methods of carrying the guns were used. In the 'box battery' or 'citadel' method they were mounted in what was basically an armoured fort in the middle of the vessel; this gave a high freeboard and therefore a seaworthy ship, but it had limited fields of fire and individual guns could only fire on one side of the ship. Rotating turrets gave a much better field of fire on both sides of the ship, but had the disadvantage of being very heavy and therefore having to be mounted near the waterline, giving a less seaworthy ship. The problem was finally solved by mounting guns on a rotating platform on top of an armoured tower, the 'barbette', which had the advantages of both the other methods. Confusingly, when an armoured gun-house was later added to protect the gunners on top of the barbette, this came to be known as a 'turret' instead.

Underwater warfare first came on the scene with the use of mines during the Crimean War, and primitive torpedoes (including ones attached to submarines) were used during the American Civil War. For the first time a small vessel had the potential of sinking even the largest ship, and this development produced specialist torpedo craft and forced an increase in the size of battleships, both to incorporate extra small guns to fight off this new threat and to increase internal subdivisions which would limit the effect of the explosion of a mine or torpedo. Initial enthusiasm for very small and very fast torpedo boats was tempered by the discovery that lack of seaworthiness, reliability and endurance severely restricted their usefulness. However, the steady increase in the size and seagoing ability of torpedo boats had led, by the end of the nineteenth century, to the evolution of the true seagoing torpedo

Top to bottom: HMS *Cossack*, the culmination of the inter-war destroyer. Pearl Harbor – the end of the supremacy of the battleship. HMS *Argus*, the first flat-topped aircraft carrier. HMS *Thunderbolt* (ex-*Thetis*), a 'T'-class submarine of the Second World War. Carrier-borne aircraft and submarines spelt the end of the big battleships and cruisers

vessel, the 'destroyer'. Originally developed as an enlarged torpedo boat armed with guns, as a counter to her smaller brethren, the destroyer soon took over their function of torpedo attack as well.

During the late nineteenth century 'cruisers' evolved from the frigate and corvette. These varied from the big 'armoured cruisers', often larger than contemporary battleships, and with greater speed and (usually) range though less protection, down through medium-sized, trade-protection vessels, to the small and fast cruisers intended for scouting for the fleet. These latter would eventually be termed 'light cruisers'.

By the beginning of the twentieth century technical developments were making great advances in warship design possible. Improvements in gun construction, explosives and fire control meant that gun ranges suddenly increased from a couple of miles to the limit of vision, and therefore made the all-big-gun 'Dreadnought' battleship not only possible but necessary. Development of the reciprocating steam engine had already made the use of sails obsolete, and now the introduction of the turbine produced much increased speed and reliability. Improvements in torpedo design kept pace with gun development, while wireless revolutionised communications at sea. The French had made the submarine into a viable weapon, and therefore made possible the development of what was to become the most effective torpedo boat of all. The appearance of the internal combustion engine started a new cycle of torpedo boat development with the MTB, and, before the outbreak of World War I, the first naval aircraft had entered service, with ships converted to act as 'aircraft carriers'.

The First World War firmly established both the mine and the torpedo as most effective weapons, threatening, though not destroying, the role of the battleship. Inevitably, this threat produced countermeasures, new types of ship were purpose-built for mine-sweeping and for anti-submarine work. By the end of the war specially designed aircraft carriers were building, and the lessons of war had caused battleships, light cruisers and destroyers to grow in size, strength, speed and seaworthiness. The old armoured cruisers, and their successors the battle cruisers, had not proved over-successful, and the naval treaties which followed the war, limiting tonnage and numbers of ships, helped to produce the 'heavy cruiser'.

Between the wars there were fierce arguments over whether the development of aircraft had rendered the battleship obsolete, but it was not until well into the second conflict that the aircraft carrier forced the battleship into second place in the major navies. From the start of the war, however, the threat of air attack proved even more difficult to counter than had been feared, and

A Russian Echo I class nuclear submarine, photographed under tow after it had broken down off Japan in 1980

light anti-aircraft guns proliferated on the superstructures of warships of all kinds. More and more attention had also to be given to countering the submarine, and out of this came the 'frigate', a specialised anti-submarine escort the size of a destroyer (and later to grow still larger). Even more revolutionary, in the long run, was the influence of electronic developments: radar, radio direction-finding and other such devices played an increasingly vital role in naval warfare and therefore took up ever more space and weight in ships. By the end of the war most new ships were optimised for countering the air or submarine threat rather than for dealing with other surface ships. For by that time developments in submarine design, particularly by the Germans, had produced vessels which could be considered true submarines, rather than submersibles capable of submerg-

ing for comparatively short times and distances. These new U-boats were much faster and more difficult to attack than their predecessors.

By 1945 the trends which were to dominate the post-war years had already made themselves obvious. The tasks the battleship could perform under the threat of air attack no longer justified the great expense of building them. The aircraft carrier was queen of the ocean, but with the submarine also achieving a new and even greater importance. Most other warships were intended to protect the former and/or to attack the latter. Electronic warfare and the guided missile had already seen action. After a period of relative stability in ship types and functions there was now to be another period of constant flux, experimentation and confusion similar to that of the latter nineteenth century.

WAR AT SEA
WARREN TUTE

Sail

Sea power can be defined in a number of ways. In essence, however, it allows free movement on the sea for oneself and inhibits, if need be, a similar capacity in others. Man uses the sea to further his interests as a land animal, and sea power is but one element of overall national authority and national strategy.

The effective force on which sea power depends is a Navy, and the potential threat – the power to inhibit, blockade and destroy – which all groups of fighting ships have sought throughout history has inevitably been put to the test from time to time. The sea battle, therefore, is often a turning-point in world events, marking the rise or fall of a nation, a decisive factor in a changing pattern of communication and trade.

The first great naval battle fought for command of the seas took place in 480 BC between the Greeks and the Persians at Salamis in the Aegean. Both fleets employed galleys, the oared fighting ship of the Mediterranean dating from about 3000 BC and used in there until AD 1717 and in the Baltic as lately as the Russo-Swedish war of 1809.

Originally propelled by oars on a single level, the galley later developed into a vessel with up to five banks of oars, giving an estimated speed of between eight and nine knots. Its weapon was the ram, a pointed spur fixed to the bow on or just below the waterline, and since, basically, it was an unstable vessel, the galley could only be of real use in calm waters. Apart from its ability to ram and sink, it also formed a moving container for soldiers, who could, however, only be effective in hand-to-hand fighting after galleys had grappled together. Later, galleys were to bear archers and later still mount guns but these could not be trained, thus firing only directly ahead.

At Salamis the Persian fleet commanded by Xerxes began with a big superiority in numbers and had trapped the Greeks under Themistocles in the bay of Eleusis by blocking the two entrance channels. The narrowness of these channels, however, combined with Persian impetuosity in attack, caused one of the earliest traffic jams on record, and the Persians, unable to manoeuvre, became a perfect target for the Greek triremes. After some hours of battle, the Persians had lost 200 warships to the Greeks' forty and Aeschylus, who was a marine on board a Greek trireme, compared the action with the

Lepanto, the last important Mediterranean galley battle, took place in 1571

catching of tuna fish, where they are driven into shallow water and then killed with any available weapon.

The effect of this first key sea battle was to induce the Persians to abandon any further attempt to conquer Greece. It also led to the flowering of Athenian political and cultural life – the golden age of Pericles and the building of the Parthenon – and to the expulsion of Persian garrisons from the Thracian coast.

Two hundred and twenty years later, in 260 BC, the Roman empire can properly be said to have started with the defeat of Carthage at Mylae on the northern coast of Sicily. Basically a land power, Rome early discovered the necessity of controlling the seas if she was to retain her expanding empire. The victory at Mylae under Gaius Duilius brought Rome domination over the whole of the Mediterranean.

Even in those days warship technology, and in this particular battle galley tactics, never stood still. Duilius had planned his attack in as military a fashion as possible and for this purpose used grappling irons and boarding bridges from which his Roman soldiers savaged the Carthaginian crews. The spectacular victory they achieved was later commemorated by a column in the forum at Rome adorned with the beakheads of the captured Carthaginian ships.

The last important Mediterranean galley battle took place over 1800 years later. This was at Lepanto in 1571 and it broke Turkish command of the eastern Mediterranean for ever. By this time oars were supplemented by sails in a compromise ship known as the galleass, a combination of oared galley and galleon which not only had a ram but was also heavily gunned. These ships, under the command of Don John of Austria, the 24-year-old half-brother of Philip II of Spain,

proved more than a match for the oared galleys, manned by slaves, of the Turkish Ali Pasha.

This battle off Cape Skrophia near the Gulf of Patras was the first sea encounter of the western world to be celebrated by artists of renown such as Vasari, Sabbatini and Andrea Vicentino, whose fresco in the Doge's Palace in Venice, together with the captured Ottoman standard, can still be seen. Coming as it did only six years after the failure of the Turkish siege of Malta in 1565, one of the most famous in history, Lepanto ensured that henceforth no Sultan would exercise paramount control at sea and that further Moslem expansion into Europe would be on land and then only into Poland and Russia.

The scale of the battle was commensurate with the result, some 200 Christian ships of the Triple Alliance or Holy League of Spain, the dominions of the Pope and the Republic of Venice defeating a Turkish fleet of 273 galleys from Moslem areas as far apart as Algiers, Tunis and Constantinople. Christian losses were 8000 and Turkish 20,000, more than double those numbers being wounded. The battle was remarkable not only for the release of some 12,000 Christian slaves from the Turkish galleys but also for the presence of Don Miguel de Cervantes, the author of *Don Quixote*, who lost the use of his left hand in the battle.

Lepanto was in a way the connecting link between the pure galley battles of Salamis and Mylae and the pure sailing battles of the Armada and later. Indeed, the Armada campaign, that initial period of English challenge to Spain's command of the Atlantic and Pacific, had begun with the Hawkins voyages of 1564 and 1567 and extended via Drake's circumnavigation of the world in 1580 to the battle itself in 1588.

Strictly speaking, the Armada was not a conventional encounter on the high seas between opposing ships of the line (as was Trafalgar, for instance) but an example of a powerful invasion fleet of 130 ships being harried downwind into a narrowing English channel by a smaller, better sailed and 'more weatherly' force, and then, when compelled to anchor off Calais on a lee shore, being attacked by fire ships so that they had to cut their cables and make sail again in order to escape a holocaust. The Armada did, however, establish certain principles about war at sea which had not been proved before but which were to apply until the end of the sailing era.

The Armada is usually credited to the genius of Drake, but in fact the English fleet was commanded by Lord Howard of Effingham. Queen Elizabeth, like her opponent Philip II of Spain, considered that only a nobleman could wield the necessary authority over such diverse, highly qualified personalities as Drake, Hawkins and Frobisher. She was right but there was a further

difference between the Spanish and English commands.

Until Drake on his famous voyage round the world eight years previously had settled for ever the paramount authority of a Captain on board his own ship, the feudal division of command had obtained in every fighting ship of every nation. Quite simply this meant that the seamen under their Master worked and navigated the ship, whilst command vested in the Knight, Captain or General in charge of the troops. In other words, sailors were subordinate to a military 'supercargo'. Drake had put an end to all that. In English ships the Captain of the ship had become the supreme and unquestioned authority on board. This gave English ships an efficiency, a flexibility and a decisiveness denied to their Spanish counterparts who were still subject to hidalgo whims. These gentlemen gave the

orders but were ignorant of the sea and were not prepared to help in the 'menial' working of the ship.

The great 'Spanish Enterprise', dubbed before it sailed as 'most fortunate and invincible', had been designed to pick up the Duke of Parma's army waiting in the Netherlands and then to invade a helpless and impotent England. A sea battle formed no part of this Spanish plan. Had it been forced upon them, they would have chosen to engage closely with their tall ships and well-disciplined soldiers, as Don John had done at Lepanto. The English knew this perfectly well. With their 'low-charged' and therefore more manoeuvrable ships they kept their distance to windward, closing in when they saw fit, to pick off a straggler and to pepper the tight Spanish formation with gunfire at their longest effective range.

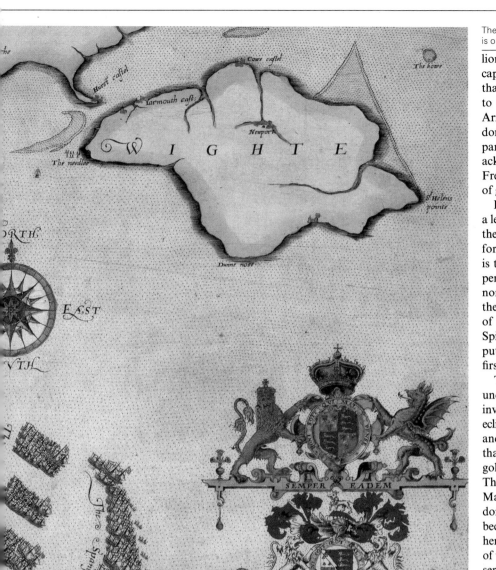

lion on the sea forces which had proved capable of severing the Spanish lifeline. From that time on the balance of investment was to change in favour of the Navy. After the Armada the English laid claim to being the dominant power at sea. In fact this was only partially so and was not in any case to be acknowledged by their Spanish, Portuguese, French and Dutch rivals until after 200 years of gruelling war at sea.

In the seventeenth century the Dutch took a leading place among maritime nations and their victories over the Spaniards extended for more than forty years. Difficult though it is to believe, a Spaniard, Federigo Spinola, persuaded his king to send a fleet of galleys north to the English channel to reconquer the Netherlands. A Dutch Admiral disposed of them off the coast of Flanders and only Spinola's own galley reached Dunkirk. That put an end to galleys as a part of Spain's first-line fleet except in the Mediterranean.

Then in 1639 a Dutch fleet of thirty ships under Tromp completely trounced a Spanish invasion fleet of seventy-seven ships. This eclipsed the power of Spain in northern waters and proved the saying that 'In gold rather than steel lies the strength of Spain. Take his gold and the Iberian's steel will not prevail.' The Battle of the Downs not only made Marten Tromp famous, it ensured Holland's dominance in northern waters. She had also become the principal European carrier. But her dependence on other nations for so much of what she needed began to involve her in a series of wars in different parts of the world. The age of empire had begun.

Over the next century and a half improvements in ship design and armament resulted in the ultimate sailing warship – the three-decker ship of the line – the battleship of the eighteenth and early nineteenth centuries, of which Nelson's *Victory* is the best-known example. They were tremendous ships, the first-rates carrying over one hundred guns. Lines of these battleships engaging each other have formed the substance of a gallery of famous pictures. Into them, as Ruskin said with mid nineteenth-century hyperbole, man had put 'as much of his human patience, common sense, forethought, experimental philosophy, self-control, habits of order and obedience, thoroughly wrought handwork, defiance of brute elements, careless courage, careful patriotism and calm expectation of

The results were devastating. Certainly luck was on the English side but when the fireships drifted downwind into the compact mass of Spanish shipping at anchor off Calais – and nothing was more dreaded in the days of sail than fire – 'the troubles and miseries we have suffered cannot be described to your Majesty,' Medina Sidonia wrote to King Philip. The fleet had perforce to cut and run before the wind, northwards up the east coast of England, rounding Scotland and the Orkneys, and then home to Spain as best it could battered by Atlantic gales. Sixty-four of the 130 ships which had left Spain were lost, wrecks being dotted in the Outer Hebrides, Donegal, Connaught, Galway and even, in one instance, off Bolt Head in Devon.

The defeat of the Spanish Armada had important and far-reaching effects in the overall story of sea power. How was it that a

virtually non-existent Navy, or at least a collection of ships cobbled together at the last moment, had toppled a fleet of much greater, longer-established force? Apart from the native daring of a Protestant island folk, the well-thought-out warship design of Hawkins must be given a major credit. As at Salamis where the smaller and faster Greek triremes had run rings round the larger, clumsier Persians, so now English terriers had caused a Spanish bull to cower.

Elizabethan sea heroes such as Drake, Raleigh, Hawkins and Frobisher started what came to be known as the Blue Water school of strategic thinking. From now on England would look to the sea in the first place for her safety and wealth. Between 1585 and 1603 Queen Elizabeth spent £4½ million on land campaigns in Europe which yielded no lasting dividend and only £1 mil-

the judgment of God, as can well be put into a space of 300 feet long by 80 broad'. It was some specification. To a certain extent it was also true.

The ship of the line and her smaller and faster sister, the frigate, conditioned eighteenth-century battles at sea. In the middle of the century the greatest single exposition of sea power, in its way a direct follow-up of the Armada campaign but this time against the ancient enemy, France, took place in the Seven Years War (1756–63). This war saw the British conquest of Canada and India and the acquisition of much other real estate to form part of the British Empire.

Of all the battles in this war, perhaps that of Quiberon Bay, combining a classic Admiral with a classic battle, is pre-eminent. Hawke's victory not merely put an invasion of Britain out of court, it humbled the French Navy under the eyes of her soldiers. A fleet of twenty-three ships of the line had chased another of twenty-one, and defeated it under its own cliffs with the direct loss of seven vessels and 2500 men for the cost of two British ships, the crews of which had been saved. It was a favourite maxim of the elder Pitt, then Prime Minister, that 'the boldest measures are the safest'. Hawke certainly proved it.

The Glorious First of June in 1794, on the other hand, was an example of a sea battle, perhaps the first major engagement to take place out of sight of land, which could be considered as a tactical victory for the British and a strategic victory for the French. This was because Lord Howe defeated the fleet of Admiral Villaret de Joyeuse but was unable to prevent an immense grain convoy from Chesapeake Bay getting through to starving France. Thus the French Admiral, far from feeling disgraced by the loss of seven ships of the line, considered that France had come off best, the more so since had the grain not got through he himself would have had an appointment with the guillotine.

The Napoleonic war showed sea power to be no longer localised but now world-wide. The battle of Trafalgar takes its place as but one incident in a pattern of sea power which lasted from 1803 to 1815 and covered the Mediterranean, Indian Ocean, Atlantic and Caribbean. The greatest sailing battle there had ever been, however, was terminal in its effect and resulted in a century of the so-called Pax Britannica during which the Royal Navy policed the oceans of the world.

The battle of Trafalgar itself was unlike other great sea battles in that Nelson in *Victory* and Collingwood in *Royal Sovereign* led their respective lines, instead of remaining conventionally in the middle, and because the tactics employed by Nelson had been worked out long before and had been rehearsed and known by all the Captains, his 'Band of Brothers' in the fleet. There were two other reasons for the British victory,

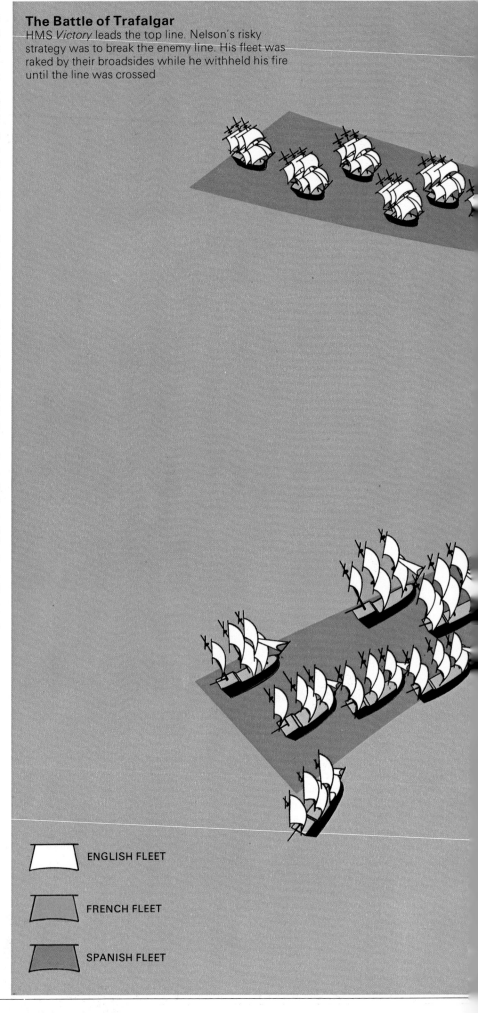

The Battle of Trafalgar
HMS *Victory* leads the top line. Nelson's risky strategy was to break the enemy line. His fleet was raked by their broadsides while he withheld his fire until the line was crossed

ENGLISH FLEET

FRENCH FLEET

SPANISH FLEET

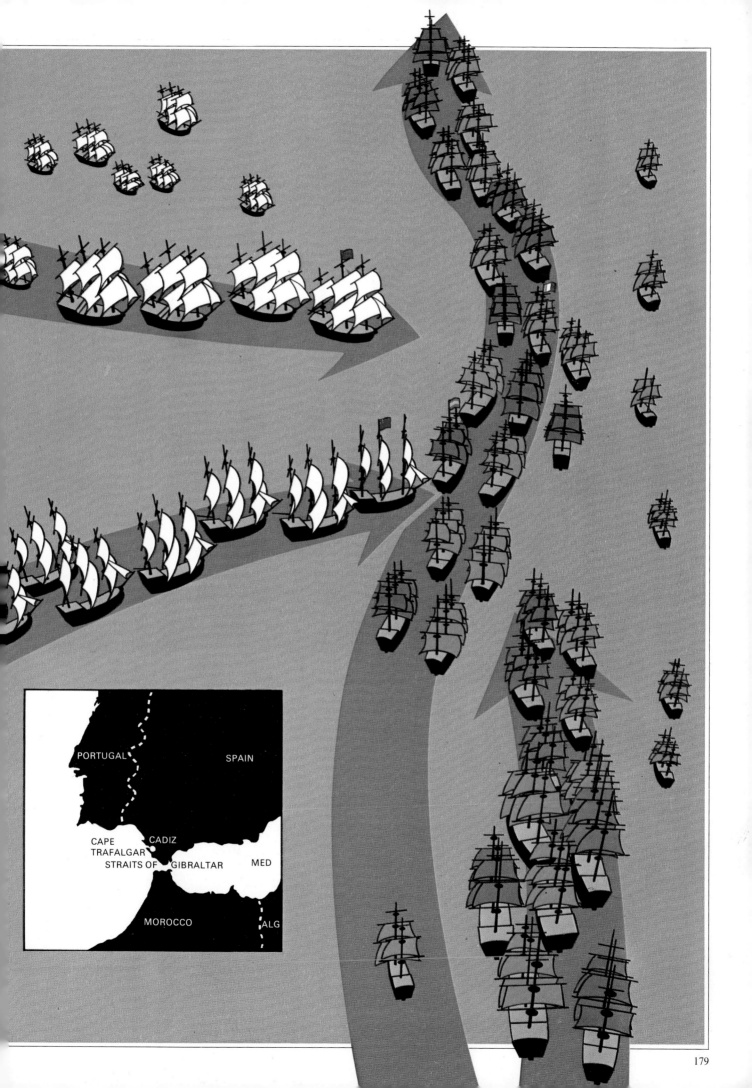

PORTUGAL

SPAIN

CAPE
TRAFALGAR   CADIZ

STRAITS OF   GIBRALTAR   MED

MOROCCO   ALG

however, one going back to Drake and the other to Monck, perhaps the foremost General-at-Sea in the Dutch wars of the Commonwealth. Drake held the view, with which every strategist since has agreed, that a war at sea should be begun as far as possible from the English coast. He believed in taking it into the enemy camp, off or even inside the enemy's own harbours. 'With fifty sail of shipping we shall do more good upon their own coast than a great many more will do here at home,' he wrote. This was a variation on attack being the best form of defence and, as succeeding Royal Navy commanders adopted the same ethic, accounts for that successful, aggressive attitude of the eighteenth century which the French and Spanish lacked, preferring to remain safely in harbour under the protection of land fortifications.

But to blockade a French or Spanish port or even merely to keep station there through winter gales on the chance that the enemy fleet might emerge entailed patience and endurance of a high order. 'If a man faint under the burden of such tediousness,' Monck had written over a century previously, '. . . he is in no way fit for enterprise because the two chief parts of a soldier are Valour and Sufferance and there is as much honour gained by suffering wants patiently in war as by fighting valiantly and as great achievements effected by the one as by the other . . . and yet it is an easier matter to find men that will offer themselves willingly to death than such as will endure labour with patience.' Nelson knew this very well, as did every British Admiral in the eighteenth century, with the possible exception of Byng who was court martialled and shot. Nelson's campaign which climaxed in Trafalgar began with a long watching spell off Toulon in 1803 and continued without a break through 1804 and much of 1805. Nelson did not set foot ashore himself for some two years.

The last battle fought wholly under sail took place at Navarino Bay, scarcely a hundred miles from Lepanto, in 1827, six years after the Greek War of Independence had begun. As at Lepanto an awkward alliance of Christian nations – Great Britain, France and Russia – undertook to settle with the Turks and secure autonomy for the newly declared Greek Republic. The allied fleet was under the command of Admiral Sir Edward Codrington, who had fought under St Vincent in 1794 at the Glorious First of June and had also been one of Nelson's captains at Trafalgar. His task was complicated by the previous activities of British naval officers not under Admiralty orders (such as Lord Cochrane who was fighting independently with the Greeks – and not much enjoying it), and also by the necessity of keeping the French and Russians apart whilst giving each a role consistent with national dignity.

On the other hand, the disposition of the Turkish-Egyptian fleet was such that Codrington decided his only course would be to take the combined fleet into Navarino harbour 'match in hand'. This he did. As he neared the entrance the Turks refused him permission to enter, to which Codrington replied that he had not come to receive orders but to give them and that the first gun fired by the Turks would be the signal for the destruction of their fleet. This duly occurred, the battle becoming general soon after 2.30 pm and being over by 6 pm. This last battle under sail hastened the liberation of Greece because, between it and the signing of the final treaty in 1829, Turkey had no principal fleet.

Above: The battle of Navarino Bay

Below: The battle of the Nile; the English ships under full sail are surrounding the anchored French fleet

Steam

The steam and steel age in naval warfare began in something of a vacuum. This was mainly because nothing of great importance happened in the nineteenth century to upset the world-wide pattern of British sea supremacy established at the end of the Napoleonic wars in 1815. The idea that 'what was good enough for Nelson is good enough for us' conditioned British naval thinking until the mid-century had passed. The British Admiralty indeed came out firmly against steam except for tugs and harbour craft, declaring early experiments 'too chimerical to be entertained', and it was only after the Crimean war had shown in a matter of minutes that the wooden walls of England were useless against steam-driven, ironclad ships and the guns they carried that Their Lordships reluctantly decided on second thoughts.

The next step forward in the concept of world sea power – and it was a major one – was the putting into service of the Dreadnought battleship in the first decade of the twentieth century. During the previous sixty years muddled thinking had produced in all navies a series of monstrously inefficient warships, none of them standardised. German naval rearmament, imperial expansion and a new imbalance of power, however, produced a long overdue revolution in battleship design. A further impulse was the development of the torpedo, the submarine, wireless telegraphy and the internal combustion engine.

An era of the 'all big gun battleship' had begun and, although Britain won the race to build the first of these monsters (the *Dreadnought* was laid down in great secrecy in

October 1905, launched in February 1906 and completed her steaming trials eight months later), Japan, Russia and the United States had all projected designs for such a ship in 1904. Japan had even laid down the first of the type, the *Aki*, in that same year but the precarious Japanese economy and delivery difficulties with her guns delayed completion.

Then in 1905 the first fleet action of the present century took place between the navies of Russia and Japan. The battle of Tsushima stands alone in history as an example of utter naval ineptitude – on the part of Russia whose defeat was total. The cause of the war was the Russian seizure of Port Arthur for use as a far eastern naval base and its subse-

quent destruction by the Japanese together with the Russian ships inside it in February 1904. The tragi-comedy which followed (the Russian Eastern Fleet assisted its own demise by blowing up its flagship and Commander-in-Chief in its own minefield) was watched with relish by the rest of the world.

To correct this situation Admiral Rozhdestvensky's Baltic fleet, after a blessing by the Tsar, sailed in October 1904 and, after firing on a Swedish merchantman, a German fishing boat and an appalled English fishing fleet off the Dogger Bank under the impression that these were Japanese craft sent to intercept them, reached Madagascar on New Year's Day 1905. There on one excuse or another they stayed till 25 March,

Eastern (above) and Western (below) views of the 1905 defeat of the Russian fleet by the Japanese in the battle of Tsushima Straits

eventually reaching the Straits of Tsushima between China and Japan on 25 May. The Japanese were waiting for them.

Two days later the action began on the anniversary of the luckless Tsar's coronation. It was soon apparent that Russian gunnery could be much improved. One by one the Russian battleships were put out of action by accurate Japanese fire. By sundown what was left of the fleet was a confused huddled mass. This was attacked by torpedo boats during the night and finished off the next day, part of the Russian fleet surrendering, later to be incorporated in the Japanese fleet. Only one small cruiser and two destroyers reached the haven of Vladivostok out of the forty which had come round the world to do battle. Thus ended the first major encounter between fleets of armoured battleships and no victory, in the opinion of the world, had ever been more complete or more humiliating despite individual Russian valour.

Until the First World War the Dreadnought was taken by everyone to be the culminating point in the exercise of sea power. It was assumed that the nation owning the largest Dreadnought fleet would rule the world virtually unchallenged, and in 1914 that nation was Britain. The war which followed proved the idea a fallacy. Battle experience showed that the Dreadnought was too costly and valuable a ship to be risked in action, and unrestricted U-boat warfare upset all previous notions about control of the sea.

The greatest naval battle of the First World War took place off Jutland on 31 May 1916. Because of errors in signals (the German High Seas Fleet was still thought to be in harbour by the British Commander-in-Chief) contact was made by accident. Once the engagement had begun it became obvious that a slight British superiority in numbers counted for little against better German gunnery and ship design. Beatty's famous remark summed it up as two of his great battle-cruisers went to the bottom: 'There seems to be something wrong with our bloody ships today.'

However, the spectacle on both sides which imprinted itself on future naval thinking, although it was to take another world war to prove its truth, was that of the battle line of both sides turning *away* when attacked. The ships were too valuable to be risked and lost. Admiral Jellicoe, the Commander-in-Chief, was the only man, as Churchill remarked, who could have lost the war in an afternoon, since the fate of the Allies depended in the last resort on the maintenance of British sea power. He therefore took no chances, for which he has been criticised ever since, and no naval battle in history has provoked more controversy.

In the context of the war as a whole, however, Jutland has rightly been assessed as a British strategic victory, bought at the cost

Above: The Battle of Jutland by Norman Howard. A bird's-eye view of the British fleet (left) deploying into line of battle, and the German fleet turning away. Such a view would have been very helpful on the day. In the foreground, the wounded *Warrior* is inadvertently protected by the *Warspite* circling with damaged steering gear
Below: The *Graf Spee* in Montevideo Harbour, after the battle of the River Plate

of 2500 German and 6000 British lives. Never again did the German High Seas Fleet challenge British control of the North Sea, and the subsequent blockade of Germany achieved an economic strangulation and the eventual ending of the war through mutinies in the Kaiser's navy.

The next fifty years of the sea-power story after Jutland saw vast technological developments both in ships and in weapons, a process speeded up by the Second World War. Big guns gave way to aircraft, the carrier in turn yielding to the guided missile. The old days of national supremacy at sea went for good and no single nation can now dominate the world through the strength and ubiquity of its Navy. Ended, too, is the concept of Empire so proudly held at the start of the First World War. Life today is too complex

for the tenure by one nation of big areas of real estate which were at one time guaranteed by naval control of sea communications. Today the threat of reprisal in the missile age ironically enough ensures the freedom of the seas to all who wish to use it.

The great battles of World War II ranged from the 'conventional' battle of the River Plate, where three British cruisers took on and defeated a German pocket battleship, to the great amphibious landings in North Africa, Normandy and the Pacific, which depended for their success on control of the sea and of the air space above it. There was the battle of the Atlantic, where highly successful German U-boats accounted in a single period of seven months from January to July 1942 for the loss of over three million tons of allied shipping. There was the hunting

based on an overestimate of their own capacity for sustaining war and an underestimate of the almost limitless resources of America.

The first Japanese failure was at Port Moresby and the second at Midway in May to June 1942. These were the first engagements in history between aircraft carriers, in other words the first actions to be fought at the range of carrier-borne aircraft instead of guns. The Japanese were further handicapped by not having radar. New techniques had rapidly to be learnt by both sides, the dive bomber proving to be a more valuable weapon than torpedo-carrying aircraft, which had until then been thought more dangerous, but which proved in the event to be more vulnerable, twenty of the twenty-six torpedo aircraft from the USS *Yorktown* being shot

down with no hits recorded, whereas the dive bombers were virtually unopposed and delivered the strikes which in the end won the battle.

Four Japanese aircraft carriers were sunk in the battle of Midway, together with the major portion of their highly trained and battle-experienced pilots. Only one of the three US aircraft carriers, the *Yorktown*, was sunk, and that after remaining afloat in a damaged condition for over two days, most of her crew being rescued.

Midway has rightly been adjudged the turning-point of the war in the Pacific. It signalled the end of the battleship as the supreme weapon afloat, the eleven Japanese battleships of Admiral Yamamoto's fleet then at sea never entering the action, which was

down of the *Bismark*, during which, with a chance salvo, she destroyed HMS *Hood*, the 42,000-ton battle-cruiser which was at that time the largest warship in the world.

But it was in the Pacific that the big set-piece battles took place which were to change the course of history. Of these the battles of Midway in 1942 and of Leyte Gulf in 1944 stand as the most important, making all earlier maritime encounters seem miniature in comparison. The Japanese began the war with a surprise attack on the United States fleet at Pearl Harbor, much as they had done on the Russians at Port Arthur in 1904. During the intervening thirty-seven years, however, the Imperial Japanese Navy, modelled largely on the British Navy, had become so powerful that in February 1941, ten months before Pearl Harbor brought the United States into the war, Churchill told Roosevelt: '. . . I think I ought to let you know that the weight of the Japanese Navy, if thrown against us, would confront us with situations beyond the scope of our naval resources.' This proved an understatement.

However, the devastating losses inflicted on the United States at Pearl Harbor in December 1941, plus the British loss of Singapore, Hong Kong and two of her newest battleships, had only a temporary effect. The Japanese High Command never comprehended the latent might of the United States until it was too late, and believing, as they did, that Hitler's Germany would triumph in Europe, they found themselves drawn into a gamble. A further expansion beyond the already overlong perimeter they had established in the first three months of 1942 – an expansion planned to run from the Aleutians via Midway, Samoa and Fiji to Port Moresby in Papua New Guinea – was

Above: USS *Yorktown* after being hit by a torpedo in the battle of Midway
Below: Anti-aircraft guns like these (photographed on the USS *Arkansas* in 1944) proliferated as attack from the air became more effective

just as well for the Americans whose nearest capital ships were at San Francisco and in any case would have been too slow to keep up with carriers. From then on the aircraft carrier was to rule the seas until the development of the guided missile after the war. The battle of Midway proved, indeed, to be one of the most decisive in history.

On weight of forces involved and on the area over which it took place, the battle of Leyte Gulf between 23 and 26 October 1944 stands as the biggest naval battle in history. By that time in the war, Anglo-American forces were back on the mainland of Europe, with Germany besieged and the Japanese, after nearly three years of island war in the Pacific, firmly on the defensive, although like Hitler they stubbornly refused to yield any ground they had once conquered without a fight. The key to this battle was the fact that from August 1944 American air strikes had been made on the Philippines and on the lonely islands of Chichi Jima and Iwo Jima which are only 500 nautical miles from Tokyo. An American reconquest of Luzon, therefore, the most northerly of the Philippine group, would constitute a direct threat to the Japanese homeland and would also cut their vital supply route through the South China sea. The Japanese had thus to act quickly to prevent the huge amphibious landing planned by the Americans from taking place.

To do this the Japanese assembled a fleet in four sections, comprising their two mammoth battleships *Yamato* and *Mushashi*, nine older battleships, six aircraft carriers, thirteen heavy cruisers, six light cruisers and thirty-one destroyers. American air power prevailed. At the end of the three-day operation Japanese losses were three battleships, four aircraft carriers, six heavy cruisers, four light cruisers and nine destroyers. This victory cost the Americans one light cruiser, two escort carriers, two destroyers and one destroyer escort, and this despite the employment by the Japanese at a critical moment in the battle of their Kamikaze corps, land-based aircraft making suicide dives on to American aircraft carriers. In addition to the sinkings, every major Japanese ship had been damaged, some of them seriously.

Although the war against Japan continued for the better part of a year and other large-scale naval operations were to take place, the battle of Leyte Gulf marked the end of serious carrier opposition by the Japanese and proved that even a weak air-striking force could hold off the most powerful battleships when unsupported by their own aircraft. From then on the Japanese Imperial Navy played only an auxiliary role in the country's war effort. Just as Lepanto saw the last effective use of oared galleys, so Leyte Gulf is likely to be the last action on the high seas undertaken by the battle fleets of two warring nations. The atom bomb and its aftermath changed the world for ever.

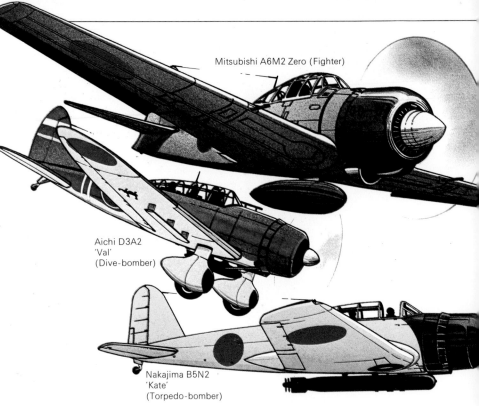

Mitsubishi A6M2 Zero (Fighter)

Aichi D3A2 'Val' (Dive-bomber)

Nakajima B5N2 'Kate' (Torpedo-bomber)

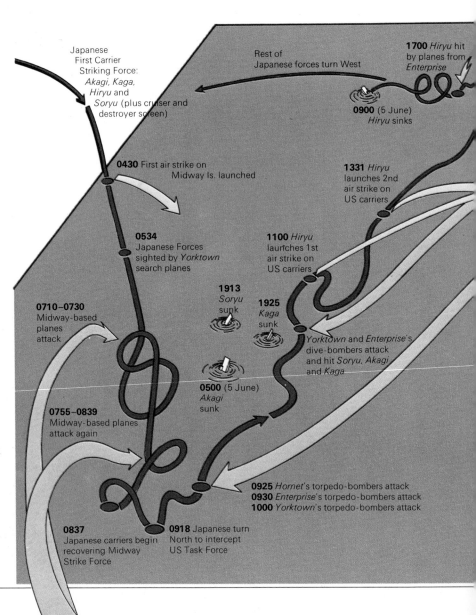

Japanese First Carrier Striking Force: *Akagi, Kaga, Hiryu* and *Soryu* (plus cruiser and destroyer screen)

1700 *Hiryu* hit by planes from *Enterprise*

Rest of Japanese forces turn West

0900 (5 June) *Hiryu* sinks

0430 First air strike on Midway Is. launched

1331 *Hiryu* launches 2nd air strike on US carriers

0534 Japanese Forces sighted by *Yorktown* search planes

1100 *Hiryu* launches 1st air strike on US carriers

1913 *Soryu* sunk

1925 *Kaga* sunk

0710–0730 Midway-based planes attack

Yorktown and *Enterprise*'s dive-bombers attack and hit *Soryu, Akagi* and *Kaga*

0500 (5 June) *Akagi* sunk

0755–0839 Midway-based planes attack again

0925 *Hornet*'s torpedo-bombers attack
0930 *Enterprise*'s torpedo-bombers attack
1000 *Yorktown*'s torpedo-bombers attack

0837 Japanese carriers begin recovering Midway Strike Force

0918 Japanese turn North to intercept US Task Force

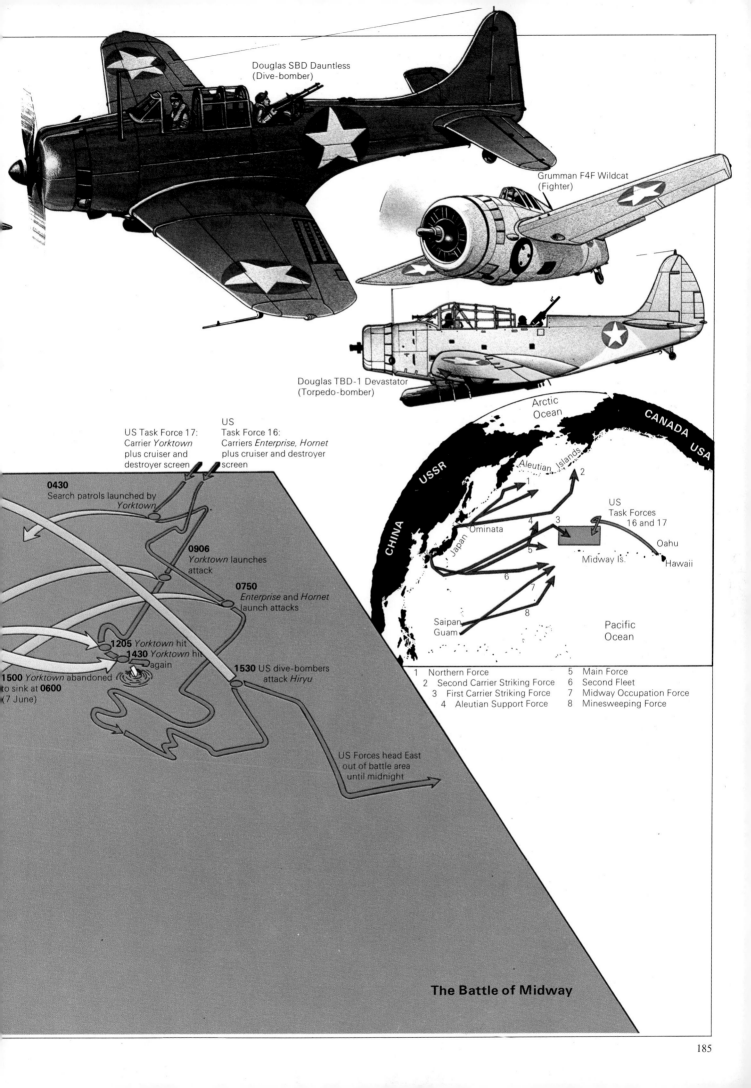

Douglas SBD Dauntless
(Dive-bomber)

Grumman F4F Wildcat
(Fighter)

Douglas TBD-1 Devastator
(Torpedo-bomber)

US Task Force 17:
Carrier *Yorktown*
plus cruiser and
destroyer screen

US
Task Force 16:
Carriers *Enterprise*, *Hornet*
plus cruiser and destroyer
screen

0430
Search patrols launched by
Yorktown

0906
Yorktown launches
attack

0750
Enterprise and *Hornet*
launch attacks

1205 *Yorktown* hit
1430 *Yorktown* hit
again

1500 *Yorktown* abandoned
to sink at **0600**
(7 June)

1530 US dive-bombers
attack *Hiryu*

US Forces head East
out of battle area
until midnight

Arctic
Ocean

CANADA
USA

USSR

Aleutian Islands

CHINA

Ominata

Japan

Saipan
Guam

US
Task Forces
16 and 17

Oahu

Midway Is.

Hawaii

Pacific
Ocean

1 Northern Force
2 Second Carrier Striking Force
3 First Carrier Striking Force
4 Aleutian Support Force

5 Main Force
6 Second Fleet
7 Midway Occupation Force
8 Minesweeping Force

The Battle of Midway

LIFE AT SEA
WARREN TUTE

To give a true picture of life at sea at any particular time must depend on the values by which you judge. The social gap between the sailor of 1914 and the sailor of today is far greater than that between the Tudor sailor and the sailor of 1914. Life at sea under sail from the fifteenth to the nineteenth centuries strikes us as all but incredible in the hardships endured and the difficulties overcome.

Certain realities and misconceptions, certain causes and effects, however, remain relatively constant. The links are there. The skills of the sea, inherited and learnt anew in each age, the psychology of the sailor, his fortitude and constancy in battle, his long tradition of belief in the greatness of his country and more particularly in the superiority of the ship in which he serves, his humour and continuing ability to suffer privation and disease for dimly seen ideals – these and many other factors have kept and keep the sailor of today in the great tradition of that anonymous mass, the 'people', as a ship's company came to be called, too often neglected by those in authority (and still to this day called 'hands'), whose prestige Nelson established with his victories and of whom he said, 'Aft the more honour; for'ard the better man'.

What then conditioned this better man and his life? How was he clothed, fed and paid? How were ships manned? Bearing in mind Dr Johnson's famous dictum – 'No man will be a sailor who has contrivance enough to get himself into a jail; for being in a ship is being in a jail, with the chance of being drowned. A man in a jail has more room, better food and commonly better company' – what made anyone go to sea at all?

The Press Gang, of course, springs to mind as an immediate answer. Indeed, it has become part of the folklore of English history, epitomising eighteenth-century brutality. Yet the process of forcing men to sea goes back to medieval times, when it was an understood part of feudal service, and forward to the twentieth century when it was called conscription. Life on board ship at any given time must be judged in the context of that time and not by the standards of subsequent ages.

In 1565, for instance, it cost fivepence a day to keep a man at sea in victuals. Twenty-two years later, the year before the Armada when the cost of living had doubled, it took sevenpence but seamen were also insisting on a gallon of beer a day. As this was beer brewed without hops it went sour and caused

Eighteenth-century engravings of the press gang, and the sailor's return

The Sailor's Return.

Just on the Beach arriv'd, with great Surprize, | But Molly's Mother, more sagacious, opes
Jack sees his Molly; Him too Molly Spies. | The wealthy Chest, on which She plac'd her hopes,
What is it Thou? with open Arms She cries. | And for the richest Prizes careful gropes.
Then drops the brittle Goods She sells for Bread, | The settled Crew gay Mirth and Love proclaim,
While all aghast beside stands Messmate Ned, | One leads aloft the mercenary Dame,
And points where flows the Bowl, & Gen'rous Red, | Who drunk, returns her Load from whence it came,
| Contemning Wealth, which they with Risk obtain,
Printed for Carington Bowles | Thus Sailors live, and then to Sea again. | in St Pauls Church Yard London.

enteritis, resulting in increased misery, a fact not really understood until it was made clear by the dietary and medical research of the twentieth century. So the sixteenth-century sailor, in this instance, gained what he wanted but in the event was no better off.

It is obvious that all ships have to be manned. Before the middle of the nineteenth century (the Merchant Shipping Act of 1854 and the Naval Reserve Acts of 1859 and 1863), the Merchant Service seaman and the Naval Rating were virtually one and the same. Without adequate manpower no vessel, let alone a warship, could put to sea, and whereas 'Rule Britannia' bravely declared that Britons never would be slaves, impressment in emergency has always been part of national life both on land and at sea. As an example of this Voltaire once described meeting a Thames waterman who boasted about the liberty of the English. The next day he was in a prison cell confined by the Press Gang.

For centuries lawyers have quoted Magna Carta as an argument against pressing, but in the context of medieval life the mariner was not a free man. He was as much a part of the ship owned by his master or lord as the standing rigging. His employment in the service of the Crown was a feudal obligation dating back to Anglo-Saxon times and, whilst there was no continuity, administrative structure or consistency in medieval naval history, the King's right to arrest men and shipping to implement service was accepted as the military basis of feudalism.

The British, being islanders, have always regarded themselves as having a natural linkage with the sea, salt being in their blood. In fact England in the Middle Ages could not be described as a seafaring nation and did not become one until the latter part of the sixteenth century, by which time the Spanish and Portuguese had been blazing ocean trails

for nearly a hundred years. Piracy or cross-Channel raiding was something else and at the end of the medieval period Richard Hakluyt (and many foreign ambassadors) made it clear that the English seaman was held throughout Europe to be 'the most infamous for outrageous, common and daily piracies'. It was out of this spirit of piracy and its cousin privateering that the Royal Navy was born.

Sailors, and especially the British, are among the most conservative men in the world. Navigation, with its newfangled charts, quadrants and astrolabes, was all very well for Spaniards and Portuguese, seamanship was what mattered to the English of the sixteenth century, and even as late as 1625 when Captain Luke Foxe returned from an unsuccessful search for the North-West Passage, he declared that he had no use for 'Mathematical seamen . . . for I do not allow any to be a good seaman that hath not undergone the most offices about the ship, and hath not in his youth been both taught and inured to all labours; for to keep a warm cabin and lie in sheets is the most ignoble part of a seaman; but to endure and suffer, as a hard cabin, cold and salty meat, broken sleeps, mouldy bread, dead beer, wet clothes, want of fire, all these are within board; besides boat, yard, top-yards, anchor moorings and the like.' It was a fair list of the duties and comforts an ocean-going sailor had then to expect.

Nor did it change except in detail, so far as food was concerned, until the invention of canning in the first two decades of the nineteenth century and of refrigeration at the end of the century. In fact, for nearly 400 years food in an ocean-going sailing ship remained poor to abysmal, mostly comprising rotten meat and hard tack (or ship's biscuits) liberally laced with weevils.

Food rather than pay or hardship was to be the cause of mutiny for over two centuries after the first recorded Court Martial in 1587. This took place in the *Golden Lion*, in which

ship Drake sent home his Vice Admiral, William Burrough, after a disagreement over tactics in the attack on Cadiz. On the way home the crew mutinied, petitioning the Captain 'to weigh of us like men, and let us not be spoiled for want of food, for our allowance is so small we are not able to live any longer on it. For whenas three or four men were wont to take a charge in hand, now ten at the least, by reason of our weak victualling and filthy drink, is scarce able to discharge it and yet groweth weaker and weaker . . . for what is a piece of beef of half a pound among four men to dinner or half a dried stockfish for four days in the week, and nothing else to help withal. We were pressed by Her Majesty to have her allowance, and not be thus dealt withal; you make no men of us but beasts.' The mutineers of 1797 said the same thing in almost the same words.

Victualling a ship was beset by two virtually unsolvable problems – the difficulty of preserving food, especially in hot climates, and the peculation of contractors. For 200 years the ration scale of the Navy remained unchanged at 1 lb of salt pork or 2 lbs of beef on alternate days, 1 lb of biscuit and 1 gallon of beer, with a weekly issue of 2 pints of pease, 3 of oatmeal, 8 ounces of butter and 1 lb of cheese. On southern voyages a pint of wine or a half-pint of brandy replaced beer, rice for oatmeal, and olive oil for butter. The Purser worked on fourteen ounces to the pound, keeping the other two as his perks, and the full measure of all articles was reduced by an eighth to compensate the purser for wastage or seepage. But even on that scale complaints were generally not as to quantity but to quality. Salt was the only preservative and contractors threw any old scrag end of meat into the barrel to make up weight. Moreover, since the Purser was in effect a civilian contractor afloat, he rarely resisted the temptation of an exorbitant profit.

The mariner's remedy when he could get it was liquor. Water in wooden casks soon

'The Point of Honour' – George Cruikshank's engraving of an imagined incident at sea shows crew and officers gathered to see punishment given

187

went putrid, as did beer and wine, though they soured at a slower pace. Brandy and rum, however, retained their efficacy and spirit of one kind or another became a staple of life at sea. Indeed, although drunkenness was severely punished (and by drunkenness was meant a state of total incapacity), most sailors kept a fair quantity of alcohol in the bloodstream to help them bear the awful conditions of life on board ship. They paid for this solace with the accidents, bruises and fighting which alcohol induces, and concussion when under the influence became extremely common in sailing-ship days.

Slops or clothing, and what the Purser charged for it, continued for long to be a contentious matter. Although officers acquired uniforms designed by George II in 1748, the lower deck had to wait until 1857. Moreover, slops were bought from a contractor ashore known as the Slop Seller and the Purser got a shilling in the pound on all sales. By overcharging both the living and the dead the Purser added to his commission and also to the overplus of stock which would become his at the end of the voyage. Men paid for their slops on tick (i.e. by ticket) which was deducted from their earnings when the ship paid off. It is scarcely surprising that the Purser was rarely the most popular man on board.

Engravings by Thomas Rowlandson: Cabin boy

Much could have been done to improve the appearance, health and morale of the lower deck had the Admiralty agreed to supply a uniform. In 1629 Sir Henry Mervyn pointed out to the Lord High Admiral, the Duke of Buckingham, that 'foul weather, naked bodies and empty bellies make the men voice the King's service worse than galley slavery'. But although six years previously the King had authorised an issue of slop clothing, 'to avoid nastie beastlyness by continual wearing of one suit of clothes and therebye boddilie diseases and unwholesome ill smells in every ship', the expense was not considered justified as the men were paid off

Midshipman

with the ship. Naval surgeons were always pressing for this reform as they realised how easily foul clothing allowed typhus to ravage a ship. But all that the Admiralty would agree to in 1757 was some sort of hospital uniform to prevent men deserting and in 1796 to an issue of soap.

Disease on board ship caused far greater casualties than enemy action. Ships were invariably overcrowded, the stench below decks was obnoxious, hygiene almost non-existent, and as nothing was known about antisepsis, any major operation was likely to prove fatal. The longer a ship spent at sea, the more acute became the dietetic problems at that time insoluble. Moreover, the incursion of northerners into the tropics laid them open to a variety of diseases, such as malaria, from which they had no immunity. Typhus would race through a ship as the bubonic plague did ashore, but the most serious disease afflicting the European mariner on long ocean voyages was scurvy.

Scurvy was known as the plague of the sea and the first recognisable description of the disease is on the Frenchman Cartier's voyage up the St Lawrence in 1534. Half the shipwrecks in history have been due to crews enfeebled by this curse, but no one knew why until the present century when the role of vitamins in diet was discovered. All that was certain in the days of sail was that after some forty days at sea on salt provisions, pimples appeared on the gums, teeth fell out, dark blotches appeared on the skin, old sores opened up and, most serious of all, a deadly lethargy overcame the sufferer. An added hazard was that any sudden movement caused by a blow or fall, both common aboard ship, killed the victim outright.

The tragedy in the story of scurvy is that, although one or two lone mariners guessed at the remedy (which was Vitamin C in the form of lemon juice and/or fresh vegetables) – just as in 1572 a merchant captain drew attention to the apparent connection between mosquito bites and malaria, nothing

was done since nothing penetrated the 'Obscurantist Portals of the College of Physicians', few of whose members deigned to serve afloat and all of whom maintained contempt for the inferior Barber-Surgeons who did. Discovery of the cause of scurvy was further delayed by conventional medical opinion which took it to be 'miasmatic' or due primarily to bad air and a noxious climate.

Altogether, the number of seamen who died in time of war by shipwreck, capture, famine, fire or sword were 'inconsiderable', wrote Dr James Lind at the beginning of the Seven Years War in 1756, 'in respect of such as are destroyed by the ship diseases and the usual maladies of intemperate climates.' The figures bore him out in a startling way. In that particular war 133,708 men were lost by disease or desertion, 1512 died in action.

Nor did the construction of naval hospitals at Plymouth and Portsmouth (Lind became the first superintendent of Haslar, at that time the largest brick building in Europe) solve any problem of health at sea, except that of accommodating the sick if and when they could be got ashore. In the eighteenth century a hospital was a place where one usually went to die. On Anson's voyage round the world in the 1740s – described as the most infamously manned and equipped on record – 1051 died out of the 1955 who embarked. After a six weeks' cruise of the Channel Fleet in 1780, 2400 sufferers from scurvy were landed at Haslar.

In view of such living conditions and likelihood of death, why did anyone other than pressed men ever go to sea? The answer is complex and only understandable in the context of the times and of life ashore. From the Conquest to the late nineteenth century, seafaring men and agricultural labourers have been the most ignored and therefore worst treated of all sections of the community. Yet go to sea they did, albeit, as the Admiralty was for ever saying, not in the right numbers at the time they were required.

Carpenter

But the eighteenth-century world was very different from that of today. A man without work could easily starve. Even the most menial job was a prized possession. Adventure was certainly to be had afloat. Some took the King's shilling for patriotic reasons, some for the prospect of prize money, but most, in all likelihood, for a combination of those reasons plus the chance of bettering yourself if you had any aptitude for the sea. Few such chances were open to you in village or town unless you were born with a silver spoon in your mouth.

Discipline was certainly ferocious whether you were an Able Seaman in a warship or a 'packet rat' in the tough ships which plied the North Atlantic on the first liner services to be organised in the early part of the nineteenth century. It had to be. The conditions of life on board a sailing ship required it. Nevertheless, it has always been true that there is no such thing as a bad sailor, only a bad officer, and the good officers of any period never had trouble in filling their ships. Not only Nelson but other great Captains of that era could pick and choose. Moreover, from the eighteenth century onwards, in time of war the British sailor was conscious – and frequently reminded in song and story – that his forebears had won ascendancy at sea over the Spanish and the Dutch. This knowledge bred in him a subconscious assurance of his own ascendancy over the sailors of France in the eighteenth century or Germany in the twentieth. This aggressive confidence made the Royal Navy take the war into the enemy's camp, proving yet again that attack is the best form of defence. The great naval commanders of both centuries, because of their qualities of leadership, enjoyed the respect and in some cases the love of the men who served under them.

The hallmark of all great British Admirals has always been that they took care of their men. Hawke's visible exertions in the Seven Years War, for example, produced better rations. Boscawen's measures for the health of his ship's company shone out in an age of darkness. Hood, Howe, Jervis and Nelson would invariably see justice done and would not rest until they were satisfied. Men would cheerfully risk death for leaders such as those. No wonder Nelson referred with pride and justification to the 'band of brothers' he had the honour to lead.

Of course money came into it too. No sailor, in his own opinion, has ever been paid the right rate for the job, possibly excepting the Captains of East Indiamen, whalers and part-owners of merchant ships. But employed sailors, never. Moreover, the volunteer 'currency', so to speak, was always debased by the availability of the dregs of humanity to be found in dockyard ports. Unskilled service afloat – and these scrapings off the floors of dockside public houses were known in the Navy as 'landsmen' – was in effect slavery under a different name, and the life of an Able Seaman (that is to say a seaman able to hand, reef and steer) was little better. The only corrective to this – and it was a big one – was Prize Money.

There is a mention of prize money as early as 1205 when King John, in ordering the bailiffs, reeves and King's representatives at various ports to send two shipmasters and 140 mariners to man two royal ships at the Tower, promised them 100 marks and half the value of any prizes taken. In Elizabethan times the prospect of making a fortune at sea had the attraction of horse racing today. Syndicates were formed, often headed by the Queen (who backed Drake), to seek out a good ship with a reliable Captain and then to fit her out as a privateer. Throughout ensuing centuries Admiralty courts were kept busy apportioning money due, the distribution of shares being as contentious a matter as union law today.

From 1708 the whole value of a prize went to its captors, the Crown waiving its share. However, this did not necessarily mean a great increase in Jack Tar's share. The value of the prize was divided into eighths, of which three went to the Captain, one to the Commander-in-Chief, one to the officers, one to the Warrant Officers, and two to the rest of the crew.

Sailor

Prize money always became a major incentive to recruitment when an outsider romped home, such as the capture of a Spanish treasure ship in the course of the Seven Years War. The treasure ship in question, the *Hermione*, was condemned in prize for £519,705, a colossal sum of money in those days when a seaman was paid £1.4.0 a month. Two frigates took this prize, each Captain receiving £65,000, every Lieutenant £13,000 and every seaman £485.

The basic seaman's wage and its payment formed the core of the pay problem. Between 1653 and 1797 the rate remained unchanged, the First Lord of the Admiralty maintaining

Purser

then (as had all his predecessors) that any rise would make 'an enormous increase to our disbursements already sufficiently burthensome'. Even Nelson when writing to his friend St Vincent, the First Lord, in 1803 considered that 'their pay and provisions cannot possibly be improved from what they are at present'.

The trouble was invariably that the actual payment of wages was bedevilled by abuses of the ticket system. For obvious reasons as little bullion as possible was carried afloat, a settlement of wages and other accounts being made on the return of a ship at the end of her commission to pay off. Out of an Able Seaman's 24/–, an Ordinary Seaman's 19/– and a Landsman's 18/– a month there were deductions of sixpence to the Royal Hospital, a groat of fourpence to the Chaplain (whose official stipend was 19/– monthly), twopence to the Surgeon (who got £5), plus a fine if the man was suffering from venereal disease. Volunteers received, in addition, their bounties and Warrant Officers were reasonably paid at £4 a month.

An added annoyance to both officers and men was that their counterparts in the Army were better paid. However, low wages might have been acceptable had they been punctually paid. The regulations called for wages to be paid every eighteen months, but before paper money a ship could only be paid off in hard cash at a recognised port after all her pay books, muster books and a multitude of forms had been passed. For that reason a ship on a foreign station could only be paid off on her return home.

As late as 1811 Lord Cochrane, like Nelson a strong supporter of his sailors' interests, was quoting ships that had been eleven, fourteen and fifteen years out East with none of her men paid at all. The crew of one 74-gun ship paid off at Plymouth had not set foot on land for six or seven years, except in the dockyard at Jamaica.

Unfortunately the aptitude of shoreside

authority – victuallers, dockyard contractors, slop sellers and Navy Board pay officers – to swindle and embezzle to the detriment of the sea-going sailor was greatly helped by the psychology of the victim himself. Money is something a sailor cannot hang on to for long. In the case of the 74-gun ship quoted above, and excluding commissioned and warrant officers, it took £22,000 to pay off the crew, yet within hours or at the most days many of these valuable, experienced men were as penniless as if they had been paid off in shillings.

Jack Nasty-face (a seaman whose real name was Robinson and a lower deck commentator of the Napoleonic war) describes a typical paying off day:

> In the early part of the day the commissioners came on board, bringing the money which is paid the ship's crew, with the exception of six months pay, which it is the rule of the government to hold back from each man. The mode of paying is, as the names are, by rotation on the books: every man when called is asked for his hat, which is returned to him with his wages in it, and the amount chalked on the rim. There is not perhaps one in twenty who actually knows what he is going to receive, nor does the particular amount seem to matter of much consequence; for, when paid, they hurry down to their respective berths, redeem their honour with their several ladies and bumboat men, and then they turn their thoughts to the Jew pedlars, who are ranged round the decks and on the hatchway gratings, in fact, the ship is crowded with them. They are furnished with every article that will rig out a sailor, never omitting a fine large watch and appendages, all warranted, and with which many an honest tar has been taken in: they can supply them likewise with fashionable rings and trinkets for their ladies, of *pure gold*, oh! nothing can be purer.

Women were officially banned from HM Ships in 1817, but the practice of taking certain of them to sea continued for at least another twenty years, nine Petty Officers' wives being known to have been on board the *Genoa*, a 74, in Codrington's fleet at Navarino, the last great battle under sail in 1827. A baby was born on board HMS *Tremendous* during the battle of the Glorious First of June and was christened Daniel Tremendous Mackenzie. Another was born at the battle of the Nile where the women were stated to have behaved as well as the men. One of them later petitioned Nelson for a pension as 'she had assisted the surgeon for eleven weeks afterwards'. That they were allowed on board at all stems from the reluctance of Commanding Officers to grant shore leave even in home ports through fear of desertion, a grievance taking pride of place with food in the 1797 mutiny petitions.

'The Sailor's Progress' by George Cruikshank

Because of this ban on shore leave, every man of war arriving in harbour would be welcomed by boat loads of ladies of the town, a scene well described in an anonymous pamphlet of 1822 (actually written by Admiral Hawkins, an 'Evangelical' officer who did a great deal to improve service conditions after the Napoleonic war was over):

> It is well known that immediately on the arrival of a ship of war in port, crowds of boats flock off with cargoes of prostitutes. Having no money to pay for their conveyance, the waterman takes as many as his boat will hold, upon speculation, and hovers round the ship until she is secured at her anchors and the necessary work done, when he, with others, is permitted to come alongside. The men then go into the boats and pick out each a woman (as one would choose cattle) paying a shilling or two to the boatman for her passage off. These women are examined at the gangway for liquor which they are constantly in the habit of smuggling on board. They then descend to the lower deck with their husbands, as they call them. Hundreds come off to a large ship. The whole of the shocking, disgraceful transactions of the lower deck it is impossible to describe –

> the dirt, filth and stench; the disgusting conversation; the indecent, beastly conduct and horrible scenes; the blasphemy and swearing; the riots, quarrels and fighting, which often takes place, where hundreds of men and women are huddled together in one room, as it were, and where, in bed (each man being allowed only fourteen inches breadth for his hammock) they are squeezed between the next hammocks and must be witnesses of each other's actions; can only be imagined by those who have seen all this. A ship in this state is often, and justly, called by the more decent seamen 'a hell afloat'. Let those who have never seen a ship of war picture to themselves a very large low room (hardly capable of holding the men) with 500 men and probably 300 or 400 women of the vilest description shut up in it, and giving way to every excess of debauchery that the grossest passions of human nature can lead them to; and they see the deck of a 74-gun ship the night of her arrival in port.

During the decade after Trafalgar the renown of the great naval victories won during the Napoleonic war improved the status and popularity of the British seaman. In the century of the Pax Britannica which followed,

In Irons for getting drunk

a Greenwich pensioner — relating his adventures

Pub'd Jan'y 18th 1818 by G Humphrey 27 St James's S'

his living conditions though never becoming ideal consistently improved. No longer despised as a social outcast, for which, it must be admitted, he was in part responsible, or pitied as the victim of an unjust system, he became admired as the chief defender of Country and Empire, basking in the sunshine of a national interest amounting to fervour from the latter part of the nineteenth century. 'Rule Britannia' became the universal secular hymn, sailor suits for children were the fashion, and it was taken for granted that every nice girl loved a sailor as she would certainly have been forbidden to do by her parents at the beginning of the century.

This promotion in national appreciation was matched by a genuine rise in the sailor's own self respect, aided by the grant of uniform in 1857, the end of impressment and the inauguration of regular pay based on long service and pension agreements, the provision in all ships of a decent diet appropriate to the climate in which the ship was working, adequate shore leave as of right, and the 'suspension' of flogging (in peacetime in 1871, in wartime in 1879, though never 'abolished' as it was in the Army in 1881). By the time of the Diamond Jubilee Naval Review in 1897, the Royal Navy, its officers and men, were held in greater esteem than they had ever been in the thousand years since Alfred first took on the Danes.

Similar improvements occurred in the Merchant Service, helped in part by the creation of the Royal Naval Reserve in 1859, which was designed to draw on merchant seamen in a crisis and by such reformers as Samuel

Plimsoll who, aided by Lloyd's, put an end to the notorious coffin ships sent to sea by unscrupulous owners for the insurance money.

The days of sail effectively ended in the 1860s and the Royal Navy and Merchant Navy as we know them today began. By 1890 the United Kingdom was building four-fifths of the world's shipping and owned three-fifths of the tonnage afloat. Perhaps of more lasting importance was the adoption of international standards of professional life at sea, set in the first place by the Royal Navy and the British Merchant Marine, and on which world commerce has built ever since.

Above: A more idealistic view of life at sea: The Captain preaching
Below: J C Ibbetson's *Sailors Carousing*. The men with the frying pan are testing their new silver watches

SEAPOWER TODAY
WARREN TUTE

The essential role of every navy remains to-day what it has always been – the maritime defence of the particular country and of its allies. The problem of what sort of navies should be built, however, and of how they are best employed, is complex, evolving and of a constant urgency. The vast fleets of Dreadnought battleships with which Great Britain and Germany entered the First World War, where strength was gauged by numbers of ships, qualified by tonnage, speed and calibre of gun, gave way in the Second World War to the supremacy of the aircraft carrier. We now live in an age of the guided missile, launched from a submarine, an aircraft or a surface ship. Nuclear electronics dictate the techniques. Scientifically-trained officers and men are required to work them. What sort of navy, therefore, do nations consider adequate to their defence in the 1980s?

First to define the task. Here world politics write the scenario, geography decrees the setting in which the drama is played, the central fact being that the oceans still comprise an immense international highway, essential to some and of strategic importance to others. Modern science has made it impossible for any one nation to control the oceans of the world in the manner the Royal Navy did in the nineteenth and early part of the twentieth centuries. But the threat of regional interference is still very much alive – the modern equivalent of colonial wars.

Nations depending on a maritime strategy are still at risk and history is very clear about what happens when such nations abandon that strategy either voluntarily through a loss of will or through defeat at sea. They go into decline. There is no exception to this rule and there never has been. Moreover all recent conflicts have shown that victory on land not accompanied by control of the seas can only be short-lived. Battles are won or lost in any environment. Wars can only be lost at sea.

The phenomenon of Russian armed might since World War II is alarming. Men under arms have increased by more than a million in the last ten years. 450,000 are in her strategic rocket forces alone. Over 10,000 new military aircraft were produced last year and a new supersonic 'Backfire' bomber goes into service every fortnight. Russia now has the largest submarine force the world has ever seen: over 450 boats are in service of which 150 are nuclear-powered. It takes five years of skilled building to make a submarine and the Soviet Union is turning one out every

Above: The *Yuri Gagarin*, a Russian satellite-tracking ship
Below: The US submarine *Nathan Hale* surfacing off the New England coast

five weeks. This is more than twice the NATO rate, for instance, and the cost, of course, is prodigious. Some 11–13% of Russia's GNP goes on defence and a quarter of that is applied to research and development. The USA and UK rates are 5.7% and 5% respectively.

In deploying her armed force, the Russian navy is backed up by a fast-growing merchant fleet, the cargo part of which is now the largest in the world. Her newest roll-on, roll-off ships currently seen in the North Atlantic are also used to supply military equipment unobtrusively to Third World clients at short notice. Her Fishing and Hydrographic fleets, too, are the world's largest and, in marked contrast to the free flow of shipping in the rest of the world, these ships are centrally controlled from naval headquarters in Moscow.

The offensive capacity of the Russian surface fleet, which numbers over 250 ships of frigate size and above, can now exert a decisive influence on certain kinds of limited conflict in distant areas of the world and this is in addition to the war-winning potential locked into its operational submarine force. All in all, the Soviet Union today has a well-balanced, modern and effective fleet, fully capable of worldwide operations.

Apart from the US first strike capability, what defence can the non-communist world put up against a possible Soviet attack?

The concern of all western navies is to prevent the first alternative. This requires an ability to be there where it matters with ships and equipment superior to or at least a match for the Russian counterpart so that it will become very clear that any escalation will inevitably lead to a situation in which the Russians are *not necessarily* going to win and will certainly suffer grave consequences if they proceed.

The first essential, of course, is to build the right ships for the job. Here consistency is the key. Nowadays it takes almost ten years to design and produce a new warship which then remains in service for anything up to thirty years. In political terms that is equivalent in the United States to ten Presidencies and in Britain to eight full Parliaments. Western naval planning, therefore, has to be based on a realistic long-term assessment of the threat and cannot respond to short-term changes of policy. New governments can hinder, delay and weaken but otherwise have little long-term effect. All are committed. Generally speaking, though, this has worked to the advantage of modern navies. The Royal Navy today, for instance, is one of the most cost-effective in the world.

All this, however, takes time, experience and money. It takes continuity in training and a highly professional determination not only to survive but to win a possible war. In the global answer to that question, geography plays a decisive part and here the West has an advantage.

The coast of the USSR is split into five distinct regions of which the arctic coastline of Siberia can be ignored because of its ice conditions. In each of the other four regions separate fleets are based. These regions comprise Murmansk, the Baltic, the Black Sea and the Far Eastern Pacific coast. There are thus four separate and powerful fleets at large in the world which the US and European navies have to oppose.

Leaving aside the Pacific and Indian oceans for the moment, the physical passage of Soviet European fleets from base to open sea is constrained by geography. Surface ships and submarines are compelled to pass through what are known as 'choke points'. The Murmansk fleet has first to penetrate the Svalbard–Norwegian North Cape gap and then the Greenland–Iceland–UK gap. The Baltic fleet must emerge through the Kattegat between Sweden and Denmark. The Black Sea's fleet must pass through the Bosporus and Dardanelles before gaining the Mediterranean, exit from which is controlled at one end by the Suez Canal and at the other by the Straits of Gibraltar. These necessities somewhat ease the problems of surveillance so that not all the aces are stacked in the Russian hand.

Once in the open ocean there are unlikely to be any more pitched battles such as Jutland or Leyte Gulf, where capital ships hurled shells or dropped bombs on each other. Today missile and anti-missile techniques condition the scene, and tactics are decreed by electronic and satellite intelligence. The single important fact is that both the US and Soviet navies can now maintain a world presence, and both are in more or less permanent confrontation in sensitive areas such as the Mediterranean and near the Persian Gulf. Nuclear submarines can circle the world without surfacing and can remain operationally at sea for months on end. Of course the objectives of thus remaining at sea are as primitive as ever – sinking enemy shipping, assault from the sea of enemy coastlines, and the capacity to land thereon with an occupying force.

Ships remaining at sea for long periods require supply, and until recently the lack of overseas bases considerably limited Soviet global maritime power. Now, however, the Russians have fleet auxiliaries capable of operating all over the world. They have also acquired valuable base rights in South Yemen (in the old British base at Aden). They are established in Cuba on one side of the Atlantic and in Angola on the other. In the Far East they benefit in Vietnam. In addition, the Soviet navy uses anchorages outside present territorial limits near Cyprus, Crete, Egypt, Libya and Tunisia. In the Indian ocean, the Russian fleet deploys around Socotra off the Horn of Africa (another former British base), Aden, Massawa and the Persian Gulf.

Logistic resupply differs considerably between the Soviet navy and those of the West. The Russians keep it to a minimum. Staple food consists of dried and salted provisions and only very occasionally are fresh vegetables bought ashore. Conscripts stay in the same ships for two and a half out of their three years' service so there is no airport requirement to shuttle men from base ports at home to the fleet. No mail is received or sent while ships are on deployment.

Conditions in the US Sixth Fleet in the Mediterranean and the Seventh Fleet in the Indian ocean are totally different. The ship's company of a 96,000-ton aircraft carrier such as the *Eisenhower* numbers 5400 in peacetime, with another 1000 in full combat condition. With an ethnic mix of whites, blacks, Puerto Ricans and Filipinos, great care is taken not to exacerbate any racial problem and a Human Resources Council on board each ship exists to oil the wheels. Food aboard is good and plentiful. 250 men supply three meals every twenty-four hours with up to 3000 loaves of bread a day being baked.

Multi-channel television, films, a comprehensive hospital and dental department, a chapel for all denominations and three separate shops selling anything from a toothbrush to an expensive camera are taken for granted, together with opportunities to continue high school or college studies under civilian teachers for the eighty per cent or so of enlisted men without previous sea experience. For service conditions the US and Russian fleets are light years apart.

Both navies, however, depend on what came to be known in World War II as 'Fleet Trains' – assemblies of auxiliary ships which can supply and repair the fighting fleet and keep it at sea for virtually as long as may be required. Both navies – and to a lesser extent the Royal Navy – have also developed a 'global limited intervention capability' – amphibious ships able to lift troops to any part of the world. In the end, though, it is the human element which will win or lose a war.

In the past ten years the size of the American fleet has shrunk from 976 ships in full commission to about 460. Numerically the Russian navy is going into the lead and the American fleet is now smaller than at any time since 1939. Numbers, however, comprise only a part of the story. As a result of decisions made several years ago, both American and NATO naval capabilities are improving significantly so that there is probably still a slim margin of superiority in favour of the West. In any case it is likely that principal warfare, if it comes, will take place in Atlantic and European waters where the fifteen nations assigning their navies to NATO will be in the front line. Of these nations Great Britain makes by far the most significant single contribution. The Royal Navy is still the third largest in the world and since 1967 virtually the whole of it has been assigned to NATO.

NATO's defence strategy, like that of the United States which backs it, is based on

Above: HMS *Renown* launching a missile during exercises off Cape Canaveral in 1974
Below: HMS *Fife* in Malaysian waters. The lack of portholes is due to the sealing off against contamination by nuclear fall-out

deterrence, and the ultimate deterrent is, of course, the strategic nuclear arsenal. In this allied arsenal the Royal Navy maintains four Polaris submarines which, together with another four from France (not in NATO but working alongside), make up the total European contribution. The USA provide a further forty-one, so that a total of forty-nine in the West stand against the USSR's eighty-nine, of which sixty-nine are nuclear-powered.

In quality the Soviet navy of today bears little resemblance to that of the early 1960s when the Western powers had a marked superiority at sea. Modernised, improved and numerically stronger, it is now in a position to tackle at least part of the strategic defence of the homeland. It also has effective control of waters adjacent to the Soviet Union. If this potential were limited to defence, there would not be much of concern to the West. However, the West's European lifeline requires more than 120 ships carrying three million tons of cargo every day of the year to replenish Western Europe. This is in addition to oil imported over and above that from the North Sea. With supply under threat what can NATO do to counter it?

NATO maritime forces have become a balanced assembly of modern, highly-efficient vessels, containing the most sophisticated and advanced equipment. These ships are designed for three distinct types of operation – Undersea, Anti-Air and Surface warfare.

NATO now places anti-submarine warfare (ASW) as its prime task in war. This is because, unlike the last war when convoys could conveniently lose themselves in the vast expanse of the Atlantic, any ship afloat can now be pinpointed in a very short time by the huge Soviet Bear Delta reconnaissance aircraft which patrol over the North Atlantic. These aircraft can remain airborne for twenty-four hours, if need be, and can sweep a 500-mile swathe of sea by radar. They are also equipped to detect and home in to radar and communication transmissions made by ships. The North Atlantic has been reduced to the proportions of a back yard.

Although the Russian submarine force is a mixed bag of offensive potential, its principal weapon is the anti-ship missile launched from under the sea. The ocean floor of the Atlantic, where anti-submarine battles are most likely to be fought, consists of mountainous ridges behind which submarines can hide and deep ocean plains which allow sound to be channelled and in which the submarine has space and freedom of action. Against that, however, nearly all shipping entering European ports must pass into UK waters and, because the English Channel is basically a funnel, enemy submarines would be contrained in shallow waters, unable to use their proper speed and performance against the rich targets passing overhead.

NATO's mix of ASW forces is already formidable and likely to become even stronger.

The hub of this is a Command ship (such as the British *Hermes* or *Bulwark*) working anti-submarine helicopters. These aircraft carry sonobuoys, active sonar, radar and a mixture of ASW weapons. Then there are the surface-ship escorts, such as frigates, which carry their own light ASW helicopters. In addition, aircraft such as the Nimrod, which are flying computer platforms, are armed with an entire ASW system of their own and can also co-operate with any other ASW unit in the finding and destruction of a submarine. Finally, if a nuclear attack submarine were to be available to operate with the ASW group, it could detect an enemy well ahead of the force and might be able to dispose of it before it could reach a suitable position for launching its missiles or torpedoes.

ASW is not only concerned with sinking submarines. Surveillance is the name of the game and in war it would, of course, go on night and day 365 days of the year. In peacetime it does so whenever there is a period of tension or when NATO needs to know where 'hostile' submarines happen to be lurking under the ocean during its exercises. This continuous peacetime surveying of the oceans for submarines and other ships inevitably impresses upon the Russian High Command the fact that the West is fully able to counter and deter aggression. Should that deterrence fail, then NATO's ASW forces are increasingly well placed to sink and destroy.

The second type of operation is Anti-Air Warfare (AAW), which is the term NATO navies now use to describe air defence operations at sea. AAW is closely linked to ASW and Anti-Surface Vessel Warfare, and all contribute to the destruction of missile-launching submarines and ships. Because of the long stand-off ranges on which threat missiles operate, a force at sea must know what is going on well beyond the horizon. Ships' air-warning radars search out aircraft within a radius of more than 200 miles but because of the earth's curvature, low-flying aircraft can escape detection until they have come in close. So NATO relies today on Airborne Early Warning, radar carried high above the sea in aircraft. Now that NATO has no aircraft carriers from which to fly fighters, external air support is essential, though the fleet will soon be able to supplement this with a small number of Sea Harriers which take off and land vertically.

In addition ships carry their own anti-missile defences. These vary from ship to ship and range from the latest Sea Dart and Sea Slug missiles to small-calibre guns. Some ships have medium- to long-range missiles (SAM systems) in order to whittle away a missile attack as soon as possible. This then simplifies target allocation for shorter-range weapons.

The inner core of surface-force defence is composed of what are called 'point defence missile systems' – radar jammers and guns.

This variety of defence is needed because some missiles are bound to get past the fighters and SAM barriers and others may be fired from within the force's outer defences. The Sea Cat was the first-point defence-missile system, small, compact and worked by seamen gunners who took great pride in the skill necessary for its control. Today, however, the Sea Cat is being replaced by the Sea Wolf system which is faster and all but automatic.

AAW is a complex operation. It calls for clear and rapid appreciation of a developing threat and the immediate and efficient co-ordination of all the different weapons available to a fleet at sea. It is a vital component in the modern navy's flexible response to aggression. It thus reduces the threat of an ultimate nuclear exchange.

The third type of operation – the destruction of enemy surface ships – used to be the only means by which sea power could be effectively exercised until the nuclear age. Today NATO relies on aircraft or submarines to deliver initial attacks on surface ships, but a surface-to-surface weapon is now also fitted in guided-missile destroyers, supplementing the conventional gun. This is the Exocet system whose missiles have a range of twenty miles, completing their final approach to the target by skimming just above the waves and thus making them difficult to destroy. Guns still play an important part in surface operations. The modern 4.5-inch gun fitted in destroyers and frigates is automatic and can be fired from the operations room without anyone in the turret or gun bay.

Today the sophistication of war at sea demands 'Command reactions' of an immediacy never before contemplated or necessary. The total fighting capability of ships must now be at instant readiness if they are to survive in war. The basis of such reaction is the computer, its facilities and what navies today call its 'interface with man'. There is no longer time to go through the hallowed formalities of bringing a warship to her action state. Now, if necessary, highly trained young officers must react correctly to any situation at any given moment and in a matter of seconds initiate action, if need be without orders from above. The sailor of today, be he officer or rating, carries a huge weight of responsibility on his back – the security, in fact, of the world.

Nautilus' trip under the polar ice cap dramatised the potential of nuclear submarines

Chapter Five

HARVEST

On the north-east coast of Scotland lies the Moray Firth, a wide inlet that bores deep into the highlands from the North Sea. On the south side of the firth, near its narrowest point, is the small garrison village of Ardersier. Until 1972 it remained relatively undisturbed, hidden off the main Inverness to Aberdeen road. The low, uncultivated marshes to the east of the village were visited by few but ornithologists. Then everything changed. The marshes were transformed into a huge pad of sand and concrete and the village was overshadowed by a series of steel structures that rose high above the land. The oil industry had come to Ardersier.

Now, in July 1979, the largest of these structures yet to be built was nearing completion. It had taken four years' planning and more than two years' building. At one time almost 2500 men had worked on it. Weighing three times more than the Eiffel Tower, it now had to be moved 285 miles north-north-east into the middle of the North Sea. This massive object was the base of an oil platform – what is known in the

The North Sea in a mood of deceptive tranquillity. Problems of oil, pollution, and over-fishing make the North Sea a test case of our ability to use the potential of the world's oceans safely

business as a jacket – and it was going to the Murchison oilfield, the most northerly yet to be exploited in the North Sea, and lying in some of the deepest water.

Although it lay on its side the jacket rose 300 feet into the sky above McDermotts' construction yard. Looking at the great web of steel, it was hard to believe it could ever be moved. Yet the plan was to shift the jacket on to a barge, tow it out to sea and launch it. It would then be upended and placed on the sea floor within feet of its designated position. If successful this would be a major achievement, for the Murchison jacket was by far the largest to be launched in this way. Yet it would only be one of a series of remarkable technological advances that have been made in the battle to win oil from below the stormy waters of the North Sea.

The unexpected discovery of vast oil and gas fields off the Netherlands, Britain and Norway in the 1960s suddenly focused attention on the North Sea. Yet for centuries this plankton-rich sea has been providing us with riches in the form of abundant fish. I had come to Ardersier not just to find out about oil technology, remarkable though it is, but to get insights into the world-wide problems which a booming population and an energy crisis have brought to the harvesting of all the sea's resources. Oilfields which would have been too expensive to exploit ten years ago are profit-making concerns; fish species which were unmarketable are now mashed into fishmeal to provide protein for a hungry world. Our demand for food and energy is insatiable, and sophisticated technology can now tap many of the sea's once inaccessible resources.

The North Sea, because it is rich in both fish and oil, is an ideal place to discover how well man is handling the harvesting of the oceans' wealth. I was about to accompany the Murchison jacket out to oilfields whose ownership has been divided fairly amicably between the maritime nations of the North Sea. I was then going to the Shetlands, where people who have long been fighting for their fair share of the fishing catch are now finding that there are less and less fish to share. Good management and wise husbandry are the cornerstones of bountiful harvesting, yet my voyages in the North Sea would show that, when at sea, man still values present riches above future rewards and has limited regard for the importance of maintaining the health and productivity of the sea. The delicate balance of life in the water is easily upset, and the chemicals and waste that are spewed into the North Sea are an ever-increasing source of serious pollution.

My voyage was starting here at Ardersier. The 540-foot-high jacket was nearing completion and would soon start its long, slow journey on to the barge, known in oil language as the 'load-out'. The 'float-out', when the barge would be edged down the man-made creek next to the construction site, and the 'tow-out', which would take the jacket to the field, would follow. Once in position a village of living, working and drilling modules would be fitted into a frame on top of the jacket, giving the finished platform a height of 866 feet above the sea-bed – well over twice the height of the Statue of Liberty. The earliest North Sea platforms stood in fairly shallow water of between 100 and 350 feet, but the jack-up platforms used there are not suitable for the northern fields with their greater depths and fiercer weather conditions. In the north you have to build a structure that the sea cannot shift. It is quite an undertaking. The Murchison jacket was going to be pinned to the sea floor by thirty-two piles. Sleeves for these piles cluster round each of the four main legs, ready to guide the seven-foot-diameter tubes of steel deep into the sea-bed.

'We call 'em bottles,' said a Texan project manager, indicating the sleeves. 'And you see the base of the legs that look like elephants' feet? They're known as cookie-cutters.'

All parts of a production platform have names which owe little to the language of civil engineering and still less to that of the sea.

'This jacket's just a way of getting real estate above the water.' The Texan thus neatly summed up the oil industry's attitude to the North Sea; it is an area of water that has to be built over, to be dominated and tamed so that oil can be extracted. Initially the sea offers a challenge, but once the platform is erected and a small area of civilisation established, you can forget it – if it will let you.

The designers had not underestimated the North Sea. With a project that had cost £70 million so far they could not afford to. The jacket itself would stand only thirty-two feet above sea level, but the module support-frame which slots on top like the basket on a supermarket trolley raises the platform over a hundred feet above the sea. This creates an air gap which allows the largest possible wave to pass underneath. In a severe storm exacerbated by tidal surge an exceptionally large wave, a 'hundred year wave', might reach a hundred feet, the crest rising more than sixty feet above mean water level. The highest possible wind speed for the North Sea had been calculated at 150 miles an hour.

These conditions are hard to imagine, yet the North Sea has been known to produce hundred-mile-an-hour storms and sixty-foot waves on several occasions. It breeds such harsh conditions because it lies near the path of the low-pressure systems which sweep across the top of the Atlantic from America. Frequently it is the northern part of the North Sea that catches the strongest winds. Furthermore, the North Sea is relatively shallow and the waves which bounce off the sea floor are steep, sharp and unforgiving. Understandably, the owners of the Murchison jacket were nervous about towing their multi-million-pound steel tower out into all this. A smaller jacket for a Brazilian field had been towed out from Ardersier and had run into bad weather; the tow had broken, the barge turned sideways, and the barge and jacket had gone to the bottom off the Scottish coast.

The weather window – the summer months when wind and sea should be moderate – does not last long at 61° North. Now, in late July, time was running short and tremendous pressure was being exerted on everyone to get the load-out under way. Anxious oil company executives were appearing at the site in increasing numbers. In overall charge of the project was the oil giant Conoco, who had a third ownership of the lease for UK Block 211/19 in which most of Murchison Field lay. Gulf Oil and the British National Oil Corporation also held one third each. Everybody was well aware that a delay could cause a postponement of the launch until the following spring and lose the oil companies millions of pounds. However, at the end of July the last of the riggers and welders finally climbed down from the web of rust-red steel, the forty giant cranes surrounding the jacket moved away, and the load-out could at last begin.

Bunches of heavy wires attached to hydraulic jacks started to haul the enormous structure along the slipways on which it had been built, and on to the giant barge, known as *H109*. The barge, 600 feet long and 155 feet wide, was the largest in the world. Inside its black anonymous hull two diesel engines pumped water in and out of the multitude of ballast tanks. Although the barge rested on a platform of sand specially built up from the bottom of the adjacent creek, the effects of the rising and falling tides and the enormous weight of the jacket slowly coming on to the barge had to be carefully evened out and counterbalanced or the barge would simply crumple under the enormous load.

Eight hours after the jacks started to inch the jacket along the ramps all activity came to an abrupt halt – one of the massive haul wires had snapped and a strand had whipped into a man's leg. Within minutes the site ambulance and the resident first-aid staff had arrived; such accidents were not uncommon. No one had actually been killed so far: 'a miracle' someone said to me. Some months before, a portal frame crane, specially built to lift the long, heavy components, had collapsed, flinging debris over a wide area and narrowly missing people and buildings. Fortunately it had happened during a meal break when the site was relatively uncrowded.

With the injured man removed, the jacket continued its slow 200-yard journey on to the barge. The giant slipways had been cleaned and covered in a thick, gooey mixture of teflon and grease to ease the passage of the 25,000-ton weight. Even then progress ranged from smooth to fitful; sometimes the jacket moved along fluidly at several feet per hour, and at other times it paused, only to jerk forward suddenly so that loose wires and equipment rattled and swayed high up on the cross-beams. Fascinated, I stood close to the slipway, trying to see the often imperceptible movement. But after one jerk, when a forgotten ladder fell with a thud behind me, I retreated to a safe distance.

After thirty-three hours the jacket finally came to a rest in position on *H109*, and the job of fixing one to the other began. The sea fastenings – 120 steel struts – were welded to jacket and barge, to hold the two together in the most extreme weather. The tow-out could now begin. It was 15 August, uncomfortably late in a Scottish summer which had not anyway been good; the Firth was usually curtained by heavy drizzle and low cloud. But it was the wind which was the critical element; the tow could not take place in winds of over twenty knots, or Force 5, while the float-out was limited to winds under ten knots; anything greater and the barge might be blown sideways as it was being edged through the narrow canal out to the Firth.

The day before the float-out was due to take place there were many worried men at McDermotts' yard. These were the executives who had to decide whether to go ahead with the operation the next day, or postpone it. They needed seventy-two hours of fine weather to deballast the barge, float it off, tow it out to the Field and then launch the jacket on to the sea floor. Once there, the platform base would be safe. But a clear seventy-two hour forecast was a tall order. There were several tense meetings, during which news came through of a bad storm south of Ireland which was causing havoc to the top event in the yachting calendar, the Fastnet Race. In Scotland the wind was slight and the outlook fair, but this was not good enough for the insurer's representative; he vetoed a tow-out on the next morning and insisted on waiting for a more certain forecast.

At the next meeting there was a further postponement: the tow master in charge of the seven tugs waiting in the Firth felt the risk of cross-winds was too high. But finally on the afternoon of 16 August, it was decided to proceed with the deballasting ready for a float-out the next morning. The relief on the faces around the yard was immense; now they could get to grips with the challenge ahead. Only the consultant meteorologist remained nervous, hoping his predictions would prove correct.

That night I took a ride on one of the smaller tugs out to the *Husky*, on which I was to sail to the Murchison Field. The *Husky*, 200 feet long with 12,000 horse power to play with, was the main towing tug. If the weather blew up it was her Dutch crew who would have the job of keeping the barge and its vastly expensive cargo safe. The captain explained that if the waves became too high they would have to turn upwind, otherwise the seas could damage the parts of the jacket that overhung the barge. If it blew a full gale and the risk of breaking a cable developed, rather than take the chance, they would try to run for shelter in the lee of the Shetlands or a Norwegian fjord until

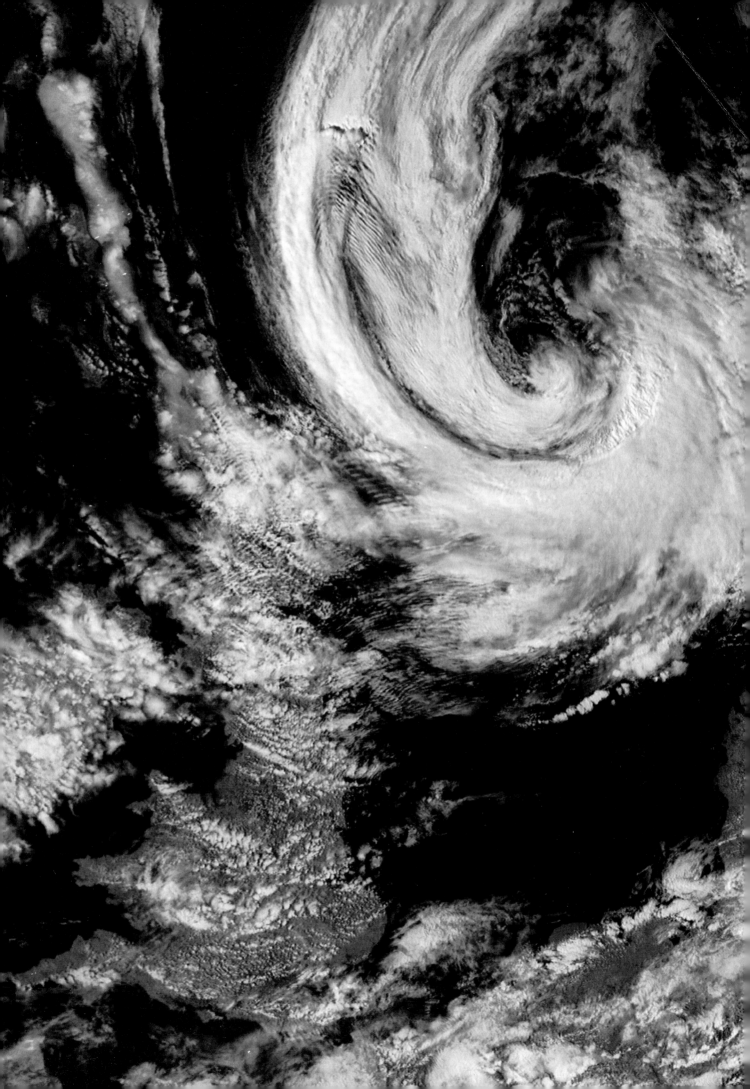

the weather moderated. The captain was matter-of-factly professional in his approach to the problems, yet he, like everyone else involved, was caught up in the excitement of the forthcoming launch, the culmination of four years' planning by the Murchison licensees and over two years' hard toil by the construction workers.

At dawn on 17 August there was hardly a breath of wind. The barge was now deballasted and riding high in the water ready for the float-out. Four small Voith-Schneider tugs took up their positions at the corners of the barge and started to edge it away from the dockside. From the deck of the *Husky* little seemed to be happening at first. Then the giant framework suddenly started to swing around, executed a quarter circle, and moved resolutely down the channel in the firm grip of the tugs. Within minutes the barge was out into the Firth and turning again, ready to take the tow. The *Husky* backed up to the *H109* until the jacket loomed high above her, the men threw a heaving line to the barge crew and then ran out the heavy double-nylon shock-absorbing rope that preceded the three-inch wire cable. By eight in the morning the *Husky* had the *H109* under tow and was sailing out of the Moray Firth towards the North Sea. The float-out had gone without a hitch. There was still hardly a breath of wind.

At McDermotts' yard the men were taking a final look at the intricate object they had created. For many it would be their last day's work for some time. McDermotts' were hoping for another large order but, in the way of the oil industry, a flood of work seemed likely to be followed by a famine.

Alongside the *Husky* another tug, the *Njord*, put out a towline to the barge, to be doubly sure the *H109* was kept under control. A third tug stationed herself a mile ahead to keep other vessels clear of the main party. Two supply boats completed the armada.

By 0900 the *Husky* had run out 800 yards of cable and was slowly building her speed up to nine knots. If she could maintain her speed – and that depended entirely on the weather – we would arrive at the Murchison Field by the following evening, well ahead of schedule. On the bridge of the tug a small group, the tow master, the Conoco representative, and the insurer's agent, all stood at the rear, staring out through the large windows over the stern, watching the barge follow obediently along at the end of

The tiny figures in the foreground give the scale of *H109*

Harvest

the cable. It seemed strange to be towing what looked like a 60-storey skyscraper. But their preoccupation was the weather and when the telex started to spit out its twice-daily weather forecast and the weather facsimile machine churned out a weather map, they examined the data with keen interest. Fortunately the low-pressure systems in the area remained benign and the outlook was good. There was relief and a visible relaxation on the strained faces around me. The operation was going to go well.

The low hills and dunes bordering the Firth were lost in steady drizzle and grey murk; only the radar showed the land falling away to starboard as we headed 056 on the compass to pass to the east of the Orkney Islands, Fair Isle and the Shetlands. Ninety miles north-east of the Shetlands lay the Murchison Field; for the moment its presence was marked only by a series of bright orange buoys.

H109 under tow

The vast oil resources lying east of the Shetlands were first discovered in 1971 and took the world by surprise. But the oil companies were quick to respond. Large fields like the Ninian, Brent, Cormorant and Statfjord were developed with amazing rapidity considering the technical difficulties of drilling and producing in depths of around 500 feet. The Murchison Field was discovered 9900 feet below the sea-bed in 1975 and was soon confirmed as a significant find by the drilling of further wells. Now, just four years later, it was only months away from production. However, it was sobering to be told that, at the planned rate of production, the platform would be in service for only about fifteen years. Then it would become obsolete, a massive dinosaur that would have to be destroyed. It was a sad reflection on man's priorities that he should put so much energy and ingenuity into perfecting a device that would serve him so short a time. Yet the ever-rising price of oil ensured that, in time, the oil companies would exploit even smaller fields with even shorter production periods.

When the Murchison Field was finally mapped it was found to extend into the Norwegian segment of the North Sea, but this was not a problem. The proportion of oil estimated to belong to the Norwegians was agreed between the companies and countries involved and the proceeds were to be shared accordingly. It was an amicable agreement, as are most such arrangements in the North Sea. This is a result of the existence of law – a basic requirement, one would think, but one which is almost totally absent in most matters relating to the sea. In 1958, when the presence of oil and gas off

Northern Europe was no more than a vague suspicion, it was agreed that countries had the right to exploit the natural resources of the sea-bed not only within their traditional three-mile territorial waters, but beyond, to the limits of the continental shelf, the area of relatively shallow and accessible sea-bed which extends about fifty to a hundred miles off the coast of Northern Europe and includes the North Sea. However, many countries could lay claim to large areas of the North Sea, and inevitably there was some argument over who got how much. For example, West Germany had a short coastline on which to base a large claim. But agreement over the delineation of each country's share was finally reached in early 1972.

The sharing out of the North Sea spoils was a great landmark in the story of the sea. For centuries men had warred to gain mastery of the oceans and now agreement in one area at least had been reached without a fight. When the vast mineral and food potential of the sea is just being realised this has enormous importance for the future.

International co-operation permeates North Sea enterprises mainly because the development of sea-bed energy resources has required huge international investment and expertise. Twelve companies from Britain, the USA and Norway share the ownership of the Murchison Field, while the workforce is collected from a dozen different countries. The fourteen modules which were to sit on top of the platform had been manufactured in France, Scotland, England, Holland and Norway.

Twelve hours after leaving Ardersier the *Husky* and her load were clear of the Scottish mainland and out into the open sea. As a north-westerly swell swept in from the Atlantic the tug started to roll her unhappy passengers through twenty degrees, but behind us the *H109* hardly moved at all, though the occasional wave reached up to touch the sides of the jacket. The waves would have to be considerably larger before the barge began to roll through the critical 20°. 'No worries at all,' smiled the captain.

However, some anxiety returned the next morning, not because the weather changed but because our progress was to be delayed. We were to meet the giant self-propelled crane barge, the *Balder*, at the Murchison Field. Without her the launch could not possibly go ahead for she had the equipment and cranes that were essential for the positioning operation. But she was delayed at the Ninian Field, finishing a job there. There was nothing for it but to slow down and delay our arrival by a day. Another day at sea could change everything; it was long enough for a gale to develop, long enough to make all the difference between success and failure. People began to look nervous again. The weather forecast for the next twenty-four hours was still good but thereafter there was likely to be a deterioration, although the Met men could not say how quickly this would occur.

By nightfall we had reached the oilfields and the sky was unlike any I had ever seen at sea. The darkness was pushed upward by the fierce glow of clustered orange lights on the horizon around us. Everywhere flare booms held up their burning flames like olympic torches, and the platforms themselves were lit brilliant white like office buildings. It was a scene from science fiction, not something a mariner would expect to find seventy miles from the nearest land, in the middle of a wide sea.

When it was agreed to extend countries' rights to include the mineral wealth of the sea-bed, the arrangement was not intended to affect the legal status of the surface water as 'high seas' that are free and unencumbered to shipping. However, safety zones of 500 metres from the outside of fixed installations like oil platforms were permitted to be closed to ships. The result is that large areas of the North Sea are in practice unnavigable, for few captains would try to weave their ships through the more clustered oilfields, particularly in bad weather. Certainly I would never attempt it in a yacht for fear the visibility might deteriorate and I would end up in the air gap under a platform, testing the strength of the mast. Fishermen complain that they have lost many of their trawling grounds as pipelines and platforms and new underwater obstructions proliferate; conservationists argue that this is a good thing, if only because it gives the fish somewhere to hide.

It seemed a serious waste of precious energy to burn flares and I wondered if the gas could not be put to use in some way. I was told gas is burnt off only when a platform first goes into production, to ease pressure and heat in the oil reservoir. Once the pressure has reached a safe level the gas can be re-injected. When the oilfield is nearing the end of its life the injection of further gas does not bring the oil up any faster, so it can then be run ashore and used for energy. In practice the oil companies have been tempted to burn off more gas than they need to, and the British Government has used its conservation powers to limit the quantity of gas flared on the well-established Brent Field.

By the Sunday morning – two days after leaving Ardersier – our speed had reduced to three knots and, having almost reached the Murchison Field, we turned south again to meet the *Balder*, now on her way from the Ninian Field. At the slower speed the tow had been shortened to prevent the cable dragging along the sea floor and eventually breaking. Contrary to popular belief, cables of that size do not whiplash back on to the deck of the tug when they break; in fact the first the tug crew would know of it would be a slackening of the cable and the sight of their tow disappearing behind them. The main danger to the crew was in turning, as we were doing now, for then the cable, swinging across the stern of the tug, may move very rapidly. The first mate of the *Husky* had seen a man cut in two that way.

The crane barge
Balder

Dense fog had been predicted and now, as we looked for the crane barge, the cloud base was beginning to descend. This made the eventual appearance of the *Balder* all the more striking, for her bulk seemed to fill all the space between horizon and cloud. Indeed, as we got nearer, I realised that most of her two crane derricks were lost in the mist. The *Balder* is one of the two largest crane barges ever built. She is 450 feet in length and 282 feet in breadth. Her working deck is 138 feet above the sea, while her two cranes rise to a height of 450 feet above the surface – it was no wonder they were lost in the fog. One of the cranes is capable of lifting 3000 tons, making it the largest in the world. Add accommodation for 550 men and a helicopter pad and the vessel is a mobile, independent construction unit. The *Balder* looks very unlike a barge; she seems much nearer to a drilling rig. Indeed the principles successfully applied to rigs have been adapted for this massive vessel so that she can operate in all weather conditions except the most severe. She is a semi-submersible; below the surface are tanks which can be ballasted with water or filled with air. From them six slim legs rise up to support the working deck high above the sea. When under way the *Balder* fills her tanks with air so that she rides high and light in the water. When in position she ballasts her tanks and sinks down until the working deck is just above the maximum wave height. Like this she is extremely stable, the ballasted tanks giving her weight and the slim legs offering least resistance to the seas. This brand-new barge and her sister ship were revolutionising work in the North Sea. Before, it had only been possible to build platforms in the summer months, but the *Balder* was now able to do the construction work – driving piles, lifting and positioning modules and module support-frames — throughout the winter, saving the Murchison licensees many months' delay and millions of pounds. Presumably the saving would be greater than the *Balder*'s fee – an incredible $235,000 a day or over $7 million a month if she is hired by the day.

Finally, the fleet arrived at the oilfield and the *Balder* positioned herself next to the platform site, ballasted her tanks, and sat down in the water. Ten of her twelve anchors were run out and the cables winched tight. Everything was now ready for the work on the *H109* to start. As twilight fell, parties of welders were transferred from the *Balder*, bright with lights and life, to the ghostly darkness of the massive black *H109* with its vast burden still draped in mist and dank cloud. By nightfall the jacket was illuminated by the flashes of a dozen oxyacetylene arcs cutting through the sea fastenings. At this stage I too prepared to transfer. I had been given permission to go aboard the *H109*, not only to see the preparations for the launch, but to witness the event itself. One thing I was going to be careful about, and that was the place I was standing when the jacket was launched. Apparently it would not actually slide off the *H109*; rather the barge would shoot out from beneath the jacket with one end submerged in the water. The manoeuvre sounded rapid and more than a little exciting.

The tug *Njord* transferred me from the *Husky* to the *H109*. It was two in the morning and pitch black. The bow of the *H109* loomed high above the tug's deck as she manoeuvred alongside. It was still calm, yet a large swell lifted the tug almost to the level of the barge's deck and then dropped her into the blackness below. A basket swung down from nowhere and, in the moment that it remained on the deck, I was pushed forward and told to grab the ropework. Like a spider on a web I clung to the outside of the basket as it suddenly shot in the air and, swinging gracefully, wove its way up on to the deck of the *H109*. Dumped unceremoniously on the steady deck of the barge, I regained my breath and asked the crane driver how he would have got everyone aboard in bad weather if it was this exciting in a calm. He thought about it but couldn't tell me how they would have done it, except that they woud have managed somehow because they *had* to.

The *H109* was buzzing with activity as dozens of men cut away the metal fastenings so that they fell with thunderous clangs to the steel plates of the deck. The barge was beginning to list as the far end was ballasted, ready for launch at dawn.

When the first thin light of the day began to illuminate the vast steel structure above my head, all but eight of the sea fastenings had been cut away. The deck of the *H109* sloped down into the water, one end fully ballasted. Wires from the four corners of the jacket had been run out, two to the *Balder* and the others to the tugs. Now, like the trick of whipping away the tablecloth without disturbing the china, the *H109* must be removed from under the jacket.

At an unseen command the last sea fastenings were cut away and everyone held his

H109 sinks beneath
the North Sea

breath. Nothing happened. I had positioned myself beside a hydraulic ram at the top
of a slipway, the bottom of the jacket just inches away. Now the operator was given a
signal and the hydraulic ram started up. Slowly, it nudged the foot of the jacket.
Slowly, almost imperceptibly, the whole wall of steel started to move down the
slipway, gathering momentum as it hissed and roared towards the water – except of
course it was we on the barge who were shooting out from *under* the jacket, but I felt
little sensation of movement, only of the barge rising higher and higher. With a muffled
crash the jacket hit the water and sent up plumes of spray and then, slowly and
majestically, it slid on and on into the sea. The base of the jacket dropped off the end of
the barge and, after rocking gently for a moment, the whole thing floated quietly and
sedately in the water, just a few feet showing above the surface. A mighty cheer rose
from the welders and the barge crew; the largest jacket yet launched had survived its
baptism.

After another tug and basket ride I arrived on the *Balder* to find all attention focused
on the upending and positioning of the jacket. Three navigation systems involving
radar, sonar and laser were being used to obtain accuracy to within three feet. On
the jacket itself four men had been dropped by crane on to an egg-like structure where
the buoyancy tank controls enabled them to upend the jacket and slowly sink it on
to the sea floor, previously cleared and smoothed in preparation for the event. Only
when the final adjustments had been made and the jacket had come to rest on the
bottom did the men who had given birth to this web of steel allow themselves to
celebrate with cheers and congratulations. The jacket was at last safe from the weather,
even now deteriorating into strong wind and rain.

Despite the size of the Murchison jacket no one was in any doubt that even larger
jackets would be launched in the future, that more complex and advanced platforms
would be built. Already this platform was to incorporate new technology in the most
fascinating area of oilfield development: in the area of subsea completions, that is,
wells that are remote from the producing platform. Rather than waste the exploratory
wells drilled years before, these had been capped and would now be connected to the

platform by flowlines running along the sea-bed. Here on the Murchison Field they were to try using double flowlines to shuttle parts to and from the well-head and to carry out certain repairs automatically. These would be similar to the air-pressure tube systems in old-fashioned department stores, using oil rather than air, and with perhaps a better chance of seeing your change returned.

During the setting-up operation they would also be using sleds to lay cables along the sea floor – anything to avoid the use of divers at these depths. The mortality rate among North Sea divers was high; only two weeks before two men on the nearby Thistle Field had died from cold after their hot water lines had become severed. Also, divers are very inefficient working in cold and darkness at extreme depths. The physical discomforts of the job were brought home to me by the unexpected sight of two small diving bells sitting next to a metal cabin on the *Balder*'s deck. Thinking they were empty I looked at them quickly and walked away. Later I was told they contained four men who had been in there for ten days, and would remain there for another twenty. These men were being 'stored' at bottom pressure, their blood saturated with nitrogen so that they would be ready to descend at a moment's notice. Once a task was done, they could be brought straight up and their bell attached to a pressurised living module where there was a little more room to stretch out and while away the time. But beyond that small world they could not move without a long period of decompression. Not a job for those with claustrophobia or a love of wide open spaces. Each man earned $10,000 a session and he deserved every penny.

Just thirty feet of the jacket was now showing above the sea. Soon thirty-two piles would be driven through the sleeves into the sea-bed and they would start to build the village for 200 men on top of it. Then would come the rush to get the platform into production; time was worth millions here. In May and June 1980 they would lay a ten-mile pipeline from the platform to the nearby Dunlin Field to join the Brent pipeline system. They would link up the existing wells to the platform using subsea completions, and soon after start to drill new wells. By the next autumn the oil should be flowing. To be sure as much oil as possible was extracted they were going to inject water at the bottom of the field. Later, when all twenty-two wells were drilled, ten of them would be used to inject water and two gas – all to push out more oil.

North Sea oil should, in theory, make Britain self-sufficient in energy for the first time, an important landmark for her economy. And yet how long will this bonanza last? At the planned rate of production this field will be exhausted in fifteen years and the known North Sea reserves in about thirty. What, everyone is beginning to ask, will then take its place? The arguments for conservation are strong, the case for rationing impressive, yet until recently nothing was done to slow down our use of this non-renewable resource. The oil companies want a fast return on investment and therefore wish to recover the oil as quickly as possible. Despite massive price rises demand shows little sign of slackening. We are hooked on energy; motor cars, central heating and air travel are so much part of our daily lives that we regard them as essentials. And so we make only feeble attempts to conserve; we pay lip-service to energy-saving. The British Government, happy at first to let the soaring oil tax revenues reduce the balance of payments deficit and increase Government revenue, has now awoken to the necessity of reducing consumption by reducing production. Without Government intervention there will be a production peak in the mid 1980s, when Britain will have enough oil for her own needs and a large excess equal to a third of her consumption for export. By ordering oil companies to curtail or delay output the Government can smooth out this peak and maintain self-sufficiency well into the 1990s. If nothing is done the country will be dependent on imports again by the end of the 1980s and all the North Sea oil will be burnt up in thirty years – just half a generation.

After the jacket launch I had a couple of hours before leaving the Murchison Field by helicopter, and took the opportunity to look around the *Balder*. Her working deck was strewn with cables, piles of steel girders and plates, and, even as I watched, a crane started to lift giant piles on to the deck from a barge that had been manoeuvred alongside. From this noisy, dirty working area the accommodation section on the stern was a complete contrast. Clean, white and sparkling, the only sound was the quiet hum of the ventilation system. Numerous cabins led off the many corridors on the three decks, each with two or three comfortable bunks and, in many cases, a shower. Over 500 men usually lived in this block and the *Balder*'s owners tried to keep them as happy as possible by providing recreational facilities, a cinema and above all good food. The spacious modern kitchens had a permanent staff of skilled chefs who turned out large meals four times a day. At each meal there was a wide choice of dishes, including a cold table which groaned with delicacies like smoked salmon and pâté. Having been up all night and missed breakfast I consumed a hot dish, a plate of cold food and two puddings, all delicious. But, as on HMS *Blake*, I was beginning to feel conspicuous by my gender. Although friendly enough, the men did not like having a woman on their ship. They preferred to keep the two worlds of ship and shore separate; one where they worked long, hard months without a break, and the other where they enjoyed women's company and spent their hard-earned money. My presence was upsetting the system and, when the helicopter arrived to take me away, I felt somewhat relieved.

Lifted high into the sky, a brave new world of rigs, flares, platforms and loading buoys spread out below me. Man-made structures seemed to spring from the sea for miles around. Hidden unseen beneath the surface two massive pipelines took the oil from this cluster of northern fields away to the west, to the quiet, isolated Shetland Islands where I was now going.

The islands lie one hundred miles north-north-east of the Scottish mainland, on the same latitude as Leningrad and the southern tip of Greenland. There are more than one hundred islands in the Shetland group, but only sixteen are inhabited. For thousands of years men have wrested a bare living from these forlorn windswept isles by crofting and fishing. As fish stocks rose and fell, so did their slender fortunes. Ironically it was during an upturn in the islands' economy that the East Shetland oilfields were discovered and the decision taken to build a giant oil terminal at Sullom Voe in the north of the main island. Now, almost ten years later, the terminal, which covers 1000 acres of bare hill and cleared peat bog, is nearing completion. Soon it will handle about half of Britain's oil production: removing water from the oil, extracting gas, and processing the gas into liquids for transportation.

Driving across the main island from the airport, the building of the oil terminal seems at first to have had little impact. Small stone cottages stand in an acre or two of fertile ground between the hills and the sea; peat is cut and loaded on to carts for winter fuel; sheep graze the bare hillsides. Yet inevitably the oil has brought great changes. The lure of high-paid jobs has taken men and women away from their traditional occupations. Some men have given up crofting, a way of life that was usually combined with fishing or another trade, because the hours they must work at the terminal preclude it. Women who knitted the traditional Shetland sweaters for small pay can now earn ten times as much cooking or cleaning for the construction workers. Young school-leavers drive lorries rather than go on to college. The influx of newcomers has put great pressure on housing and schools where there was none before. Also, not surprisingly, the incomers have brought new ideas and attitudes. The Shetlanders enjoyed a society of small communities where everyone knew and cared for each other; where time was slow and this job or that could wait until the next day. The oil philosophy with its desire to get things done quickly at all costs was quite alien.

Oil has brought some great benefits to the Shetlanders. They are extremely well compensated for the upheaval to their communities. The oil companies pay generously for the privilege of using Sullom Voe. They try to employ Shetlanders in long-term jobs whenever possible, thus keeping people on the islands who might otherwise leave. However, talking to local environmentalist and broadcaster Dr Jonathan Wills, I discovered that there is at least one major issue still dividing the islanders and the oil men: the problem of pollution. Just a month after the terminal opened there was a large spillage of oil in Sullom Voe which killed nearly 4000 seabirds. But more worrying, because it is a continuing problem, is tank-cleaning. This has been a major source of pollution ever since oil began to be transported by sea. It has accounted for more beach pollution and bird destruction than all the accidental spillages from sinking or damaged ships put together. The crux of the problem, like so many concerning the sea, is lack of international law enforcement. Although tankers are not meant to clean out their tanks in preparation for taking on a new load anywhere but in specially designated areas well out to sea, there is little to prevent them doing it close to land under cover of darkness. And the more unscrupulous captains do. With so many ships under flags of convenience and difficult to prosecute, with the facts anyway difficult to establish, little can be done after the event. But the effects can be catastrophic on seabird-rich coasts like those of Scotland and Shetland. However, some steps have been taken. When the islanders asked that tankers be made to follow certain routes around and approaching the Shetlands, this was agreed by the industry, although they were not bound by law to do so. Furthermore, it was agreed that ships who were known to have washed out their tanks near land should be refused entry to Sullom Voe. It was a small beginning. But the whole battle is not likely to be won until public pressure forces the oil industry and governments to spend the money and pass laws which will effectively prevent pollution.

The other major users of the North Sea, the fishermen, remain unhappy about the presence of the oil industry – although paradoxically they rely heavily on oil to carry out their work. The Shetland fishermen complain that the pipelines running into Sullom Voe cross some of their best fishing grounds, making them unworkable. They also maintain that the pipeline casings are not strong enough to withstand the strong currents near Shetland, risking an oil leakage. Above and beyond these individual complaints there is a widespread feeling that oil interests are riding roughshod over those of the fishermen. Geordie Hunter of the Shetland Fishermen's Association told me that the fishermen feared their industry was being allowed to run down through this infatuation with the short-term benefits of oil. He pointed out that in spite of oil, fishing was still Shetland's most important industry. Once the oilfields were exhausted the islands would have to rebuild an economy based on renewable resources.

But the question now being asked is how renewable are these resources? How long will fish stocks remain large enough to sustain the enormous catches currently being landed? And even if the Shetlanders want to maintain an economy based on fish, will they be able to do so? The history of fishing in the North Sea – and many other parts of the world – is a sad tale of greed and self-interest. In contrast to the story of oil, there

Cleaning up in Brittany after the *Amoco Cadiz* disaster

The herring industry at its height: steam drifters about 1927 and
herring packing in Lerwick about 1930

has been little or no international co-operation in the management of fish stocks. Indeed, during the hundreds of years that the coastal waters of Europe have been yielding large quantities of food, fishing has been marked by international discord and massive exploitation with scant regard to the effects on stocks. The Shetland fishing industry accounts for nearly a third of Britain's total catch, yet the islanders have grave fears about their future.

Typical of the smaller Shetland fishing boats, the *Orion* is a sixty-nine-foot trawler with a crew of six. For the second of my North Sea voyages I was to join her for a day's fishing off the west coast of Shetland. The boat was based at Hamnavoe, a village of under 500 people on the island of Burra, off the west coast of the main island. Hamnavoe has always been a fishing village, its close-knit community bound inexorably to the sea. Sometimes a boom in fishing or boat-building has brought prosperity; just as often, times have been hard. Walking through the village today it looks much as it must have done a hundred years ago, the small stone cottages snuggling deep into the gentle hillside that rises from the voe. Only telephone lines and television aerials reveal the presence of the twentieth century.

At five in the morning I joined the *Orion*, a wooden, black-painted fishing boat built in Scotland over twenty years before. Her skipper, John David Henry, introduced me to the six crew who are also co-owners. Shetland boats are generally worked on the share system, rather than men working for wages from an absent owner. A good catch and they all do well, a bad one and no one makes any money. Also on board for the day were Geordie Hunter, to give me the fishermen's story, and Jonathan Wills, the fierce exponent of conservation.

At five-thirty the *Orion* felt her way out of the voe in darkness and headed southwest to the Scalloway Deeps. By seven the seine net was cast and the *Orion* was steaming slowly against the tide, rolling heavily in the beam seas. The skipper was after whiting; a catch of a hundred baskets would be a good return. When finally the net was pulled in over the stern, even I could see it was going to be far short of that. The catch was in fact three baskets. The next catch and the one after were not much better. No one looked surprised. Only I looked astonished as nearly half of the fish caught were thrown back over the side. They were too small, I was told, and it was illegal to land them. But shouldn't the large mesh size ensure that they escaped? Not, apparently, when fishing with seine nets. The large fish block the mesh holes and the small fish are trapped. By the time the net is hauled aboard all the fish are dead from suffocation. What then is the point in throwing the small ones back for the seagulls to eat? The crew shrugged: tell that to the bureaucrats who make the rules! It was a mad, illogical situation, but really just another symptom of the general malaise: chronic and extensive overfishing.

Fish, unlike oil, has long been regarded as a renewable resource, and one which should be freely available to all, irrespective of territorial rights. Man has always hunted fish rather than harvested it. As Jonathan Wills put it, he has reaped and reaped – and never sown. For hundreds of years catches in the North Sea were generally counterbalanced by natural restocking. Fishing methods were simple and, by modern standards, inefficient; lines had to be painstakingly rebaited by hand and sailing boats could not follow fish far afield. Drift netting for herring developed, but was always extremely selective. As the fish rose to the surface at dusk the nets trapped only the large mature fish. The arrival of steam much improved the catches, but never seriously affected the total stocks. From as early as the sixteenth century large foreign fleets would periodically arrive to exploit the rich grounds off the Shetlands. First the

A seventeenth-century
Dutch herring boat

Dutch and later the Faroese and the Scots arrived in even larger and more efficient craft that took larger quantities of fish. The Shetlanders never liked these invasions, but learnt to tolerate them and to learn the new, more efficient techniques of the invaders.

However, no one was prepared for the full onslaught of modern technology that arrived with the Norwegian purse-seine fleet in 1965. The large modern ships used sonar to locate shoals of herring, place the net around them and then drew the purse strings tight, thus catching entire shoals.

The effects of this new technique were far-reaching. At first, herring were caught on an unprecedented scale. This resulted in a significant diminution of stocks. By 1971 conservation measures were introduced, but proved ineffective. Finally, in 1978, herring fishing was completely banned. The Shetlanders had been forced to stand by and see one of their most important species hoovered up before their eyes. Some had tried to emulate the Norwegians by investing in purse-seiners, but most had been able to do nothing.

Nowadays the Shetlanders mainly fish for white fish like haddock and whiting. However, here again stocks are under pressure, this time from industrial trawling. The Danes in particular are catching vast quantities of fish, using fine-mesh nets which trap all and any fish irrespective of size. The main species caught is pout, but five per cent of their catch is allowed to consist of immature protected species. Thus, large quantities of young fish are mashed up into fish meal before reaching any kind of maturity; five per cent of a catch is not much, but when the fish are young and tiny it constitutes millions of fish.

What, I asked Geordie, was the fish meal used for? 'Huh!' he exclaimed in disgust, 'it goes to feed all the pigs they sell back to us as Danish bacon!' Eighty per cent of the Danes' total catch is used to feed animals and provide the overfed European world with meat. Used in this way much fish protein is as good as wasted, because animals give a poor return for the amount of protein they consume.

The continued indiscriminate catching of fish irrespective of size and to a great extent species will, it is feared, aggravate an already serious situation. It is not just a case of banning the fishing of a certain species, Geordie Hunter suggested, it was also a matter of creating the conditions whereby that species could breed again – and little was known about the interaction of species or of what precisely was required for prolific spawning. Despite the fishing ban, no one had yet shown that the herring would ever recover and it was possible that irreparable damage had already been done.

The *Orion*'s last catch of the day lay at our feet. It was even smaller than the last. Again, at least half the fish were thrown back. Surely something was being done – had already been done – to conserve these dwindling stocks?

Both conservationists and fishermen agree that too little has been done too late. The three-mile limit around the coast was not sufficient. Neither was the current quota system ideal because it resulted in men having to throw back certain species once their quota was full; another wasteful exercise.

The whole crux of the conservation problem revolves around the question of ownership of fish stocks. Fish are migratory. Unlike oil reserves, they do not remain within the territorial waters of any one country. One month they may be off Norway, and another off Shetland; why then should not Norwegian boats catch 'their' fish off Shetland? Several countries in the European Economic Community argue that the fish off Europe are communal property and should be shared according to need rather than coastline length or other arbitrary factors. Which countries should be allowed to fish in the North Sea is as bitterly disputed as the question of how much fish should be caught. Neither problem will be easily resolved, particularly when several EEC countries are blatantly ignoring the quota and mesh-size agreements. Although banned, herring are being landed quite openly in certain French ports, and trawlers sit in harbour with small-mesh nets visible on their decks. The officials who are meant to police the agreements conveniently turn a blind eye, whereas the regulations are being rigidly enforced in British waters. As a result many continental trawler fleets are prospering while an unprecedented number of British trawlers are being forced out of business.

As the *Orion* headed back to port in a freshening wind and with little chance of finding more fish on the Scalloway Deeps, Geordie told me how the Shetlanders would like to see these problems settled. They wanted a quota system which gave Shetland at least twenty per cent of the catch. The number of boats would be limited by licensing, and preference given to local vessels. The system would be enforced by the Shetlanders themselves so that they could become the keepers of their own fish stocks. However, Jonathan Wills argued that it would take a lot to change fishermen's attitudes. Traditionally they were poachers and now, to save the fish, they must become harvesters and gamekeepers. And the Shetlanders were, in some ways, as bad as the Danes they criticised, for the Shetland fleet of purse-seiners was currently down in the south-west poaching mackerel from the Cornish. Geordie quickly replied with 'If you can't beat 'em join 'em', an attitude that Jonathan called 'despairing' and Geordie 'realistic'.

An agreement which met local needs and which also reduced the total allowable catch would inevitably result in several countries having to accept much lower quotas. This they are not prepared to concede without a battle. However, if a solution to the fishing problem is not forthcoming, there will undoubtedly be trouble. There was talk of blockades and direct action. Certainly there will be much bitterness.

Whatever the outcome there can never be a return to the past with its total lack of controls. Old methods might be used again; there was hope that limited herring fishing might be allowed, using the old, selective system of drift netting. 'Mind you,' said Geordie, 'let's hope we never return to the drudgery of hauling those nets by hand – it was slave work!'

Geordie had seen most fishing methods in his time, from hand lines to steam drifting, from trawling to seine-netting. As a skilled seaman he had also been in demand away from home. Like many other Shetlanders before him, he had gone whaling, in its time the harshest and toughest occupation of the sea. During the second half of the nineteenth century the whaling ships heading for the Arctic regularly stopped at Shetland to pick up crew. Geordie himself had gone down to the Antarctic before the Second World War to catch the still numerous blue whale. He had returned for one more season after the war and witnessed the death knell of the big whale. A wartime invention, Asdic, allowed the whalers to track their prey under water, just as warships had tracked submarines. The whales no longer had a chance and wholesale slaughter began. Before 1864 men had caught whales with longboats, a simple harpoon and long lines. Then came the explosive harpoon, which stunned and injured and tired the whales more quickly. Finally, with the introduction of powered craft and tracking devices, the last resort – the long, deep dive – was lost to the whale and nothing stood in the way of large-scale killing. Even today, when the large whales are almost gone, the weight of public opinion has been unable to stop two countries – Russia and Japan – from continuing to hunt them. The history of whaling is sad and, significantly for the fishing industry, one marked by a lack of international planning and control.

The *Orion* steamed into Scalloway Harbour to unload her catch for the market to be held the next morning. There were eight baskets of white fish – whiting, halibut and cod – one of monkfish, which would be used for scampi, and one of flat fish such as plaice and sole. And that was about it. Some dogfish and squid had been thrown back because they were unmarketable. It had not been a good day and, after sniffing the breeze, the skipper cast a seaward eye. He thought he might go straight out again and try his luck much further to the west. As usual, all depended on the weather. It was autumn now; soon the high winds would be blowing and he would lose many days fishing. He must take every opportunity while he could.

One hundred and twenty miles to the north-east, half-way to Norway, the Conoco project managers were also taking the opportunities the weather offered. The autumn of 1979 did not offer many. The wind reached seventy miles an hour on several occasions and nearly 100 miles an hour during a storm; gales were frequent and seas high. Progress on the Murchison platform was slow. Completion of the piling and installation of the module support-frame were delayed by days, while the fitting of the modules themselves was held up for six weeks. Unable to pick up the modules from an attendant barge because of the seas, the *Balder* finally had to sail for a Norwegian fjord and load them there.

Bad weather and delays continued well into 1980. In March the North Sea oil industry suffered its worst disaster with the capsize of the offshore oil rig *Alexander L. Keilland* during a gale. Moored next to a platform in the Norwegian sector, the semi-submersible rig was being used as a hotel when one of its five legs broke away and caused it to overturn; 137 of the 228 men relaxing in the accommodation block died.

When I next flew out to the Murchison Field, in the summer of 1980, the platform was finally complete, slotted together like a vast Meccano set. It was a twentieth-century village over the sea, busy with activity as the 200 men who lived there prepared to drill the first well direct from the platform. I had thought that wells were always drilled straight down, but not so. The first one is, but the twenty or so later wells to be sunk from this platform will be angled outward so that, after curving through the 9900 feet of rock, they will enter the oil reservoir as far as two miles from the platform, fanning out like the spokes of a wheel to draw oil or inject water and gas at the very perimeter of the field. The drilling platform was a scene of deafening noise, constant vibration and flying mud. Heavy machinery, drill bits, and drilling pipe swung crazily about, brilliantly handled by the team of roustabouts who move with the agility of cats. Anything less than perfect co-ordination and they would lose a finger or an arm; they do not often make mistakes. As the drill bites into the rock beneath, the dislodged rock fragments are washed out with a mud-like substance pumped down the drill pipe. This mud covers everything from men to machinery in a thick layer of oozy, slippery clay which, despite frequent hosings, makes the drilling floor like a skating rink.

While the first two wells were being drilled from the platform they were laying the flowlines to the subsea completions – the three exploratory wells capped with 'christmas trees' on the sea-bed. Christmas trees are cylinders bristling with 'branches' of valves which are placed at the top of a well to control or cut off the flow of oil and prevent blow-outs. However, the main risk of blow-out comes at the drilling stage, before a christmas tree can be fitted. Here at Murchison, as the first well was being drilled from the platform, the rare but not impossible event of a blow-out added to the tension. Usually a blow-out can be contained by plugging the hole with a ram; sometimes, unhappily, it cannot. Then a high price is paid for the oil. In April 1977 there was a blow-out at the Bravo Field in the North Sea and for over a week oil poured into the sea at the rate of 3000 to 4000 tons a day, producing a slick of 2500 square miles. Spillages of this dimension are disastrous to bird and marine life. Dispersants which break the oil into tiny globules may save some of the birds, but they can be lethal to fish.

The drilling platform complete

The food chain of the sea is not yet fully understood. As one species of fish or plankton is damaged or killed or becomes laden with petroleum hydrocarbons, we have little understanding of how this affects other species, and particularly the few on which we rely for food. There is a theory that the oceans are one large laundry which can absorb, cleanse and break down the metals, the radioactive matter, the hydrocarbons and the rubbish we put into it. However, to compare the total amount of waste products to the total area of water is misleading, for waste products are normally dumped in great concentrations. Thus, the spillage from the Bravo Field was small compared to natural seepage of oil, or to pollution from tank-washing, but it was extremely concentrated and therefore deadly. Similarly, heavy metals and chemical waste are usually dispersed into individual rivers or processing plants, not into the ocean. Thus, small areas of sea are slowly overcome by pollutants and the life poisoned. For example, it is not safe to eat shellfish caught near Naples or Minimata Bay in Japan. The fish near the Windscale nuclear reprocessing plant in Cumbria, United Kingdom, have a higher than normal level of radioactivity. It is estimated that over five million tons of oil a year is spilt or washed into the sea, cutting out light and oxygen and inhibiting growth of marine life. Even human waste products are harmful; large quantities of raw sewage causes plankton to blossom and upset the natural ecological balance. Litter, too, is a great problem. During my voyages around the world I have seen vast quantities of man-made litter that the sea has difficulty in absorbing, particularly plastics. At present, there are no regulations to prevent ships from dumping all their waste into the ocean.

Clearly an industrialised world cannot produce its goods without producing waste products, but soon we will be forced to decide exactly how high a price we are prepared to pay for our standard of living. We want oil, we want plastics, we want chemical pesticides, but not presumably at the price of our fish and our healthy productive oceans.

Like the story of fishing, the control of pollution has been marked by a high degree of self-interest and a reluctance to sit around a conference table. Only recently have countries started to agree measures to save the great rivers they share. In 1979 Holland, West Germany and Switzerland reached agreement on anti-pollution controls for the Rhine – although France, the remaining river-user, was not yet ready to sign. Gradually countries are trying to bring dead rivers back to life, to find a balance between progress and pollution. On the high seas pollution control is harder to achieve, for no single country can usually bring effective measures to bear. After the disastrous *Amoco Cadiz* tanker spillage on the north Brittany coast, the French attempted to police the two-lane shipping highways off Ouessant and ensure laden tankers kept in lane well clear of the land. But it was an uphill task; even if rogue ships could be identified, it was often pointless to prosecute them when owners were frequently hidden behind flags of convenience.

The cleaning of oil tanks at sea remains the major source of oil pollution, but this could be drastically reduced by the wider use of the new Load on Top (LOT) system whereby seawater used for cleaning is kept in the tanks and the oil floats to the surface to be added to the next cargo. Again, the difficulty is implementation. The oil companies are increasingly aware of their responsibilities to the environment and are keen to introduce LOT to the tankers they own. However, many of the tankers they use are chartered from owners hidden behind agents in flags-of-convenience countries, owners who are unlikely to introduce such systems unless they are forced to do so. As the Shetlanders successfully argued for safety zones around their islands and for the banning of rogue tankers, so pressure groups elsewhere may be able to force measures through. It would be best achieved by international agreement, but this would seem to be a long way off yet.

The price we have to pay for progress in terms of pollution and damage to our environment is, many say, far too high. As oil becomes increasingly scarce it is argued that more risks will be taken to extract the precious commodity. On the other hand, looking at the rapidly advanced technology here at the Murchison Field and elsewhere in the North Sea, it would seem that safety can only improve with time. Pollution emanating from land-based industry and from great cities would appear to present the greater long-term threat.

Although the North Sea is today the scene of the most dramatic developments in man's harvesting of the ocean's resources, the eyes of the oil- and food-hungry world are beginning to turn elsewhere, to the place which promises riches greater than those of any other ocean on earth: the Antarctic coastal waters. These cold and inhospitable seas have always been rich in plankton, producing large quantities of food for baleen whales and a host of other sea creatures via the intricate food chain. Now the larger species of plankton, particularly the shrimp-like crustacea known as krill, are being investigated for potential exploitation as fish protein for human consumption. Krill is considered to be a vast new resource that could actually double the present sustainable world intake of fish.

The Antarctic is also thought to contain large quantities of oil. Extraction from the continent itself would be so difficult and expensive that it is unlikely to prove economic for many years. However, the North Sea experience has pointed the way to removing oil from under the Antarctic continental shelf, despite the enormous problems of ice, weather and sea temperature.

One major difficulty still stands in the way of Antarctic exploitation, and that is the one that has haunted the harvesting of the North Sea and other areas rich in fish and minerals: the inter-dependent problems of ownership, law and control. No one owns the Antarctic. At present it is divided into dependencies administered by six countries, and many more, including the US and USSR, have research bases there. Little has yet been done to suggest a formula whereby the riches of the Antarctic can be shared equitably between the nations of the world. Yet the oil sharing in the North Sea has shown what can be achieved in terms of international co-operation.

During my last visit to the Murchison Field in the autumn of 1980 the first oil was beginning to flow along the pipeline to Sullom Voe. The platform was in production at last, more than a year after the momentous voyage from Ardersier. The flare boom, standing out from the platform like the arm of the Statue of Liberty, held a bright orange flare that flamed high into the sky. As dusk fell I watched migrating birds circle the ball of light. One flew into the flame and fell, a small pathetic bundle, on to the platform beneath. It was a tiny bird, but it now lay dead, a small victim of our need for oil.

The balance between exploitation of the sea and maintenance of its resources is still to be established. In the future we are going to have to conserve and harvest the sea if we are to gain maximum benefit from it. Oil must be shared and used wisely, life must be nurtured and protected from pollution. In the future a mixture of old harvesting methods, new ideas for intensive fish farming, and the use of the sea for energy generation, could make the oceans the greatest provider of all. This challenge would be the theme of my last voyage.

OIL
WARREN TUTE

The story of drilling for oil in the sea is little more than forty years old. The first off-shore oil well, a simple wooden platform affair, was sunk a mile off the Louisiana coast in the Gulf of Mexico in 1938. The North Sea saga started with the discovery of a giant gas field in the Netherlands in 1959. Geologists studying this new Dutch asset pointed out that the Groningen Field must necessarily stretch out into the southern North Sea. Intensive exploration in comparatively shallow off-shore waters began.

Before the Second World War drilling the sea-bed in the middle of the North Sea would have been inconceivable. Divers, who then worked in cumbersome metal helmets and breastplates derived from the diving dress invented by Augustus Siebe in 1819, or from diving bells fed by air under pressure, could not work much below 200 feet. Underwater completion would have been impossible.

Nor was undersea drilling thought necessary. At that time the world's supply of petroleum came from wells on shore, the first of which, drilled in fifteen days in Pennsylvania in 1859, had gone down just under seventy feet. As oil became scarcer and more expensive – land wells of today average 5000 feet, the deepest in Oklahoma is 30,000 feet – the hazards and expense of deep-sea drilling became worthwhile.

Early North Sea rigs were of the 'jack-up' type. These still remain in use today in shallow water near to the coast: they are towed to the site, their extendable legs then being telescoped down on to the sea floor and the platform jacked up well above the surface of the sea. The purpose of the rig is to provide a fixed point on the surface of the sea from which the sea-bed can be drilled. It has to be able to withstand the maximum wind and wave pressures known to be possible in a given place. This was not too difficult with the shallow-water jack-up rigs.

However, the greater depths of water in the higher latitudes of the North Sea, where the weather is also more severe, require dead accurate anchoring of a semi-submersible rig or the drill string will snap. Moreover the drilling bit, the business end of the drill string, has frequently to be changed. It is no good pulling out the drill string for this purpose if you cannot replace it in the same hole.

Until recently marine drilling was only practicable in depths up to 300 feet. Today we can get down to 800 feet and drilling experiments are under way in waters over 10,000 feet in depth. Already the mechanical anchoring of earlier submersible rigs has been replaced by computer-controlled multi-directional propulsion units. These counter-

Above: A drilling rig in the Murchison Field. Below: A welder at work on a North Sea platform

act drift and maintain the pinpoint position required.

A drilling rig works on the same principle as a carpenter's drill and the process is essentially the same whether on land or under the sea. A cutting point called a 'bit' is screwed to the end of a steel pipe made up of thirty-foot lengths. This is known as the 'drill string'. The bit is of hardened steel with inserts of tungsten carbide and sometimes diamonds and it is put to work inside a larger diameter pipe used to guide it to the right spot on the sea-bed.

Special and variable chemical substances known as 'drilling mud' are then pumped down through the drill string and up again through the annulus between drill string and borehole. This mud lubricates the system and can also be used to seal formations which the bit penetrates and which prove to have oil or gas under pressure, thus preventing an escape. Mud chemistry is complex and for any given well the properties of the mud will be changed as the drill progresses down. The

Below: The *Alexander L. Keilland*, after its collapse during a storm in March 1980. 137 lives were lost

mud coming back to the platform carries with it cuttings which reveal whether there is oil or gas in the formation and whether it is worth continuing to drill in that particular place.

Once oil in quantity has been discovered and it is decided to develop a field for production, the mobile exploratory rigs are replaced by semi-permanent ones and a platform is normally installed supported on legs from the sea floor. Two types of production platform have been developed for North Sea use. One is concrete, the weight of which, anything up to 30,000 tons, holds it down on the sea-bed. Concrete platforms usually contain oil storage tanks below sea level. The advantage of this is that when bad weather rules out tanker loading from a buoy, production into the storage tanks can continue uninterrupted. The other kind of platform is of steel supported on legs driven deep into the sea-bed.

All production platforms end up as small lonely townships stuck out in the middle of the sea since accommodation, workshops, derricks and a huge electricity generator are necessary to service the thirty or forty wellheads each platform is designed to cover. Equipment to remove contaminants and burn off gas which cannot be piped ashore is also required.

The high cost and complexity of these platforms, whether of steel or concrete, has led to the development of alternative systems in which production wells are now sunk from drilling or exploration platforms, the wellheads being set on the sea-bed. These are known as 'sub-sea completions'. From them oil and gas are taken by pipeline to a simpler collecting platform for transport to shore.

Getting the oil and gas ashore by pipeline or tanker depends upon the distance from land, the quantity produced and its cost. The capital cost of laying down a pipeline is really only justified if a number of small fields lie close together and can combine economically to share the expense. Otherwise offshore loading into tankers is used, vessels being moored to a buoy which is itself connected to the production platform by about a mile of sub-sea pipeline.

Abandoning a well follows a set pattern. Any area not covered by casing is first plugged with cement. Where the well has been perforated, cement is forced under pressure into the formations. Mechanical or cement plugs of several hundred feet in length are placed in the well bore immediately above the area perforated and above the point where each casing string ends. Finally any casing or other steel work is cut off at least ten feet below the sea-bed. Eventually the North Sea wells which now make us self-sufficient in oil and gas will all be sealed. The feats of engineering of the North Sea oil-men have however given us a breathing space in which to develop alternative sources of energy.

A drilling rig is floated out and righted. A cone of bore holes pene

Being flooded
Already flooded

reservoir below.

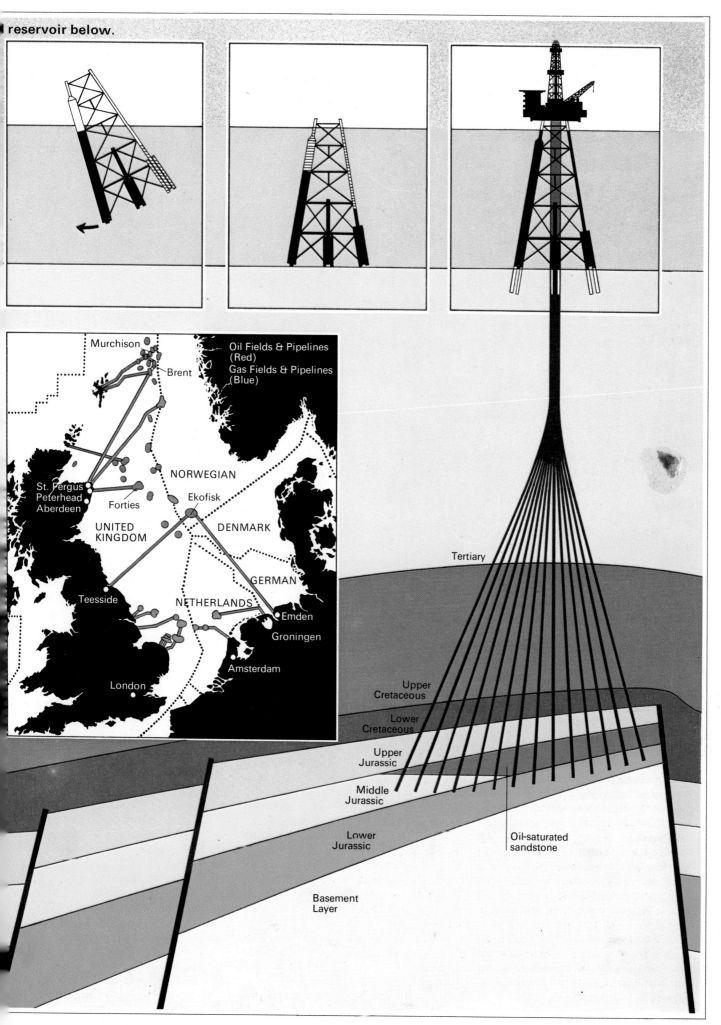

Oil Fields & Pipelines (Red)
Gas Fields & Pipelines (Blue)

Murchison

Brent

NORWEGIAN

St. Fergus
Peterhead
Aberdeen

Forties

Ekofisk

UNITED
KINGDOM

DENMARK

GERMAN

Teesside

NETHERLANDS

Emden

Groningen

Amsterdam

London

Tertiary

Upper
Cretaceous

Lower
Cretaceous

Upper
Jurassic

Middle
Jurassic

Oil-saturated
sandstone

Lower
Jurassic

Basement
Layer

SHETLAND
CLARE FRANCIS

The Shetland Islands appear low, dark and barren when approached from the sea. There are no trees to be seen, nor a pattern of cultivated fields. The strong winds from the Atlantic and the Arctic sweep over the land, taking everything in their path. Almost vertical cliffs rise out of the sea where the land has been attacked by the waves. Rocks and small islets, inhabited by thousands of screaming seabirds, lie scattered around the larger islands.

Of the hundred or so islands of the Shetlands only sixteen are inhabited. Most live on the 351-square-mile Mainland, which is by far the largest island. In recent years the total population has been in the region of 20,000.

The Shetlands lie over a hundred miles north-east of Scotland and two hundred miles west of Norway, yet despite this remoteness they have been inhabited since the Stone Age. The first settlers were probably people moving north from the British mainland. Some hundreds of years after they arrived they appear to have been threatened by invasion, for they built spectacular stone fortresses known as brochs. Eventually, by about AD 300, the islands became part of the kingdom of the Picts, a Celtic tribe who inhabited parts of the north and east Scotland.

Nothing is known about the boats these early seafarers used, but fishing was clearly practised for weights and hooks dating from early times have been discovered.

In the eighth century the history of the Shetlands was changed dramatically by the arrival of the first Viking raiders. Over the next two hundred years more of them followed until, by the eleventh century, few traces of the Picts remained. The Norse settlers called the islands Hjatland, a name which was eventually anglicised to Zetland and finally Shetland.

In 1469 the Danish king who reigned over Norway, Denmark and Sweden mortgaged the islands back to Scotland to raise money for his daughter's dowry. However Shetland remained Norse in character until as late as the nineteenth century. Norn, the ancient Norse language, was spoken and the laws and customs were predominantly Norse. Even today the islanders consider themselves as much Norse as Scottish and many still speak a dialect drawn from the old language and the new.

The Norse settlers were quick to exploit the natural resources of the islands; the fertile land that lay in a narrow strip between the cliffs and the hills was used for growing crops, the hills for grazing sheep, and the sea for

catching fish. This combination of crofting and fishing remained the mainstay of Shetland life until early this century.

Traditional Shetland fishing boats bear a strong resemblance to the ships used by the Vikings centuries ago. The oldest type of fishing boat known in Shetland is the yoal, a light double-ended clinker-built craft with little draught and low profile. It was rowed by a crew of three, although a small sail could be raised if the wind was fair. Fishing in these frail craft was confined to coastal waters, using baited hook and line to catch ling and cod. In the seventeenth century the Shetlanders traded some of their fish with Hanseatic merchants from Germany, though it was left to the Dutch to exploit the bountiful herring fisheries offshore.

In the late eighteenth century the inshore fishing grounds began to fail – possibly climatic conditions caused the fish to move out to sea – and the Shetlanders were forced to fish further from the land. For this purpose

they developed the sixerne, a larger version of the yoal propelled by six oars. The fisherman's life on the sixerne was a hard one. Throughout the summer they made two trips a week, spending two nights at sea on each, without room to sleep, no cooking facilities, and largely exposed to the elements. When the catch was brought in it had to be gutted, salted and dried.

The sixerne was not an ideal craft for off-shore fishing since it was completely open and required skilled handling to avoid swamping in heavy seas. Inevitably there was steady loss of life and occasionally a terrible disaster. On one day, in 1832, thirty-one boats and 105 men were lost in a storm. In 1881 ten boats were lost and fifty-eight men perished. Shortly after 1881 the Shetlanders began to abandon sixernes in favour of safer, fully-decked boats bought from the East Scotland fleet. With these boats they caught herring in summer as well as the traditional ling and cod in spring. Improved links with

mainland Scotland also created a new market for fresh haddock, previously regarded as an inferior fish. By this time Shetland was a key centre of the British fishing industry.

The coming of steam brought changes, however. Few of the crofter-fishermen could afford the expensive new steam drifters and the occupations of crofting and fishing became largely separated as fishermen were forced to specialise. Crofters still went fishing, but on a small scale using traditonal Shetland boats in coastal waters.

The herring was the mainstay of the Shetland fishing industry during the first half of this century, although the catches varied considerably from year to year. In 1905 there was a record catch but then, for no apparent reason, the number of herring greatly decreased for ten years. These variations were probably caused by climatic changes.

But it was in 1965 that a major change occurred for which the Shetlanders could not be prepared. A fleet of Norwegian boats began to fish the rich herring banks around Shetland using purse-seine nets. These nets were devastatingly efficient, taking up whole shoals of herring that had been located by sonar. Later, in the 1970s, the Danes came with equally efficient trawlers to sweep up vast quantities of white fish. The Shetland fishing industry has been overwhelmed by these onslaughts and has suffered a setback from which it is still recovering. Nonetheless fishing is still the Shetland's principal industry.

Crofting, too, remains important to the islands. Shetland knitwear and wool are important exports and peat is still dug from the bogs and hillsides for winter fuel. The greatest changes in recent years have been the develop-

Left: Shetland. Oil rigs beyond crofts – jobs in the oil industry have changed the economy of the islands which used to depend on crofting and on fishing – both dangerous inshore waters like those below, and, as competition increased, offshore as well

ment of the tourist industry and of course the surprising and spectacular arrival of oil. The islanders drove a hard bargain over Sullom Voe, the giant oil terminal nearing completion in the north of Mainland, and they succeeded in gaining a high degree of control over the extent and area of oil-related developments, as well as financial compensation for the upheaval to a balanced and independent community. Some have welcomed the oil industry as an important boost to the Shetland economy. Others look on it as a temporary nuisance which is drawing the islands' resources away from the development of the fishing industry and thus endangering the islands' future prosperities.

The Shetlanders are an independent and self-reliant people who have long been dependent on the sea and the croft for their livelihood. Most have little doubt that, once the oil has run out, so they will be again.

Shetland as it was
Top: Sixernes at Fethaland in North Shetland in the 1880s
Middle: The herring fleet leaving Lerwick in 1890
Above: Yoals – being sailed and rowed
Right: The crew of the sail herring boat *Queen Adelaide*

FOOD FROM THE SEA
WARREN TUTE

Almost all fish caught and consumed in the world today are to be found in sea areas above the 200 fathom (1200 feet) mark. Whilst marine life provides food for coastal people in every part of the world, major fishing grounds are concentrated in a few well-defined regions such as the seaboards of the United States, Japan, Malaya and South Africa. The oldest and most highly developed of these areas, however, is the continental shelf of north-western Europe – the North Sea, the British Isles and Iceland – bounded on the east by the land mass of Europe and on the west by the Atlantic deeps.

Fishery is of two kinds, pelagic and demersal. Pelagic includes all creatures of the upper, open waters such as herring, mackerel and sprats. Demersal, which simply means 'living near the sea bottom', includes cod, haddock, whiting, hake and the various flatfish such as plaice and sole. Crustaceans and shellfish – oysters, mussels, lobsters and crabs – are also demersal but require special-ised fishing, as do salmon and eels.

The story of fishing starts when man first began collecting shellfish off a rocky shore or building simple stone enclosures low down on a beach in which fish would be trapped by the falling tide. Archaeologists have dis-covered great mounds of sea shells alongside prehistoric man's earliest dwellings, and both oysters and salmon were a staple food for the poor until very recent times. Although the types of fish landed have not much changed through the ages, the quantities show great fluctuations caused by over-fishing, changes in taste, and developments in the way fish are caught and marketed.

Primitive trapping was improved by flexible fences made of plaited mats strung on poles. Such V-shaped constructions are still in use today in Finland and Sweden. Salmon nets off Scotland and eel pound nets off Denmark, which trap the silver eel as it migrates from the Baltic, are also much the same today as they were in the middle ages.

The next advance was when man went to sea in coracles or small rowing boats to hunt with nets and lines rather than wait for the fish to come to him. Multi-oared rowing boats then gave way to sail and in the last century to steam or diesel. There is a continuous history of inshore fishing, but commercial fishing in the North Sea only dates from late medieval times.

Gutting the catch on a modern trawler

The problem has always been how to preserve the catch. Until refrigeration in the late nineteenth century, the disposal of the day-before-yesterday's catch – other than back into the sea – was always a chancy business. The art of fish curing by drying, smoking or the use of salt and spice had been known for thousands of years, but the fish had first to be landed, for curing was rarely practised at sea until, early in the fifteenth century, the Dutch built ships of a sufficient size for the job. After the great Baltic shoals disappeared between 1416 and 1425 the Dutch virtually took over the North Sea herring fishery from the Hanseatic League ports.

The Dutch three-masted herring busses were really the first factory ships. They were able to catch and cure fish at sea. As soon as the herring were hauled on board, they were gutted, carefully covered in coarse salt, and then packed head to tail in wooden barrels with a layer of salt between each layer of herring. The barrels were then made as airtight as possible and branded with the date caught. This method allowed the fish to be kept in an edible state for up to a year.

The Dutch virtually monopolised the North Sea trade for well over two hundred years. They did this not by force of arms (though this was resorted to later), but by meticulous care for quality and by commonsense regulations they imposed on themselves in order to maintain the high quality of the cure. These regulations covered the mesh size of the herring nets, the type of salt, the size of barrel and the way it was made. Most important of all, perhaps, they limited the fishing season to approximately six months of the year. No fish could be caught before the feast of St John the Baptist on 24 June each year. The season ended shortly after Christmas, when the fleet of herring busses which had worked south from the Shetlands to the Thames estuary returned to Holland to rest and refit.

By 1669 30,000 fishermen and 450,000 others, a fifth of the population of the Netherlands, were employed in the herring industry. The Scottish and English industries never came near this figure, despite bounties and other royal encouragement, mainly because the boats were too small and for most of the year were unable to reach the main herring shoals.

The British Fisheries Society was established in 1788 and revived the East Anglia herring industry from Yarmouth and Lowestoft, also building the town of Ullapool for the fishing centre of Loch Broom, to ease unemployment and depopulation in the Highlands. By the mid-nineteenth century there were fleets working from Wick, Helmsdale, Peterhead and Fraserburgh in Aberdeenshire in addition to those from English ports in the south. The British herring fleet had come into being.

However, white fish, such as haddock, became even more valuable than the migrating

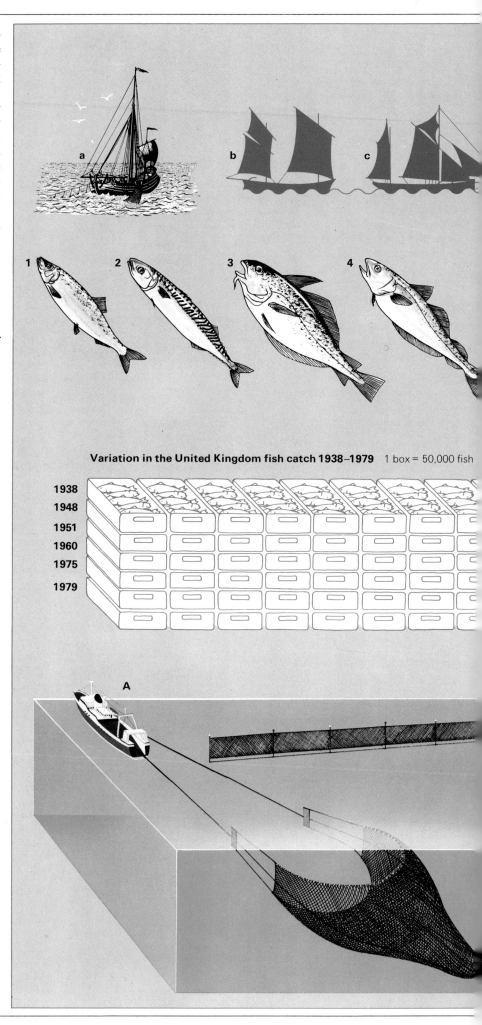

Variation in the United Kingdom fish catch 1938–1979   1 box = 50,000 fish

1938
1948
1951
1960
1975
1979

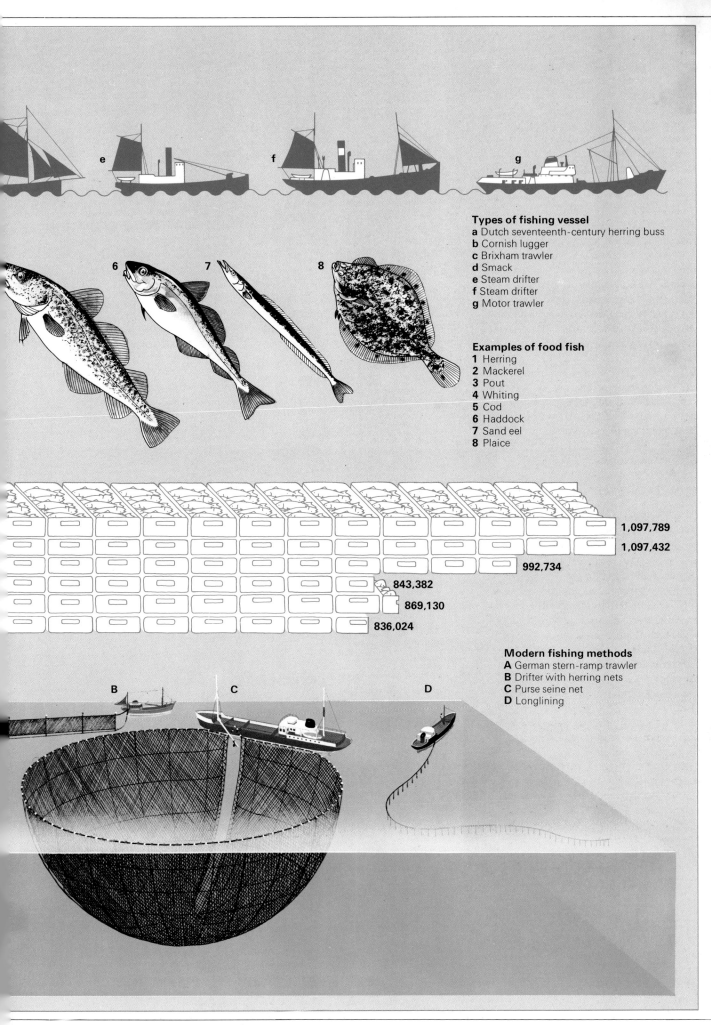

Types of fishing vessel
a Dutch seventeenth-century herring buss
b Cornish lugger
c Brixham trawler
d Smack
e Steam drifter
f Steam drifter
g Motor trawler

Examples of food fish
1 Herring
2 Mackerel
3 Pout
4 Whiting
5 Cod
6 Haddock
7 Sand eel
8 Plaice

1,097,789
1,097,432
992,734
843,382
869,130
836,024

Modern fishing methods
A German stern-ramp trawler
B Drifter with herring nets
C Purse seine net
D Longlining

and seasonal herring because they could be found all the year round on inshore fishing grounds. Little special equipment was necessary other than boats since white fish not sold fresh in the ordinary way can be dried unsalted to produce stockfish in the cold, dry and windy climate of the north, and salted or pickled in the wetter climate of the south. Herring cannot be preserved by drying: they are too oily and go rancid.

In any case an outside factor was profoundly to affect the fishing industry in the second half of the nineteenth century. This was the advent of the railway which provided a growing network of quick transport throughout Europe. Two coincidental developments also took place: the 'invention' of the kipper by John Woodger of Seahouses, Northumberland, in 1843; and the nationwide phenomenon of the Victorian fish-and-chip shop. The era of cheap food which was to last a century in the British Isles had begun.

The latter part of the nineteenth century also saw sail give way to the steam drifter and the steam trawler. Human muscle was replaced, thankfully, by the powered winch for hauling in the nets, and refrigeration began to extend the time a ship could stay at sea.

A massive exploitation of the North Sea got under way. The results were predictable. Records of west European fishing go back over 1000 years and the cyclic fluctuations of herring, for instance, have been well documented. However, greed and the vastly increased catch then available made people turn a blind eye to the consequences. We are paying for this today.

The net and its size of mesh became crucial to this exploitation. Four different kinds of net were developed in commercial fishing – the trawl, the drift net, the seine and the purse seine. All in a sense derive from the trawl which was originally tried in the North Sea in the twelfth century. The correct net to use depends on the type of fishing – pelagic or demersal – and the depth of water. In addition, baited long-line fishing, with one end anchored to the sea-bed and the other attached to the ship, effectively covers all depths on an individual-hook basis from bottom to surface of the sea.

The change brought about by steam can be seen from a few figures. In 1860 820 sailing smacks worked out of Grimsby. By 1902 all but twenty-nine had been replaced by 500 steamers. In 1860 4500 tons of fish were landed at Grimsby. Forty years later the catch had risen some thirty times to 134,000 tons. By 1913, the year before the First World War, 420,000 tons of fish were being landed each year in United Kingdom ports. Sixty-five years and two world wars later (and in both wars fishing greatly diminished, thus allowing stocks to recover), a total ban on herring fishing in the North Sea has been reluctantly agreed and partially enforced.

We are now into an era of new technology which includes fish location by echo-sounder, the freeze trawler and the multi-thousand-ton factory ship. World consumption of fish has enormously increased, over twenty-two million tons being taken each year from the overfished Atlantic alone, with a similar amount from the much larger Pacific ocean.

The local effect in the North Sea and North-eastern Atlantic is close to disastrous. Cod taken by all nations from the Icelandic area declines every year by about 8000 tons because the stock is no longer there. To add to Icelandic concern other species such as haddock, redfish, plaice, Greenland halibut and herring are now threatened with extinction. All in all it is time we woke up to the facts of life.

Ullapool, 1980. Foreign factory ships which are not allowed to fish these waters wait out beyond the harbour to buy the catch from local boats

ECOSYSTEMS
WARREN TUTE

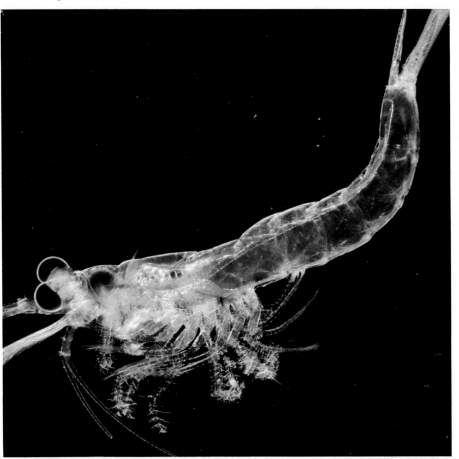

Top: Crustaceans like this one feed on phytoplankton, the tiny plants that form the base of the food chain, which are in turn eaten by larger fish

Bottom: Mackerel caught in a gill net: one of the most common members of a family which includes the giant bluefin tuna

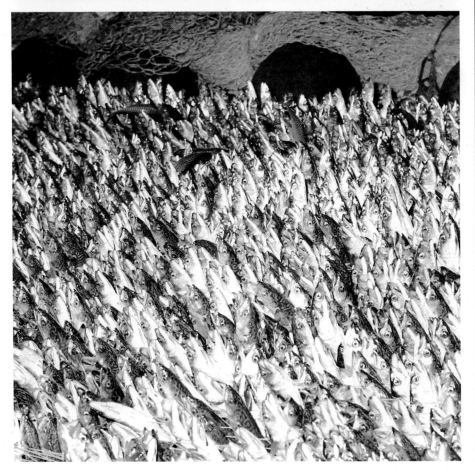

The oceans and seas of the world form one continuous body of salt water. Yet each ocean appears to have an identity of its own. The Atlantic, Pacific, Mediterranean and North Sea differ from each other both in size and characteristic. The ecologies – the biological relationship between organisms and their environment – are distinct.

The North Sea and the adjacent Baltic and English Channel have a special identity determined by a mixture of geography, biology and the politics of man. This rich area of continental shelf has been used as a moat, a highway, and a fishpond.

The physical nature of the North Sea – its comparative lack of depth and the fact that the rivers of Northern Europe drain into it – make it a valuable depository of minerals and one of the richest fishing grounds in the world. How did this come about?

Two hundred million years ago America, Europe and Africa are thought to have comprised a single land mass. This gradually split and drifted apart so that after some 165 million years what had been a dip or plain between mountains sank and became inundated. A shallow young sea thus came into being.

To set its size into perspective, the Atlantic ocean is roughly thirty-one million square miles in extent, the North Sea less than a quarter of a million. The average depth of the Atlantic is 11,000 feet, the North Sea 300. The volume of water in the Atlantic give or take a bucket or two is seventy-seven million cubic miles, that of the North Sea a mere 13,000. The relationship is that of a bath to a cup.

The North Sea sports only one major relief feature: the Norwegian trough which goes down over 2000 feet. The virtually flat bottom of the North Sea is covered with 20,000 feet of sediment; in their depths lie the oil and gas we have recently begun to extract.

Most forms of life feed on some other form of life. At sea the single cell phytoplankton is the building brick for the whole maritime ecosystem. Solar energy becomes fixed into myriads of these microscopic plant cells, which free float in the upper surface waters. Only along the seashore, that strange frontier between two elements, are there large standing seaweeds and other algae forming a marine ecology in some respects resembling its land counterpart: the deep ocean phytoplankton are the basic converter of sunlight and minerals into living tissue.

They are in turn consumed by a mass of tiny herbivores. These then provide the food for ocean carnivores such as whales and sharks at one end of the scale and tiny zooplankton at the other. This planktonic life as a whole maintains a vast, rapid and efficient turnover in the upper realms of the sea.

Despite its ceaseless motion, the marine environment is one of great stability. The sea acts as a buffer and because there are no violent temperature changes or wind storms below the surface as there are above on land, few marine creatures have developed tough outer skins. The sea, therefore, harbours some of nature's longest-living and most successful creatures. There may not be coelacanths in the North Sea – that extraordinary looking marine creature thought to be extinct for sixty-five million years but rediscovered in the Indian Ocean in 1939 – but the North Sea is unique in the prolific variety of marine life it supports.

Fish have no insulating layer of blubber, hair or feathers next to their skin. They therefore have no mechanism for regulating their body temperature and are entirely dependent on the surrounding water for whatever they need to exist.

The North Sea is special because it is shallow, semi-enclosed and temperate and because into it drain rivers such as the Rhine, Elbe and Weser carrying dissolved nutrients from a quarter of the European land mass. Another key factor is the Gulf Stream drift, one branch of which runs in through the Straits of Dover whilst another enters from the north between Shetland and the Faeroes. Thus the area is constantly being refreshed and stocks the northern cold-water fish such as cod, haddock and herring and the southern warm-water fish such as pilchard, anchovy and mullet.

The North Sea ecosystem includes, of course, the human beings who lay claim to the offshore waters, the open sea, the sea-bed and what lies under it. The problems are complex and here again the North Sea is unique in that many of the basic concepts governing world-wide offshore control have been formulated in north-western Europe. These factors have a long history and cover the complicated nature of the coasts and islands, the presence of rich fishing grounds in nearby waters, early interests in trade and navigation, and the varied questions of neutrality, smuggling and war prizes.

Until today matters in dispute have usually been settled by force of arms. The successful development of North Sea oil marks the possible opening of a new era where agreement can be reached without going to war. We need now to apply these new methods of control to the food resources of the sea and to the problem of pollution. It can be done.

In the North Sea early claims to offshore waters for trade and fishing were settled by treaty. For instance, by the end of the thirteenth century Norway had passed a law to prevent foreigners from sailing north of Bergen without a royal licence. Iceland had been joined with Norway in 1264 and both countries passed to the Danish crown in 1380

so that control of the whole area north of the Iceland–Faeroes–Shetlands–Bergen line rested in Danish hands until the end of the sixteenth century. Neither England nor Scotland, both concerned in this matter, went to war about these fishing and trading rights. They settled it by treaty in 1432.

Unfortunately this did not last. Improvements in ship design, skill in navigation and

above all the gun opened the door to greed. Certain nations such as the Dutch became much more expert at fishing and the preservation of the catch than others in whose territorial waters the fish were so often found. The controversy between 'free' and 'closed' seas began, the Dutchman Grotius maintaining in 1609 that the sea could not be subject to private ownership and the

Top: Herring gulls: one of 285 species of seabird
Bottom: A puffin with a beakful of fish

Top: Pilot whales are found in the Atlantic, Pacific and Indian Oceans. They grow to about twenty-two feet
Bottom: Grey seals. All seals are carnivorous mammals; they are protected from the extreme cold of their habitat by a thick layer of blubber beneath the skin

Englishman Selden claiming the opposite in 1619. Later in the seventeenth century four savage wars between England and Holland took place, none of which settled the matter in any lasting way. However the three-mile limit to territorial waters, based on the maximum range of cannon and therefore capable of being policed, had been generally accepted by the North Sea nations by the end of the eighteenth century.

Since then trading and fishing wars have proliferated. Primitive man hunted and moved on, leaving a desert behind him. The same process has been applied to fishing. The more we know the less responsibly we seem to behave. Today the polluted Mediterranean and Baltic and the badly overfished North Sea almost shout at us to learn before it is all too late. We can now destroy the environment in which we live, indeed we are already doing

so without apparently being aware of the almost immediate consequences. Hunting can never be abolished but it can be controlled. We must now learn to farm the sea. The international co-operation and investment which have made the North Sea oil and gas industry the success it is must now be extended to the entire ecosystem. It can be done but the time is short.

Chapter Six

THE LAST RESOURCE

You'll be going down to about 6000 feet,' said the pilot. 'That's over a mile down – half our maximum operating depth.'

We turned the corner of the building and there, in a small hangar, was the craft in which I would be making the last of my voyages. Her name is *Alvin*. Strictly speaking she is a submersible, but some call her a submarine or just sub. By any standards she's strange – more like an insect than a boat, with a short bulbous body, a tail which supports a large white propeller, antennae and sensors and, stretching out ahead, two long, clawlike arms which can reach out and pick objects up off the sea floor. Here in the hangar the team of pilots and technicians who tend *Alvin* were beginning to strip her down, ready for a major overhaul. The foam-filled buoyancy chambers and racks of heavy-duty batteries were lifted off the main frame. Then the forward section of the body was removed – a bright silver sphere made of titanium alloy, capable of resisting over 360 atmospheres (pressure of more than two tons per square inch). The sphere, just six feet across, carries a pilot and two scientists. In a few months' time, when *Alvin* made a routine dive off Nassau in the Bahamas, I would be going down as an observer.

Normally I like to stick to the element I know – the surface of the sea. In fact I'm a person who usually avoids putting so much as a toe into sea-water. When I swim I prefer a swimming pool – guaranteed free of kelp, crabs and sea-urchins. I have a fear of sea-water which stems from childhood when I swam into a thick bed of weed and panicked. But I had no need to fear a dive in *Alvin*. Not only does the two-inch-thick titanium keep the enormous outside pressure at bay, but conditions inside are near normal: one can breathe and move freely – and remain quite dry. But even if there had been disadvantages, it was such a fantastic opportunity that it was not to be missed. Few people have gone down into the deep and seen what is the last virtually unexplored part of our planet. The size of the deep sea is vast – larger in area than all the land put together – and scientists have examined only a minute part of it. Yet in recent years they have made discoveries that have revolutionised our knowledge of the earth, of its formation, its life processes, and its riches. At a time when the resources of the relatively shallow continental-shelf areas are being exploited on an ever-increasing scale, this knowledge about the deep sea has extended commercial and political interest beyond the coastal regions and into the oceans themselves. The world is becoming aware that the sea is our last great untapped resource.

At the centre of this increasing attention are the scientists who are trying to discover how the many different facets of the sea work, how they are related and how they change. A leading centre of oceanography in the United States is the Woods Hole Oceanographic Institution. Situated on the south-western tip of Cape Cod in Massachusetts, Woods Hole is famous for two things: the ferries which sail to the off-lying islands of Martha's Vineyard and Nantucket, and the Institution. The village is typically New England; pretty white pastel-painted clapboard houses form a gentle patchwork of colour against the surrounding woodland. On three sides of the small inner harbour, known as Eel Pond, there are larger buildings which house laboratories and offices of the Institution. Facing Nantucket Sound there are quays for research ships like the 245-foot *Knorr*, which carries twenty-five crew and twenty-four scientists, while close by are workshops and hangars for repairs and overhauls. It was here that I first saw *Alvin*, which is operated by the Institution and chartered to a variety of scientific projects. Jack Donnelly, in charge of *Alvin* and her mother ship *Lulu*, told me that the sub is always in great demand. There are just a handful of submersibles in the world, and only *Alvin* is available to US scientists on a permanent basis. Not all oceanographers need to examine the deep sea, but there are enough biologists and geologists studying it to keep *Alvin* booked up for years ahead.

Fred Grassle regularly dives into the deep. He is a marine biologist who is studying the many small animals that inhabit the thick mud on the ocean floor. Ruth Turner, another biologist, is investigating wood-eating creatures which feed off the timber that floats out to sea and sinks to the bottom. The animals these two scientists study are small – many are just a millimetre or so long – and look just as you would expect: long and worm-like, round and louse-like, or many-legged like a centipede. It is difficult at first for an outsider to appreciate why scientists are interested in this multitude of small animal life. There is pure scientific curiosity, of course, but it is more than that. Although it has been known for more than a century that the deep sea contains some fish life, little more was discovered until recently. It was thought that the ocean floor was arid, rather like the surface of the moon. Certainly it looks it. At his Woods Hole laboratory, Fred Grassle showed me photographs of the sedimentary mud which covers millions of square miles of the sea-bed. It is a flat, monotonous area, looking about as interesting as the Utah salt flats. The life down there is very sparse, yet on and under the surface live an extraordinary variety of animals. 'It's a storehouse of variety,' says Fred. 'It's comparable to a coral reef or a rain forest. The diversity of life is quite extraordinary.' It will take many years for Fred and his colleagues to build up a picture of how the many life-forms are interrelated, how they eat, migrate and reproduce. Yet it is important that they do. 'Basically we are studying how fast things can, and do, grow down there,' explained Ruth Turner. 'Then we can begin to determine what's normal so that, should the deep-sea environment be disturbed, we can measure the effects.'

Woods Hole is involved in pure research, yet inevitably their work has far-reaching political implications. 'Governments are going to have to make various decisions about the sea floor,' says Fred, 'decisions concerning the various uses of the sea – waste disposal, mining and so on – issues which are going to be extremely important in the future. We need to know how these deep-sea communities adapt to disturbance, how they are related to surface life, if at all. But so much is still unknown – we still have a long way to go.' People like Fred Grassle and Ruth Turner are under increasing pressure to answer questions on which political arguments can be built. The environmentalists search for evidence that the sea will be irreparably damaged by some of the uses proposed for it, while commercial interests want scientific backing for widespread exploitation.

Whatever the arguments, one thing is certain. The sea is going to be used as never before. Thirty years ago, most attempts to take new food, energy and mineral wealth from the sea would have been regarded as impractical and financially unrewarding. Yet many ideas that seemed unlikely, preposterous even, in the past are today being developed or seriously investigated: oil and gas are being extracted from increasingly deep waters; the vast deposits of minerals that litter the sea floor are being studied with a view to mining them, probably within the next ten years; the harvesting of shrimplike creatures called krill is being tried, an industry which could, it is said, double the protein yield of the oceans; and numerous ideas are being tested to extract the boundless and inexhaustible energy from the water and the waves. All these assets exist in very large quantities and, if we can make use of them, will go a long way to augmenting the declining resources of the land.

However, three barriers stand in the way of all this wealth. The first is technological – getting at the resources, removing them, and utilising them efficiently. But, just as the problem of removing oil from under the North Sea has been overcome in a few short years, so we will undoubtedly find ways of extracting the other resources we want. Oil from the Antarctic, minerals from the deep-sea floor, and krill, which float in profusion in the Southern Ocean waters – all these can probably be exploited on a large scale once the full force of science and industry is applied to the problem. To be attractive to industry, the prices will have to be right, but it is argued that in time food, mineral and energy resources will be in such short supply, that even the most expensive propositions will be worth pursuing.

As the world wakes up to the sea's full potential, the second barrier looms up – and it is more formidable than the technological one. This is the thorny question of who owns the ocean. Most of the minerals, the oil and the krill, and indeed a large proportion of the world's diminished fish stocks, lie outside traditional territorial limits which, for many years, were fixed at three miles around a country's coast, the range of an eighteenth-century canon. Everyone wants a share of the ocean's wealth, but who shall lay claim to it? It is argued that geographical luck and the possession of a long coastline is no reason to claim a disproportionately large share of the sea's resources which have been described as the common heritage of man. Others maintain that we have never shared the land's resources, so why should we share the sea's? They believe that those with the means and the knowledge to extract the resources should be allowed to do so – an argument that favours rich countries over poor.

Although this question may lead to conflict, it is at least capable of solution – politicians, governments and electorate willing. The third and possibly the greatest problem has no real solution, and it is a problem that will not go away. Life as we know it cannot go on without industry, and industry breeds waste products. Somehow a balance must be found between the benefits of progress, which we all want, and the costs of the damaging, life-destroying waste elements of that progress which we all want to avoid. In the past man has been using the seas as a giant sink to take away the unpleasant by-products of industrial processes. The question is not whether the sea should do this job at all – it has to because the alternatives are far too expensive – but how much it should be asked to absorb. At present it takes effluent from rivers and outfalls, and it absorbs much of the considerable airborne pollution from chimneys and exhausts (if anyone doubts the distance this travels, they have only to remember that the ash from the erupting Mount St Helens floated from one side of the United States to the other). In some areas the sea is already overburdened with toxic materials and it is essential for scientists to determine what the danger levels for the life and health of the oceans are. It would be appalling management if we were to bite the hand that feeds us. The sea, through evaporation and rain, forms a single system with the air, and for life on earth to thrive, it must be kept healthy. The future uses of the sea will place further burdens on its ability to adapt and to withstand interference. It is argued that the oceans are so vast that it will take years before they are seriously affected by pollution, but no one can be sure. Moreover, certain kinds of pollutants like high-level nuclear waste are, in the case of accident, immediate and deadly in their effects.

Institutions like Woods Hole are deeply involved in these questions. Only scientists can identify and quantify the problems accurately. Oceanography is a two-edged sword: it shows us the way to find and exploit the wealth of the sea, but it also indicates how we may damage and change the ocean's myriad of interrelated systems.

The director of Woods Hole is Dr Steele, a Scots-born mathematician. He heads an Institution that has grown from a dozen people and a budget of $85,000 on its formation in 1931 to an organisation of 1000 employees, six ships and a budget of $30 million. It is an expansion that reflects the growth of oceanography as a science. Only twenty years ago it was a young science, explained Dr Steele, and even now it is adolescent. 'It's difficult for us to establish an identity. We embrace so many basic disciplines – chemistry, physics, biology and so on – that the only thing oceanographers have in common, they say, is a love of the oceans.' On a practical level, the science faces the difficulties of breadth and scale. The subject is so vast and the sea so intertwined with the air and the earth that it is impossible to get a complete picture of how the sea works. As Dr Steele put it, 'there will be always areas of uncertainty'.

But ask people when oceanography was born, and they do not hesitate to answer 'With the *Challenger*'. The voyage of this famous ship took place more than 100 years ago, yet it is still a vivid source of inspiration to scientists today. As he talks about his work, Fred Grassle credits the *Challenger* expedition with the beginning of deep-sea research. Ruth Turner elaborates: 'Among the expedition's objectives were three of major importance – to prove there was life in the deep sea, to define the chemistry of the water, and to map the bottom. Only now, all these years later, are we achieving these things!'

HMS *Challenger*

HMS *Challenger* sailed from Portsmouth, England, in 1872 with a party of scientists sponsored by the British Government. In a voyage lasting two years and seven months, the three-masted, auxiliary-powered corvette circumnavigated the world, sailing a total of 68,000 miles through every major ocean. The research was meticulous and far-ranging, covering climate, current and wild life as well as deep-sea data. The equipment available for the gathering of samples and information was, of course, limited. Nevertheless, the expedition was extremely successful. Not only did it establish that a variety of life existed in the deep sea, but that minerals in the form of manganese nodules littered much of the ocean floor. The vast process of charting the sea-bed was begun, although it would be many years before the large variations in depths were satisfactorily explained – and found to be highly significant.

Only with the development of modern technology could the riddles of the sea start to be solved – and riddles they were. How was the sea formed? Where did the minerals come from? Why are there great ridges in the sea floor? Why doesn't the chemical make-up of the oceans add up?

Robert Ballard is a geologist based at Woods Hole. His field is providing some of the most exciting discoveries in oceanography today, discoveries that would not have been possible without sonar charting techniques, deep-sea cameras towed on sledges, and submersibles like *Alvin*. On the wall of his office, Dr Ballard has a map of the world's sea-bed. It's a dramatic picture which shows a great mountain range, 40,000 miles long, weaving its way around the world through all the major oceans, rather like the seam on a baseball. This range is the largest single feature on the earth and covers twenty-eight per cent of its surface. But there is more to this extraordinary ridge than just mountains: it holds the answers to some of the fundamental questions about the earth and how it works as a total system.

Back in the nineteenth century the Mid-Atlantic ridge was discovered by cable-laying expeditions and named Telegraph Plateau, but it was not until the 1960s that geologists realised the ridges of the oceans were a single basic feature of the earth and extended 40,000 miles through every ocean. Finally the theory of plate tectonics emerged – a theory so revolutionary it has been described as 'one of the major upheavals in the history of man's knowledge'. Bob Ballard explained that the mid-ocean ridge is a site where the earth's crust is actually separating. The earth is trying to give off its heat; and the ocean floor, which is heavier and floats lower on the molten magma than the continents, is the place it tries to do it. The heat forces the ocean floor to separate and the earth 'bleeds', so that molten magma rises, cools, and hardens to form new tissue. But what is separating must necessarily be going somewhere. In fact, the separating ocean plates are pushing out against other plates or against continents. They either collide and form mountain ranges, like the Andes or the Himalayas, or, being heavier than the continents, they slip underneath the land and are remelted in the furnace of the earth's molten heart. There are twelve principal plates floating on the earth's mantle – and they are all going somewhere. It is believed that once there was one single supercontinent which has been called Pangaea. Gradually the continent split into pieces and the segments of land started to float around, a system of movement that has been going on for some 200 million years. India was tucked into the Antarctic before it moved away and collided with the Asian continent. A section of California which includes Los Angeles is moving steadily towards San Francisco on a plate that will disappear under the Arctic in the Aleutian Trench. The way Bob Ballard talks you would think it was all happening rapidly, but to geologists a few hundred thousand years is nothing.

It was not until 1973 that men saw the oceanic ridge for the first time. In a joint Franco-American project named Famous, *Alvin* and two French submersibles dived on to a ridge area in mid-Atlantic near the Azores. Evidence of past volcanic activity was found in the axis of the ridge, which looks something like the Grand Canyon. Dating of the sides showed it was a mere 100,000 years old – very young – and that the two plates, the American and the African, were moving apart at about one inch per year.

But what happens in places where plates are moving apart much faster? The answer took Bob Ballard and other geologists to a point off the Galapagos Islands in the East Pacific. It had been discovered that the deep water here was warmer than normal and, since the plates were separating at a fast 2.4 inches per year, there was a good chance of finding signs of recent volcanic activity in the form of geysers or hot vents. When *Alvin* dived into the rift in 1977 that is just what the scientists found, but they also discovered a lot more. As they measured water gushing up at temperatures of 61 degrees Celsius, the geologists and chemists were amazed to see profuse animal life around the vents, including many species never previously known. It was a discovery that was to turn the ideas of marine biologists upside down. The picture of life in the deep sea which was being so painstakingly constructed by scientists like Fred Grassle had to be redrawn. It now appeared that there was one kind of life in the flat sedimentary muds of the ocean plains and quite another in the mountain rifts.

Before the Galapagos discovery, biologists had been using *Alvin* to investigate areas of the deep sea which had been chosen for convenience of access as much as anything else. When so little was known, one starting point seemed as good as another. So vast is the area concerned there was no possibility of examining more than a minute fraction anyway. If the deep sea is arbitrarily defined as starting at a depth of 1000 feet, it covers sixty-three per cent of the earth's surface and holds seventy-five per cent of the total volume of sea-water. No light penetrates the waters and the temperature is normally only a few degrees above freezing. The pressure increases about one atmosphere with every ten metres of depth and reaches over seven tons per square inch in the deepest trenches. The development of submersibles gave men the chance to see the life of the deep at first hand. Many creatures disintegrate when brought to the surface from great depths – their cells expand and collapse with the enormous reduction in pressure; while others, though they may survive on the surface, do not thrive. Being able to go down and view animals in their habitat was a great breakthrough. At first, Ruth Turner says, 'our work was observational: we just went down and looked at things'. Then an incident occurred which completely changed the biologists' approach. *Alvin* had an accident and sank.

In 1968 she was being prepared for a launch from mother ship *Lulu* when a wire broke and she toppled off the launch platform, filled with water through her open hatch, and sank in 5000 feet of water. Fortunately she was empty save for a few items the crew had put aboard prior to the dive – some clothing, personal belongings and sandwiches. *Alvin* sat on the ocean floor for ten months before a rescue operation could be mounted using another submersible, the *Aluminaut*. When the craft was recovered, biologists were intrigued to discover that, after all those months in the water, the crew's lunch was intact. In surface waters the sandwiches would have been quickly devoured by bacteria and small organisms. Why, it was asked, hadn't this happened in the deep sea? The question led biologists to branch into a whole new world of experimentation. As Ruth Turner puts it, 'The loss of *Alvin* was not a complete disaster: in fact it was a great boon to biologists'. In a series of controlled experiments using bottom stations to which *Alvin* regularly returned, it was discovered that the deep sea works at a completely different pace from the surface waters. The sparse though varied life of the sedimentary mud grows and moves very slowly. The deep-sea environment turned out to be gentle and benign, very far from hostile, as some had thought.

With Ruth Turner examining samples of wood retrieved from the sea floor by *Alvin*

It was to one of these bottom stations that I would be diving in a few months' time. Fred Grassle explained why they had chosen the Tongue of the Ocean, the trough west of New Providence Island, for a station. It was deep but conveniently close to land, and a good place to go in winter when rough seas prevented access to the more northerly bottom stations. Also the environment was different from the waters off New England. The water contained less food matter but a greater variety of life, and they would like to understand why. He told me that life in most of the deep sea is based on photosynthesis, just like life elsewhere on the planet. Not directly, of course, for no light penetrates the deep, but via dead organisms that float down from the surface waters. In other words, life in the deep sea is dependent on life above. For a while it was believed that this was universally true. It seemed a perfectly reasonable assumption. After all, how else could life possibly exist?

Then came what has been described as the major find of the decade: the Galapagos hot vents. What Bob Ballard first saw, and Fred Grassle and his colleagues came to examine later, were large, vivid, quick-growing creatures which broke all the rules about the deep sea. Six-foot worms encased in white tubes and tipped with bright red plumes grew in profusion near large clams with blood-red meat – creatures that were quite unknown before. Another new kind of worm, new families of crabs and mussels, and a dandelion-like creature related to the Portuguese man-of-war were also found in large quantities. It was like coming across a lush oasis of exotic new plants in the midst of an almost barren desert. The world of oceanography was stunned, not only by the profusion of new life, but by the million-dollar question: what do all these creatures live on? Clearly it must be something produced by the hot vents, and not by food floating down from the surface. It could not therefore be based on photosynthesis. But what else was there? The microbiologists found the answer: the waters around the vents are dense with bacteria which use not light but hydrogen sulphide in their metabolic process. The hydrogen sulphide is brought up in the hot water from the depths of the earth. Directly or indirectly, the larger life forms live off these abundant bacteria, forming a self-sufficient community around each vent.

The full implications of this discovery will not be established for some time, but everyone agrees they will be far-reaching. When I was visiting Woods Hole the community was a-buzz with the publication of a paper suggesting that chemosynthesis, as this life process is called, was originally the basis of all life.

The hot vents have also provided geologists and chemists with some new insights into the way the planet works. After investigating the Galapagos site, Bob Ballard and fellow scientists went to look at even hotter vents at 21°N, off the Mexican coast. Here they found water gushing out at an incredible temperature of 350 degrees Celsius, so hot that it melted *Alvin*'s temperature probe. (The water doesn't actually boil because of the immense pressure.) Rising up with this superheated water are dissolved minerals which, on hitting the cool ocean water, solidify and form deposits around the vents. The minerals are rich and abundant: silver, zinc, copper, lead, cobalt, mercury and manganese. Immense wealth – if only it could be mined. Bob Ballard explained how places like Cyprus, which has been mined for its minerals since Roman times, was once at the edge of a plate, most of which sank under the continent leaving only this fragment of its riches behind. 'Plate tectonics shows us the best place to look for minerals. Right now I can tell you that a good place would be near Easter Island where the plates are separating really fast – at eighteen centimetres a year.' With increasing pressure on the land's resources, it won't be long before mining of the sea-bed is an economic proposition.

Ever since chemists have been analysing sea-water they have been mystified by a chemical imbalance in its make-up. Even allowing for what the rivers bring down off the land and for other factors, the sea contains too much manganese and not enough magnesium. For decades scientists were bothered by this question – until the hot vents were discovered. Now it is believed that sea-water seeps down into the earth's mantle through fissures and cracks on the sides of the great ridge system and loses magnesium on the way. Heated by the hot magma under the earth's crust it then shoots up through the vents, taking manganese with it. It has been calculated that every drop of sea-water will go through this vast circulation system every ten million years or so.

The Galapagos discoveries have been, in the words of Ruth Turner, a major impetus to marine science. This detached phrase describes what is a dramatic and very exciting landmark for many oceanographers. It can be likened to Darwin's discovery of the extraordinary life on the Galapagos Islands, just to the west of the vent area. Or to the opening of Tutankhamun's tomb for archaeologists. But it is not just the discoveries themselves which have been attracting attention. At a time when the sea is already being viewed as a major new source of food and inexhaustible energy, it is the implications of these finds for the location of minerals that are making governments and big business take notice. Scientists may find that their work is an end in itself, but the rest of the world always wants to know: is this knowledge also of practical use? At Woods Hole the range of study is wide and, though some of the work can be described as pure science, much is directly relevant to such wide-ranging applications as fish farming, medicine, and waste disposal, as well as mining and energy.

Tube worms and mussels photographed near one of the hot vents in deep water off the Galapagos Islands

In November the Bahamas are popular with holiday-makers; the temperature is a warm seventy-five degrees and the gentle trade winds cool the skin during the heat of the day. As *Alvin*'s mother ship *Lulu* took on stores in Nassau, ready for the forthcoming eight-day diving trip, I talked with Dr Carl Berg, a colleague of Ruth Turner and one of the scientists who would be diving to the Tongue of the Ocean. He told me how he had become involved in a project that had direct practical applications which could prove useful to the inhabitants of the Caribbean. He and other scientists had made a study of the queen conch, one of the largest marine snails and a major source of food to the islanders for centuries. In recent years the queen conch has been seriously overfished, with the result that prices are very high and stocks so low that fishermen must go many miles to collect a meagre load. To counter this trend, studies have been made into rearing conch in tanks until they are large enough to escape most predators. These experiments could be extended by scattering young conch, raised in hatcheries, from aircraft flying low over the shallow waters where the conch live and feed.

Fish farming is nothing new, of course; the Chinese kept fish in ponds as long as 3000 years ago. But aquaculture, as the idea is now called, will probably develop along much more intensive and commercial lines in the next few decades. So far only high-value fish and shellfish like salmon, oysters and shrimps have brought profits to private enterprise, but as other breeds of fish dwindle, many more types might be raised successfully in artificial conditions. What Carl Berg hopes is that more governments will become interested in restocking their overfished species. There is probably no profit as yet to be made out of breeding queen conch commercially, but it is in the interests of every Caribbean government to examine such schemes for the benefits they could bring to the local economy. Dr Berg is acting as an adviser to a scheme aimed at restocking Bahamian conch, which are much in demand to feed not only the islanders but the large numbers of tourists on which the country's economy depends. Based on research at the University of Miami, conch are being raised under a variety of conditions, in pens, cages and pools on a Bahamian island and, once the best rearing method has been established, it is hoped to extend the scheme to a national basis.

Many believe that artificial rearing of the more common species of fish should not be necessary. Given proper management of the ocean's fish stocks and the harvesting of new food species, it is argued that the seas will continue to produce abundant protein. However, as I had seen in the North Sea, gross overfishing has led to fast-dwindling stocks in popular fishing grounds. In the Bahamas some of the deep-sea species have shown a sharp decline in numbers. A local boatman told me how numerous the famous bluefin tuna used to be. During their annual migration from the Caribbean Sea through the Florida Straits into the Atlantic, many a bluefin was caught by a wealthy tourist from a sports fishing boat. But the Bahamian and Florida fleets were not the only ones after the fish. As the tuna continued their migration into the North Atlantic they ran the gauntlet of a second fleet off New England and, as the fish arrived in the Mediterranean at the end of their journey, yet a third fleet swept up most of the survivors. Such intensive fishing could not continue and now the bluefin is hard to find.

Optimists have high hopes that the new 200-mile fishing limits, which most countries are likely to adopt soon if they have not already done so, will do much to prevent overfishing by excluding foreign fleets from home waters. However, migratory and ocean fish will still be largely unprotected. As fish yields have fallen in recent years, prices have risen and this has resulted in an increase in the number of fishing fleets rather than a decrease. The higher prices have led to more intensive fishing, rather than a decline in fishing effort. With more ships chasing fewer fish the risk of permanent damage to stocks becomes more acute.

However, not all parts of the oceans are overfished. On the contrary, there are many areas which are under-utilised, particularly in the more remote regions of the southern hemisphere. If the price of fish rises sufficiently, it could become worth while to build more ocean-going fleets capable of fishing remote waters for months at a time.

Another answer is for people to eat more species of fish so that less have to be thrown back into the sea as unmarketable – a complete waste since, with modern trawling methods, once caught they are dead anyway. Only a few types get on to our plates although there are many more which are perfectly good to eat. The problem with nations who can afford to pick and choose is that they are very conservative in their eating habits. In the US one does not often get offered squid, red crab, or grenadier. In Northern Europe spider crab, octopus, squid and monkfish are not popular. If you are like me, you've tried squid once or twice but haven't exactly rushed off to buy it. The Eastern palate is far less fussy. The Japanese, Koreans and island people eat a wide variety of food from the sea, and accept new species more readily.

In the last twenty years the Russians, and more recently the Japanese, have been harvesting a new kind of food, Antarctic krill. This crustacean, which looks like a small shrimp, is just four to seven centimetres long, hardly large enough to fill one's mouth. Yet these creatures exist in such abundance that it is predicted they could yield 100 to 150 million tons a year – about *double* the existing world fish catch of 60 million tons. In a world with a fast-growing population short of protein, this fishery could bring about a dramatic increase in the supply of food. The Russians and Japanese have developed a number of processes to make krill palatable: there is krill meal, krill paste, krill butter and krill cheese; the Japanese market a fish sausage in which part of the fish is replaced by krill. The crustacean can also be used as animal feed, to ease the demand on overfished species currently used to produce animal protein. Having tried krill myself – from a can bought in Japan – I cannot see Westerners taking to *Euphausia superba*, as the creature is properly called, with anything like enthusiasm. It tastes – well, salty, and not much else. Nonetheless, it could well be popular as a food supplement, and be added to fish cakes or fish fingers, rather as soya is to meat.

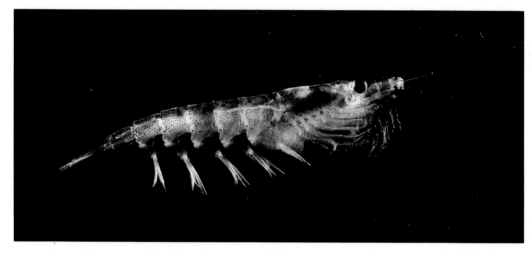

Euphausia superba

In quantity at least, krill would seem to be the answer to the shortage of fish protein. However, many questions hang over the future of this industry. Krill lives in the icy waters close to the Antarctic continent and fishing is restricted to the summer months; even then the weather is stormy and unpredictable, reducing fishing time considerably. There are also problems involved in processing: krill deteriorate quickly and must be frozen or canned immediately. Trawlers have to be specially built for the industry and the costs are probably as high as those for popular species caught nearer home. But for commercial fisheries the greatest uncertainty concerns the amount of krill available for harvesting: the figure of 150 million tons a year could be fifty per cent out. The distribution of the creatures is also very patchy: trawlers have brought up many tons in a few minutes, or gone for hours without any.

For the oceanographer the main drawback of a large-scale krill fishery is the damage it may do to the abundant Antarctic life. The ecosystem around the southern continent is unusual; all the higher life-forms are dependent on one creature at the bottom of what is a relatively simple food chain. That creature is krill. Whales, seals, penguins, birds, fish and squid all live off the small crustacean, either by eating it directly, or by eating another creature which eats it. The principal consumer of krill used to be the baleen whale which came to the Antarctic in vast numbers in the southern summer to feed and breed. With the dramatic and, many believe, tragic decline in the whale population, it is calculated that there is enough uneaten krill to produce the projected 150 million tons of harvest. However, birds, seals and penguins seem to have taken advantage of the food supply and have been increasing in numbers, so the surplus available to man may not be as large as people think. What environmentalists fear is a fast build-up of the krill fishery which could cause long-lasting damage to the vulnerable life of the Antarctic. Uncontrolled high-level catches could endanger the survival of the remaining baleen whales and result in significant reductions in the populations of all the other dependent species. What is needed, they say, is a slow, controlled build-up of the fishery so that scientists can measure the effects and make recommendations for the future. One soon appreciates that this is the cry of scientists everywhere, in all branches of oceanography. Do what you want to do, they are saying, but please do it slowly and do it carefully, so we can tell you what the effects are before it is too late!

The Antarctic possesses another great asset which is attracting attention, and that is oil. Although no one can yet be sure it exists, the deep-sea drilling ship *Glomar Challenger* has found indications of oil in the continental slope. Despite the difficulties of extracting it from such an inhospitable place, the quantities involved could be large enough to justify very high initial costs. The possibility of an Antarctic sea covered with oil platforms fills the hearts of environmentalists with dread. Oil pollution could affect not only the rich and varied wildlife of the region, but could be spread to all the major oceans by the Southern Ocean currents.

One place which is about to be exploited for its oil is the eastern seaboard of the United States, including the area off the north-west tip of the Bahamas. However, exploration off the archipelago is still in the early stages, and there is no guarantee that the Bahamas will become an oil-producing nation. Marine geologists can tell oil companies where there is a good chance of finding oil and gas, but they cannot point to the exact spot. They can also be pretty definite about where *not* to look. As Bob Ballard said, 'You never look where the earth's crust is very young, near the ocean ridges; you look where it's very old and the sediments are very thick, for example around the perimeter of the Atlantic where the continents separated almost 200 million years ago.'

The theory of plate tectonics may also help locate the highest densities of manganese nodules which litter the sea-bed. No one completely understands how these extraordinary clusters of minerals were formed, but it is thought that manganese and other minerals thrown out by the hot vents may solidify into balls and roll down the sides of the great ridge system, eventually covering vast areas of the ocean floor as the plates move apart. For many years the possibility of mining these nodules has been examined. The main difficulty is, of course, technical: the nodules sit on the sea-bed several thousands of feet down. Even assuming the minerals can be brought up, the scale of the operation will have to be very large indeed to make it pay. Nevertheless several mining consortia have expressed the serious intention of starting such mining within the next ten years.

Bob Ballard believes the emphasis will change, however. Now that geologists have discovered immensely rich sulphide deposits forming at the hot vent areas, he thinks that interest may well move away from manganese nodules to more selective mining close to the vent areas. But whichever deposits are exploited first, there seems little doubt they will be mined soon. In June 1980 the United States passed a law permitting

Oil wells in the Gulf of Mexico.

commercial companies to start deep-sea mining in 1988. This move appears ordinary enough, but at the time it created concern abroad.

What the United States was effectively saying was: we have the right to mine the deep sea, to take the minerals, and to keep the benefits for ourselves; we claim this right because we have the technology, the expertise and the money to invest in the equipment – and we do not recognise any other basis for laying claim to the deep-sea resources. The extension of the argument is that anyone is free to take the minerals if they care to make the enormous investment. In practice, only the developed nations will be able to afford to.

What upset the other governments of the world was that for no less than seven years the United Nations Conference on the Law of the Sea (known as LOS) had been trying to establish international agreement on this and other vital matters concerning the future uses of the sea. After long, complex and delicate negotiations, during which the many factions sometimes seemed poles apart, the negotiating arm of the Third World countries managed to pull off a *coup* and create agreement on all the major issues. One of the chief negotiators was Ambassador Koh of Singapore, who came to Woods Hole in June 1980 to lecture scientists on the outcome of the talks. Among the principal points agreed are: countries' territorial limits to be fixed at twelve miles around their coasts, but vessels to have rights of innocent passage within those limits; the exclusive economic zone of coastal states to extend to 200 miles around their shores (thus confirming the rights to fish and oil that many countries have already claimed); landlocked and geographically-disadvantaged states to have a share of living resources in the 200-mile zone and to have guaranteed access to the sea. The last of the twenty or so principles, agreed after perhaps the longest and most difficult negotiations, was the one governing the mining of minerals outside the 200-mile limit. The Third World claims that manganese nodules are, like the sea itself, the common heritage of mankind and not the property of those who can afford to mine them. Eventually the Western powers agreed that there should be a system of 'parallel' mining, whereby an internationally-managed sea-bed authority, largely financed by the West, should mine side by side with multinational companies, who would have to pay profit-sharing taxes and heavy licence fees to operate.

Thus by mid-1980 it seemed that the impossible had been achieved: East, West and Third World had agreed on how to share out the ocean's wealth. All that was then required was ratification of the treaty, which could probably be achieved within two to three years. Then the United States made its unilateral declaration of intent to mine, come what may, and now certain groups within the US are campaigning for non-ratification of the treaty. They include some of the mining companies seeking greater freedom for their operations, and certain scientists. The proposed treaty includes a clause which prohibits scientific exploration and research within the 200-mile economic zone without permission from the country concerned. Scientists see this as a threat to scientific freedom and the exchange of knowledge.

Sitting in the warm Bahamian sunshine in Nassau Harbour, from where *Lulu* would leave for the diving zone next day, Ruth Turner explained what this clause would mean to her and other oceanographers. In the past, she said, they always used to take local scientists on expeditions on an informal basis and exchange photographs and information with them afterwards. This worked very well and kept everyone happy. But if formal permission had to be applied for and the country concerned insisted on a large number of special requirements, then it would merely result in the expedition being conducted outside the 200-mile limits. 'We will always find a way to continue our research,' she added, 'but on this basis it may cost more.' The Galapagos expedition had been a case in point: because of difficulties encountered in using Equador as a base, a location outside their 200-mile limit had been chosen, and personnel and supplies were transported from other countries. 'But the really sad thing,' said Ruth Turner, 'is that we can no longer work side by side with scientists from certain countries, and this can only have a detrimental effect.'

Dr Steele, director of Woods Hole, echoed this concern. Under the proposed treaty a large portion of the oceans would come under the control of individual countries – and that portion covers many areas which are vital to oceanographic research. Dr Steele could foresee the Institution having to hire a full-time diplomat to negotiate bilateral agreements with a variety of countries.

Despite the scientists' justified concern, there are those who see this as a minor point which should not stand in the way of what they regard as a vital international treaty. If the US fails to ratify, then the proposed law will not come into being and a major portion of the earth will be open to anarchy, commercial over-exploitation and international conflict.

Woods Hole,
Massachusetts

Just before dawn *Lulu* left Nassau Harbour and began the three-hour journey to the point above the scientific bottom station at 24° 53′.25 North and 77° 40′.25 West. *Alvin*'s mother ship is a strange-looking craft. Two ex-US Navy pontoons, originally designed for minesweeping operations, have been used to form a giant catamaran by the addition of two archways and a deck topped with a bridge. In the middle of the deck area is an elevator platform by which *Alvin* is raised from the water up to the deck level between dives. The catamaran's 105-foot length accommodates nine officers and crew, as well as ten technicians and pilots who tend the sub, and up to eight scientists. Most of the living quarters are situated deep in the pontoons, and the remainder on deck in small units. Other units house machinery, workshops and laboratories. From a distance *Lulu* looks like a squat drilling platform never intended for sea; indeed, she has a reputation for making all but the best sailors seasick. But she is well designed for her job of getting *Alvin* safely launched, recovered and maintained.

While *Lulu* steamed towards the station, *Alvin* was being prepared for the dive. Enormous care is taken to ensure that every system on the sub is checked and doublechecked for faults. The men who pilot and maintain the craft during operations are the same men who take her apart for overhauls; they do not like to leave any jobs to outsiders. Their painstaking approach has paid off. Since her launch in 1964 *Alvin* has made more than a thousand dives without injury or loss of life. Not that her career has been without exciting incidents. In 1966 the submersible joined other deep-sea craft in the search for the missing H-bomb off Palomares, Spain, and after a month combing the sea floor, it was *Alvin* which managed to locate the weapon. In 1967 the sub was attacked by a 200-pound swordfish which left its sword embedded in the main frame. In 1968 the now famous *Alvin* sandwich incident occurred, and the sub spent over ten months on the sea-bed before she was recovered. Since that time the diving has been more or less trouble-free, except for one occasion which the chief of *Alvin* operations, Jack Donnelly, will not easily forget. During the expedition to the Mid-Atlantic ridge near the Azores, Donnelly was guiding the sub along a split in the rock face on the side of a giant canyon when she became stuck; the fissure had narrowed and an overhang prevented *Alvin* from moving up or forward. It took an hour and a half of patient manoeuvring to work her free, by wriggling and inching her out, stern first.

Alvin in one piece looked sleeker and less insect-like than she had at Woods Hole. She reminded me, irresistibly, of Walt Disney's cartoon tug Little Toot, with her bulbous body and miniature conning tower. The sub is twenty-five feet long and the sphere in which the pilot and two observers must live during each eight- to ten-hour dive is just six feet across. Ralph Hollis, the pilot who would be taking me down in three days' time, pointed out the viewing ports through which the passengers can see the ocean floor. The Plexiglas is several inches thick; like everything else it is built to withstand that more than two tons per square inch of pressure it meets two miles down. I ask how often they test the sphere. 'The best way possible – we use it,' answered the pilot. But he omitted to mention that an identical sphere was tested to a depth of 22,500 feet – more than four miles down – and suffered no problems.

Once on her way to the bottom of the sea, the submersible is independent of her mother ship. The large stern propeller gives her forward motion – maximum speed is $1\frac{1}{2}$ knots – and the two smaller ones give her lift to hop along the sea floor. Overall buoyancy is created by sections of glass foam attached to the main frame, and pump-operated ballast tanks enable the sub to vary her depth during a dive without recourse to the system used by the early submersibles, whereby petrol, which is relatively buoyant, was pumped out to gain depth, and steel shot released to lose depth. However, getting enough negative buoyancy to make the initial dive from the surface down to the sea floor is still a problem. It is such a long way down that, using the ballast tanks alone, it would take many long hours to descend. To make the journey faster *Alvin* uses heavy metal weights which are jettisoned on the sea floor. Nevertheless, it takes her an hour to reach 6000 feet, and two hours to reach 12,000 feet. To ascend, further weights are dropped and, in case of emergency, the large banks of batteries which drive the multitude of electrical systems can be released for a fast trip to the surface.

A wide range of functions can be carried out from *Alvin* on the sea floor: using the claw-like arms, samples are collected and placed in baskets; trays, cages, pieces of wood and food matter are left at bottom stations for experiments; temperature and current are measured; a video television camera records the terrain and life of the deep; and the observers can take photographs through the viewing ports. *Alvin* is a far cry from the early days of submarines, when, though men dreamed of possessing an independent pressure-proof craft, few boats succeeded in getting more than a few feet under the surface.

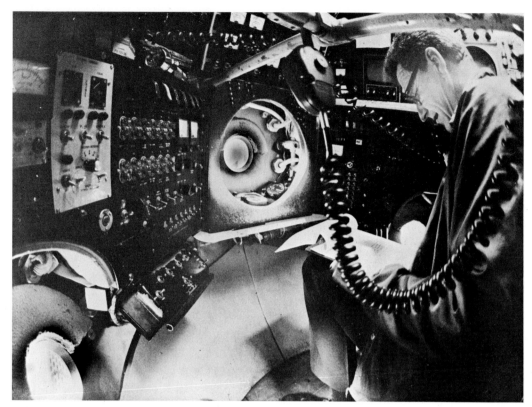

Inside *Alvin*

As long ago as 1578 a British naval officer, William Bourne, had the idea for a navigable submarine, which would be made of leather and wood and rowed along under the surface. The hull would have flexible sides which could be pushed out or pulled in by means of large screws. By winding in on the screws the crew could decrease the boat's volume and let it sink, and by winding out increase volume and let it rise. Air was to be provided by a long wooden pipe. A simple principle, but one that never got as far as the drawing board. Leonardo da Vinci, whose extraordinary inventions ranged from guns to flying machines, developed some ideas for diving but, foreseeing that underwater operations could be used to destroy enemy ships, refused to publish them.

In 1620 Dutchman Dr Cornelius Van Drebbel persuaded King James I to provide funds for the development of an underwater boat and, after some experimentation, succeeded in building the first submarine. Primitive buoyancy chambers made of pigskins were used to make the watertight wooden craft sink or rise in the water. The necks of the pigskins were connected to the outside of the craft through watertight flanges and were allowed to fill with water in order to make the boat dive. The crew then used wooden twisting devices to squeeze all the water out of the bags and make the boat rise to the surface and float. While submerged the craft was propelled by oars protruding through holes in the hull, which were kept watertight by means of leather sleeves banded with brass. Not only did the design work, but the king himself took a trip lasting several hours under the waters of the Thames. How Van Drebbel solved the problem of replenishing air when submerged is not known, but it is possible that a primitive carbon dioxide scrubber in the form of soda ash was used.

This early success was never put to practical use and, for some 150 years, no significant advances were made in the development of a mobile submersible. However, diving bells were used successfully during the sixteenth and seventeenth centuries, often to salvage valuable articles from sunken ships. Most worked on the simple principle that air will remain trapped in an upturned barrel and, if the barrel is ballasted sufficiently, a man can stay submerged until the air runs out. A major improvement was brought about by the addition of an air supply pumped down from the surface through a pipe. However, the first recorded attempt at an endurance record ended in disaster. In 1774 one John Day descended to the bottom of Plymouth Harbour with the intention of staying at 130 feet for twelve hours. His underwater boat went down all right but, amid much speculation as to what had gone wrong, it never reappeared.

The first truly independent and self-powered submarine to appear since Van Drebbel's was built in 1775. Like many inventions, the idea was born from necessity – in this case, the desire of American revolutionaries to blow up some of the British fleet anchored in the Hudson River. A brilliant farmer, David Bushnell, designed and built a submarine that was driven by a hand-cranked propeller and could dive and surface any number of times by means of hand-pumped ballast tanks. The wooden craft had a small conning-tower with glass windows so that the crew of one could see where he was going, but for the planned night assault on the British flagship a compass illuminated by phosphorescent fungus was used. Bushnell had also invented the first limpet mine – a barrel of explosives triggered by a clock mechanism and designed to screw on to a ship's bottom. Using the sub to place the mine, it was hoped to accomplish the first act of submarine warfare. After long months of development, the *Turtle*, as the strange, oval-shaped boat was called, eventually set out for HMS *Eagle* under cover of darkness. However, someone had got the tidal calculations wrong and by the time the sub arrived under the ship it was almost light. After failing to place the mine, the pilot abandoned the mission and, as he made his way back to the shore, was spotted by the enemy. Jettisoning the mine, he cranked furiously and reached safety in time to watch the mine explode near the British fleet. Although it did not sink any ships, the explosion was large enough to make the fleet panic and scatter. The *Turtle*'s extraordinary voyage was a success after all.

By 1902 the prototype of the modern submarine had been developed, using petrol engines on the surface and battery power beneath. However, no ordinary submarine could dive very deep because of the immense problems posed by water pressure. It was not until the 1930s that Otis Barton and William Beebe launched the first bathysphere and, after suitable trials, made a dive to a depth of 800 feet. In subsequent years the two men took the sphere, made of $1\frac{1}{2}$-inch-thick steel, to depths of first 2200 then 3028 feet, more than half a mile down.

Barton and Beebe's bathysphere was raised and lowered by means of a steel cable running to a winch on the surface tender, which made the diving system both simple and vulnerable. A man who believed he could improve on this idea and build the first really independent submersible was the Swiss balloonist Auguste Piccard. Eventually, in 1953 after many trials and setbacks, he and his son Jacques took their third prototype, the *Trieste*, to more than 10,000 feet. The submersible consisted of a pressure-proof sphere, to which was attached a float to provide buoyancy. Since an air-filled float would be crushed by the water pressure, the compartment was filled with petrol which is light but uncrushable. Negative buoyancy for the initial dive was provided by weights, which were released on the bottom to bring the vessel back to the surface.

Once the principles for diving into the abyss had been established there was no limit to the depths to which men could descend. Having bought the *Trieste* in 1958 the US

Navy planned an assault on the deepest part of the oceans – the Challenger Deep in the Marianas Trench off Guam, where the ocean floor sinks to 38,000 feet under the sea. In a race with the French, who were also planning some deep dives in their new bathyscaphe, the *Archimede*, the US obtained a new sphere for the *Trieste*, with walls five inches thick to withstand the pressure it would meet more than seven miles under the sea. In 1960 the *Trieste* succeeded in reaching a depth of 35,800 feet.

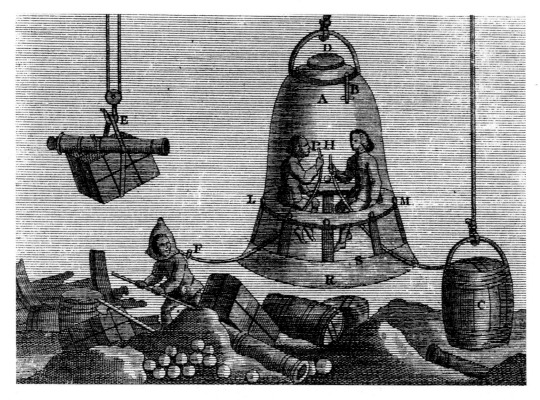

Halley's diving bell (1690): the first solution to the problem of replenishing the underwater air supply

Very few parts of the ocean are anything like as deep as the Marianas Trench. Much of the sea floor is within *Alvin*'s range of 12,000 feet, so the submersible from Woods Hole has plenty of area for study. After more than three hours at sea *Lulu* had now arrived over the bottom station in the Tongue of the Ocean. Captain David Landry had the task of positioning the catamaran as close as possible to the exact location. Using the various navigation systems on board – satellite navigation, radar fixes, Loran-C and precise depth measurement – he manoeuvred on to station, ready for *Alvin*'s launch. On deck the sub's crew were going through the last pre-dive checks with meticulous care. No launch could take place until the crew chief, the pilot, the surface controller and Captain Landry had signed the consent form. The size of the waves had to be under eight feet and the weather prospects fine – recovery of *Alvin* can be the most hazardous part of the entire operation. Finally, at half past eight in the morning, all was ready and Fred Grassle and his assistant, who were to make the first descent, stood waiting as the giant elevator platform bore *Alvin* down into the water. Crew members held the sub steady with ropes as the pilot and observers stepped from one of the catamaran pontoons on to *Alvin* and down through the hatch into the sphere. The hatch was closed and locked and, with two divers standing on her deck, the sub was manoeuvred out from between *Lulu*'s pontoons. The divers untied the holding lines, swam clear, and *Alvin* floated free, just her small conning-tower visible above the wavelets rippling the surface. Up on *Lulu*'s bridge, the surface controller was in contact with the pilot on VHF radio.

'*Lulu*,' came the message from *Alvin*, 'my hatch is closed, no leaks or grounds, my tracking pinger and underwater phone are on. Request permission to dive.'

'Roger, *Alvin*,' the surface controller replied. 'You are clear to dive. Present water depth is 2040 metres. Good luck.'

The sub began to dive; there was a brief flicker of white, a burst of bubbles, and then she was gone. She would be down about eight hours, surfacing shortly before darkness.

It takes the submersible more than an hour to reach the depth of one mile, descending at almost a hundred feet a minute. During that time the pilot is in frequent communication with *Lulu*; once on the bottom telephone communications will be less frequent, but never more than thirty minutes apart. On the mother ship's bridge the sub's position is constantly checked. Although *Alvin* has certain navigational aids, the pilot relies on *Lulu* to give him his position. On this expedition a simple navigation system is being used: by means of precisely-timed sonic pings emitted from *Alvin*, *Lulu* knows the distance and bearing of the sub. The pilot then relays his depth and, with the help of a small computer, the surface controller solves the geometric triangle. This system is adequate for most purposes, but when precise location is required – when trying to locate thermal vents, for example – a triangle of sonic 'lighthouses' is used. Three transponders are dropped and moored to the sea floor and, using their signals and those from *Alvin*, the surface controller can give the pilot course and distance to the place that is to be investigated.

On this first dive *Alvin*'s pilot must search for the bottom station which was last seen more than two years before. 'It can take minutes – or hours to find,' Fred Grassle had told me. The principal guide is a metal reflector beside the station, which will show up strongly on the sonar screen. Once the site is located, a small pinger will be put down nearby so that on subsequent dives *Alvin* can home in on the station immediately.

For Ruth Turner, Carl Berg and the other scientists on board *Lulu*, there was little practical work they could do until some samples and experimental material were brought up from the sea floor. Ruth explained how various pieces of wood had been left on the bottom during previous visits. When they were brought back to the surface during the next few days she expected to find them largely eaten away. 'Everyone thought I was wrong when I suggested that wood was an important source of food in the deep sea. They pointed out that wood had seldom been found there. My argument was: of course it hadn't – because it had been eaten!' Wood-boring creatures have long fascinated Ruth Turner. In the past she has studied a worm with which I am well acquainted – the teredo, for centuries the sworn enemy of masters of wooden ships. It can reduce solid planking to a honeycomb of long cylindrical holes within a few months. Nowadays strong antifouling paints discourage these bivalve molluscs from attacking wooden yachts. The work carried out from *Alvin* has shown that wood and other nutrients support a surprising diversity of life in the deep sea, life that was hardly suspected until this series of experiments began.

In the late afternoon we heard that *Alvin* was on her way up. During the hour-long ascent her progress was carefully monitored. As she neared the surface *Lulu* moved away; the sub could be seriously damaged if she came up under the mother ship. With just thirty metres to go everyone scanned the water near the expected arrival point. The Boston whaler, a small open boat, was ready with engine running and crew aboard to get to the submersible as soon as she surfaced. Suddenly the red dome of *Alvin*'s unmistakable profile broke the sparkling blue Caribbean waters some 300 yards away. The whaler sped across and put a pilot aboard to guide the sub back to *Lulu*. Soon the small white craft was safely over the submerged elevator platform and the three passengers emerged, smiling but anxious to exercise their cramped limbs. The bottom station had been found and the first sample boxes recovered. Fred Grassle and the other scientists carefully took the boxes from the receptacles under *Alvin*'s claws and carried them to the laboratory for preliminary work – mainly dissecting and preserving. More detailed study would be carried out using the facilities at Woods Hole.

As he sieved sedimentary mud, Fred Grassle described some of the findings that were emerging from this and related research programmes. Under normal circumstances, he explained, there are no large-scale disturbances on the floor of the deep sea. As a result, the life on the sea-bed is quite unused to adjusting to disturbances; it is therefore vulnerable. It is believed that any large change would result in the extinction of a large number of animals from a particular site. Manganese nodules are likely to be mined by means of large and very powerful suction dredges which will kill most of the animals in their path. The sediment picked up by the dredges would be put back into the sea, spreading over a large area. 'Until we have a better picture of life in the deep sea, we can't begin to measure the effects of such disturbances.'

There is one major use for the sea that scientists – and governments – must be able to monitor very carefully, and that is as a dumping ground for nuclear waste. In the past, certain low-level radio-active waste, set in concrete inside metal barrels, has been unceremoniously thrown overboard from ships and left to sit on the sea-bed. This kind of dumping is clearly unsatisfactory because the waste is left lying on the sea floor, its exact location unknown, and the radioactivity around it cannot be properly measured. The disposal envisaged for the future is very different: canisters of waste – including high-level waste – would be buried deep in the ocean floor, in an area where the clay sediment is very stable and capable of containing radioactivity should there be any leakage. The exact location would be recorded and the surrounding sediment and water carefully monitored so that a faulty canister could be identified and dealt with – though no one seems to know exactly how.

The instinctive reaction of all who care for the sea is why choose the oceans to dump this most deadly of materials? Why not somewhere else? Unfortunately, the alternative to the ocean is the land, and for almost every area of land that might be chosen, there are people who will say, 'But this is where we live and we don't want it here'. For small countries like Japan, Britain and the Netherlands, there are no land sites that are remote enough for consideration anyway.

Before any sub-sea-bed sites are chosen there is a great deal of research to be done, not only into the clays in which the waste canisters would be buried, but into the deep-water currents, the life of the creatures who inhabit the sediments, and the movement, if any, of deep-sea inhabitants towards the surface. As Fred Grassle says: 'We must know whether radioactive material could be transported in food chains. And if so, how rapidly it would get back to man.'

The ideal solution would be to do without nuclear energy. There are many who believe that within the next half-century we will manage to harness an immense source of energy which is not only limitless but is also free of harmful waste products that have to be disposed of. That source is the sea. The oceans possess many forms of energy: tides, which rise and fall by as much as fifty feet; waves, which in many offshore regions are sufficiently large for enough of the time to produce almost continuous power; stronger currents, such as the Gulf Stream; heat differences between surface and deeper waters; and, for ships themselves, auxiliary sail power to reduce their oil consumption. Most developed countries have research programmes investigating the feasibility of harnessing these different forms of energy. At the moment the enormous

The Last Resource 255

investment required is prohibitive and, apart from the Rance tidal energy project in France, no major schemes have been launched on a commercial basis. But once existing energy sources become sufficiently expensive or, in the case of nuclear power, unacceptable, then more research and development will doubtless bring about economically-viable schemes.

No alternative is without its drawbacks. At sunset, I looked towards the wide expanse of red-tinged sea to the west and tried to imagine it covered in long booms rocking to the rhythm of the waves, or in massive structures supporting underwater turbines to catch the currents – in addition to the oil and gas platforms that are already appearing. Perhaps we will have a sea regimented like the skies, with commercial sea lanes controlled by operators behind radar screens, and no-go areas kept clear for the generation of energy. National parks would be declared for leisure pursuits such as sailing, and pleasure boats would have to be equipped with sophisticated navigation aids to ensure they kept within the park boundaries. It is not a picture that will appeal to those who cherish the freedom of the seas.

After three days aboard *Lulu*, it was now my turn to prepare for a dive in *Alvin*. On the second day, our cameraman, Charles Lagus, had gone down with Fred Grassle to record what I was now going to see for myself. This was the only way we could film the event, because of the very limited amount of space in the submersible. The evening before the dive, I reported to pilot Ralph Hollis for the pre-dive briefing. Climbing down through the hatch, the sphere didn't look big enough for three people, but once we were in our respective seats – mine was a piece of foam rubber on the floor – the space appeared much larger.

For forty minutes, Ralph Hollis took me through the workings of the instruments that line the inside of the sphere. The interior looks rather like an aircraft's flight deck: there are display read-outs, switches, levers, dials and screens. These electronics reveal height above the sea floor, depth below the surface, each with its duplicate system. The sonar 'looks' ahead from as close as ten feet to as far as 1500 yards. A gyro compass gives direction, while the sonic pulser emits signals every two seconds to tell *Lulu* where we are. For the scientific work there is a temperature sensor and current meter. The two claws, properly called manipulators, are controlled differently, one by electric power, the other hydraulic. Powerful lights can illuminate the scene around the sphere, so that the video camera can take its record of each dive.

In the extremely remote chance of the pilot falling ill, each observer must know how to get the submersible to the surface. Ralph Hollis showed me how to release the electro-magnetically held weights to give the sub positive buoyancy. If, by an even remoter chance, *Alvin* was stuck, I was also shown how to release the banks of heavy batteries. If everything else failed and desperation set in, then the sphere itself could be released from the main frame, to rise to the surface like a cork. 'But we try to avoid that!' the pilot commented with a smile.

I had been told that the pre-dive briefing was the moment when people discovered if they were claustrophobic. Eight hours in a six-foot sphere is a long time but, though conditions would obviously be cramped, I did not think it would bother me. At eight in the morning Ralph Hollis, Fred Grassle and I climbed down into the sphere for the dive itself. I checked that I had my warm sweater and hat, my lunch and camera equipment. Above my head the hatch clanged shut, shutting out the warm sunlight, and I felt a touch of anxiety. Logically I knew that everything would be all right but, like most people who sail on the surface, I prefer unlocked doors and open spaces. My overactive imagination links closed hatches to watertight compartments on sinking ships. Thankfully the feeling lasted only a moment and, after concentrating on what was going on around me, I forgot to worry about going one mile down into the sea, locked in a small bubble.

Alvin at work

Alvin was driven from between *Lulu*'s hulls. The waves started to roll her gently and without ventilation the inside of the sphere became rather warm – all conducive to seasickness. But just as my stomach and I became uneasy, the divers cleared the last of the lines, I saw one of them finning away, and we were given permission to dive. Suddenly we were on the way down; the rolling was replaced by a beautiful calm. Outside, the water turned from bright sunlit blue to strong azure blue, then to rich dark velvet, the colour of night. After sixteen minutes it was pitch black outside the portholes and the only illumination came from the dim instrument lights inside the sphere. Ralph Hollis was talking on the underwater telephone, going through the procedures that he had been through a hundred times before. Fred was staring out of his porthole, watching for life in the mid-waters. Sitting there in the subdued light, staring out into the darkness, I was reminded of sailing at night. *Alvin* felt comfortingly safe, a small warm cocoon in a sea of black.

Fred pointed at the viewing port and told me to watch for luminescence. Peering out, I saw streaks of silver passing the small window. Descending at twenty inches per second there wasn't much time to take a good look at the creatures which were producing these strange flashes of light, but now and then I could identify individual organisms. Phosphorescence is one of the most beautiful and admired phenomena of the sea. Anyone who has looked over the stern of a ship on a dark night will probably have seen the disturbed waters sparkling and flashing in the wake. In the 1870s a scientist on HMS *Challenger* wrote:

> There was no moon, and although the night was perfectly clear and the stars shone brightly, the lustre of the heavens was fairly eclipsed by that of the sea. The unbroken part of the surface appeared pitch black, but wherever there was the least ripple the whole line broke into a brilliant crest of clear white light.

The Last Resource

Phosphorescence or, as scientists call it, bioluminescence has proved to be very useful in medical research. The process by which creatures ranging from tiny microscopic organisms to large fish can emit light is based on a chemical reaction which, unlike most light-creating processes, does not produce heat. The study of how this chemical energy is converted to light energy is helping medical researchers to understand how the energy-conversion processes of our bodies work, whether they be muscular, electrical (the nervous functions), or transport (kidney function). Bioluminescence can also provide a sensitive measurement of the effects of drugs and anaesthesia.

This is not the only way in which marine and medical research are interlinked. The giant squid has provided much of our knowledge about the nerve cell because it possesses a giant nerve-fibre system that is easy to examine. Skates and crabs are used for studies into the workings of the eye – the horseshoe crab has a long, easily-accessible optic nerve, while the skate's eye is responsive to light but not colour or detail. Study of the sea-urchin's reproductive system has relevance to cancer research and fertility control.

As *Alvin* continued downward the luminescence disappeared but, Fred Grassle said, we were likely to see more nearer the bottom. He explained that some fish have luminescent patches on their bodies, possibly to signal to each other, possibly to identify themselves or to navigate. One fish I knew of was the angler fish, which uses a lighted lure to attract its prey. Others, it seems, use a light to confuse predators, illuminating themselves quickly then squirting away.

After fifty minutes we were still diving. Yet the bottom here was just a seventh of the depth of parts of the Marianas Trench. The concept of vast depths like endless space is difficult to grasp and I stopped trying. Inside the sphere it was colder now – about 60 degrees Fahrenheit – and I put on my warm sweater. The others told me that our body heat would prevent the temperature dropping any further.

Ralph Hollis announced we had just 100 metres to go. He switched on the floodlights and the sonar. A minute later the descent weights were jettisoned and we stopped falling. To reach the bottom the variable-direction propellers were switched on and angled for downward motion. I peered through the port and with excitement realised I could see a wide expanse of ocean floor. At first there didn't seem much to see; for a few yards there was mud, then the lights failed to penetrate the thick blackness. Then Fred Grassle pointed out creatures on the sea floor. First a sea-urchin, then, as we began to move gently towards the bottom station, guided by the sonic pinger, there were holothurians or sea cucumbers.

Ralph Hollis drove *Alvin* very gently over the bottom. It was important not to disturb the sediment as we approached the bottom station. Eventually the lights picked up objects ahead and we settled on the bottom, just in front of some trays and baskets. Fred had decided on his programme the night before; the first job was to retrieve a tray next to one of Ruth Turner's wood towers, to see what life has been attracted to the vicinity of the wood. He also planned to take some core samples of the mud at varying distances from the wood. These would be put through a sieve later and the animals counted and identified. The work took time. The mechanical arm was manipulated to pick up an empty core sampler from the sample tray, swing it out to the required position, push it into the mud, then spring the door shut, before lifting it and dropping it back into the tray. While the others worked I tried to imagine what life was like 6700 feet under the surface. The pressure here was 3070 pounds per square inch – more than one metric ton. No light penetrates the deep and the temperature is near freezing; to man, it is as alien an environment as outer space. It even seems empty of

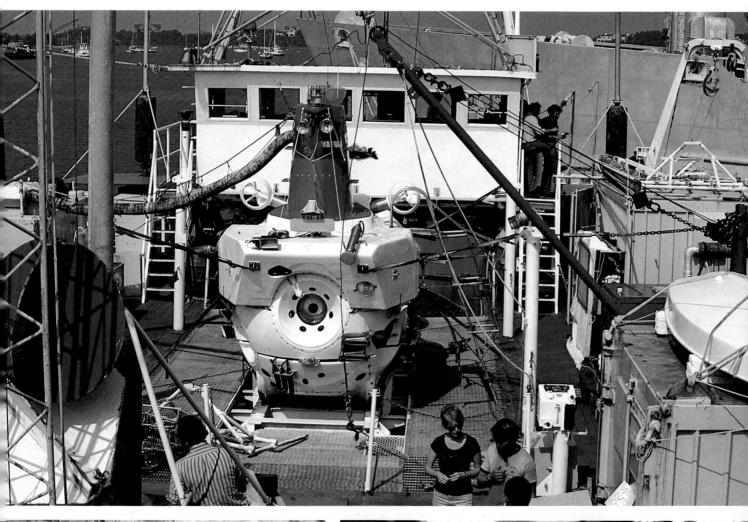

p: *Alvin* on the deck of *Lulu*. Bottom right: *Alvin*'s dive is monitored on board *Lulu* by Bob Ballard. Left: Undersea lava flow from the mid-Atlantic ridge, and *rotenthis octoped* photographed from *Alvin* in the Cayman Trough

fish, but Fred told me that if we put bait out it would soon attract scavenging fish and other predators lurking beyond our bright lights. At one point I thought I saw a large-mouthed fish on the periphery of vision but then it was gone, a grey shape melting into the black beyond. Fish are not plentiful in the deep, Fred told me. Compared to the surface, the waters here are low in oxygen and food is hard to come by for the relatively large creatures.

Time passed very quickly inside the sphere and, after picking up another set of samples, I found we had been on the bottom for four hours. On this trip the time on station was being cut short so that we could travel across to the wall of the trough in which we were diving, and make our ascent to the surface beside it. The escarpment on the east side of the Tongue of the Ocean rises thousands of feet from the flat ocean floor to less than a hundred feet below the surface. As we approached, *Alvin*'s sonar easily found the massive wall of rock. Ralph Hollis released the two 250-pound ascent weights and the sub started her long journey to the light. As we glided upward just feet from the rock face I saw squid squirt away. Occasionally there were fish or glass sponges. Rocky outcrops suddenly protruded outwards as if to touch us but, with a light touch on the controls, the pilot guided *Alvin* skilfully round them. The great wall climbed ever onwards, like a cliff in the Grand Canyon. Smooth rock gave way to deep fissures and steep slopes to overhanging ledges, and I became aware of how deep we had descended.

Less than fifteen minutes to the surface there were sea-urchins and starfish; we were entering the realm where tiny particles of daylight begin to penetrate, although, with *Alvin*'s powerful lights on, one was not aware of it. Soon, however, we turned the lights off and I could see a glimmering of shape and texture in the wall. Gradually colour emerged and sparse plant life appeared on the rock. The water turned a dark royal blue, then, as we went steadily higher, it grew rich and vivid. I found myself looking up through the pilot's viewing port towards the surface, but it was some time before I saw the sparkle of the sun on the top of the water. Ralph Hollis slowed our ascent by flooding the ballast tanks and, just short of the surface, he stopped the sub and awaited final clearance to come up. When *Lulu*'s permission was received, he readjusted the ballast and *Alvin* rose gently towards the warm fresh Caribbean air.

Safely aboard the catamaran once more sitting in the yellow sunshine of the late afternoon, visions of the cold dark waters of the deep sea stayed sharp in my memory. To the pilots and scientists who regularly travel in *Alvin* diving a mile down is routine, but for the first-time observer like me it was an experience which for ever changed my view of the sea. Until then depth had been a remote and intangible concept; I had thought of the deep sea as a black lifeless pit. Now I would never sail an ocean again without remembering it possessed mountains, plains and animal life; that far beneath the surface there was another world, benign, vulnerable, and full of secrets still.

It is the unknown characteristics of the sea which concern the scientists most. Three days later, with *Alvin*'s work on the bottom station finished, we discussed the future uses of the sea and the effects they are likely to have. It seems that, whether we like it or not, the oceans are going to be used on a large scale, both for what we can get out of them, and for what we can dump in them. For biologists like Fred Grassle the problem is one of time. 'We haven't yet got the basic information on the rates of processes in the deep sea. We can't begin to predict what will happen under disturbed circumstances. Really, we don't know much about the deep sea at all!' This had been echoed by geologist Bob Ballard: 'The area we most want to study, the mid-ocean ridge, is 40,000 miles long – and we've seen just a few hundred metres of it.'

It seems that, having sent men to the moon, we know more about the area around our planet than the waters of the sea. Recent discoveries have solved some of the riddles of the earth and the formation of the continents, but other mysteries remain. It is thought that the sea floor may hold clues to the causes of glacial cycles, for example. The rate at which the sea uses up oxygen is still unknown. And one of the most urgent questions of all – what are the long-term effects of pollution? – cannot be answered with certainty. It is now believed that the creatures of the deep sea may actually help to hide the effects of pollution by stirring up the sediment and burying toxic matter which floats down from the surface. Nonetheless there must be limits to the amount the sea can absorb. Through atmospheric fall-out, coastal and river effluent, spillage and dumping we have already put an uncomfortably heavy load on some areas. Substances like mercury and lead are found quite naturally in the sea, but the water must be given time to assimilate large additional quantities. Similarly, oil seeps up from the sea-bed and is absorbed; it is only when it is poured over the surface in a concentrated stream that it kills and destroys. The ocean can adapt to many things, given enough time. Scientists enjoy pointing out that, if someone suggested putting a pipe down into the ocean and releasing water superheated to a temperature of 350° Celsius and loaded with chemicals, the Environmental Protection Agency would never allow it. Yet that is just what has been happening at the hot-vent sites for millions of years. Everything, scientists stress, depends on the time the oceans are given to adapt to change.

Certain substances are, however, difficult for the sea to absorb, and these include the family known as halogenated hydrocarbons – synthetic organic chemicals which include the now notorious DDT, which was found to interfere with the life processes of birds and animals. Although the use of DDT has been curtailed, the harmful effects of related substances are coming to light. For example, we use chlorine to disinfect our water supplies, yet when released into lakes and rivers it forms into organic compounds which are strongly suspected of causing cancer and mutations. Rivers which flow from heavily populated areas bring these chlorinated organic compounds into the sea, where they are believed to be harmful to food chains. At the same time chlorine has been immensely beneficial to mankind; when it was first added to water supplies it almost eliminated waterborne diseases like typhoid overnight.

'Biology is not black and white,' says Ruth Turner. 'We can't say definitely: Don't do this! We can only measure the effects and let the people decide.'

Dr Steele, director of Woods Hole, had stressed this problem. 'When we are faced with the two extreme views – shall we do something or shan't we? – we cannot give firm answers. The solution is somewhere in between. The oceans can assimilate a certain amount and we have to find out how much by trial and error. The important thing is to keep our options open.'

As far as highly toxic or cancer-forming substances are concerned, one idea is to collect them and bury them under the sea floor along with the nuclear wastes. This would be a less harmful solution than washing them into sea-water or trying to dispose of them on land. (I was told that, due to lack of legislation, control and facilities, many tons of toxic wastes are dumped on to America's highways from moving trucks under cover of darkness.) Ruth Turner summed up the problem. 'Man has to decide how he can live best, while doing the least damage.'

The decisions about how we are going to use the sea, both as a provider and a refuse-disposer, are political. Each government has to decide how it is going to use its own coastal waters; whether it is going to allow its fish stocks to replenish themselves, or harvest them to the point where they are exhausted; whether it is going to take minerals and oil from the sea and how it will protect the environment from the effects; whether to use the ocean's boundless energy for power and how to make the best use for it.

However, many of the sea's riches lie outside the 200-mile limits. Unless the proposed Law of the Sea treaty is ratified, then no step will have been taken towards ordering and controlling people's use of the oceans; no framework will exist to protect the major part of the sea as a provider of food, minerals and energy; the possibility of agreeing conservation measures for endangered species and for vulnerable ecosystems will be that much more remote.

The ocean has been likened to the Wild West of the nineteenth century. It is today's last frontier: an immense area ripe for exploitation by those who dare risk its dangers, yet a place without effective laws to settle disputes over ownership or rights to natural resources. Even should international laws be agreed, the question of who is to police the oceans then arises. If the sea floor becomes a waste-receptacle, regulations will be passed governing acceptable levels of radioactivity and toxicity on the sea-bed. Scientists may decide what levels are acceptable, but who is to make sure these levels are adhered to?

If, as seems certain, the ocean is to provide much more for us in the future, then it must necessarily cease to be a free place which men may travel and harvest as they please. Like the land, it will have to be governed and controlled so that it can give up its wealth without being robbed of its lifeblood. Possibly a United Nations sea-going force will have to be formed to enforce fishing quotas, monitor mining operations and measure pollution levels.

For myself, I look forward with infinite sadness to a sea which is ruled and regulated like the land; the freedom of the sea is one of its most alluring characteristics. At the same time I want all the benefits the sea can provide for me: energy, food and natural resources. I also want the oceans kept healthy so that they can continue to play their part in the sea–air–rain–water cycle on which life depends. All in all, I prefer the idea of having a few sheriffs and lawmen on the frontier to leaving the place open to overexploitation and short-term profit. It is too late to prevent the savage slaughter of the whale whose numbers, like the bison's, have dipped almost to extinction level; but there are myriads of other life forms which can and must be protected soon.

When I imagine coasts lined with oilwells, fish farms and wave-energy machines, and the lonely beautiful Southern Ocean busy with krill-fishing boats and suction-mining vessels, I remember that, even if we build ten times as many ships as we have now, even if we construct a hundred thousand devices for extracting energy, there will still be large areas of the oceans that will resist our efforts to utilise them. However hard we try, we will never control the sea itself; vast distances, waves, storms, ice and great depths will always prevent us from achieving mastery. If we are immensely careless we are capable of destroying much of the life in the sea, but we can never destroy its power.

In the long story of man's relationship with the sea, he has learned to take food from it, travel across it, fight over it, and remove oil from beneath it. But at best it has always been a tolerant master, at worst a ruthless adversary. Even the man who lives and works on the sea is but a visitor on its surface and a guest in its waters.

OCEANOGRAPHY
MARGARET DEACON

Scientist at work on board a research ship
belonging to Albert I of Monaco

The origins of oceanography can be traced back to the seventeenth century, when scientists now more famous for their work in other fields, such as Robert Boyle and Robert Hooke, first attempted to found a science of the sea. They experimented with apparatus designed to measure the depth of the ocean and to sample water at any given depth, to see whether it was salt all the way to the bottom. Such information would provide valuable clues about the nature of the earth but they also expected practical benefits. At a time when maritime affairs played an increasing part in national life greater understanding might promote safety at sea.

Plagued by uncertainties over apparatus and the necessity of relying almost entirely on others to make their observations, they made slow progress, and for the next 200 years marine science developed piecemeal. Nevertheless, important work was done and new ideas proposed. The first comprehensive book on the sea, *L'Histoire Physique de la Mer*, by the Italian engineer Marsigli, appeared in 1725. In 1772 the French chemist Lavoisier published the first analysis of seawater. Alexander Marcet, Swiss but living in London, improved on his results in 1819 and showed that variations in salinity occur in different parts of the world. On a Russian circumnavigation of the 1820s, the physicist Lenz made the most far-reaching observations up to that time of the vertical distribution of temperature and specific gravity within the oceans. James Rennell's *Currents of the Atlantic* (1832) was based on fifty years' careful collation of data on surface-water movements.

In 1847 Matthew Fontaine Maury began publishing *Wind and Current Charts* using information derived from logbooks deposited at the United States Naval Observatory. These were welcomed by sailing-ship masters facing growing competition from steam. Maury envisaged extending the work on an international basis, with all ships, naval and merchant, keeping registers of observations. His plan was adopted by a congress held in Brussels in 1853, but Maury's work came to

an end with the outbreak of the American Civil War.

Maury was also involved with the search for a route for the first Atlantic submarine telegraph cable in the 1850s. Until that time deep-sea sounding had been laborious and uncertain. With the aid of steam and new technology it now became possible to take accurate soundings in deep water and to lower and retrieve apparatus.

Marine biologists were the first to appreci-

ate the new possibilities for science. Their work had gradually extended from the seashore to the shallow waters of the continental shelf, using the naturalist's dredge, but there had been few opportunities to work at greater depths. This did not much matter while it was believed that the inhospitable depths of the ocean were empty of life, but as contrary evidence began to accumulate scientists became eager to take advantage of the surveyors' new expertise. Two British scientists, W.B. Carpenter and C. Wyville Thomson, sailed in HMS *Lightning*, under the auspices of the Royal Society, in the summer of 1868. The results of the voyage were so interesting that they made further cruises in HMS *Porcupine* in 1869–70, and live animals were dredged from the then enormous depth of nearly 15,000 feet.

For Carpenter it was only a short step from observing the effect of varying temperature on the distribution of species in the deep sea to curiosity as to the cause of these changes. Improved deep-sea thermometers showed that the depths of the ocean, even in the tropics, contained water so cold that it must have originated in polar regions. To account for its presence Carpenter revived the idea that the oceans have an internal circulation based on differences of density in the water. This theory was opposed by those who saw the winds as the only cause of ocean currents. To collect further evidence, as well as to extend the search for new animal life in the sea, Carpenter planned a new expedition, devoted entirely to the exploration of the sea. This was the origin of the voyage of HMS *Challenger* 1872–6, with a team of civilian scientists headed by Wyville Thomson. This ambitious round-the-world expedition aroused international interest, both in the voyage and its subsequently published results, and modern oceanographers rightly look back to it as one of the key points in the foundation of their science.

On board *Challenger*

But although by the early twentieth century oceanography had achieved recognition, its development was still uncertain because of the expense of sending out new expeditions or founding research institutions. Much was done by wealthy individuals, in particular Prince Albert I of Monaco who devoted much of his life to research and founded the Musée Océanographique in Monaco (1910) as well as an institute in Paris. In Scandinavia physical oceanography, as well as marine biology, flourished in the universities. In Germany state support was forthcoming for a series of expeditions, culminating in the voyage of the *Meteor*, 1925–7, which extended the work of the *Challenger* to show the pattern of circulation of the great water masses of the Southern and Atlantic Oceans. In other countries scientific societies founded marine stations,

Exploring the ocean depths and the life found there

Features of the ocean floor – continental slope, abyssal plain, mid-ocean ridge and deep troughs – can be seen in the 'drained' hemisphere and the (laterally much condensed) section below. The geological history of the ocean floor has been revealed in cores drilled by *Glomar Challenger* (right)

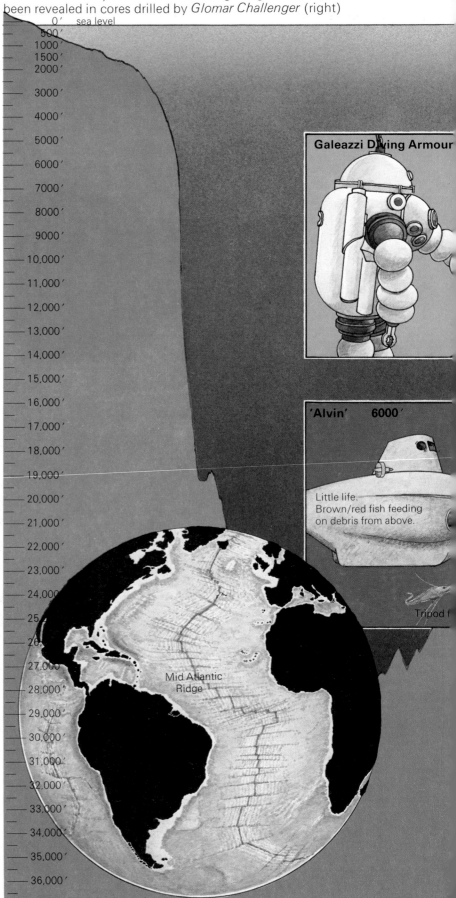

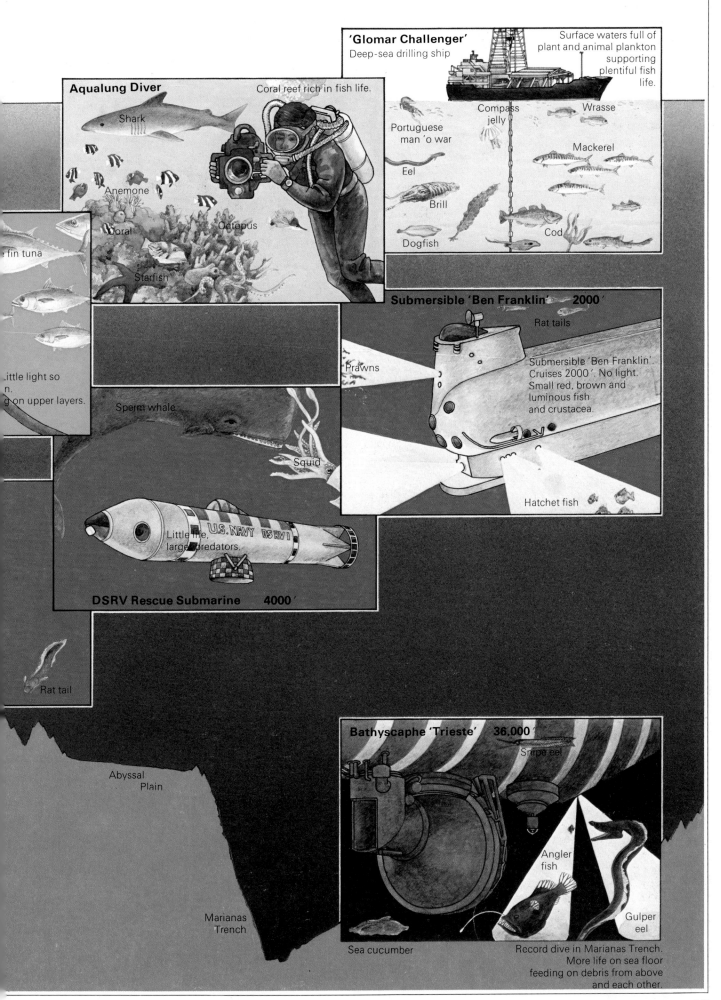

'Glomar Challenger'
Deep-sea drilling ship

Surface waters full of plant and animal plankton supporting plentiful fish life.

Aqualung Diver

Coral reef rich in fish life.

Shark

Anemone

Coral

Octopus

Starfish

Compass jelly

Wrasse

Portuguese man 'o war

Mackerel

Eel

Brill

Dogfish

Cod

fin tuna

little light so
n.
g on upper layers.

Submersible 'Ben Franklin'   2000'

Rat tails

Prawns

Submersible 'Ben Franklin'.
Cruises 2000'. No light.
Small red, brown and
luminous fish
and crustacea.

Sperm whale

Squid

Hatchet fish

U.S. NAVY DSRV 1

Little life,
large predators.

DSRV Rescue Submarine   4000'

Rat tail

Bathyscaphe 'Trieste'   36,000'

Snipe eel

Abyssal
Plain

Angler
fish

Marianas
Trench

Gulper
eel

Sea cucumber

Record dive in Marianas Trench.
More life on sea floor
feeding on debris from above
and each other.

265

of which some, from very small beginnings, have grown into international centres of research.

This transformation has come about partly as a result of changing attitudes to scientific research. For a long time governments were largely interested only in financing research of obvious importance to the national economy, such as fisheries. This led to much useful work being done, for example the research in the 1920s and 1930s by *Discovery* and investigations on the life history of the whale, but ignored the need for wider understanding, which only basic studies could give. These have been made possible during the last forty years by a great expansion of oceanographic research which in turn has come about because of the experience of two world wars, in which submarine operations were crucial, as well as growing peacetime needs, and because of the modern pattern of government involvement in scientific enterprises.

Like their earlier counterparts, twentieth-century oceanographers have made good use of technological innovations. Modern developments in electronics and communications have been most important. Continuous recording apparatus has made available, for example, much more detailed information about the water movements in the ocean and many new discoveries and ideas have resulted. Biologists have been able to operate their nets with greater accuracy to study the distribution of individual species, the detailed kind of work which is needed to obtain a wider ecological understanding of the life of the oceans where every creature – from the minute plants of the surface layer, deriving nutrients from the sea-water and energy from sunlight, through the small creatures feeding on them (plankton), to the great fishes and whales – forms a link in the chain of dependence. Perhaps the single most surprising development of the last twenty years, and certainly one which has attracted much attention, has been the field of plate tectonics, or continental drift as it was at first known, which arose from sea-floor studies of the 1940s and 1950s and which has revolutionised geological thinking. Great advances have been made in the study of waves and tides and the knowledge gained has been put to use in many ways, not least in the offshore oil industry, fulfilling the prediction of the early scientists that greater understanding of the oceans would bring practical as well as theoretical benefits.

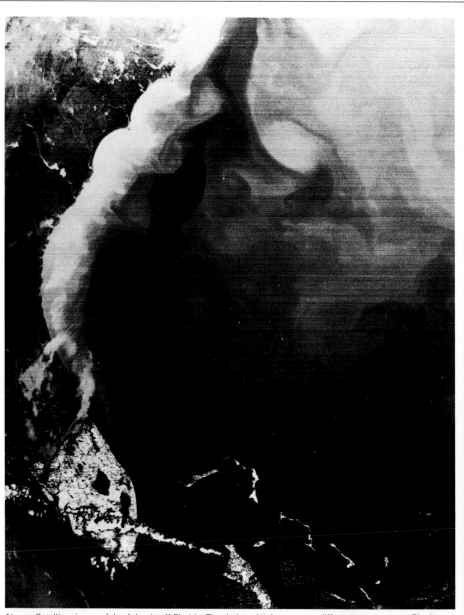

Above: Satellite picture of the Atlantic off Florida. The dark and light areas are different temperatures. Pictures from satellites can show directly what earlier oceanographers had to work out in much less detail from mapping and sampling
Below: *Challenger*'s launch on dredging trip

On board *Challenger*

ANTARCTICA
ANN SAVOURS

'Lands doomed by nature to everlasting frigidness and never once to feel the warmth of the sun's rays, whose horrible and savage aspect I have no words to describe. . . . Whoever has resolution and perseverance [to proceed] further than I have done, I shall not envy him the honour of the discovery, but I will be bold to say that the world will not be benefited by it.' Captain Cook penned these words two centuries ago in the journal of his second great voyage, during which he came so near to discovering Antarctica. It is interesting to consider how much the world has benefited, and will benefit in the future, from the frozen continent, which even at the beginning of this century was only known from the sightings of sealers, whalers and explorers in ships under sail.

The greatest gain has been in the increased knowledge of our own planet, and its atmosphere, flora and fauna, particularly since the International Geophysical Year of 1957–8, during which scientists of many nations combined to work in the laboratory of the far south. As a result of this successful demonstration of international co-operation, the United States proposed that an antarctic conference should be held between the participating countries to ensure that Antarctica 'shall be open to all nations to conduct scientific or other peaceful activities' and to ensure the continuation of co-operation in a treaty which would not affect the legal *status quo*, by freezing all territorial claims. The Antarctic Treaty (dealing with land areas and ice shelves south of 60°S) was signed in 1959 by Argentina, Australia, Belgium, Chile, France, Japan, New Zealand, Norway, South Africa, USSR, the United Kingdom and the USA. Since that date, other nations active in Antarctica have acceded to the treaty, which has worked harmoniously, providing for the exchange of scientific personnel, programmes for scientific work, data and the conservation of living resources, through the holding of consultative and scientific meetings. Sites of special scientific and historic interest have been designated. An example of the former is the Emperor Penguin rookery at Cape Crozier, and of the latter the Scott and Shackleton huts from the 'heroic age' of antarctic exploration; furthermore, antarctic seals have been protected. The treaty is of considerable interest from the point of view of international law and may be a hopeful pointer for the future.

The question of the development of the antarctic regions for the exploitation of minerals, fisheries, tourism, and so on, is one which is urgently being considered by the treaty nations. One eminent authority has

Iceberg in the Southern ocean. The feasibility of towing icebergs from the Antarctic to arid parts of the world has been seriously considered

suggested that they could become responsible trustees recognised by the United Nations, acting on behalf of a much wider group of countries. Oil operations in the Arctic have shown that it is technically feasible to work in the hostile polar environment. Licences might be issued by the Antarctic Treaty nations and the revenue ploughed back into scientific research. The question of the harvesting of fish, and in particular of krill, the shrimp-like food of the baleen whales, upon the high seas (which is not subject to the treaty) is of great concern to a hungry world. A potential annual harvest of over fifty million tons is spoken of, although at present no more than some 200,000 tons are taken each year. Biologists are now co-operating, in an international programme involving fifteen ships from eleven countries, to discover how much krill there is, so that they can estimate the maximum sustainable yield, i.e. the amount which can be safely taken from the Southern Ocean.

There is a great danger that unregulated overfishing of krill will not only lead to its disappearance, but will endanger the existence through starvation of higher forms of life in the Antarctic. It would be a terrible tragedy if the penguins, seals, albatrosses and other creatures wonderfully adapted to the harshest of environments should perish as a result of man's unenlightened self-interest, in the pursuit of an even more deadly harvest than that wreaked upon the great whales. It was to prevent the development of such an unregulated industry that the Convention for the Conservation of Antarctic Marine Living Resources was concluded in Canberra in May 1980. The Antarctic Treaty countries are acutely aware of the threat that uncontrolled krill fishing represents to the other species in the Antarctic, and for this reason the new Convention is concerned not only with the sustainable yields of krill, but also with the effect various levels of harvesting might have on the other predator species. This 'whole ecosystem approach' is unique among conservation agreements.

The midnight sun colours the Antarctic ice at Halley Bay: a harsh environment and a fragile one. Studies of the Antarctic fauna suggest that exploiting the krill or the oil of the Antarctic will require the most careful monitoring of short- and long-term effects. The pencil drawing of Emperor Penguins at Cape Crozier (below) is by Edward Wilson, who accompanied Captain Scott on his South Pole expedition. Left: A Rockhopper Penguin. Overfishing of krill would affect penguins, seabirds, seals and whales

LIFE IN THE DEEP SEA
PETER J. HERRING

Little more than a century ago it was confidently believed that marine life could not exist more than a few hundred fathoms below the surface. Although it did not take long for this belief to be dispelled it has only recently become possible to journey into the ocean depths for the express purpose of investigating the activities and abundance of its inhabitants.

It is difficult for us, as part of the terrestrial environment, to comprehend the extent of the oceans. Land organisms are restricted to the thin layer of surface vegetation; the oceans not only cover seventy-one per cent of the earth's surface but also have an *average* depth of 3.8 kilometres. Organisms of all sizes, from the microscopic to the gigantic, permanently inhabit this vast volume while others dwell upon its floor. The overwhelming characteristic of the deeper regions is their uniformity. Though there are gradients of all physical features there are no major discontinuities throughout most of the deep sea in space or time. Water deeper than one kilometre is uniformly dark and at temperatures of 0–5°C, though at shallower depths there is a more marked vertical 'structure' in terms of density, oxygen content and light.

Some of the features of this unique environment are apparent during a submersible descent. Daylight is rapidly attenuated, becoming a deeper blue as the depth increases and disappearing at 800–900 metres in even the clearest ocean waters. The temperature falls rapidly in the upper few hundred metres, while outside the vessel the pressure increases steadily by approximately one atmosphere for every ten metres of depth. Though more life is likely to be seen by a coastal Scuba diver than by the descending aquanaut, some indications of layers of animals are usually observed. Marine 'snow' is commonly seen; this is a manifestation of the slow rain of organic material from the surface to the depths. At the lower levels of the dive the blackness outside is broken by the flashes and glows of luminous animals, though the sources are likely to be elusive.

The physical gradients are vertically compressed compared to horizontal variations of the same magnitude, and it is not surprising to find this reflected by a similar vertical structure in deep-sea life. The rapid absorption of all wavelengths of solar radiation has a critical consequence for all life in the ocean: photosynthesis by the largely unicellular phytoplankton is confined to the well-lit surface waters, particularly the upper hundred metres, and solar heating is similarly restricted to the surface. Animal life is almost entirely dependent on the productivity of these tiny plants just as the land fauna is dependent upon the vegetation. Herbivores graze the phytoplankton necessarily in the upper layers. Only carnivores and detritus feeders can live permanently at great distances below. As the conversion of food into animal tissue is only about ten per cent efficient, only a very small fraction of the surface productivity remains available for deep-sea carnivores two or three links further along the food chain. The biomass in the deep sea is therefore very low and its few inhabitants must either adapt to the nutritional poverty

or migrate towards the richer surface to feed.

Recent advances in our ability to sample the oceans have shown just how complex is the vertical distribution pattern so dimly perceived from the submersible. Nets can be opened and closed remotely by acoustic triggers and their performance continuously monitored from the surface. The catches show clearly that individual species have particular depth ranges. The depths of the population maxima of even closely related species are separated even if only by a few tens of metres. This daytime stratification alters at night. Many animals within the zone affected by overhead changes in light intensity move towards the surface at night. Different species move at different rates and times but the trigger for these daily vertical migrations is the change in light intensity at dusk and dawn. Transient events such as solar eclipses or sudden cloud cover may also precipitate short-lived vertical movements. Many fish and shrimps migrate over ranges of several hundred metres each night, and even small animals travel considerable distances. The advantages of moving nearer the surface to feed are obvious. Calculations indicate that migrants who feed more efficiently in the warm surface waters at night, when they are less vulnerable to visual predators, and then migrate back to the daytime obscurity of colder, deeper water to assimilate their food, achieve an energy bonus much greater than

Left: Deep-sea angler fish. Below: *Pseudoscopelus* – a deep-sea species that can eat prey larger than itself

the cost of the journey. A similar layering of the animals occurs at greater depths, though information is still scanty and daily vertical migrations probably do not occur.

The apparent eccentricities of structure and colour of the animals in a deep-sea trawl are the result of a very great adaptation to the demands of a highly competitive environment, characterised by considerable physical uniformity. These animals are bizarre only on the deck – in their own habitat they are magnificently efficient. The scarcity of food imposes two overriding requirements: the capture and consumption of whatever prey is accessible and the conservation of such hard-won energy. Each species has evolved its own compromise between the two.

Animals within the daylit regions have the most marked vertical differences in appearance. Those in the upper 100–200 metres either adopt the transparency typified by jellyfish, squids, fish larvae and crustaceans, or are highly silvered. A large active animal cannot achieve complete transparency for many of its tissues are necessarily opaque. In the larger fishes stacks of minute crystals are so aligned within or beneath the scales that constructive interference produces a near perfect reflective surface. Dorsally the animals are dark, and the ventral counter-shading provides an effective camouflage in the prevailing light conditions. The ventral surface still presents a silhouette to a predator below, but this hazard is reduced by its compression into a keel and appropriate orientation of the reflective plates. In deeper waters (400–700 metres) further reduction in the ventral profile is achieved by great lateral flattening of the body, typified by the hatchet fishes in which the flanks form perfect vertical mirrors. The whole ventral margin is provided with rows of luminous organs from which the fish emits light of the same colour, angular distribution and intensity as that of the down-welling daylight – and the last traces of a silhouette are obliterated. The significance of the silhouette is clearly indicated by the number of animals with upwardly directed tubular eyes, including the hatchet fishes themselves. Bioluminescence

Hatchet fish. Lateral flattening and reflective flanks make it almost invisible from below in the deep waters where it lives

cannot match the light intensities in surface waters so the strategy is only practicable at midwater depths. At depths below the effects of daylight ventral organs are no longer effective and are reduced or absent. Camouflage now involves merging into the black background and most fishes have velvety-black non-reflective surfaces. The body shape need not be compressed and is more nearly circular in cross-section. Luminous organs are present elsewhere on the body and serve a variety of functions. Some act as lures, others as headlights, sexual signals or deterrents to predators. Beebe and others have described the alarm response of deep-sea shrimps which discharge clouds of luminescence should they make contact with the ports of the vessel, while recent observers have noted how a flash of a submersible's lights will evoke answering flashes from the water around. Light emission is an important ability of deep-sea animals, for any function served by colour in an illuminated environment can be served equally well by light in a dark one. Animal light is predominantly blue, like residual daylight, and it is to this colour that the eyes of deep-sea animals are particularly attuned. In these conditions the red pigment of deep-sea crustaceans is as effective a camouflage as the black of the fishes.

The more an animal reduces its energy expenditure the less food it requires. Swimming in order to maintain position is a particularly costly activity. Many animals reduce the cost by achieving near neutral buoyancy. Gas provides the most effective buoyancy but is very compressible. A gas-filled swimbladder offsets the negative buoyancy of the skeleton and muscle of most active surface fishes. Midwater fish undertaking vertical migrations face the difficulty of maintaining a constant volume of gas in the swimbladder against the depth-related pressure changes. To achieve this deeper living fishes have developed an increasingly long countercurrent system of blood vessels which supply the gas gland. The layer of silvery crystals impermeable to gas which lines the swimbladder is thicker in deeper species. Some siphonophores and the mesopelagic squid *Spirula* also use gas spaces for buoyancy. Many other deep-sea squids and crustaceans achieve neutral buoyancy by increasing the volume of tissue fluids and replacing some of the 'heavier' ions (e.g. calcium and magnesium) with 'lighter' ions. Such increases in body volume or lipid content and reduction in the denser tissues (skeleton and muscle) do achieve neutral buoyancy – but at the cost of mobility. Deep-sea fishes also have a lower oxygen capacity in the blood, smaller heart, more anaerobic white muscle, reduced or absent swimbladders and a lower metabolic rate commensurate with their reduced organisation. In one study fish and crustaceans from 900–1300 metres had an oxygen uptake per unit weight only one tenth of that of similar

A trawl being lowered from the research vessel *Discovery*

animals from 0–400 metres. Vertical migrants, however, need an adequate swimming ability and tend to differ from the relatively watery and less mobile non-migrants. The nutritional significance of these differences is shown by the fact that a 40-gram *Anoplogaster* (an active midwater predatory fish) could survive for thirteen days on a 2-gram migrating lanternfish but for only $2\frac{1}{2}$ days on a 2-gram watery non-migrant fish (*Sagamichthys*). The same 2-gram fishes would sustain the reduced metabolic demands of a 40-gram deep-sea *Borostomias* (a less active more watery fish) for twenty-five and five days respectively.

Large watery carnivores with reduced muscles cannot fulfil the role of fast active predators. They must adopt a different lifestyle more dependent on stealth than speed, with methods for luring and trapping their prey. Where food is scarce animals cannot

A crab trap is being used to gather specimens from one of the communities of creatures that have recently been discovered to live in the hot water rising from vents in the Galapagos rift

may provide an unappreciated food source for a large population of scavengers. The rapid attraction of fish and crabs to artificial bait laid on the deep-sea floor supports this speculation. The discovery of the Galapagos rift ecosystem has provided another unexpected source of energy. Hot water containing dissolved inorganic material is vented through volcanic fissures in the sea-bed. Bacteria utilise the energy in these compounds for their growth, this process of chemosynthesis paralleling the surface use of solar energy in photosynthesis. The bacterial populations supply the nutritional needs of a remarkable associated fauna of worms, bivalves, crabs and others. This ecosystem is quite independent of solar energy.

We still lack knowledge about most aspects of deep-sea life. Physical gradients rather than discontinuities have made it difficult to relate animal distribution to oceanographic features. More detailed sampling and better analytical techniques now provide a basis for the confident recognition of ocean communities. Particular communities are associated with the great mid-ocean gyres. The effects on the deep-sea communities of seasonal and longer-term fluctuations in surface productivity are not yet clear. In the gyres, however, where the surface waters are relatively impoverished, species of midwater fishes are stunted when compared to specimens below richer waters. Doubts remain about the factors controlling the reproduction of sea-floor communities. We do not really know how much our views about the ocean fauna are biased by our sampling methods. Animals which are either very active, very fragile, very large or very small are inadequately sampled by nets. Most information about large squids derives from the stomach contents of sperm whales, while the importance and abundance of delicate gelatinous animals has only recently been revealed by open ocean Scuba divers. Direct observation and photographs of bottom communities are providing information unobtainable with nets. The versatility of *Alvin* and other submersibles has enabled scientists at Woods Hole and elsewhere to mount biological experiments on the sea-bed. Nevertheless, our understanding of the lives of most deep-sea animals is very meagre. For example, we have little idea how the high pressures in the deep sea affect the distribution of animals.

The technology for disturbing the deep-sea communities by drilling, ocean-floor mining or dumping of radioactive and other industrial waste has outstripped our understanding of the long-term consequences of such action. The vast three-dimensional scale of the ocean environment which provides the main hurdle to its investigation has also been regarded as a sufficient buffer to the effects of man's intervention. The more information that is acquired, the less tenable does this comfortable assumption become.

afford to be too selective. The jaws and teeth of deep sea fishes are enlarged to cope with large prey while the pharyngeal basket can still filter out small organisms. Many have jaw articulations that can be dislocated (like some snakes) and very elastic stomachs, so that they can take prey larger than themselves. Angler fishes provide prime examples of this strategy, the females having large bulbous watery bodies with black skin, huge mouths and stomachs, small fins and a luminous lure. They are living baited traps. The males are tiny with no lure but large eyes and nostrils. They probably recognise the female by sight and scent and then attach permanently to her body becoming sexual parasites. The investment in living tissue is thus concentrated in the female. This is also the case in other deep-sea fishes which first mature as males but as they grow change into females.

Although the deep-sea animals of the midwater realm are carnivores, a change occurs as the bottom is reached. The residual rain of organic material from above accumulates here and consequently many of the bottom community are devoted to sediment feeding. The echinoderms (sea cucumbers, starfish and urchins) are often the dominant examples though worms and filter feeders such as bivalve molluscs and ascidians are also important. Deep-sea species of the latter two groups have also developed methods for the capture of live prey.

Many of our original concepts about deep-sea life have had to be modified. It has proved difficult to equate the energy requirements of bottom populations with the known input from above. Substantial populations of near-bottom fishes appear to belie the scarcity of food. The rapid descent to the bottom of large food packages (whales, large fish, etc.)

FISH FARMING
PETER HJUL

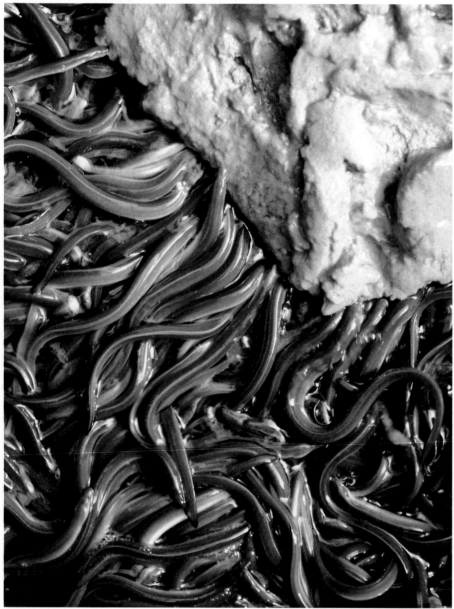

Fish farming is one of the oldest and, paradoxically, one of the newest of food-producing activities.

There is nothing very complicated about the raising of living organisms in water. Early man probably learnt soon after he had begun to trap fish in a fast-flowing river, or spear them in a shallow pool, that those remaining alive could be held for a while to be eaten later, or perhaps even left to grow.

Still among the leaders in cultivating fish in fresh water, the Chinese can trace written records of pond farming back to the eleventh century BC. The first known manual on carp farming was written by a Chinese called Fan Li some 2400 years ago. Carp was the fish usually kept in the stew ponds of medieval monasteries to be readily available on fast days.

But these on-growing methods were what is known to modern aquaculture as 'non-intensive'. Although confined, the fish (or sometimes lobster, prawn or mussel) is left with enough space to feed on naturally-occurring plants and organisms. It is a way of farming that still forms the broad base of aquaculture. Boosted by initial fertilisation of ponds, by the intelligent use of areas of brackish water interacting with the sea, or by alternating fish with an agricultural crop (such as rice in paddy fields), non-intensive culture will continue to have an important place in the future of fish raising.

It is the newer, industrial phase of aquaculture, however, that has caught the popular imagination over the past decade. This packs fish in concentrations five, ten and more times those of the earlier farms, in ponds, tanks, silos, flowing-water raceways or cages in lakes or sheltered sea inlets. The fish have to be fed artificially (mostly with diets that consist largely of protein from fish), the water has to be aerated, expensive farm structures have to be built and maintained, a careful watch has to be kept to prevent and control disease. Biologist, geneticist, chemist, engineer and vet work alongside the husbandryman to perfect an efficient food-production system.

Linking the two basic methods, and using the best features of each of them, is the ranching of certain species which can be grown under control in hatcheries and then released to feed and grow in the open sea or in large lakes. Salmon is the ideal fish for ranching. Along the coast of the North Pacific there are now hatcheries from California round to

Alaska, and in Japan and the USSR. Pacific salmon returning to spawn and die are stripped of their eggs which are hatched in incubators. The fry are held until they develop to fingerlings or smolts and are then released. Two, three or four years later, according to species, those that survive return to where they first made contact with salt water. Survival rates of two to three per cent are enough to make most hatchery operations worthwhile; improved to four or five per cent, they would enormously increase the stocks of salmon.

The first small steps are being taken to try and ranch the atlantic salmon, and experiments are also being carried out in the transfer of salmon from one ocean to another.

In the south of Chile, an American fish-farming company has set up a hatchery to

Young eels feeding in a Japanese fish farm (left) and sea ranching in Laguna de Bay in the Philippines. The fenced enclosures are for growing milk fish. Below: Salmon have been under some degree of cultivation along the US North Pacific shore since 1877. 'Sea ranching' from release and capture stations is building new salmon populations

incubate coho salmon eggs flown to it from North Pacific streams. The first mature salmon have returned to encourage further tests towards the possible eventual seeding of the Southern Ocean with a valuable fish that might thrive on the krill that once fed the great whales.

But, tempting as it is to dream of a future abundant with salmon, farming and ranching presently provide only a small share of the world supply of fish and other seafoods. The estimate by the Food and Agriculture Organisation of the United Nations is six to seven million tons of an acquatic harvest of around seventy-five million tons. The share could be even less than this now that we have a more accurate idea of how much is farmed in China, which was once thought to be producing around two million tons of farmed fish a year. A report for FAO from China in 1980 indicated a figure below one million tons. Japan is producing 600,000 tons or more, India 250,000 tons, and the USSR over 200,000 tons. The United States farms about 90,000 tons of catfish, trout, oysters, salmon and numerous other species.

For Western Europe, one recent estimate is that the EEC countries will be producing 100,000 tons of rainbow trout a year by 1985, plus some 500,000 tons of farmed shellfish. In Norway there are now around 400 small farms (and one very large farm) producing Atlantic salmon. Production in 1979 was just over 4000 tons; this was expected to rise to 8000 tons in 1981 and 15,000 tons in 1985. Considering that in 1979 the total catch of hunted Atlantic salmon was around 8000/9000 tons, this expansion in Norwegian farming, plus the increasing production of farms in Scotland, will have a heavy impact on a high-price gourmet market.

Here it is possible to support the view of one prominent fish farmer that this activity, on an intensive scale, 'is a commercial reality with a quite extraordinary potential for growth'. Grow it certainly will, but not at the pace nor in the ways indicated by many of the more blithely optimistic views of aquaculture. And it may be a long, long time before the farm equals the fishing boat as a supplier of quality protein from the sea.

Aquaculture science and technology have only just started to break through some of the earliest and most obvious barriers to large-scale development. Farmers are learning to control fish in increasing concentrations in an aquatic environment. The day of the fish vet is arriving although the good fish pathologist with experience over the many species that are being cultured is still a rare individual. Fish medicines are gradually being perfected, as are fish foods.

But aquaculture has not developed as much as it needs if it is eventually to rank with agriculture and fish hunting. More than ninety species of fish, eight to ten of crustaceans, many varieties of oysters, mussels, clams and

Hawaii
Above: A research laboratory where selective breeding of fish and crustacea for farming is being carried on
Below: An oyster farm – the aim is production of three million oysters a month

other shellfish, and numerous sea plants are presently being cultivated. Geneticists have produced successful hybrids from some of these species; large fish have been raised like prize cucumbers or champion bulls. As yet, however, the fish farm has no aquatic equivalent of the domestic animal. The farmer has to work with wild creatures, the most marketable of which are flesh-eating predators that have to be fed on protein if they are to survive and grow.

But experience is accumulating and the skills are increasing. The domestic fish will come and with it the big farm able to convert abundant and readily available foods into millions of tons of edible fish, lobsters, prawns, oysters, clams and mussels. The forecasts of the mid-1970s that aquaculture might be contributing twenty million tons and more to world fish supplies by the turn of the century may prove to have been too optimistic. It does, however, have the potential for expansion (and it offers the challenge) that must recommend it to governments and other authorities looking ahead to the food needs of expanding populations, and improving tastes.

ENERGY
DAVID ROSS

The ceaseless, raging motion of the waves has aroused the imagination of everyone who has stood on the deck of a ship or walked along a beach and watched the sea thundering out its message in a majestic but wasted expense of energy. The problem of capturing that energy has been recognised formally for nearly 200 years. It was on 12 July 1799 that the first-known patent for a wave energy device was filed in Paris by a father and son named Girard. Their scheme was to moor a ship off the shore, fit a gigantic lever to it, with the fulcrum on the beach, and drive pumps and bucket-wheels from the other end of the see-saw. The patent argued: 'The enormous mass of a ship of the line, which no other known force is capable of lifting, responds to the slightest wave motions.'

The Girards had a sound concept of the problem. A casual observer, watching a line of white horses gliding towards the shore, can get the impression that the waves – like rivers and currents – travel in a single direction and that one could capture this motion by siting a water wheel in the sea. But in reality each particle of water travels in a circular motion, returning almost to the point from which it started. If you throw a bottle into a river, it will be swept away rapidly. If you throw it into the sea, it will drift with the current but the stongest movement is up and down as it is bounced by the whirl of the waves. The problem is to capture that motion.

The Girards' patent was followed by 341 others in Britain alone; but they remained paper ideas. There was one practical development. In the 1920s Trinity House had the bright idea of boring a hole up through the middle of its navigation buoys and perching a whistle on top. As the waves rose and fell, a

The Cockerell raft

bubble of air was pushed out and sucked in (to fill the resultant vacuum) and this blew a warning whistle blast. It took a long time before anyone realised that this was to be the forerunner of 2000-megawatt power stations which, in the words of Mr Glyn England, chairman of the Central Electricity Generating Board, could 'supply the whole of Britain with electricity at the present [1978] rate of consumption'.

It was in the 1950s that the first attempts to capture wave energy were carried out. They happened in two island communities – Mauritius and Japan. In Mauritius a civil engineer, A.N. Walton Bott, who had learned about the power of water while working on hydro-electric schemes in Scotland, arrived to set up an electricity board. He observed a fringing reef off the shore, studied wave power, and devised a plan to build two walls at right angles to the reef and create a huge lagoon. The waves would at times overtop the ridge and would then be allowed to run back into the sea, driving turbines as they went. Mr Bott was helped by the Hydraulics Research Station at Wallingford, Oxfordshire – the most experienced organisation in the world at designing things which stand up in the sea – and his plan would have been a

forerunner for numerous countries. But in 1966 the price of oil actually started to fall and it was decided to abandon work, on the grounds that diesel generators were cheaper.

In Japan, a former Naval commander, Yoshio Masuda, was experimenting with a device similar to Trinity House's. But instead of a whistle on top of his buoys, he put an air turbine there and this drove a generator which charged a battery and powered a flasher unit and the lamp. It was also used for lighthouses and produced 70–120 watts. More than 300 of these were stationed in the Pacific, and Trinity House itself is now buying them – the first three are stationed off Harwich, Great Yarmouth and Dover. In 1976 the Japanese provided Masuda with a grant of $39.5 million over seven years to build and test a 500-ton ship, the *Kaimei*. She was moored for nine months off the coast with eleven generators on her deck. One of them was provided by Britain at a cost of £300,000 under an International Energy Agency programme. Nothing like it had ever been built before and it worked beautifully. It spins at up to 1800 revolutions per minute, producing between 100 and 170 kilowatts. The whole ship was officially rated as a two-megawatt power station and was plugged into the grid, lighting up Japanese homes with the fuel coming from the sea.

In Britain, meanwhile, there were two major developments. Stephen Salter, an engineer at Edinburgh University, devised the most catchily named wave-energy generator of all, the Duck. It happened when the oil crisis of 1973/4 was making everyone aware that the world had a growing energy problem. Mr Salter's wife Margaret asked him why he didn't find a new energy source 'which would be clean and safe, would work in winter in Scotland and would last for ever'. He later commented: 'It's a good thing for an engineer to have the design objective clearly specified.' Even better, he proceeded to fulfil the request.

He experimented with a flap but, as anyone who has ever paddled his or her own canoe can testify, a piece of wood dragging through the water will not absorb the energy;

The Japanese floating power generator, the *Kaimei* ('Light from the sea')

on the contrary, it will create reflected waves (like a breakwater) and following waves. These represent wasted energy. Mr Salter then arrived, after an arduous search, at the design of a cone. The point of it is the Duck's beak and the rounded bottom follows the circular motion of the waves and thus avoids displacing water and losing power. Mr Salter tried his device in a laboratory tank and was rewarded by the spectacle of an artificial wave hitting the Duck – and calm water behind it. All the energy had been captured.

Around the same time, Sir Christopher Cockerell, inventor of the Hovercraft, had been wrestling with the same problem. He put his own money into the early experiments and devised a power station called the Raft. It started as a string of seven pontoons, linked by hinges, which followed the contours of the waves – 'a ship with a broken back,' as he called it. It has since been improved and now has only two pontoons, the rear one heavy and held down by moorings so that it is relatively stable, while the smaller, lighter, front one (divided in two) bobs up and down. The movement of the front pontoons drives a pump on the rear one, sucks in sea-water and then drives it at high pressure into a turbine. This, in turn, drives a generator and electricity flows.

In April 1976, the British Government announced its first investment in wave energy – a sum of only £1.01 million. This has been increased in several instalments, and total expenditure, spread over about ten inventions, totalled £12 million by 1980 – still way below Japan's expenditure on one device. But the money has enabled great progress.

The Masuda design has been improved by the National Engineering Laboratory at East Kilbride, near Glasgow. Masuda's ship floats with the bows facing the incoming waves and the holes (or air chambers) under the ship. The NEL device will be fixed to the sea-bed so that none of the power will be lost by the ship itself bobbing in the waves. In addition, the openings will be broadside-on to the waves, like portholes in the sides of a ship, so that they receive and capture more of the energy.

One idea being explored is to build small units, like harbour walls, off the fishing villages of Sri Lanka, generating electricity for refrigeration plants so that the catches can be frozen and sent inland.

The Mauritius plan has come to the forefront again, thanks to the rising cost of oil. Sir Alexander Gibb and Partners, consulting engineers, who are exploring the possibilities, have demonstrated convincingly that wave electricity would cost considerably less than, for instance, diesel power, with the gap widening in favour of the waves as the high, initial capital cost is paid off. The Crown Agents, who have been active around Mauritius from the start, have been investigating the possibility of similar schemes for Fiji, Western

Tidal Power
As the rising tide fills the reservoir, it powers a turbine which generates electricity. Just before the tide turns, the turbine blades are reversed to pump an extra head of water into the reservoir. As the tide falls, water from the reservoir powers the turbine. The extra water pumped in at high tide can give several times the energy it took to get it there

Cock
Raft
A larg
moore
has tw
attach
wave
ponto
a van
and e
coupl

Salter's Duck
The rocking motion imparted to the Duck's 'beak' by the waves is used to drive gyroscopes, which convert the slow wave motion into the high angular velocity needed to drive a generator

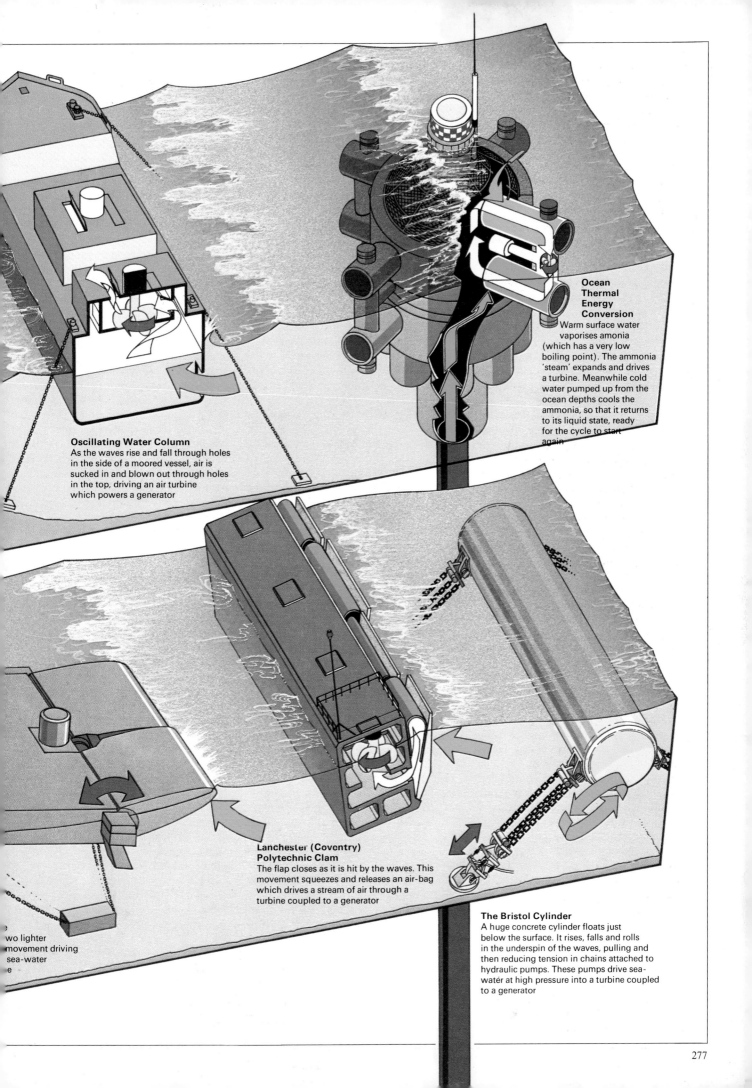

Oscillating Water Column
As the waves rise and fall through holes in the side of a moored vessel, air is sucked in and blown out through holes in the top, driving an air turbine which powers a generator

Ocean Thermal Energy Conversion
Warm surface water vaporises amonia (which has a very low boiling point). The ammonia 'steam' expands and drives a turbine. Meanwhile cold water pumped up from the ocean depths cools the ammonia, so that it returns to its liquid state, ready for the cycle to start again

Lanchester (Coventry) Polytechnic Clam
The flap closes as it is hit by the waves. This movement squeezes and releases an air-bag which drives a stream of air through a turbine coupled to a generator

The Bristol Cylinder
A huge concrete cylinder floats just below the surface. It rises, falls and rolls in the underspin of the waves, pulling and then reducing tension in chains attached to hydraulic pumps. These pumps drive sea-water at high pressure into a turbine coupled to a generator

wo lighter
movement driving
sea-water
e

Samoa, Tonga and the Seychelles, with the original inventor, Mr Bott, on their team.

Salter's Duck has been vastly improved by the use of four gyroscopes inside the cone. They solve the problems of power take-off and storage, both of which were regarded only a year or two ago as insuperable obstacles. The Duck no longer has to be part of a string of 20–30 units but can function alone, producing a steady output of 600 kilowatts for one small community.

In addition, a second generation of devices has come along. The first was the Lancaster Airbag, designed by Professor Michael French and favoured by the British Government because it was estimated to produce electricity more cheaply than its rivals. Rubber bags are attached to a concrete beam and they squeeze out and suck in air as the waves rise and fall. The passage of the air drives air turbines. A development of this is the Lanchester (Coventry) Polytechnic Clam, which gets its name from its clam-like movement. It is a coffin-shaped box with a flap on one side which opens and closes as it is hit by the waves. The movement of the flap pulls and squeezes a line of air bags which, again, drive air through turbines. Both these devices differ from the Masuda invention in that they use enclosed-air systems. This creates problems when there is a puncture but saves the mechanism from damage by jetsam, flotsam, ice and seaweed.

A completely different idea is the Bristol Cylinder, a huge concrete container shaped like a dustbin, which floats just below the surface, thus avoiding the worst buffeting of the sea. As it bounces in the underspin of the waves, it drives chains connected to hydraulic pumps on the sea-bed and these drive seawater at high pressure into a turbine.

At Queen's University, Belfast, the Masuda invention has been developed into a device with a name that sounds like an Irish folk song – the Belfast Buoy. It is a circular structure, shaped like a Greek vase, which can accept energy from any direction. Its major contribution has been its turbine which was invented by Professor A.A. Wells, FRS, and is self-rectifying – it can receive a stream of air from above or below without any need for flap valves and works equally well whether the waves are rising or falling. It has been so successful that the Japanese have bought patent rights so that they can use it on their marine buoys in place of their own less efficient design. The Japanese also decided to convert the *Kaimei* and adopt the design of the National Engineering Laboratory.

Another invention came from the US. Lockheed designed what they call Dam Atoll – because it has some of the properties of both a dam and an atoll. It is a dome-shaped island, 250 feet in diameter, which floats just below the surface. Waves enter a gap at the top and are led down in a spiral for sixty feet, driving a turbine at the bottom.

It is also Lockheed who are experimenting with a completely different method of winning the sea's energy: Ocean Thermal Energy Conversion (OTEC). It is designed for use in the tropics where the water on the surface can be 40° F warmer than at the sea-bed. A huge tube, 100 feet in diameter and 2000 feet in length, and shaped like an upright loop, is moored in the ocean with ammonia inside it. At the (warm) surface the ammonia vaporises, expands and drives a turbine (just like the steam in a conventional power station). It is cooled as it falls towards the icy water on the sea-bed and then starts out again on its unending travels through the loop. A 50-kilowatt pilot plant has been tried out off Hawaii, and has convinced Lockheed that full-scale power stations can be built.

Finally, the sea offers tidal power – something that many people confuse with wave energy. The tides come in once every twelve hours while the waves break every ten seconds. But, as every swimmer knows, the tides contain tremendous power. The limitation is that there has to be a large tidal range – the difference between low and high tide – and sites for this are limited. They occur usually where the sea is funnelled and squeezed by the coastline – La Rance off Brittany, in the Bay of Fundy off Canada's east coast and in the Severn estuary in south-west England.

Tidal power was first used on a small scale for milling by the Romans in Britain in the eleventh century. The problem – for them and for the vast modern schemes now being contemplated or, in La Rance, actually in use – is to obtain sufficient height between the water in the upper millpond or reservoir and the depth to which it falls before driving a waterwheel or turbine. Without a sufficiently high head of water, the power is insignificant. The answer is to build a barrage with sluice gates and pumps. This means vast capital expenditure – the Severn barrage is estimated to cost £4000 million at least. And this is a once-off operation, with no diminution in cost from serial production, as happens with wave energy, because of the limited number of suitable sites.

This is why wave energy is usually regarded as the most attractive device for capturing the energy of the sea. But it, too, requires heavy capital expenditure and in 1980 the British Government cut back on its commitment by reducing the number of devices which it was backing from nine to three.

What problems are presented? The only serious objection so far has been on grounds of cost. The first official estimates, by a consulting engineer in the summer of 1978, quoted figures like 20p, 40p and even 60p per kilowatt hour compared with the notional cost of 2p (in Britain) for conventional electricity. In the short period since then, the official costing for four of the devices has already come down to less than 10p, with at least two of them in the area of 4–5p. During the same period, with the cost of oil shooting up, the actual cost of electricity has been rising and 4p is a more realistic figure in Britain. For those areas which are not linked to the grid and depend on diesel generators – such as the Western Isles – the cost is around 25p a unit.

Even these figures understate the case. Part of the attraction of wave energy is that it is modular – that is, the same devices are mass-produced and they come down in price as serial production gets into its stride. They also have the advantage over standard power stations in that they start producing electricity as soon as *one* unit is at sea. With a normal power station, the whole building has to be put up first. So even before the next inevitable rise in the price of oil and coal, wave energy is competitive.

But we should not be talking just about money. We know that the world will sooner or later run out of fossil fuels and uranium, even with a fast-breeder reactor. We know also that even the most favoured countries, such as oil-rich, coal-rich Britain, should not be using up their capital wealth at the present criminal rate. And we know that traditional British industry, much of which is standing idle in the slump, is ideally suited to making wave energy generators – our shipyards, engineering, construction and electrical industries are ideal for manufacturing the huge clanking turbines and generators needed.

What sort of monsters are we thinking about? They would be the size of giant oil tankers. To provide *all* of Britain's electricity would need perhaps 600 miles of them (though no one is suggesting that we should shut down all other sources). The thought may worry some people, and the environmental impact is being carefully studied by the Wave Energy Steering Committee. So far, no deleterious effects have been discovered. After all, there's plenty of room at sea.

But for those who favour small units, the waves can cope with them. We can now contemplate a range of devices from the navigation buoys which light up a 40-watt bulb to the 600-kilowatt Duck, to the two-megawatt Japanese ship, the *Kaimei*, to the 2000-megawatt power stations which would provide our basic needs.

Our engineers and scientists have taken us to a stage where we could well be on the eve of a new industrial revolution with an advanced society run on electricity which does not depend on burning coal, oil, gas or uranium. The waves will be a clean, benign, non-polluting source of energy. Renewable energy, because the waves go on for ever.

David Ross is author of Energy from the Waves *(Pergamon)*.

INDEX

Page numbers in *italic* refer to the illustrations

13

(910.45)